The publisher and the University of California Press Foundation gratefully acknowledge the generous support of the Simpson Imprint in Humanities.

The publisher gratefully acknowledges the generous support of the Director's Circle of the University of California Press, whose members are:

Melva and Stephen Arditti
Nancy Boas
John Geiger
Lorrie and Richard Greene
Arlene Inch
R. Marilyn Lee and Harvey Schneider
Celeste Meier
Anthony Nicholas
Alejandro Portes
Rowena and Marc Singer

Adventures of a Jazz Age Lawyer

Adventures of a Jazz Age Lawyer

Nathan Burkan and the Making of American Popular Culture

Gary A. Rosen

UNIVERSITY OF CALIFORNIA PRESS

University of California Press
Oakland, California

Library of Congress Cataloging-in-Publication Data

Names: Rosen, Gary A., author.
Title: Adventures of a Jazz Age lawyer : Nathan Burkan
    and the making of American popular culture / Gary A.
    Rosen.
Description: Oakland, California : University of
    California Press, [2020] | Includes bibliographical
    references and index.
Identifiers: LCCN 2019020046 (print) |
    ISBN 9780520297371 (cloth : alk. paper) |
    ISBN 9780520969759 (ebook)
Subjects: LCSH: Burkan, Nathan. | Copyright—Music—
    United States—History. | Copyright—Performing
    rights—United States—History. | Copyright—Artistic
    performance—United States—History. | Performing
    arts—United States—20th century—History.
Classification: LCC KF3035 .R63 2020 (print) |
    LCC KF3035 (ebook) | DDC 340.092 [B]—dc23
LC record available at https://lccn.loc.gov/2019020046
LC ebook record available at https://lccn.loc.gov
/2019980732

Manufactured in the United States of America

28 27 26 25 24 23 22 21 20
10 9 8 7 6 5 4 3 2 1

For Lisa, Emily, and—in loving memory—
Gregory Nathan Rosen

Our songs and cities are the best things about us. Songs and cities are so indispensable. Even if we go into darkness, the time will come when people will want to know how these ruins were made—the essence of the life we made.

—Jane Jacobs

Contents

Nathan the Wise

More than two thousand mourners packed New York City's cavernous Temple Emanu-El on Tuesday morning, June 9, 1936. An overflow crowd of several hundred more, herded by forty police officers, gathered on the sidewalks along Fifth Avenue and 65th Street. It was a remarkable display of affection and esteem for a man who had devoted most of his life to the private practice of law, Nathan Burkan. "Today he will be buried and a legion of humans in all walks of life who knew him intimately will pause," one columnist wrote that day. "A great void has come into all our lives."

Led by Mayor Fiorello LaGuardia and his archrival, the former mayor James J. Walker, the political elite of New York had come to pay final respects to Burkan. Senator Robert F. Wagner and former four-term governor Alfred E. Smith, the 1928 Democratic presidential nominee, were there to bid farewell to a political protégé. They had first aligned with Burkan in the progressive faction at New York State's constitutional convention of 1915, and they had been expecting to be seated with Burkan in the New York delegation at the upcoming Democratic National Convention in Philadelphia, which would renominate President Franklin D. Roosevelt two weeks hence.

The leadership and rank-and-file of the Society of St. Tammany—"Tammany Hall" to supporters and detractors alike—were there in force. For two decades, Burkan had been the leader of the Wichita Democratic Club, the seat of Tammany's waning, but still formidable, power in a melting pot precinct that included portions of Spanish, Jewish, and Italian Harlem. Political reporters never quite knew what to make of Burkan, a financially independent professional of unimpeachable integrity playing a role usually filled by plebeians whose livelihoods depended on kickbacks for dispensing patronage and other means of mulcting the public purse. "'The travail, the pangs, the agony of politics!'" one newspaper profile began. "The speaker, being a Tammany district leader, has to be Nathan Burkan. The rest of the boys would just say, 'The game is a headache.' Burkan has vocabulary."

Burkan had formed his allegiance to Tammany Hall as a boy on the Lower East Side, where it was an indispensable social service organization for newly arrived immigrants. He saw his role not as ward boss for a political machine, but as unpaid champion of the obscure and friendless. To Tammany's antagonists—Roosevelt's New Dealers and LaGuardia's Republican reformers—Burkan's loyalty to Tammany had been perplexing and exasperating. Just a few months earlier, Roosevelt was reported to be considering Burkan for a federal judgeship, as a way to ease him out of the political arena.

The pols were by no means the most famous personages in the congregation that day. Nor, arguably, were they the most powerful. The film industry's financial nerve center, still based in New York, had all but shut down for the morning so that East Coast moguls could attend the service. Will Hays, the industry's gentile public face, was there with a contingent that included honorary pallbearers Joseph Schenck of the newly merged Twentieth Century–Fox Film Corporation, Nicholas Schenck of Metro-Goldwyn-Mayer, Jack Cohn of Columbia, Arthur Kelly of United Artists, Eugene Zucker of Paramount, and independent producer Samuel Goldwyn. Burkan, at his death, was a director of both United Artists and Columbia and a member of the Academy of Motion Picture Arts and Sciences. He had been a player in many of the mergers, spin-offs, and bankruptcies that, in their messy totality, had given birth to the Hollywood studio system, which was at the height of its glory in 1936.

Expressions of sympathy and condolence had been pouring in from Hollywood since the news of Burkan's sudden death, at age fifty-seven, began to circulate three days earlier. Widely syndicated columnist Louella Parsons wrote that "many of Hollywood's most famous stars, directors, and producers have good reason to remember Burkan, whose wise counsel played such a part in their success as well as in the success of this industry." Foremost among those stars was Charlie Chaplin.

"I love him, but I'm afraid of him," he once said of Burkan, with tongue only partially in cheek. "We would be such good friends if he were not a lawyer. . . . I might fire him and then get acquainted."

In reality, as Parsons knew, Burkan was "not only Charlie Chaplin's personal attorney, but probably closer to him than any other friend." Burkan had guided Chaplin's rise from contract player to powerful auteur and had extricated him from multiple career-threatening predicaments, providing a safety net that the Tramp's high-wire act would sorely miss in the years that followed.

As trusted counselor to the famous, wealthy, and powerful, Burkan had often found himself enmeshed in cases that probed the tawdry, prurient underbelly of show business, café society, and the nouveau riche. "One or two newspaper writers," it was said, "can always be found mulling about for any crumbs that may be picked up from under Burkan's polished mahogany desk." As circumstances required, he could be the hard-boiled enabler of a powerful cad with feet of clay, the chivalrous knight in shining armor for a discarded wife, the merciless avenger of a cuckolded husband, or the tenacious defender of a third party in an amorous triangle. In attendance at his funeral was Gloria Morgan Vanderbilt, whose licentious lifestyle had cost her custody of daughter "Little Gloria" in an emotionally draining 1934 trial that was Burkan's most sensational defeat. It was likely the fallen socialite's first visit to a Jewish house of worship.

After a long and seemingly chaste bachelorhood, Burkan had married late in life, and now left behind a thirty-eight-year-old widow and a five-year-old son. Outside of his young family, it was the music industry that was experiencing the most acute sense of loss that June morning. Burkan had devised the strategies and spearheaded the legal battles—in all three branches of government—that set the stage for a revolution in the American popular music business, transforming it from a somewhat disreputable purveyor of sentimental ditties and ethnic novelties, sold as sheet music to home musicians, into the powerful economic engine behind the first golden age of the American popular song, heard worldwide on records, over the airwaves, and at the movies. Irving Berlin, a founding member of Burkan's most treasured legacy, the American Society of Composers, Authors, and Publishers (Ascap), was seated in Temple Emanu-El along with Ascap's staff and many of its other members, for whom the Great American Songbook was, in 1936, still a collective work-in-progress.

The choir sang a selection from Mendelssohn's *Elijah* oratorio, and the rabbi read the 90th Psalm. Then Gene Buck, a lyricist for the Ziegfeld Follies in its heyday, and since 1924 the president of Ascap, delivered the eulogy. Buck recalled that he had first been introduced to Burkan by composer Victor Herbert. Herbert, he said, "loved Nat because he found in him a young crusader":

> Thirty years ago, in the Halls of Congress, as a young attorney, he stood at the side of Herbert, Mark Twain, and John Philip Sousa and pleaded for them and others because he saw that in this nation those who created songs, and books and plays—things that may live possibly a few hours or a hundred years—should have some protection.

Burkan, Buck continued, was "the greatest copyright protector that this nation ever had."

Burkan was indeed the veritable Moses of copyright law in the United States. He was one of the draftsmen of the epochal Copyright Act of 1909 and the guiding spirit behind Ascap. Together with the Hollywood studio system, the 1909 Copyright Act and Ascap formed the legal and institutional infrastructure upon which the United States became the world's leading generator and exporter of creative energy in the early twentieth century. Burkan was there at the creation, one of the principal architects of this durable complex.

Following Buck's eulogy, the cantor chanted "El Mole Rachamim," the Jewish prayer for the soul of the departed. Ninety honorary pallbearers led the recessional from the Romanesque sanctuary. The funeral motorcade paused by the Wichita Democratic Club on West 114th Street before heading to Union Field Cemetery, part of a vast Jewish necropolis on the Brooklyn-Queens border.

"Crusader" and "friend" were words on many lips that morning and in the days that followed. "Underneath his force and brilliance, he was a sentimentalist," Buck had said in the eulogy. "I never knew a man of greater heart. I know of hundreds of cases where he wanted to help, and did help, and they never received from this man a bill, a suggestion or an idea of the cost, if the cause was right." According to one reporter who mingled with the mourners, "Stories of the man's capacity for friendship were legion. Those who knew him best liked to tell and re-tell his many kindnesses, his ever-constant desire to help the low as well as the mighty." "He was fearless, yet friendly; his heart was as great as his brain," lamented Samuel Goldwyn. "The film world has lost one of its real leaders and I my closest friend." "Mr. Burkan," another tribute noted,

New York City Mayor Fiorello LaGuardia and former Mayor
James J. Walker lead ninety honorary pallbearers out of Temple
Emanu-El, June 9, 1936. (The LaGuardia and Wagner Archives,
LaGuardia Community College, City University of New York)

"was remarkable in his freedom from embitterment and bias, remarkable in his ability to engage in professional conflicts without aftermaths of rancor."

These were not just nostalgic postmortem reassessments. Nine years earlier, a newspaper man had observed that "an endless capacity for friendship, an agreeable personality, and a fine wit are largely responsible for Mr. Burkan's private and personal vogue." Fellow lawyer Louis Nizer had extolled him in life as "serene in manner, dynamic in thought, emotional in appraisal, logical in speech, sincere in everything."

"He is said to know just when a motion picture actress should pull out her handkerchief and cry," wrote one reporter, "and he is likewise said to be able to see the joker in a contract a mile away." Burkan was, to be sure, a courtroom pit bull and a maven of legal loopholes. But when wags cracked Nathan Burkan jokes, they did not play off those timeless stereotypes. The conceit of a Nathan Burkan joke was the lawyer as a preternaturally wise and trusted counselor, a paragon of diplomacy, sagacity, and bonhomie. Even if it was not a premise rich with comedic possibilities, there was much truth and only slight exaggeration in the quips that made the rounds. What do you do with a particularly intractable business dispute? "Before it reaches the stage of actual warfare, someone should place it before the Supreme Court, the League of Nations, or Nathan Burkan." Anyone who knew that Burkan was the consummate dealmaker—that is to say, everyone who knew him—could get a chuckle over the incongruous image of "Nathan Burkan trying to negotiate a merger between his driver and the golf ball but failing to get the principals together." Such jests were far more enlightening than the bland descriptor that journalists invariably attached to the name Nathan Burkan: "theatrical lawyer and Tammany leader."

Burkan's career provides a revelatory perspective on America, ascendant and decadent, in the first third of the twentieth century. The list of his friends, clients, adversaries, and legacies reads like the contents of a time capsule from an era too vivid and influential to be dismissed as "bygone." The sensational courtroom battles, the scandalous escapades of the rich and famous, and the momentous clashes of powerful political, economic, and cultural forces in which Burkan played a central role illuminate the coming of age of a distinctly American popular culture.

PART ONE

Leg Shows and Longhairs

CHAPTER I

Immigrant Passages

Nathan Burkan was eight years old when he left Iași, in what is today Romania, bound for New York City with his mother, Tillie, and brothers Joseph and Benjamin. They steamed past the newly dedicated Statue of Liberty aboard the *City of Berlin* on December 20, 1886, alighting at the Castle Garden immigration station. The head of the Burkan household, Moritz, had already settled on the Lower East Side, where he would operate a succession of luncheonettes and pool rooms in the heart of the red-light district. Although they hailed from an important center of Jewish culture, where they were subjects of the emperor of Austria, in the hierarchy of New York Jewry the Burkans were on the low rung, reviled as "Russian" greenhorns by the tonier and better-established "Germans."

Nathan, the middle son, owed his swift ascent into the professional class to two of the most potent engines of assimilation and upward mobility the city had to offer. After passing a highly competitive entrance examination at age fifteen, he enrolled in tuition-free City College. There, long before the school became a Jewish bastion, he survived a punishing weeding-out process (the attrition rate hovered around 90 percent) and graduated in three years. By then a fourth son, David, had been born and the Burkans had moved to the Jewish "suburb" of Williamsburg, Brooklyn. Nathan, however, remained in Manhattan, where he had found an unlikely second family in Tammany Hall.

To its foes, such as Charles Parkhurst, the pastor of Madison Square Presbyterian Church, Tammany Hall was "not so much a political party

The Burkan family, circa 1888. Nathan, age ten, is on the right.
(Courtesy, Nathan Burkan Jr.)

as a commercial corporation, organized in the interest of making the most out of its official opportunities." But for New York's growing immigrant population, its primary significance was neither political nor commercial. "Tammany Hall's leaders delivered social services at a time when City Hall and Albany did not," writes journalist Terry Golway. "For generations of immigrants and their children in Manhattan, the face of government was the face of the local Tammany ward heeler. And it was a friendly face."

Tammany was also a vehicle for identifying and advancing the ambitions of able young men who lacked social pedigree. Burkan had been taken under the wing of Martin Engel, the Tammany leader for the downtown Eighth Assembly District—"De Ate," in the local dialect. Engel was the first Jewish district leader in what was historically an Irish political machine. For lads with little to recommend themselves except raw ambition, Engel could find a place in the prostitution and gambling rackets that he protected; for those with ambition and a modicum of scruples, he might arrange a bureaucratic sinecure through

Tammany's vast web of patronage. The select few who were ambitious, scrupulous, *and* blazingly intelligent, such as Nathan Burkan, were groomed for higher callings.

A Jewish boy like Burkan angling for Engel's favor, in Irving Howe's words, "made himself visible in the clubrooms, he peddled chowder tickets, he put placards in store windows. He rooted himself in the neighborhood," generally providing the shoe leather that Tammany's political outreach to newly arrived Jews required. In exchange, Burkan enjoyed such perks as invitations to Engel's sumptuous formal balls at Tammany's headquarters on Union Square, the "Wigwam," where he could mingle with "gorgeously gowned women" amid "the popping of champagne corks, the whirl of laughter, the swish of silk and satin and the crash of the big band playing ragtime two-steps." Tammany Hall taught Burkan how the levers of power worked in New York City and gave the tenement kid his first tantalizing glimpses of how the other half lived. But it was another immigrant of 1886 who would truly open the door for Burkan to enter the world of early twentieth-century New York's upper crust.

Victor Herbert first arrived in New York a few months before the Burkans, in starkly different circumstances—as the trailing spouse of a celebrated diva. Frau Therese Förster-Herbert, a Wagnerian soprano, had been recruited by the Metropolitan Opera to bolster its German repertoire. She joined the fledgling company as one of its prima donnas, while her twenty-seven-year-old husband relinquished a plum job as principal cellist of the Court Orchestra of Stuttgart to take a $60-per-week seat in the Met's string section.

An orchestra pit could not for very long contain Herbert's prodigious musical talents, his ebullient personality, or his Falstaffian appetites. Herbert was a garrulous and witty raconteur, a loyal and generous friend, and by all accounts an extraordinarily jovial and capacious drinking and dining companion. His upbringing and education in Germany endowed him with impeccable musical credentials along with the cosmopolitan self-confidence and continental bearing of a man of the world. With "his robust charm, his ready Irish ribaldry, and his enthusiasm which equally embraced his art and his fellows," biographer Neil Gould wrote, Herbert "created a world centered on the lodestone of his magnetic personality."

A leisurely performance and rehearsal schedule at the opera house allowed Herbert to pursue solo and chamber engagements, to teach at the National Conservatory—where Antonín Dvořák was the director— and still have plenty of time left to kill in New York's beer gardens and cafes, where he mixed easily with the city's cultural elite. He soon made the helpful acquaintance of another newcomer to New York, James Gibbons Huneker, a young music and literary critic on the rise. Huneker was every bit Herbert's equal in gluttony and carousal, and they formed a lifelong bond. Their social circle included the three conductors who dominated orchestral music in America at the close of the nineteenth century, Theodore Thomas, Anton Seidl, and Walter Damrosch, for each of whom Herbert became cello soloist of choice. When Seidl conducted the world premiere of Dvořák's *New World Symphony* in 1893, Herbert was the featured cellist, as he had been when Thomas gave the American premiere of the Brahms Double Concerto for Violin and Cello in 1889. Contemporary listeners invariably remarked on the precision of Herbert's technique, the purity of his tone, and his ability to coax the finest shades of emotion from his instrument.

Herbert had begun composing for cello and orchestra while still in Germany, and not long after he arrived in the United States some of these youthful works received their U.S. premieres under Damrosch and Thomas. In 1894, he gave the world premiere of his more mature Cello Concerto No. 2 with the New York Philharmonic. Dvořák was in attendance and was inspired to compose his own cello concerto, a repertory staple ever since.

Young Herbert, audiences and critics agreed, was a world-class artist on the cusp of a magnificent career, destined to be—in the widely quoted but wildly premature appraisal of his Pilsner-swilling buddy James Huneker—the "Irish Wagner."

The next stepping stone for Herbert in the ordinary course of events would have been leading a symphony orchestra of his own. Despite his compelling résumé (he had also served as assistant conductor to Thomas and Seidl and conducted the prestigious Worcester Festival orchestra), no such opportunities were on the horizon. The number of "permanent" symphony orchestras in the United States—those with an institutional existence, dependable funding, and a stable roster of musicians—could be counted on the fingers of one hand.

As he reached the age of thirty-five, Herbert's rapid rise to the top of the classical music world had stalled, even as his financial imperatives were mounting. His ever more epicurean lifestyle collided with a severe national recession, the pinch tightened further by his wife's decision to retire from the operatic stage and devote herself to raising the couple's two American-born children, managing Victor's career, and presiding over their bustling, servant-filled residence and salon on Park Avenue.

Though short on symphony orchestras, the United States at the fin de siècle was awash with military-style brass bands. In 1893, a vacancy opened at the helm of one of the best, the 22nd Regiment Band of New York, better known as "Gilmore's Band." The group was celebrated for both its disciplined musicianship and its raucous showmanship (its take on Verdi's "Anvil Chorus," replete with dozens of anvils and cannon fire, was legendary), but it was struggling after the sudden death of its leader, Patrick Gilmore. As key personnel were defecting to the newly formed rival band of John Philip Sousa, Herbert assumed Gilmore's mantle, trading in the evening dress of a symphony orchestra player for the fitted tunic and regalia of a tin-pot militia commandant.

Herbert embraced the lowbrow conventions of his new role with grace, even gusto, programming crowd-pleasing light classics, charging popular prices, and serving with boyish glee as drum major when the ensemble marched to its engagements. Herbert quickly revitalized Gilmore's Band musically and commercially, while smoothing over some of its excesses. "It was as Gilmore's successor," writes Neil Gould, "that Herbert first achieved the status of a musical superstar."

By 1894, Herbert was reported to be making more money than any other person in America whose vocation was music, but leading Gilmore's Band neither exhausted his energies nor fully satisfied his pecuniary needs. Just a few weeks after the successful premiere of his second cello concerto, Herbert's compositional career veered onto an entirely new course. He entered into a contract to provide a score for an operetta to be produced on Broadway and taken on tour by the leading American light opera company of the day, the Bostonians.

Herbert's show, *Prince Ananias,* was a flop, burdened by "an inept and inane libretto that clouded appreciation of the music's worth," writes Gerald Bordman. ("This," he adds dryly, "was to be the case with many Herbert shows.") But no one doubted that Herbert had the right stuff. "When he knows the operetta field better," one critic wrote, "he will make his melodic framework smaller and stick to the elementary song form which is easily within the grasp of operetta audiences."

It soon became clear that in light opera, especially of the comic-romantic variety, Herbert had found his métier. Over the next four years and five shows, Herbert honed the tricks of his new trade, learning how "not to write over the heads of his audience." His breakthrough as a theatrical composer came in 1898 with *The Fortune Teller*, which went on to be one of Herbert's greatest successes, its "Gypsy Love Song" his first stand-alone hit song.

Both the show and the song benefited from Herbert's new affiliation with an upstart music publisher, M. Witmark & Sons. Purveyors of sentimental waltzes, two-steps, and "coon songs," the Witmarks had just opened a new office on Manhattan's West 28th Street, planting the first flag on the block that would soon be known as Tin Pan Alley. The Witmarks gave Herbert the promotional razzle-dazzle needed to put his theatrical scores over to the masses who bought sheet music for their parlor pianos. Herbert gave the Witmarks a touch of class that set the firm apart from the rest of the Tin Pan Alley crowd. Together, Herbert and the Witmarks would raise to new heights the art of "turning cheap sheets of music paper into thousand-dollar bills."

Herbert found no shortage of kindred spirits on Broadway. In 1896, he was elected to membership in the Lambs Club, a louche, preening fraternity of actors, playwrights, and other theatrical personages and hangers-on. The Lambs, Theodore Dreiser wrote, did not "lay claim to any extraordinary purposes or plans or even an elevating influence." Their principal activity in those years was entertaining each other with "Gambols" performed in their private theater. "Current plays, monologues and specialties were travestied (in many cases by professionals who burlesqued their own parts)," an internal club history states, adding with characteristic self-regard, "the Lambs' Theater became the center of the wit and humor of New York Bohemia." Once each year, as a fundraiser to address the club's chronic indebtedness, the Lambs would rent out a Broadway-class theater to present a Gambol open to the ticket-buying public.

Not long after Herbert joined, when the club was in especially dire financial straits, the Lambs decided to take an "All-Star Gambol" on a multicity tour. Herbert was the musical director for this production, which combined blackface minstrelsy with sophomoric sketches that both parodied and promoted the members' stage hits. At each stop on the tour, the entire troupe, led by Herbert and his brass band, paraded from the train station to the theater clad in buckled top hats and double-breasted linen frocks with ruffled collars, the spectacle on the whole suggesting a Thanksgiving pageant put on by Leprechauns. Even for a public accustomed to the sight of Victor Herbert costumed in cheesy military decorations, this deliberately buffoonish getup was an arresting image to say the least.

The arrival of a Lambs Club All-Star Gambol, led by music director Victor Herbert and his fifty-piece brass band, was a spectacle not soon forgotten. *(Chicago Tribune)*

Victor Herbert now inhabited the dissolute realm of popular entertainment with the same charisma he had so recently brought to the rarefied world of "longhair" high culture. Voluntarily and without reservation, he had taken a path previously reserved for those who could not make the grade as "serious" artists. He would soon have an opportunity to test whether that was a path of no return.

Nathan Burkan graduated from New York University Law School in 1899, after completing a two-year course of study offered at the time to college graduates. Still several months short of his twenty-first birthday, he was too young to sit for the state bar examination that year. In the interim, he took a job as a stenographer with lawyer Julius Lehmann.

Lehmann had a busy office on the site of the present-day Woolworth Tower, near the state and federal courts in which he appeared regularly. His practice was typical of the mix of legal work that was relegated to the small clique of Jewish lawyers in New York City's highly stratified bar at the turn of the twentieth century—mostly low-status matters such as criminal and civil litigation, bankruptcy, and matrimonial law.

Lehmann raised his profile in the legal community with newsworthy work on behalf of prominent artists, including some of Victor Herbert's earliest musical associates. He represented Walter Damrosch in multiple cases arising out of the messy affairs of his short-lived German Opera Company. He represented the flamboyant Jewish violinist Nahan Franko (Herbert's concertmaster at the Metropolitan Opera) in a series of tabloid-friendly disputes with his gentile in-laws—brewery magnate

Jacob Ruppert and family—which culminated in a grisly fight over possession of the corpse of the young Ruppert heiress who had eloped with Franko shortly before she died of typhoid fever. Victor Herbert, as he rose to the top ranks of New York's musical world, quite naturally hired Lehmann to look after his legal interests.

It was, as far as can be determined, sheer fortuity that Burkan found himself apprenticed to a lawyer with a theatrical clientele. Burkan was not himself artistically inclined in any way, nor does it appear that he possessed any taste for music or theater beyond that offered in the crudest variety and burlesque halls. Lehmann, however, was a solid Tammany man, active in Lower Manhattan's Jefferson Democratic Club. It was almost certainly this political connection that led to Burkan's situation with Lehmann, not some affinity, conscious or subconscious, for what would become his life's work.

Upon being admitted to the bar in 1900, Burkan threw himself into all aspects of Lehmann's practice, the glamorous and the mundane, with equal diligence. Burkan had been a licensed attorney-at-law less than a year when Victor Herbert walked into Lehmann's office with the case that would launch a brilliant legal career.

CHAPTER 2

The Pittsburgh Troubles

The events that brought the disparate immigrant paths of Nathan Burkan and Victor Herbert into an unlikely and fateful convergence began in 1898, when Herbert embarked on a new phase of his career in Pittsburgh, Pennsylvania.

A few years earlier, flush with the steel fortunes of Carnegie and Frick, Pittsburgh had become the fourth American city to join the permanent symphony orchestra movement. After three artistically desultory and fiscally insolvent years under the leadership of a local organist, the Pittsburgh Symphony Orchestra's financial guarantors demanded a change. Victor Herbert was offered the job of conductor, it appearing that his ambitions and financial circumstances dovetailed perfectly with the orchestra's. "My operas and other work have made me independent financially," Herbert told the press. "It was not money that brought me here. It is my ambition to make the orchestra second to none in the world."

Classical music's gatekeepers did not rush to welcome the prodigal son back into the fold. Even in Pittsburgh, civic pride over attracting America's maestro-in-waiting was tempered with apprehension that the goods had spoiled on the shelf, "that his brass band work and his light opera antics have changed him greatly from the Victor Herbert who achieved some reputation as the cellist of Theodore Thomas' orchestra." Under the title "Bim-Boum and Pilsner," the *Pittsburgh Press* reported that commentators were "lamenting Herbert's 'vulgarity' as a composer and his absorbing passion for the effects produced by a big drum." His "chief distinction," it was being said, "lies in his being the 'only living Irishman who drinks Pilsner.'"

The most strident voice among the Herbert skeptics could be found in the pages of the *Musical Courier*, the very journal where James Huneker had anointed Herbert the "Irish Wagner" only a few years earlier. Under editor Marc A. Blumenberg, an astute and highly opinionated businessman who was well versed in the fine arts, the *Musical Courier* of the 1890s was the world's most comprehensive and profitable weekly periodical devoted to music. A contemporary writer put his finger on the source of its appeal:

> The Musical Courier affords a great variety of interesting matter, and the treatment is light and brilliant rather than earnest and dignified. It is the tone of the club man after dinner . . . Accordingly, it has a large following of what might be called the "worldly element" in music. It fills a place, and it would not be impossible to remove from its columns everything against which gentlemanly taste would rebel without in the act depriving it of the source of its real power.

Stripped of circumlocutions and double negatives, this was a good Victorian's way of saying that much of the *Courier*'s criticism, especially when anonymously penned by Blumenberg himself, trafficked in gratuitous snark and mean-spirited gossip. His writing was notorious "for the violence of its antipathies." Blumenberg's penchant for colorful invective made him countless enemies in the music world. When combined with his reputation for sharp business practices, it gave rise to a widely held suspicion that the paper's editorial judgments were for sale.

Blumenberg was a complicated man. He was an unapologetic defender of the American "genteel tradition"—a term coined in 1911 by George Santayana, and later appropriated by cultural critic Gilbert Seldes, to describe an intellectual mindset that discouraged open appreciation and serious criticism of the popular arts. Classical music and popular music, in Blumenberg's view, especially American popular music, were fundamentally incommensurable enterprises, the latter being unsusceptible to and unworthy of critical appraisal. The *Courier*'s mission, Blumenberg said, was to turn the American public "not radically, but gradually" from treating music as a form of entertainment to appreciating it as an art, which would in time lead to the extinction of popular music.

Blumenberg's commercial unsavoriness and his deeply felt musical elitism coexisted in an uneasy equilibrium. Huneker, who wrote for the *Cou-*

rier from 1887 to 1902, apparently without editorial interference, was unstinting in vouching for Blumenberg's devotion to the arts and artists. Near the end of a life in which he had befriended many of the leading artists of the early twentieth century, Huneker wrote of Blumenberg:

> His faults, no doubt, were many, but he boasted virtues that some of his opponents could not. Above all, he was not a hypocrite. If he called the kettle black, he cheerfully admitted the sootiness of the pot. I never came in contact with a more agile intellect, nor with a cheerier nature than his.

Huneker wrote laudatory reviews of Victor Herbert's work throughout his time at the *Courier*, while Blumenberg lambasted Herbert in the harshest of terms, sometimes within a few pages of Huneker's bouquets of praise. Herbert's work with Gilmore's Band, for example, was praised in one issue of the *Courier* for its "scholarly, musicianly manner," and excoriated a few weeks later as "generally trashy and extremely noisy."

Herbert's appointment to lead the Pittsburgh Symphony elevated Blumenberg's vitriol to new heights. "Pittsburgh will find out about Victor Herbert for itself," Blumenberg warned. But he could not resist poisoning the well: "Herbert is anything you like but a good conductor.... His beat is wild and amateurish, his musical conception commonplace, and he lacks the greatest of all requisites of a conductor: He has no personal magnetism." When Herbert announced that he would continue to lead Gilmore's Band and reside in New York for half of each year, Blumenberg translated for his readers: "That is, symphony in Pittsburgh and 'All Coons Look Alike' in New York." The allusion was to a then-current M. Witmark & Sons hit song; Herbert's guilt by mere association with Tin Pan Alley was sufficiently damning that, in Blumenberg's eyes, his point required no further argumentation.

In an unfortunate coincidence, the Lambs Club's All-Star Gambol rolled through Pittsburgh shortly after the announcement of Herbert's appointment as orchestra conductor in the spring of 1898. "The people of Pittsburgh will get a first-class idea of how Band Leader Herbert will conduct Beethoven symphonies next season," another unsigned *Courier* piece warned, "when he heads the parade of the Lambs Club." If Herbert's leadership of a respected military band was suspect in Blumenberg's worldview, his participation in this traveling minstrel show was patently disqualifying:

> The same man who conducts a brass band, who is at the head of a theatrical frolic, marching at the head of a street band through the thoroughfares of a city, the hero of the gamins, is selected to conduct the supposed reposeful,

aesthetic concerts dedicated to symphony, to Beethoven, to Mozart, to John Sebastian, to Tchaikovsky! Is it a wonder that we Americans are a laughing stock of civilization?

Once Herbert actually ascended the podium, the Pittsburgh public and press rallied to his cause. Herbert put the demands of the Pittsburgh Symphony at the forefront of his activities, and he adhered scrupulously to the norms of the polite world of classical music. He moved his principal residence to Pittsburgh, ended his association with Gilmore's Band, and after completing existing contractual commitments took a hiatus from Broadway and turned his attention back to composing concert works.

Herbert's diligent work, promising results, and faultless deportment with the Pittsburgh Symphony may not have mollified Blumenberg, but for several years it kept him relatively quiet. The *Courier*'s coverage of Herbert's first three seasons in Pittsburgh was mostly fair and sober.

That came to an end in the early summer of 1901, when two seemingly unrelated pieces of gossip reached Blumenberg's ears. First, word came that a London production of *The Fortune Teller* had closed after a somewhat disappointing run. Second, Herbert announced his intention to take the Pittsburgh Symphony on a "pops" tour the following spring, a for-profit venture that Herbert would underwrite out of his own pocket. In Blumenberg's mind this was proof of what he had warned of all along: that putting a brass bandmaster in charge of a symphony orchestra was an act of cultural self-immolation.

Blumenberg's July 17, 1901, editorial entitled "The Pittsburgh Troubles" may be the most bizarre and disordered verbal fusillade ever fired in the cause of musical snobbery. Any attempt to coherently summarize it requires some departure from Blumenberg's jumbled sequence of thoughts. After declaring it a self-evident truth that "our standards of taste are based on European decisions," Blumenberg cannot conceal his delight over the news out of London:

> This paper long since declared not only that the *Fortune Teller* had no merit whatever, but that all of Victor Herbert's "written to order" comic operas were pure and simple plagiarisms. . . . The whole Herbert repertory is stone dead, and London merely acted on rhythmic impulse when it rejected this agglomeration of puerile piracies and refused to countenance them.

"Everything written by Herbert is copied," it goes on; "there is not one original strain in anything he has done."

Ignoring Herbert's exemplary background in classical music, Blumenberg writes that "he became popular suddenly by attaining command of a brass band and joining a rollicking club of actors and Bohemians known as the Lambs." The Lambs, lacking "any musical comprehension," made Herbert their musical director, and "American fashion immediately paralleled him with serious-minded composers."

"But what has all this to do with Pittsburgh?" Blumenberg asks rhetorically. He answers: "From the very outset it could not be understood by equipoised minds how a writer of comic operas (and American comic operas at that), and a conductor of brass bands accustomed to parade at the head of militia and processions, could possibly be the director of a symphony orchestra. How Pittsburgh intelligence could ever select this clever bandmaster as its symphony director passes comprehension." In conclusion, Blumenberg asserts that "the great symphony conductors are not drafted from the ranks of the composers of the shoddy American farces, alias 'leg shows,' nor are they taken from the leaders of the parading military bands."

The *Musical Courier* had not, in fact, previously accused Herbert of musical piracy or plagiarism. It had written that Herbert's theatrical scores were "almost beneath criticism," that he was living proof that "a man cannot successfully compose, conduct and play 'cello," and that Herbert should "pause in his mad flight after the shining dollar and cheap applause," but assertions of plagiarism and piracy are of an altogether different category. They go beyond subjective criticism of the art to impugn the character and integrity of the artist, ostensibly on the basis of known but unstated facts. Herbert, who had ignored Blumenberg's imprecations for years, understood the difference. He had his lawyer, Julius Lehmann, demand a retraction. When none such was forthcoming, the case of *Herbert v. Musical Courier* was formally commenced on October 21, 1901, the plaintiff seeking $50,000 in damages for defamation. To do the legal spade work that taking on a well-financed, ideologically committed defendant entailed, Lehmann turned to Nathan Burkan, his twenty-two-year-old associate.

At the turn of the twentieth century, New York State still followed the English common law of defamation, which was (and remains to this day) friendly terrain for plaintiffs. Blumenberg's accusations of piracy and plagiarism constituted libel per se—words that by their very nature and on their face would tend to hold Herbert up to public scorn, impugn his integrity, and/or injure him in his vocation. Herbert could therefore collect damages for reputational and emotional harm without proving any actual monetary loss. And if the jury was satisfied that the libel was published with malice (in careless or reckless disregard of the truth, or with ill will), it could also award punitive damages. The dollar amounts required to compensate the plaintiff and punish the defendant would be entirely within the discretion of the jury.

New York law recognized a privilege for fair criticism, but this required that the critic "confine himself to criticism and not make it the veil for personal censure, nor allow himself to run into reckless and unfair attacks merely for the purpose of exercising his power of denunciation." As a New York judge once charged a jury, "The critic can call a painting a daub and an abortion, but he cannot call the painter himself a low, discreditable pretender and an abortion."

Lehmann and Burkan correctly surmised that when the case came to trial the court would not even submit the question of privilege to the jury. That would leave the *Musical Courier* with only one defense: truth, or, in legal parlance, "justification." Under the common law, the defendant would bear the burden of providing proof "as broad as the charge . . . proof of the truth of one out of many charges does not constitute a justification." Lehmann and Burkan surely gamed out that proving the literal truth of Blumenberg's categorical charge that Herbert had written *nothing* original—that "there is not one original strain in anything he has done"—would require laborious dissection of every measure Herbert had ever composed, a practical impossibility. Blumenberg would have no choice but to prove out his core thesis that American popular music, by its very nature, *could not* be anything other than the by-product of plagiarism and piracy. *Herbert v. Musical Courier* would put the genteel tradition itself on trial.

Herbert and his legal team would be ready. Above all, they would not bow to Blumenberg's brand of Eurocentrism. Quite the contrary, the plaintiff would proudly wrap himself in the red, white, and blue. Just one week before the start of trial, Herbert, by then already a resident of the United States for sixteen years, went to the federal courthouse in Pittsburgh to take the oath of citizenship.

As the case moved quickly toward a trial date, Lehmann and Burkan received a bracing preview of what might be in store for them. In the summer of 1901, the great African American minstrel team of Bert Williams and George Walker had a hit with a cakewalk called "Good Morning, Carrie," the publication of which had, fortuitously, coincided with a spike in public attention to Carrie Nation's temperance campaign. The publisher of an earlier, less successful cakewalk, "It's Up to You, Babe," sued for copyright infringement. Lehmann was engaged to defend. Burkan collected affidavits from prominent musicians and composers arguing that "Good Morning, Carrie" took nothing from "It's Up to You, Babe" that was original; the alleged similarities, they said, would be found in comparing any two examples of "what is technically called in the music trade a 'coon serenade.'"

At a temporary restraining order hearing, Judge E. Henry Lacombe of the federal district court in Manhattan confessed his ignorance of "ragtime" and refused to listen to recordings of the two songs. When another court official offered to play the tunes for him on the fiddle, Lacombe "shoved the papers in his safe and hurriedly left the building." The *Times* ran an editorial applauding Lacombe, agreeing that he "had better use for his brain endowment than to fritter it away in drawing nice distinctions between musical compositions which admit of no other classification than 'drunk and disorderly.'" (Elsewhere, editorials were more explicitly racist in tone: "Coon songs, like coons, are all very much alike.") The case was a wake-up call for Lehmann and Burkan. The court eventually denied a restraining order, but the persistence of the genteel tradition in the judiciary and the press had to be worrisome.

One more pretrial jolt awaited Herbert's legal team. On May 22, 1902, Julius Lehmann, age thirty-six, died unexpectedly of complications from surgery for an ear abscess. Nathan Burkan, just three years out of law school, not yet two years at the bar, received a battlefield promotion to counsel of record, a vote of confidence from Victor Herbert that would be vindicated many times over in the years to come.

CHAPTER 3

To Victor Belong the Spoils

The trial of *Herbert v. Musical Courier* began on October 22, 1902, in the Old New York County Courthouse—a storied monument to Tammany Hall corruption often called the "Tweed Courthouse"—on Chambers Street in Lower Manhattan. With a jury and an elected New York State Supreme Court justice presiding, Herbert's popularity with the public figured to be a valuable asset. (In the New York court system, confusingly, the "Supreme Court" is a lower trial court.) Burkan made sure the courtroom was conspicuously "packed to the doors with musical and theatrical folk" each day. In a stroke of luck, the judge assigned to the case, Charles Truax, had been a friend of Julius Lehmann and was reported to be an inveterate Broadway first-nighter.

Burkan lined up some of the leading lights of American music to testify on Herbert's behalf, including Walter Damrosch and Henry Hadley, the most widely performed American-born orchestral composer of the day. In a concession to his own youth and inexperience, Burkan engaged a veteran trial lawyer, Arthur C. Palmer, a Connecticut Yankee known for eloquence inside and outside the courtroom, to serve as "first chair."

To defend the *Courier,* Blumenberg hired Abraham Hummel, the self-educated junior member of New York City's most notorious law partnership, Howe & Hummel. The firm was then nearing the end of a nearly forty-year run as, in *New Yorker* writer Richard Rovere's words, "the mouthpieces, if not, as was often asserted, the brains" of New York's underworld. Profiling the firm nearly four decades after it had dissolved,

Rovere found that Howe & Hummel anecdotes were still staples of New York City legal folklore. "Blackmail, subornation of perjury, the corruption of public officials, and the fabrication of evidence were part of each day's routine." In his attitude, appearance, and penchant for quibbling, the diminutive Hummel conformed closely to the "literary stereotype of a shyster." Palmer and Burkan had every reason to gird themselves for some outrageous courtroom shenanigans. For what other purpose would Marc Blumenberg have engaged Abe Hummel?

Herbert's case-in-chief was perfunctory. A stream of his friends and associates testified about various occasions on which they had witnessed Herbert in the act of composing music without apparent reliance on source materials. Herbert took the stand briefly to deny that he had copied any of his music. On cross-examination, Hummel tried to get him to admit that *The Fortune Teller* had indeed been a failure in London. Herbert denied it, attributing the shortened run to a period of mourning following Queen Victoria's death. Hummel, standing about five feet tall and tipping the scale at less than one hundred pounds, bore in on the corpulent witness: "I am not versed in the history of *your* queen." The newly naturalized Herbert seized this opening to declare to the jury: "I'm an American!"

Before the trial began, Hummel had been promising that he would present an all-star line-up of expert witnesses, including composer Pietro Mascagni and the conductors of the New York Philharmonic and Boston Symphony. None of these notables showed, leaving the defense to rely on a few B-list experts who shared Blumenberg's low opinion of Herbert. Speaking in dialects that the newspapers of the era felt no compunction about crudely caricaturing ("What a peety eet ees zat I talk wiz a man who never knew ze music!"), they analyzed no more than a half-dozen isolated phrases in Herbert scores that they thought closely resembled previously published works of others:

Palmer. Then what struck your notice [in Herbert's full-length operetta *Wizard of the Nile*] was what?

Witness. Four measures.

Q. That they were similar to something in a waltz song that you cannot remember the name of, the composer of, nor where you heard it?

A. If you choose to put it that way.

The jurors never heard a single note of either the originals or the alleged copies performed, but instead were treated to a seminar on music taught by hopeless pedants. "Mr. Hummel, who says he has taken lessons in music for months as a preliminary to the trial, used at least fifty-seven technical musical terms at the opening day's session," one reporter noted. "The expressions on the twelve jurymen's faces were painful to look at." Even if the jurors had found the isolated examples identified by Blumenberg's witnesses convincing, they fell far short of the required "proof as broad as the charge" that Herbert had written *nothing* original.

Herbert's experts testified that the resemblances the defense relied upon were all on the level of what copyright lawyers would call "scènes à faire"—themes, rhythms, and harmonies so native to the genres in which Herbert was working as to constitute common property freely available to any composer, the use of which constituted no evidence of copying at all. The originality of Herbert's music, they testified, resided in the realm of coloring and style, in his uniquely "Herbertian" development of commonplace elements. In this respect, he was not different from most serious composers, excepting only the most protean of musical geniuses, such as Mozart, Beethoven, and Wagner.

By all accounts, "Walter Damrosch was the most enlightening witness to the lay mind." Damrosch pointed out that he and Herbert were rivals as conductors, but he was generous in his praise of Herbert's compositions and emphatic in rejecting the charge of plagiarism, analogizing the similarities that the defense had seized upon to those between two stories beginning "once upon a time" or sharing a setting in Paris. "The sonorous tones of the symphony leader filled the courtroom like a huge cathedral organ," wrote the *New York Herald*. "The jurors had been nodding at the tiresome iteration of previous witnesses about themes, melody, point and counterpoint. As Mr. Damrosch's resonant voice rang out, they sat up jerkily and leaned forward."

The defense would rise or fall on Marc Blumenberg's ability to sell the jury on the proposition that the charges he leveled against Victor Herbert were not mere empirical facts—the types of facts that a courtroom trial is reasonably suited to determining—but rather logical corollaries that followed from what he deemed to be a priori truths: Music written under contract to appeal to a musically uneducated American audience, in exchange for money, by definition *could not* be original or meritorious, and furthermore, anyone who has shown an ability to catch the public's fancy with such works "*cannot* legitimately aspire" to compose or conduct classical music. "Such a man cannot be in an aesthetic condition and artistic mental condition that enabled him to devote his time to great classical work." "The two pursuits are contradictory." The artistic balancing act that we have come to call "crossover" was, to Blumenberg, simply an impossibility as a matter of logic.

On the witness stand, Blumenberg seemed nonplussed by the very idea that he should have to prove propositions he knew to be axiomatically true. As to his central allegation that every line of Herbert's music was copied, he insisted that "there is no necessity for verifying it unless you please to do so, when you hear the composition you know it at once." He made dogmatic pronouncements of the type that often appeared in the pages of his publication—it is a "natural conclusion" that "money kills inspiration," true musical genius "never" copies, European opinion in the arts is "paramount"—but he became flustered when pressed on their implications or presented with counterexamples. Herbert's music, he said at one point, could not meet his exacting classical standards "because he is living, it takes longer than his life to fix itself":

> *Palmer.* Is it true in all cases, that before a man's music can be considered classical, he must die?
>
> *Blumenberg.* In nearly all cases the history of music shows it.
>
> Q. Was Wagner considered classical before he died?
>
> A. Yes, except in some countries they did not recognize him until after his death.
>
> Q. And Verdi was another?
>
> A. Verdi became very old and outlived it.
>
> Q. How was it with Mozart?
>
> A. He was recognized in Austria where he lived, but not to the extent that he was until 10 or 15 years after his death.

The longer Blumenberg spoke, the more mystifying his distinctions became. Herbert was "not a good composer as a composer," he testified, "but he was a good musician as a composer."

Even without knowing the eventual verdict, one might infer that Blumenberg's testimony came across no better in the courtroom in 1902 than it does on the printed page more than a century later, since his lawyers found it necessary to request an instruction to the jury "that any physical or mental peculiarities of Mr. Blumenberg have nothing to do with the issues in this action."

Blumenberg's testimony did not support a defense of justification. Nor did he help his cause on the issue of malice. In the face of prose that oozed with animus, questioning how "Pittsburgh intelligence could ever select this clever bandmaster as its symphony director," he preposterously stated that his editorial was written with friendly feelings toward Herbert and that he had not intended to suggest that Herbert should be removed from his position. He argued that the charges of plagiarism and piracy meant only that Herbert had drawn upon familiar strains that he carried around in his head, that his copying was likely "unconscious." This was, in effect, a substantial retraction of the editorial at issue. Blumenberg would hardly have been the first to observe that Herbert's music was "reminiscent," nor would such a charge be libelous per se. The fact that Blumenberg had refused to make this concession in print, after receiving a demand for a retraction, only strengthened the inference of malicious intent.

The one witness who might have credibly vouched for Blumenberg's good faith, James Huneker, did not appear. After a fifteen-year association, he had resigned from the staff of the *Courier* just one week before the start of the trial to become the full-time theater critic for the *New York Sun,* telling Blumenberg he was "weary of the atmosphere of petty intrigue, personalities, and futile bickering that disgrace the profession of weekly musical journalism." Huneker never commented publicly on *Herbert v. Musical Courier,* but the timing of his departure leaves little doubt as to where he stood.

Burkan could not have imagined that the trial would be such a walk in the park. Damrosch had been articulate and engaging. Blumenberg had bombed on the stand. Huneker was not there to smooth Blumenberg's rough edges. Abe Hummel, but for some sarcasm and minor histrionics, had been a model of courtroom decorum, his cross-examinations utterly ineffectual. Victor Herbert's attorneys had come prepared for a brawl, not the well-mannered class in music theory that was transpiring. Their failure to adjust their tactics accordingly proved costly in the end.

Playing off Blumenberg's reputation for trading favorable reviews for advertising dollars, Palmer and Burkan presented evidence showing that Herbert had last advertised in the *Musical Courier* in 1898, and that prior to that time he had received many good notices. The timeline, however, was not compelling; there had been bad reviews before that date and good ones after. To juice up their theory, they resorted to what, even then, was one of the oldest tricks in the book. Over Abe Hummel's vociferous objections, Palmer and Blumenberg had the following exchange:

Palmer. Did you say to Mr. Weil [Otto Weil, Herbert's one-time agent] that if Herbert did not continue to advertise, you would pound him, because it was business?

Blumenberg. Never in my life. I never made a remark of that kind.

Q. You were trying to get Victor Herbert to advertise again?

A. Never.

Q. Never to anybody?

A. No one.

Q. And you never said to Mr. Weil in substance that it was business and you were going to pound Herbert?

A. Never in my life. I never could use such a remark as that.

Weil had already been on the witness stand, but Palmer had not asked him about any such conversation. This was dirty pool, using a question to plant in the jurors' minds a highly prejudicial "fact" for which there was no competent evidence. Hummel had probably done this hundreds of times himself and knew how effective and damaging it could be; his objections were well taken. Justice Truax's tolerance of this gamesmanship, and his refusal to give the jury a curative instruction, cast an unnecessary shadow on the proceedings.

Naturally, Palmer's closing argument treated the advertising blackmail, for which there was no evidence at all, as proven fact. With this subtext and a disconcerting dollop of casual anti-Semitism thrown in, Palmer argued that it was Blumenberg the highbrow critic, not Herbert the composer for hire, who was the true mercenary, a "snake in the grass, ready to pounce" on vulnerable, sensitive artists:

> Do you believe he is the great philanthropist he pictures himself to be, laboring to elevate the art of music, or do you believe he has a shrewd, misdirected mind, that plans to turn to commercial account everything that he does? Look at him, does he look like an inspired man? If I ever saw the embodiment of the commercial spirit, I see it in him! There is only one question regarding the field of music that interests him: How much is in it for me? How much can I get for advertising?

The courtroom spectators, who had hissed and laughed during the defense's closing, now burst into applause. Justice Truax gaveled the courtroom to order, gently admonishing that any further outburst would cause him to clear the courtroom. The defense was justified in complaining on appeal that the "mild way in which the judge rebuked these manifestations" sent an unmistakable signal that his sympathies were with the plaintiff.

The jury of twelve men (New York did not allow women to serve on juries until 1937) deliberated for only an hour and forty minutes before returning a verdict of $15,000—well short of the $50,000 Herbert had sought in his complaint, but still a hefty sum, amounting to $425,000 in inflation-adjusted 2020 dollars. Herbert, his trial team, and his supporters celebrated that night at Lüchow's Restaurant, a Hofbräu and schnitzel emporium on Union Square frequented by show people and politicians. The dais was festooned with a floral wreath from M. Witmark & Sons bearing a card reading, "To the Victor Belong the Spoils."

Herbert v. Musical Courier continued to be litigated in the press for weeks on end. Blumenberg was defiant. He assured his readers that the setback was temporary and that in any event criticism "will continue to be published in this paper on the basis of its attitude during the past twenty odd years. . . . Every aggressive paper necessarily invites hostility, but its existence and its prosperity are evidences in themselves that its expressions on the average must be satisfactory."

Blumenberg cleverly turned his own disrepute into an argument for overturning the verdict. If the law allows "any musician who feels as if he or she had been wounded because of a remark made in any paper to go before a lay jury and get a money verdict, the editors of newspapers will feel themselves in a very insecure position." Papers of general circulation, according to Blumenberg, would find it economically unviable to publish music criticism that risked causing offense—that is, any music criticism worth its salt—and investors would be loath to back new music publications. Ironically, then, the field would belong solely to the established, deep-pocketed *Musical Courier,* which considered libel lawsuits to be valuable advertising and badges of honor.

Blumenberg's competitors were having none of that. Editorial opinion in both the general and trade newspapers uniformly applauded the *Herbert* verdict and saw nothing in it that threatened their business models. The *Brooklyn Eagle* opined that while phrases such as "stone dead agglomerations of puerile piracies" might be "good enough to run some risks for, whether the joy of coining it was worth $15,000 may be left to the man who must pay the bill." The *Times* remarked that the "scurrilous and 'slang-whanging' style of criticism" that the *Courier* directed at Herbert "is so old-fashioned and out-of-date in respectable periodicals that it may, happily, be called obsolete."

Blumenberg's appeal slowly wended its way through the courts. The New York Supreme Court's Appellate Division, by a 2–1 vote, affirmed the judgment on the condition that Herbert accept a reduction of the damages to $5,000. Neither the majority nor the dissenter provided a written opinion explaining this ruling, but presumably the two-thirds discount reflected a compromise between discomfiture over the plaintiff getting away with the advertising blackmail innuendo and satisfaction that rough justice had nonetheless been meted out.

New York's Court of Appeals, the state's court of last resort, affirmed the reduced judgment on December 30, 1904, also without written comment. Young Nathan Burkan, it turned out, was not averse to gloating. He let it be known that he had received payment of the judgment and court costs in "five crisp $1,000 bills, one $500 bill and four $100 bills." It was not an insubstantial sum, but if Marc Blumenberg was chastened rather than simply embittered by this loss, one would not know it from the pages of the *Musical Courier* during the remaining decade of his editorship. And it was a foregone conclusion that he would, at a time of his choosing, seek to exact revenge on Burkan.

Herbert v. Musical Courier was no landmark in the law of defamation. Its significance lies elsewhere. Most importantly, it was a repudiation of the genteel tradition and a victory for the up-until-then heretical ideas that popular culture could be original and worthy of serious critical attention, that a creditable artist could indeed provide scores for leg shows and lead brass bands through the streets, that worldly compensation and artistic inspiration were not wholly incompatible.

Far from bringing about the demise of popular music in America, Blumenberg had hastened the coming of its golden age. "Although the stated intention of the arbiters of high culture was to proselytize and convert," one scholar has written, "their attitudes often had the opposite effect." By insisting on the "sacralization" of the arts, snobs like Blumenberg stirred resentment in the general populace. "The term 'highbrow' was still young when it became a term of popular derision."

Crisp bills or not, $5,000 was not a life-changing sum for Victor Herbert. By 1909 he was said to be pulling down twice that amount in a week. But the verdict was a vindication of his artistic worth and integrity. It liberated Herbert to pursue commercial ventures unabashedly. He left the Pittsburgh Symphony in 1904 and, except for a few programs with the New York Philharmonic during the 1905–6 season, never again conducted a major symphony orchestra. Instead, he embarked upon the most productive and lucrative phase of his career, composing more than thirty theatrical works over the next twenty years, including such iconic operettas as *Babes in Toyland, Naughty Marietta,* and *The Red Mill.* He toured the country almost constantly with the peripatetic Victor Herbert Orchestra, giving musical programs that adhered to his philosophy that Bach and Wagner should not be foisted upon "those who enthuse over simpler music."

Herbert's judicially certified credibility served as the popular music industry's calling card in every important legal and political battle of the next twenty years, a crucial period during which the disruptive technologies of recordings, film, and broadcasting transformed popular music artistically and commercially. No longer would judges (or congressmen) cover their ears and run away at the sound of ragtime. Nathan Burkan would be at Herbert's side every step of the way.

The jury in *Herbert v. Musical Courier* may never have heard Burkan speak, but industry insiders knew where credit for the victory belonged. Their regard for Burkan bordered on idolatry. After the trial, Herbert's publisher, Isidore Witmark, told reporters, "I don't know that he is any relation to Nathan Hale, but he surely has some similar traits of character." Quite by happenstance, the American popular music business had found in Victor Herbert's young lawyer the crusader who would lead it to the promised land.

PART TWO

A River of Nickels

CHAPTER 4

Tin Pan Alley

The bond that Burkan formed with Victor Herbert was deep and lasting. By the time he had collected Herbert's winnings from the Musical Courier Company, early in 1905, he was representing the maestro's interests in a broad range of legal matters. Despite the twenty-year difference in their ages, they had become close friends and regular dining companions, most frequently and famously at Lüchow's. Just off Union Square, then the heart of the entertainment district, and a few steps from Tammany Hall headquarters (where Burkan's stock was continuing to climb), Lüchow's was the central node in Burkan's expanding professional and political networks. He was also a regular guest at Herbert's summer retreat in the Adirondacks, Camp Joyland, where the city-by-way-of-shtetl boy made valuable connections and developed an appreciation for the rejuvenating powers of the great outdoors, with a special fondness for horseback riding and golf. So closely did he identify with his famous client, for a time, while still in his twenties, Burkan even sported a Victor Herbert paintbrush moustache.

As if Herbert's own affairs were not enough to keep a young lawyer fully occupied, members of Herbert's vast circle—collaborators, cast members, fellow Lambs—came to Burkan with their contracts, lawsuits, divorces, and bankruptcies. With his newfound prosperity, Burkan, like many an upwardly mobile Lower East Side Jew in the nineteen-aughts, moved uptown to East Harlem, where he lived with his now-widowed mother (Moritz Burkan had died in 1901) and younger brothers

Benjamin, a pharmacist, and school-aged David. It was a manageable commute via the Third Avenue El to the bustling law office he had opened in a landmark cast-iron building at the corner of Nassau and Fulton Streets, near the downtown state and federal courthouses where he was becoming a familiar presence.

By far the most important of the clients that spilled over from Victor Herbert's world was his publisher, M. Witmark & Sons, a firm founded and managed by three Witmark brothers, Isidore, Julius, and Jay. (Their father, Marcus, lent his name to the enterprise as a legal formality while his entrepreneurial sons were still teenagers.) The Witmarks had published their first song, "Grover Cleveland's Wedding March," written by Isidore, the eldest, in 1886. By the first years of the twentieth century, the "House of Witmark" was the largest, and some would say classiest, of the music publishers on Tin Pan Alley.

Signing Victor Herbert in 1898 had been a coup for the Witmarks, bringing them prestige and an entrée into the lucrative business of licensing scores and librettos for professional and amateur theatrical productions. (The Tams-Witmark Music Library remains, to this day, one of the powerhouses of the field.) But that was a sideline. Their stock-in-trade, like that of other Tin Pan Alley publishers, was the thirty-two-bar popular song, sold in the form of sheet music for less than a quarter at wholesale.

The geographical Tin Pan Alley, a cluster of publishing offices on West 28th and 29th Streets, between Broadway and Sixth Avenue, was short-lived. The Witmark firm's brief tenancy there, from 1893 to 1903, roughly demarks the beginning and end of the otherwise nondescript neighborhood's reign as the epicenter of the popular music business. The Tin Pan Alley business model, however, endured until the late 1920s, when the Witmarks and many of their competitors were swallowed up by Hollywood studios hungry for musical content after the introduction of synchronized sound.

Tin Pan Alley songs should not be confused with the standards of the vaunted Great American Songbook which, for the most part, came along later. Conformity and simplicity were valued over originality and artistry on Tin Pan Alley. The target consumers were modestly skilled home musicians, often self-taught, who played the parlor piano and sang barbershop harmonies for their own amusement. The financial rewards for the creators of these ditties were meager, an up-front payment of a few dollars or a running royalty of a penny or two per copy. Harry von Tilzer ("Bird in a Gilded Cage"), Charles K. Harris ("After the Ball"), and Paul Dresser ("On the Banks of the Wabash") all made their names as Tin Pan Alley songwriters—but they made their real money as music publishers.

Even the best Tin Pan Alley songs were harmonically simple, easy to learn and remember, and required no great vocal or instrumental sophistication to perform satisfactorily. Songs that readily lent themselves to social singing, whether sober or drunken, were the most durable. Perhaps the Tin Pan Alley song most frequently performed today, and one representative of the genre, is the 1908 waltz "Take Me Out to the Ballgame." "Sweet Adeline" and "When Irish Eyes Are Smiling" were among the biggest Witmark hits of the early 1900s.

Tin Pan Alley churned out such numbers by the hundreds each year. Most were abysmal failures. The economics of the business depended on a select few not magically *becoming* hits, but being actively *made into* hits, selling tens or hundreds of thousands of copies, through a relentless form of marketing known as plugging. "Plugs," in Tin Pan Alley's argot, were simply public performances of a song, whether by sots in a beer garden, ringers planted in a theater balcony, well-coached demonstrators in a department store, or hurdy-gurdy men on the street. In a world without mass media, any opportunity to let potential sheet music purchasers hear a song was a valuable advertisement, and publishers went to great expense to secure them, sending their pluggers to dozens of venues in a day.

The most coveted plugs were professional performances by popular vaudeville stars who might take a song on the road and give it national exposure. "Our business is run scientifically," one of the Alley's founders, Edward B. Marks, said. "We do not boom songs until they have made a pronounced hit in whatever shows they are being sung. Then and only then do we send it out to dealers and say, 'This song is a winner.'" The cost of such plugs might be as little as providing free orchestrations and other in-kind favors, or as much as a large cash stipend. On Tin Pan Alley's ledgers, public performances were an expense item, not a source of revenue. Its history is littered with the bankruptcies of firms caught in a financial squeeze between two countervailing "evils" that the Alley was never able to eradicate, despite numerous attempts at self-policing: cut-throat price-cutting on the one end (like any commodity, Tin Pan Alley songs competed on price), and bidding wars for the best plugs on the other.

There was one tried-and-true way to reduce the risks and costs of producing a hit: copying a proven formula. "The publishers of popular music all have their places of business in a radius of five blocks in the borough of Manhattan," one witness in the "Good Morning, Carrie" case testified. As a consequence, each firm watched the others closely and "was familiar with the successful publications of its competitors." This geographical and competitive proximity, when combined with the rather small set of shared materials available for constructing simple melodies with instant and widespread appeal, guaranteed that copying would be rampant on Tin Pan Alley. "If a songwriter is ethical," Edward B. Marks said, "he will not cop a tune within three years of its publication." Copyrights were the principal asset of the Tin Pan Alley publishers, and copyright infringement litigation, or the mere threat of it, was simply the continuation of the music publishing business by other means.

Article I, section 8, of the U.S. Constitution grants Congress the power to "promote the Progress of Science and useful Arts, by securing for limited Times to Authors and Inventors the exclusive Right to their respective Writings and Discoveries." "The immediate effect of our copyright law is to secure a fair return for an 'author's' creative labor," Supreme Court Justice Potter Stewart wrote in 1975. "But the ultimate aim is, by this incentive, to stimulate artistic creativity for the general public good." When the "limited time" expires, so too does the "exclusive right," and the "writings" enter the public domain, freely available to all. The history of our copyright law has been a gradual process of Congress and the federal courts assigning expanding meaning to the words "limited times," "exclusive right," and "writings," and putting sharper teeth into the remedies for infringements of copyright. The evolution of the American entertainment industries has closely tracked these developments in copyright law in a symbiotic cycle, sometimes responding to changes in the law and sometimes triggering them.

In the Copyright Act of 1790, styled "an act for the encouragement of learning," the first Congress took a rather narrow view of its constitutional authority, providing that the authors of "maps, charts, and books" could, by complying with certain formalities, obtain "the sole right and liberty of printing, reprinting, publishing and vending" for a period of fourteen years (renewable for another fourteen years if the author was still living). In 1831, the initial term was extended to twenty-eight years, the right of renewal extended to widows and heirs, and the list of protectable writings expanded to include "prints," "engravings," and "musical compositions." For the first time, purely aesthetic objects, neither textual nor informational, qualified as "writings," opening the door to protection of all sorts of matter that, whatever their artistic merits, have only the most attenuated connection to "progress in science and the useful arts."

In an 1856 amendment, Congress extended protection to "dramatic compositions" and conferred on the authors of such works, in addition to the exclusive right to publish and sell them in book form, "the sole right also to act, perform, or represent the same . . . on any stage or public place." This was another significant conceptual leap, the first grant of an exclusive right over the reproduction of a writing in an intangible and impermanent medium of communication—a "performing" right.

In the waning days of the Civil War, as Matthew Brady's work was gaining recognition for its artistry, above and beyond mechanical representation of objective reality, Congress extended copyright protection to photographs, and in 1870 to paintings, drawings, and statuary. When Brady's successor as America's leading portrait photographer, Napoleon Sarony, brought suit against an unauthorized reproducer of a photograph he had taken of Oscar Wilde in 1882, a picture that helped establish Wilde as a fashion icon, it was argued that a photograph was not a "writing" within the meaning of the Constitution. The Supreme Court, however, upheld the copyright, stating that "writings" could include anything "by which the ideas in the mind of the author are given visible expression." In posing, dressing, and lighting Wilde as he did, Sarony had created a visual expression of his own intellectual conception and was entitled to a copyright on it.

The 1870 act also expanded the bundle of exclusive rights to include dramatization and translation, a humble beginning to what we now call the right to make "derivative" works, a catchall that includes the merchandising and adaptation rights that undergird multimedia franchises such as Harry Potter and Spiderman, manifested in everything from school lunch boxes to theme park attractions.

An 1897 amendment recognized that the ephemeral nature of dramatic performances resulted in many infringements going undetected and unpenalized, and that therefore a more effective deterrent was needed. It provided that if an infringing performance was "willful and for profit," the violator could be imprisoned for up to a year. Dramatists and theatrical producers had lobbied hard for this bill. In addition to the enhanced penalties, they sought a clarification that the exclusive right of public performance applied to theatrical works with music as well as to straight dramas. Through the vagaries of the legislative drafting process, early language that granted an exclusive performance right in "dramatic or operatic compositions" morphed into the much broader "dramatic or musical compositions." The vast implications of this language, which would apply as forcefully to a vaudeville rendition of "Take Me Out to the Ballgame" as to a fully staged Victor Herbert operetta, seem to have gone largely unnoticed at the time.

In December 1902, Oliver Wendell Holmes Jr. took a seat on the U.S. Supreme Court. Less than two months later, he handed down the first of his many important copyright opinions. The case concerned the validity of a copyright on an illustrated circus poster. Holmes rejected the argument that copyrightability of a work could be defeated by its commercial origins or lack of artistic pretension: "If they command the interest of any public, they have a commercial value—it would be bold to say that they have not an aesthetic and educational value—and the taste of any public is not to be treated with contempt."

Such was the state of play as the century turned, and just as revolutionary new technologies of mass entertainment were arriving on the scene.

Publishing the sort of commodified music that Tin Pan Alley specialized in would surely have been a losing business proposition absent copyright protection. No genius was required to produce these tunes, and the economic barriers to entering the business were trivial. Yet despite its existential dependence on copyright, Tin Pan Alley in its early years was an unusually passive special interest group.

Other copyright-intensive industries had become highly effective in getting their voices heard on Capitol Hill—where copyright bills were constantly on the calendar—and in launching litigation to advance their institutional interests. The nascent film industry acted early on to establish copyright eligibility of its productions under the statutory category "photographs," and book publishers and theatrical producers pounced on the film industry as soon as it began adapting their copyrighted works for motion pictures. Music publishers, in contrast, were a relatively fractious and shortsighted lot. Their business was selling music in printed form and their vision for the future was one in which they would continue to do so indefinitely. Neither the possibilities nor the challenges posed by new technologies seemed to stir their hidebound imaginations.

In 1895, the Witmarks and a few other leading Tin Pan Alley firms joined with some old-guard publishers of "standard" music (that is, classical, traditional, and liturgical music) to form the Music Publishers Association of the United States. The minutes of this group's early meetings

read like burlesques of a well-intentioned but hopelessly ineffectual chapter of the Rotary Club. "Interesting reports of the various officers were
read and approved and ordered placed on file," a typical entry went.
"These show the association to be in excellent condition and well fitted
for the important work before it." Year after year, committees were
formed, plans were hatched, no measurable progress was achieved, pro-
fuse expressions of gratitude and self-congratulation were exchanged,
and the cycle of futility was repeated. The president's annual message
regularly included an assurance to the effect that, while "it would seem at
times as though the association was standing still, such is not the fact."
The secretary annually lamented that despite hundreds of membership
applications having been mailed out, only a handful had been returned.

One of the association's most intractable problems, also revisited every
year, was counterfeit sheet music. Copyright law, by capturing not only
exact, literal copies, but also imitations "varying, adding to, or diminish-
ing the main design with intent to evade the law," was useful for enforcing a minimal ethos of nonplagiarism within the trade. The penalties
available, and the cost of litigation, were enough to give a legitimate competitor pause before knocking off a hit. Not so with fly-by-night operators who trafficked in counterfeit sheet music. Without any royalty obligations or promotional expenses, their cost of doing business was so low
that they could easily absorb an occasional seizure of their inventory.
Money judgments against them were generally uncollectible.

Frustrated with the Music Publishers Association's torpid pace, the
Witmarks brought their dynamic young lawyer to the eleventh annual
meeting, held at the Broadway Central Hotel in New York on June 13,
1905. Nathan Burkan arrived with fresh, actionable ideas on counterfeiting and other nettlesome issues. He left as the first general counsel to
the music industry's most important, and now newly energized, trade
association.

Burkan's plan for dealing with the problem of counterfeit sheet music
was simple in concept. The civil remedies available under federal copyright law had proven insufficient, but the New York State Penal Code
made it a crime to sell "an article of merchandise" bearing a *trademark*
that falsely identified its source. Sheet music counterfeiters who hoped
to sell their wares through legitimate channels needed to make exact
copies, including any publisher trademarks. If they could be caught and
prosecuted under the New York law, conviction would be relatively
easy and jail time would be an effective deterrent to others.

The difficulty with the plan was that it required enlisting law enforcement to prosecute. The Manhattan district attorney, William Jerome, was a reformer and a tireless crusader against vice and political corruption; he would be reluctant to expend his resources on behalf of a victim class that was itself considered somewhat unsavory, especially at the behest of a Tammany Hall man. Burkan would have to engage private detectives to collect evidence against perpetrators who were careful to cover their tracks. Then he would have to take the laboring oar beside whatever junior assistant district attorney was assigned to accompany him to the seediest, most sharp-elbowed courtroom that he would ever set foot in, Manhattan's Tombs Police Court.

Burkan needed one showy case that would intrigue Jerome and make a big enough splash to send a message to the counterfeiting underworld at large. Enter one Garrett J. Couchois.

Couchois was an American original, a self-published songwriter with a few modest successes to his credit, the inventor of patented designs for whistles played through the nostrils—"nose flutes"—and a talented forger. His counterfeit sheet music was virtually indistinguishable from the authentic originals, and the phony invoices that he printed were good enough to overcome any doubts his customers might have as to the provenance of merchandise that was being offered to them at low, low prices. The forgeries were so convincing that some of Couchois's customers didn't think twice before availing themselves of their right to return unsold copies to the actual publishers, which included several members of the Music Publishers Association. They alerted Burkan, whose detectives traced the fakes to the Couchois home in Rutherford, New Jersey, where they could see the suspect, through his kitchen window, unpacking boxes containing thousands of counterfeits.

Burkan maximized the impact of the Couchois case by getting the district attorney to issue a series of indictments, one for each song he counterfeited, and having Couchois re-arrested with great fanfare each time he made bail on the prior charge. In the face of the bulletproof evidence Burkan's detectives had marshaled, Couchois's only defense was the legal argument that sheet music was not "merchandise" under the terms of the state penal code. But if Tin Pan Alley had accomplished anything, it had conditioned Americans to think of music as merchandise, just like soap or shoe polish.

Couchois spent only a few months in jail, but the music publishers were thrilled to have scored such a high-profile victory, to have finally flexed some legal muscle. The association ran triumphal announce-

CONVICTED OF PIRACY

GARRETT J. COUCHOIS

OF RUTHERFORD, N. J.

was found GUILTY and sentenced to a term in prison and a fine by Associate Justices Olmstead, Duell and Wyatt in the Court of Special Sessions in New York City, October 25th, for printing, publishing and selling spurious copies of "HEARTS AND FLOWERS."

Criminal prosecutions for infringing other publications are now pending.

The case of the people and publishers against

GARRETT J. COUCHOIS

was ably prosecuted by Nathan Burkan, Attorney for the Music Publishers' Association of America, and District Attorney Jerome, through his able assistants, Robert S. Johnstone and Charles C. Nott.

The Publishers of the United States will prosecute to the fullest extent of the law all infringements of their Copyrights, and will also vigorously prosecute any person or persons who may handle, sell, or offer for sale, any spurious copies of their publications hereafter.

(SIGNED)

MUSIC PUBLISHERS' ASSOCIATION

Burkan and the Music Publishers Association made Garrett J. Couchois an example for all sheet music counterfeiters. *(Music Trade Review)*

ments in the trade papers, the first of many such ads, over many years, placed by many clients, to invoke the name Nathan Burkan as half bogeyman, half avenging angel. The music men never forgot the zeal with which Burkan seized control of those dingy courtrooms, combining the street smarts needed to survive in the anything-goes culture of the Tombs with legal erudition and oratory that would have been at home in the hallowed halls of the U.S. Supreme Court. As far as the publishers were concerned, Burkan had already secured his legend at the tender age of twenty-seven.

As lawyer for the Music Publishers Association, for one of its most prominent member-publishers, the Witmarks, and for that publisher's most important composer, Victor Herbert, Burkan found himself in a situation rife with potential conflicts of interest. Pulling off this kind of balancing act would become a hallmark of his career. Burkan's seemingly casual representations of conflicting interests can seem mystifying to lawyers who have come of age in the late twentieth and early twenty-first centuries. But the American Bar Association did not adopt its first code of legal ethics until 1908, and even that regime, in the words of one study, emphasized the "lawyer's moral autonomy in the attorney-client relationship," an ethical view that allowed lawyers "to reconcile within their own consciences the differing interests of their clients." In any event, Burkan's clients trusted him implicitly, almost blindly. If an actual conflict arose, they figured, who better to iron it out than good ol' Nate?

The veneration Burkan received from his clients may have been, at this stage of his career, disproportionate to his actual accomplishments. The fruits of his victories over Marc A. Blumenberg and Garrett J. Couchois were more psychological than tangible. But the almost cultish devotion of his clients meant that Burkan was uniquely well positioned to take his place on a national stage and to play a pivotal role in the epochal copyright law developments about to unfold.

CHAPTER 5

Canned Music

On May 31, 1905, just two weeks before Burkan was named general counsel of the Music Publishers Association, Librarian of Congress Herbert Putnam had convened the first of three planned conferences to consider a comprehensive revision of the copyright law. (The Copyright Office is a part of the Library of Congress.) The need to modernize and codify the patchwork of copyright statutes adopted over the previous 115 years was widely recognized. "Our copyright laws urgently need revision," said President Theodore Roosevelt, a close friend of Putnam's, in his 1905 message to Congress. "They are imperfect in definition, confused and inconsistent in expression; they omit provision for many articles which, under modern reproductive processes are entitled to protection; they impose hardships upon the copyright proprietor which are not essential to the fair protection of the public." The modern technologies Roosevelt was referring to included two mechanical means of reproducing music that had only recently become commercially important: player piano rolls and phonograph records.

Putnam had invited twenty-six trade associations to send delegates to the conference with authority to discuss and vote on proposals for a draft bill that would be submitted to the appropriate congressional committees. Putnam's invitations only went to associations that were interested in copyright reform in what he deemed to be "an affirmative way." His list included organizations representing writers, publishers of books and periodicals, theatrical producers, artists, architects, librarians, photographers, and lithographers, among others. It was a conclave predisposed by design to support expansion and strengthening of copyright in all forms. Near the top of Putnam's agenda was giving copyright holders an exclusive right of mechanical reproduction. He did not invite any representatives of the piano roll and phonograph record manufacturers.

The Music Publishers Association received the sole invitation to represent the music industry. By this time, musicians had begun to inveigh against "canned music," to use the epithet popularized by John Philip Sousa. But the music publishers were complacent, even though they were receiving not a dime in royalties on piano rolls and records. The association's delegates to that first Library of Congress conference politely demurred to suggestions that the new law should include an exclusive right to reproduce musical compositions mechanically, explaining that, in their view, "the present law will be sufficient to protect us." This act of apparent self-sacrifice amid a prevailing spirit of logrolling was undoubtedly puzzling to the other delegates, all of whom were aggressively bellying up to the trough in the hope of getting their constituents' carefully crafted wish lists enacted into law.

When the Music Publishers Association met two weeks later, James Bowers, its longtime president, and never one to say a discouraging word, reported that the association, through its delegates, had "acquitted itself splendidly, and stood well with the fine body of men who made up the conference." Burkan, however, was determined to stiffen the association's spine on the mechanical reproduction issue. He had another influential client whose views on the matter were far more militant than the music publishers'. Victor Herbert's compositions were mainstays of early piano roll and record catalogs, and there was no doubt in Herbert's mind that their use, without his permission and without compensation, constituted outright theft of his intellectual property. It was not just a matter of money— mechanical arrangements and recordings, over which he had no quality control, did not always present his compositions in a positive light.

Burkan had attempted, just a year earlier, to shut down one such source of Herbert's irritation. The Zonophone record label had released recordings of Herbert compositions performed by an ensemble credited as "Victor Herbert's Band." But Herbert had never entered a recording studio nor granted permission for any of his works to be recorded. The group performing for Zonophone was apparently a remnant of the Gilmore Band that remained active for several years after Herbert had resigned as its leader.

Burkan successfully sued Zonophone's parent company, Universal Talking Machine, under a newly enacted New York State "right-of-privacy" statute, which prohibited the use of an individual's name for advertising purposes without written consent. When the offending Zonophone recordings of his compositions were simply rereleased as performances of the "Zonophone Concert Band," Herbert was dismayed to find that he had no recourse under the copyright law of the United States.

In need of a new cause after vanquishing the *Musical Courier,* Herbert and Burkan fastened on the mechanical rights issue. Despite the support of the president and the librarian of Congress, and despite the evident logic and justice of protecting musical compositions against unauthorized mechanical reproductions, this would be a battle royal. To understand why, a few pages of history, as Justice Oliver Wendell Holmes once wrote in another context, will be "worth a volume of logic."

The first Pianola came off the Aeolian Company assembly line in 1898. Soon thereafter, the Melville Clark Piano Company introduced the Apollo. These were automatic devices that played standard piano keyboards with piston-like mechanical "fingers," a configuration known as the "push-up piano player." Within a few years, both companies had integrated their automatic playing technology with the piano action itself, and the "piano player" became the more familiar "player piano."

Pianolas and Apollos, and many other instruments in the fiercely competitive automatic player market, were controlled by interchangeable rolls of perforated paper. As the roll unspooled at a rate of about six feet per minute over an array of pneumatic ducts, the apertures selectively permitted air to enter, the change in pressure causing the appropriate piano keys to be depressed for the appropriate number of beats. Competing manufacturers sold rolls that were compatible only with their own instruments and their catalogs quickly ballooned into the thousands.

The content ranged from public-domain classical compositions to the latest popular songs protected by copyright. No permission to use the latter was sought from copyright owners and no royalties were paid. The copyright law granted copyright owners the exclusive right to print, publish, and copy musical compositions. Perforated rolls, the industry insisted, were component parts of their proprietary musical instruments, unintelligible to humans and unusable for any other purpose, not "copies" of "musical compositions" within the meaning of the law. A single lower federal court precedent from 1888, *Kennedy v. McTammany,* which involved a crude precursor to the automatic piano player, the "Organette," supported the roll-makers' argument.

Music publishers might not have agreed with the roll-makers' legal position, but they were not disposed to argue about it either. Sheet music sales were continuing to climb even as the automatic players gained in popularity. When automatic players began appearing in public gathering places, the publishers saw them as cheap, indefatigable pluggers. Many publishers proactively requested that roll-makers cut their copyrighted numbers, putting in advance orders large enough to cover the manufacturers' fixed costs. They did not ask for or receive any royalties.

Paradoxically, it was the Aeolian Company, the largest supplier of players and piano rolls, that decided to challenge the status quo. Aeolian made the calculation that it would be good business to pay a royalty on copyrighted music, provided that it could corner the market on the most popular numbers (and consequently on the machines exclusively capable of playing them). It offered a deal to the members of the Music Publishers Association, who controlled a large percentage of the most valuable music copyrights: Aeolian would pay a 10 percent royalty on each copyrighted roll it sold in exchange for an exclusive license to a publisher's entire catalog. The deal was contingent on two things. First, a "satisfactory" number of publishers (at the sole discretion of Aeolian) would have to sign on. Second, because the exclusivity being granted would be meaningless if not legally enforceable against Aeolian's competitors, a lawsuit would have to be filed, "against some manufacturer other than the Aeolian Company," to obtain an authoritative legal decision that perforated piano rolls were indeed "copies" of "musical compositions" as those terms are used in the copyright law. Aeolian agreed to bear the expense of prosecuting a test case, which, it was assumed, would eventually go all the way to the Supreme Court of the United States.

The publishers not only found this an offer too good to refuse, they evidently found it too good to even haggle over. The terms were exceptionally one-sided. There were to be no retroactive royalties paid. The publishers' obligation to license their copyrights to Aeolian was to continue for a term of thirty-five years. Aeolian's exclusivity was not contingent on maintaining any minimal level of production or sales. The deal was brokered by the association's president, James Bowers, whose interests in the matter were not in complete alignment with the interests of his membership. Bowers's company, Lyon & Healy of

Chicago, was more prominent as a retailer of music and musical instruments than as a music publisher, and it was Aeolian's exclusive sales agent in the Midwest.

On May 5, 1902, Aeolian gave notice that the requisite critical mass of publishers had signed on to the contract. By the end of that month the test case had been filed in the federal court in Manhattan. The nominal plaintiff was White-Smith Music Publishing Company, a Boston firm and charter member of the Music Publishers Association. The defendant was the Apollo Company, distributor of the Melville Clark Piano Company's players and rolls. White-Smith, of course, was just a proxy for the Aeolian Company; like its fellow music publishers, it sat back and passively waited for the royalty checks to start rolling in.

It would not turn out to be that simple. The Aeolian contracts, even though they never entered into force, proved to be an enormous albatross around the publishers' necks.

The perforated piano roll was the first commercially successful medium for making a library of "recorded" music available for home entertainment. The phonograph record followed close on its heels. Since the 1870s, Thomas Edison had marketed his "talking machine" as just that: a device for recording and playing back speech. Edison's low-fidelity wax cylinders were far better suited to taking office dictation than to capturing the sound of music, which might be drowned out by noisy motors and springs on playback anyway. In contrast to a Pianola, which could pass as an attractive sideboard when not in use, the early Edison phonographs were ungainly pieces of industrial equipment that clashed with the delicate warmth of the Victorian parlor.

Most prerecorded musical cylinders produced in the late 1800s were sold to public arcades for coin-operated phonographs. "The idea of recorded sound was still quite a novelty," writes Tim Brooks, a leading authority on the history of recorded sound. "For only a nickel one could hear, through a pair of ear tubes, selections by all manner of bands, singers and monologists." As late as 1900, says cultural historian David Suisman, "the player piano was widely seen as having transformative potential, while the phonograph was generally dismissed as a clever but idle amusement." The annus mirabilis for the phonograph as a home accoutrement was 1904. By then, two aggressive competitors had emerged that would eventually overtake Edison and dominate the record business for many decades: the Columbia Phonograph Company and the

Victor Talking Machine Company. Columbia and Victor both made big splashes at the 1904 St. Louis World's Fair with their attractive, quiet equipment and flat-disc records featuring such major stars as Victor's Enrico Caruso. The range, timbre, and warmth of Caruso's voice were ideally suited to the acoustic recording technology of the day. The great Neapolitan tenor was the phonograph's first killer application.

Although Tin Pan Alley tunes and other copyrighted music (such as Giacomo Puccini's arias) were staples of the record business from the beginning, the phonograph initially caused little consternation in the publishing establishment. The coin-operated arcade machines were, after all, another cheap and effective plug. As the market for home phonographs began to take off, the publishers may have been expecting that it was just a matter of time before Edison, Columbia, or Victor would drop an Aeolian-style deal in their laps.

One publisher, however, took matters into its own hands. Joseph W. Stern & Company (later renamed, as it is still known today, for Stern's better-known partner, Edward B. Marks) was an innovative and cussedly independent force on Tin Pan Alley. So excited had Stern and Marks been at the prospect of plugging their numbers by phonograph that they opened their own recording studio in the late 1890s, making prerecorded Edison cylinders under the name Universal Phonograph Company.

Initially conceived as just another plug for sheet music, the record company became a small profit center in its own right. Universal's first set of releases included a popular vaudevillian, Stephen Porter, performing compositions that he had sold to the Stern company. When ragtime pianist and composer George "Rosey" Rosenberg self-recorded and self-released his own arrangements of the Porter tunes, Stern and Marks saw it as direct competition to their promising record business. They sued Rosey for copyright infringement.

Stern v. Rosey was dismissed summarily. The federal appellate court for the District of Columbia, writing in 1901, noted that the "precise question here presented for decision is a novel one because of the comparatively recent invention of the phonograph." Nonetheless, it disposed of the case succinctly:

> It is not pretended that the marks upon the wax cylinders can be made out by the eye, or that they can be utilized in any other way than as parts of the mechanism of the phonograph. . . . These prepared wax cylinders can neither substitute for the copyrighted sheets of music nor serve any purpose which is within their scope.

As such, the court concluded, "the ordinary signification of the words 'copying,' 'publishing,' etc., cannot be stretched to include it."

The precedents of *Kennedy v. McTammany* and *Stern v. Rosey* loomed over *White-Smith v. Apollo*. Phonograph records, like perforated rolls, and like music boxes and hand organs before that, were seen as manifestations of a single phenomenon. If the issue of copyright infringement turned on whether the medium of copying is decipherable by the human eye and a functional equivalent for sheet music, then all forms of mechanical reproduction would seem to fall outside the law's reach.

This result was hardly inevitable under the language of the copyright law, which imposed no explicit requirement that a copy of a musical composition be first perceptible by the human eye rather than immediately by the ear. The difficulty the *Stern v. Rosey* court found in stretching the words "copy" and "publish" to cover phonograph records seemed to result from an unspoken premise—that a "musical composition" under the law *was* the physical sheet music routinely deposited with the Copyright Office as one of the formalities of obtaining a copyright registration. If, instead, a "musical composition" is understood to be a mental conception, then any tangible medium by which the composer's idea can be transmitted to others for their enjoyment, whether print or mechanical (or, later, digital), should qualify as a copy or publication of the composition.

The Supreme Court would have the last word on how those statutory terms should be interpreted. But Aeolian was in no rush to get that legal question before the Supreme Court, nor did it care whether it set a precedent that would apply to phonograph records, if it could win the case on narrower grounds. Aeolian, as one of Apollo's attorneys complained, "poured out money like water" into the case. Its lawyers went out of their way to draft a complaint against Apollo that did not even mention that the copying at issue came in the form of perforated rolls, thereby guaranteeing that there would not be a quick dismissal on the pleadings and expedited trip to the appellate courts to settle the legal question.

Rather, Aeolian undertook the laborious task of creating a record that distinguished *Stern v. Rosey* on the facts. Over a period of more than a year, testimony was gathered by deposition as Aeolian sought to prove that a perforated roll was an alternate form of musical notation, one of many such systems that have been devised over the centuries. Aeolian's learned experts—professors, composers, conductors, music critics, and historians—insisted that with practice a pianist could read a perforated roll as readily as conventional notation. (A few attempts to demonstrate this feat, however, misfired abysmally.) One expert claimed that the roll was superior from the musician's perspective, because it eliminated the need to turn pages by hand.

Aeolian did make the more viable argument that the perforated roll was a *commercial* substitute for sheet music and therefore threatened the livelihood of the very creators that the copyright law was intended to motivate and reward. This speculation, though, was buried in an avalanche of hard evidence that many publishers were paying roll manufacturers to cut their numbers for promotional purposes and that sheet music sales were on the upswing. Apollo noted pointedly that it came with poor grace for the music publishers—notoriously rapacious in their dealings with all but the most prominent composers—to try to exploit the plight of the journeyman tunesmith to make out their case.

Even worse for Aeolian, this line of argument opened the door for the introduction into evidence of its contract with the music publishers. Apollo argued that Aeolian's exclusive access to the most popular copyrighted music would put competitors out of business, leaving both the public and composers at Aeolian's mercy. Coming during the height of President Theodore Roosevelt's trust-busting campaign, invoking the specter of monopoly was a potent line of defense.

After three years of litigation, and just days after Burkan was named general counsel of the Music Publishers Association, on June 21, 1905, the federal district court ruled on the legal issue at the heart of *White-Smith v. Apollo*. The effort and expense that Aeolian put into equating perforated rolls with sheet music was for naught. Judge John Hazel gave the argument the back of his hand: "The impracticability of reading a perforated sheet of music for the purpose of singing or playing the composition represented is not seriously disputed." Judge Hazel was content to follow the holdings of *Kennedy v. McTammany* and *Stern v. Rosey* as settled law, agreeing that a copy of a musical composition, under the plain import of the copyright law, refers to a "tangible object that appeals to the sense of sight." If that interpretation allowed mechanical reproducers to deprive the author of "the fruits of his labors," the court suggested, it was a matter for Congress to address by statutory amendment.

Librarian of Congress Putnam scheduled a second conference on copyright law revision for the first week of November 1905. This time, Burkan was in charge of the Music Publishers Association's preparations.

Judge Hazel's ruling strengthened his hand. The association's delegates at the first conference had instructions not to agree to anything that might nullify the Aeolian contracts (which would be triggered only by a favorable court ruling on mechanical reproduction, not by legislative action). But Burkan was not especially interested in preserving the Aeolian deal. "If I had been attorney," he later said, "no such contract would have been made." He shaped an important compromise. The music publishers would now support congressional enactment of an exclusive mechanical reproduction right, but with the proviso that it would apply only to compositions copyrighted after the effective date of the new law, ensuring that the *White-Smith v. Apollo* case, on which the Aeolian contracts hinged, would not be rendered moot on appeal.

Burkan was decades younger than the other participants in the conference, which included such grizzled warhorses of American arts and letters as playwright Bronson Howard, sculptor Daniel Chester French, painter Francis Millet, and publisher Charles Scribner. Still, he made his presence felt. There was virtually no opposition to the mechanical reproduction right, but considerable reluctance about enacting Burkan's other priority, a "misdemeanor" clause that would criminalize any willful, for-profit copyright infringement, with a penalty of up to one year in prison. Many delegates considered this draconian and unnecessary, but Burkan's well-told war stories about the Couchois counterfeiting case turned the tide and the clause was approved unanimously.

By the close of the third and final conference, in March 1906, consensus had been reached on many other far-reaching reforms: an extension of the copyright term from a maximum, with renewal, of forty-two years to a single term of the life of the author plus fifty years; vastly enhanced civil remedies for infringement; and a relaxation of legal formalities that had frequently resulted in the inadvertent forfeiture of copyrights. The Copyright Office was tasked with drafting the actual legislation. There were handshakes and backslaps all around, with some participants expressing the belief that the hard part was over. Because they represented all "interests which are likely to be benefitted or injured" and had achieved substantial unanimity, one delegate predicted, the bill about to be placed before Congress would "pass without any query."

A rude awakening awaited the conferees once they stepped outside the protective bubble the librarian of Congress had erected for them.

CHAPTER 6

Mr. Burkan Goes to Washington

The public got its first look at the bill drafted by the Copyright Office when it was introduced in both houses of Congress on May 31, 1906. Joint hearings before the Senate and House Committees on Patents were scheduled for the following week. (Until the 1940s, each house of Congress had a "Committee on Patents" whose jurisdiction included copyright law.) If the proponents of the bill thought they could steamroll those who did not share their "affirmative" interest in copyright reform, and who had therefore been personae non gratae at the Library of Congress conferences, another think was in order.

Brimming with confidence, the music publishers waived their opportunity to state the case in favor of the mechanical reproduction right, resting instead on brief appearances from the twin colossi of American music, John Philip Sousa and Victor Herbert. Ten years earlier they had been rival composers of both brass band music and light opera, but by 1906 each had settled in as undisputed king of his respective domain. Herbert assured the committees that the two were speaking on behalf of "many hundreds of poor fellows who have not been able to come here— possibly because they have not got the price—brother composers whose names figure on the advertisements of these companies who make perforated rolls and talking machines, and who never have received a cent, just as is the case with Mr. Sousa and myself."

Sousa was candid to a fault about his personal stake in the matter. To him it was self-evident that composers possessed a divine right to reap all pecuniary fruits of their intellectual labors. When one congressman tried to steer him toward a discussion of the public interest at the heart of copyright law, Sousa was facetious:

> *Mr. Campbell.* Is not the real reason that if it protects you and other composers, there is an incentive to you to compose?
>
> *Mr. Sousa.* Oh yes; I can compose better if I get a thousand dollars than I can for six hundred. [Laughter]

While the committee members good-naturedly bantered with their celebrity guests, the opposition was belatedly gathering in Washington. The mechanical manufacturers had been blindsided by the rapid-fire unveiling of the bill and scheduling of hearings, but they were making up for lost time. The parade of witnesses hurriedly arrayed to speak against the mechanical clause included several who had been directly involved in *White-Smith v. Apollo* (which had been affirmed by the court of appeals a few days earlier) and others who were equally able to quote chapter and verse from the extensive evidentiary record that had been compiled in that case.

When their opportunity came, the opponents complained that the bill-drafting process had been rigged against them, a "star chamber proceeding." (The chairman of the House committee, Representative Frank Currier of New Hampshire, was sympathetic; a few weeks earlier he had observed that the librarian of Congress's conferences had excluded 80,000,000 citizens. "This committee will try to represent those people," he pledged.) The opponents argued that Congress lacked constitutional authority to apply copyright to mechanical media, because they were not "writings." They contended that composers received all the incentive they needed when they collected royalties on sheet music sales, and that the advertising that piano rolls and records provided was of incalculable value in increasing those royalties.

Their most riveting testimony, however, dealt with the Aeolian contract. Applause rang out through the hearing room when one witness referred to it as "a complete monopolistic octopus, in which the Aeolian Company forms the head and brains, the Music Publishers Association the body, the independent publishers the writhing arms, and the composers the suckers and baiters." Another called it a scheme "so ingenious that it does not violate any law whatever except one, the golden rule. You cannot square the Aeolian scheme with the Sermon on the Mount, but . . . you can square it with every statute on the statute books." The mechanical reproduction right, its opponents argued, was a money grab by a select few at the expense of a dynamic young industry and the music-loving public.

Burkan, who had not planned to speak, was reduced to making sputtering interjections. He seemingly had no prior inkling that the Aeolian contract would play so poorly in the political theater. He was flailing like a callow youth tormented by grown men.

When he was granted a few minutes to offer rebuttal at the very end of the four days of hearings, a Saturday morning session, the southerners and westerners who dominated the joint committees seemed confused as to whom he represented. They showed little patience for a New York City Jew they had never heard of before, and they justifiably took umbrage when Burkan insulted their intelligence with an "innocent" explanation of the Aeolian contracts that glossed over their most damning features. He was cut off abruptly. On the biggest stage of his career up until then, Burkan had laid an egg.

The mechanical reproduction right, which seemed within easy grasp when the Library of Congress conferences adjourned, was now in peril. There was talk of separating the mechanical right from the larger reform bill, which would have almost certainly killed its prospects. At the next round of hearings, scheduled for the December 1906 lame-duck session, its proponents would need to lay to rest any doubts about its constitutionality and make a more compelling case that it was sound public policy, that its purpose and effect would be to stimulate creativity, rather than just satisfy the greed of parasitic middlemen. The Aeolian contracts, if they couldn't yet be declared void (Aeolian had appealed the *White-Smith v. Apollo* case to the Supreme Court, where a ruling was not expected for another year), at least had to be rendered less politically toxic.

Keeping the coalition behind the Copyright Office bill together would be difficult for Burkan. Literary groups were being told that they ought to ditch the music people, whose cause seemed "doomed." To keep them in the fold, Burkan drafted an amendment to clarify that the exclusive right of mechanical reproduction was not limited to musical works, but would apply also to poetry, lectures, and any other literary works. He prodded the music publishers to adopt the more sophisticated forms of copyright advocacy that authors, dramatists, book publishers, and other stakeholders had long since mastered, so that the other copyright industries would come to see the music men as valuable allies.

To lift the music publishers' stature and solidify their place in the copyright community, Burkan organized a testimonial dinner for T. P.

The Music Publishers Association feted Irish MP "Tay Pay" O'Connor on October 19, 1906, an event that heralded the arrival of the music industry as an effective political force. Seated *(l. to r.):* music publisher Leo Feist, playwright Bronson Howard, Burkan, Victor Herbert, O'Connor, music publishers James Bowers, H. R. Stern, and George Furniss. Standing *(l. to r.):* Isidore Witmark, Pianola inventor Edwin S. Votey, and author John Kendrick Bangs. *(Music Trade Review)*

"Tay Pay" O'Connor, a celebrated Irish nationalist politician and journalist who was touring the United States in the fall of 1906. O'Connor, a member of Parliament, had recently sponsored a law that criminalized music counterfeiting in the United Kingdom. In addition to the membership of the Music Publishers Association, Burkan invited and gave speaking slots to prominent copyright advocates from other fields. Much of their oratory that evening was devoted to inspiring anecdotes about obstacles they had overcome in enacting copyright reforms past and to teaching the gathered music publishers, by example, how one speaks in polite company of the higher public purpose of copyright that transcends mercantile profits and losses. The event was widely reported and enhanced Burkan's reputation considerably.

Burkan was undergoing a Pygmalion-like transformation. He knew he had fumbled the June hearings. Although he had been a busy member of New York's copyright bar for several years, his cases had been relatively routine matters, usually rather one-sided legally and factually. It hadn't been necessary for him to develop a deep, scholarly mastery of copyright law. He now applied himself to that task, thoroughly familiarizing himself with the history and theory of copyright, domestic and foreign. And he sought out guidance on the ways of Congress, mysteries for which neither the politics of Tammany Hall nor the rough-and-tumble of Manhattan's lower courts had fully prepared him. Two members of the House Committee on Patents gave Burkan valuable advice and support: William Sulzer of New York City, a Tammany man with eyes on the New York governorship, and Andrew Barchfeld, a first-term congressman from Pittsburgh, where he had been a drinking companion of the city's former symphony conductor, Victor Herbert. That left just 384 members of the House and the entire Senate still to be won over.

As he arrived in Washington for the next set of hearings on December 6, 1906—with an entourage that included Sousa, Herbert, and authors William Dean Howells and Samuel Langhorne Clemens—Burkan was confident and ready to seize control of the debate. During breaks in the committee hearings over the next several days, Burkan completed his initiation rites at the other branches of the national government. He strolled over to the Old Senate Chamber, where the Supreme Court sat, to be formally admitted to practice before the high court. Escorted by Representative Barchfeld, he paid a well-publicized courtesy call on President Roosevelt with Herbert and Sousa.

When the time set aside for arguments on the mechanical right arrived, the proponents exercised their prerogative to go first, and their presentation was choreographed with great care. It centered on Burkan, who offered a magisterial argument in support of Congress's constitutional authority to grant the mechanical right. Drawing seamlessly from English common law, colonial American law, the Federalist Papers, prior acts of Congress, and Supreme Court precedent, he shredded the notion that the proposed mechanical right exceeded the enumerated power under Article I of the Constitution to secure for authors the exclusive right to their "writings."

The term "writings," Burkan argued, restricts the subject matter that is eligible for copyright protection but not what forms of reproduction can be prohibited under the copyright law. It does not mean that a "writing can be protected against another writing only, or that the author's rights are restricted to reproducing his writings in writings only." Rather, if it is to stimulate creativity, the exclusive right secured to the author can and should include *any* profitable use of a writing. He cited the exclusive right of public performance of a dramatic work, first enacted in 1856 and never challenged, as precedent for protecting authors against unwritten forms of reproduction.

Alternatively, Burkan argued, a perforated roll or phonograph record from which a musical composition can be reproduced for the ear, even if only with the aid of a machine, is indeed a "writing" within the meaning of the Constitution. "Writing," he argued, referred to any material embodiment of an author's intellectual conceptions.

> It is the intellectual production that is entitled to protection, and not the means or the vehicle for indicating to the senses the ideas embodied therein. The purpose of printing is to indicate to your senses the ideas embodied in the paper; a perforated roll or phonographic disk is but another method of conveying to the mind the ideas of the author embodied therein.

When the Supreme Court, in the case of Sarony's Oscar Wilde photograph, said "writings" were the means "by which the ideas in the mind of the author are given visible expression"—language that opponents of the mechanical right relied upon—it meant not that the author's ideas are perceptible by the eye, Burkan argued, but by the mind.

Like students in a graduate seminar overly eager to impress, the committee members jumped in to complete their instructor's thoughts:

> *Mr. Bonynge.* Then it became a reproduction of an intellectual idea, the same as the performance of a drama is the reproduction of an intellectual idea, the same as a perforated roll when it is put into a machine becomes a reproduction of an intellectual idea.
>
> *Mr. Burkan.* Yes, precisely.
>
> *Mr. Chaney.* It has a visible expression when it is reproduced.
>
> *Mr. Burkan.* Yes, it becomes intelligible to the mind.
>
> *Unidentified Voice.* Suppose you take a blank sheet of paper and you use some invisible ink, you have to use some acid or some light in order to reproduce it.
>
> *Mr. Burkan.* Yes. It would be entitled to copyright, provided it represented an intellectual conception.

Unidentified Voice. That it is visible to the eye has nothing to do with it.

Mr. Burkan. No.

Mr. Bonynge. It is visible to the intellect. That is the point.

In the very room where they had manhandled Burkan just six months earlier, congressmen were now eating out of his hand. It was a bravura performance. It erased memories of Burkan's earlier miscues and guaranteed that there would be receptive audiences for his many more congressional appearances over the next thirty years.

John Philip Sousa had not been given a formal speaking role at the December 1906 hearings, but as a certified American icon he exercised carte blanche to interject and heckle others. "The whole bugaboo of this matter," he blurted out, "is found in this infernal Aeolian business!" Opponents of the mechanical right had barely begun their testimony and Sousa's frustration was already palpable.

Burkan and his witnesses had done all they could to neutralize an issue that they considered a red herring. They had explained that the Aeolian contracts could be triggered only by a favorable Supreme Court ruling in *White-Smith v. Apollo,* a prospect that now seemed remote. Rumors that Aeolian and the Music Publishers Association had a side agreement dealing with legislation were unfounded. And the contracts, they insisted, had no application at all to phonograph records. (A representative of Columbia Phonograph, however, swore that he had seen Burkan carrying around exclusive contracts between the Music Publishers Association and Victor Talking Machine in his jacket pocket.)

Still, as a bugaboo Aeolian was so useful, opponents of the mechanical right would not let go of it. Aeolian's conspicuous absence from the proceedings and seeming indifference to whether the legislation was enacted were taken as sure signs that its intentions were nefarious. "They know the charges made against them," one witness pointed out. "If anybody's ears would tingle, theirs ought to." One way or another—the mechanical people had various theories as to how—Aeolian would satisfy its "hankering" to monopolize the music trade if the bill passed.

Although the mechanical interests were now organized to fight the bill under the umbrella of the "American Music Copyright League," they did not put up an entirely unified front. Some seemed resigned to the notion that composers had a just claim to some compensation, while others were adamant that the advertising that recordings provided was compensation enough. All professed to having the goal of uplifting the masses by bringing them classical music, but all complained that without access to the "cheap" or "bum" popular hits, their businesses would be destroyed. Those who were not dead set against paying any "tribute" at all for copyrighted music began to coalesce around a concept that would require copyright holders to give all manufacturers, not just Aeolian, equal access to publishers' repertory—the "compulsory license."

Opposition to the idea of a license that a copyright holder was *required* by law to grant, which would be something entirely new in the U.S. copyright system, was intense. It came not only from the music publishers, but also from authors and artists. They argued that a requirement to license a copyright would exceed the constitutional authority of Congress to secure to writers "the exclusive right" to their works—there could be no such thing as a nonexclusive copyright. And they argued it was unworkable. How would the royalty be determined and how would a composer be protected against irresponsible or unscrupulous manufacturers who didn't pay up? Worst of all, it was un-American. Robert Underwood Johnson, editor of *Century* magazine and a longtime copyright activist well known to the committees, insisted that a manufacturer has no more right to use the copyrighted music of another "than it has the right to have the horse of the Chairman. There is a communistic principle back of all this agitation for a license to do something with a man's work which the Constitution has reserved to him, and I tell you, gentlemen, that you cannot trifle with that principle!"

Proponents of the mechanical right had won the debate on the merits, but the politics looked grim. The player piano and the phonograph had spawned large and growing industries, representing enormous capital investment, tens if not hundreds of millions of dollars in sales, and thousands of employees. That was a powerful political constituency. The music publishers, comparatively speaking, were mom-and-pop operations with collective sheet music sales of $6 million per year. A witness speaking for a dozen independent mechanical manufacturers at the hearings had been blunt in expressing his side's contempt for the music publishers:

> Did you ever hear of any of them before, gentlemen, as having a place in the business of the country? Are they men of standing and position in the community—these music publishers? Did you ever hear of them? They put forward John Philip Sousa, who is known to everybody and loved by everybody, to take their chestnuts out of the fire. [Laughter]

The music publishers did not command much sympathy or respect, and their claims to speak for the interests of starving composers had been met with deserved derision. Composers, not publishers, were a sympathetic political constituency. They would have to become the public face of the mechanical right if it was to become law. Nathan Burkan, with his interlocking clientele, was the perfect person to execute this pivot.

After the December hearings, Isidore Witmark and Burkan hatched a plan to bring the voices of the "cheap" and "bum" composers into the mix. The Witmarks had maintained index cards, numbering more than five thousand, with the name and address of every songwriter who had submitted manuscripts to the firm over the years. It was likely the most comprehensive such list to be had, given M. Witmark & Sons' standing in the field. Witmark circulated a petition in support of the Copyright Office bill to every one of the rejected songwriters, with a cover letter disingenuously suggesting that "if the music publishers received the revenue due to them from the sales of mechanical reproductions, they would be in a position to publish more music." Just after the new year, Burkan submitted to Congress petitions signed by, he claimed, "nine-tenths of the composers of the country."

In a written brief that Burkan submitted with the petitions, he rather abruptly tossed the music publishers aside. Once again addressing the Aeolian issue, he made a new argument. Under standard songwriter agreements, publishers "had no right to dispose of the mechanical rights," Burkan wrote, "for they hold the copyrights as trustees for the composers." This, in fact, was a controversial proposition that would be a point of contention between publishers and songwriters for decades to come. But if true, it meant that the Aeolian contracts were legal nullities. Notably, Burkan signed this brief without indicating specifically on whose behalf he was filing it.

The 59th Congress would adjourn, and all pending legislation would expire, on March 4, 1907. That left less than sixty calendar days after the holiday recess for the copyright bill to be reported out of committee, debated, and voted on. It was during these frenetic weeks that Victor Herbert truly emerged as the champion of the American songwriter. A charm offensive was needed, and charm was Herbert's strong suit. Herbert not only could speak from the heart on behalf of his less fortunate brother composers, but he had learned to speak the language of copyright theory—and he was immensely likable to boot. Through Representative Barchfeld, Herbert gained access to an exclusive Capitol building speakeasy called the Inner Sanctum, where he befriended potentially influential members of Congress, including President Roosevelt's new son-in-law, Nicholas Longworth, a musician and future Speaker of the House.

The House and Senate Patent Committees reported out their respective bills during the last week of January 1907. Both bills followed the Copyright Office draft in overall form and in many particulars. Disagreement over the mechanical reproduction right was the biggest obstacle standing in the way of a modern, liberal copyright code for the twentieth century. A bare one-vote majority of the Senate committee, led by its chairman, Alfred Kittredge of North Dakota, endorsed a mechanical right as broad and unqualified as Burkan could reasonably have hoped for. But the dissenters, ominously including Senator Reed Smoot of Utah, who would chair the Committee on Patents in the next Congress, adopted the alarmist rhetoric of the mechanical instrument makers. "Manufacturers who have invested many millions, relying upon the existing statutes," the Senate minority report said, "should not be despoiled for the benefit of the few" and "the public should not be exploited for the benefit of a group who apparently intend and expect to obtain complete control of these industries."

The House committee reported a bill that did not address the mechanical right at all, the majority stating that in light of the pendency of *White-Smith v. Apollo* in the Supreme Court, "further legislation regarding this matter should be postponed until we can know what construction the court will give to the existing law." There was, initially, no minority report filed on the House side.

"The divergence of views on the subject is so marked," one newspaper reported, "that no legislation this session is considered possible." Burkan's Washington contacts stressed to him the importance of putting a minority report before the House, so Burkan ghost-wrote one. It was filed in the closing hours of the 59th Congress by Representative Barchfeld. Burkan's House minority report introduced new, composer-centric arguments for the mechanical right and is notable for its prescience. In it, Burkan envisioned a future in which mechanical reproduction has done away "with the laborious studying and tiresome practicing that are necessary to master instruments played by hand from written or printed scores," making the "mechanical form of reproducing music the rule and the use of sheet music the exception."

Without a mechanical right in such a world, Burkan argued, composers would naturally be discouraged from pursuing their art, whereas enactment would "attract to the writing of music a great many having musical talent" and "keen rivalry and competition among the manufacturers to obtain good music will bring out the greatest efforts of composers." Far from being at the mercy of music publishers, the mechanical manufacturers would "have it in their power to contract, as they may desire, for new or current music, or to engage staffs of composers to write especially for them; and they will find the number of composers available for their purpose increasing every day, their ranks being sure to be swelled by the incentive of this new demand." Burkan had stumbled upon a vision of a future in which mass media of entertainment, not Tin Pan Alley publishers, would serve as popular music's gatekeepers.

Burkan was just beginning to understand the commercial and creative dynamics of modern communication technologies. And with that he was finding his voice as a forceful and creative copyright advocate.

CHAPTER 7

The Two-Cent Solution

The mechanical reproduction controversy would be on a slow simmer until Congress and the Supreme Court returned to Washington in the autumn of 1907. Meanwhile, long-standing tensions within the Music Publishers Association were reaching the boiling point. In forging a strategic (if somewhat cynical) alliance with songwriters, Burkan and Witmark were not operating with the organization's approval. Witmark, for his part, believed that President James Bowers's affiliation with Aeolian left him hopelessly compromised. In anonymous comments attributed to "a publisher whose opinions are held in the highest regard," Witmark complained to a trade paper that the Music Publishers Association's handling of the copyright bill was being "badly bungled" and that, compared to the well-heeled and well-organized mechanical interests, the association "cuts very little ice" before Congress.

Witmark, who was funding the copyright battle with almost no financial support from his fellow publishers, believed he had a pledge from Bowers not to seek reelection at the association's June 1907 meeting, but Bowers reneged. Lacking the votes to oust Bowers, Burkan and Witmark did not bother to attend. "Despite the anticipation of a war over the election of officers, especially on the part of the so-called popular publishers of New York, the dove of peace descended, and the proceedings of the thirteenth annual meeting were as smooth as a mill pond."

Burkan and Witmark, in league with Victor Herbert, continued down their separate path. Witmark used his mailing list to solicit members for a sketchy, faux-grassroots organization that he christened the "Authors and Composers Copyright League of America." For a $1 fee, members received a card "entitling them to work their heads off for the Cause!" wrote Witmark. "It was no trouble to get that dollar. Wasn't it worth it from the member's standpoint to be in the same organization with Herbert, [Reginald] DeKoven, and Sousa?" Burkan, who had previously kept his distance from *White-Smith v. Apollo,* sought and received the Supreme Court's leave to file a brief on behalf of Herbert. His petition listed seventy-five Herbert numbers that were in the Apollo piano roll catalog and argued that "the composers are more direct parties than the music publishers" and that the case "will be more adequately argued" if Herbert were permitted to participate.

While Witmark toiled away as the man behind the curtain of the Authors and Composers Copyright League, writing broadsides for the press and orchestrating letter-writing campaigns from an empty floor of the Witmarks' building that he dubbed "the propaganda department," a group of successful Tin Pan Alley songwriters organized the "Words and Music Club." Primarily a fraternal organization, it was inevitably drawn into the copyright debate as a small, but authentic, voice for professional songwriters.

Although Burkan and Witmark had spent much of the preceding winter together in Washington working on the copyright bill, they did not seem to tire of each other's company. The two bachelors spent a long weekend in Atlantic City in April 1907—a sojourn that had no discernible business purpose—and they spent the better part of July and August touring Europe. It was Burkan's first trip abroad and he took advantage of the opportunity to introduce himself to copyright experts in London and on the continent, as Witmark signed up foreign representatives for his company's catalog and acquired U.S. publication rights for European operettas. "My friend and legal advisor, Nathan Burkan, was always there," Witmark told a reporter after they returned to New York by steamship, "whether for sightseeing, copyright confidences, or when contracts were to be drawn, and together we returned, being pleased with our trip, yet withal glad to be home once more." After Isidore Witmark married in 1908, his lifelong bachelor brother Jay took his place as Burkan's regular travel companion for many years.

Aeolian had allowed its appeal in *White-Smith v. Apollo* to languish on the Supreme Court's docket, but with the House Committee on Patents recommending a hold on legislative action until the high court spoke, the case was front and center when the court's October 1907 term began. Oral argument was scheduled for January 1908. The parties' briefs, described as "elaborate" by the court, were indeed treatise length, but they trod what was by then very familiar factual and legal ground.

The court of appeals had acknowledged that a mechanical reproduction right would be of the "same class" as the exclusive rights explicitly mentioned in the copyright laws, and that "the reasons which led to the passage of said statutes apply with great force" in the case of perforated rolls. Nonetheless, the court felt it could not construe the word "copy" broadly to encompass a mechanical reproduction, citing the old legal saw that a statute which creates new rights, and therefore is "in derogation of the common law," should be construed strictly.

Burkan, in his brief, gamely tried to change the terms of the discussion. He argued that the federal copyright acts did not create new rights at all, that at the time of the Constitutional Convention of 1787 all states recognized copyrights as part of their common law. The Constitution merely gave the central government the power to "secure" those already existing rights more effectively. Federal copyright law was therefore "remedial" in nature and, under an equally ancient legal canon, should be construed liberally to effectuate its purpose. The word "copying," Burkan argued, had been included in the copyright acts specifically because of its elasticity, to cover forms of reproduction not captured by narrower terms such as "printing" or "engraving." "Notation serves as one means to the end of making possible the reproduction of a composition to the ear. But if the result is obtained by other means, the purpose of reproduction is equally realized." If mechanical reproduction is not covered, he concluded, "composers would be without protection as against the most extensive and profitable use of their compositions" and musical copyright "would cease to promote the musical art."

Burkan could have saved his ink and paper. The very fact that an "extensive and profitable" industry had grown up in reliance upon such cases as *Kennedy v. McTammany* and *Stern v. Rosey,* without Congress taking any action, led the Supreme Court to show unusual deference to those lower court precedents. Justice William Day's opinion for the unanimous court in *White-Smith v. Apollo,* announced on February 24, 1908, adopted what was probably the narrowest construction of "copy" that any party had proffered: "a written or printed record in intelligible notation." The copyright law, as it stood, protected music only in a form that appealed to the eye, not the ear. "It may be true that the use of these perforated rolls, in the absence of statutory protection, enables the manufacturers thereof to enjoy the use of musical compositions for which they pay no value," Day wrote. "But such considerations properly address themselves to the legislative, and not to the judicial, branch of the government."

Justice Holmes wrote a separate concurrence. Though unwilling to dissent given the long line of precedent, he felt the court's holding gave copyright "less scope than its rational significance and the ground on which it is granted seem to me to demand." He defined a musical composition as "a rational collocation of sounds." "On principle," he concluded, "anything that mechanically reproduces that collocation of sounds ought to be held a copy, or, if the statute is too narrow, ought to be made so by a further act."

The ball was back in Congress's court. At the opening of the 60th Congress in December 1907, Senator Reed Smoot (the new chairman of the Senate Committee on Patents) reintroduced his bill, which included language explicitly exempting mechanical reproductions from copyright infringement liability. To the surprise of many, Chairman Frank Currier of the House Committee on Patents, whose previous bill had been silent on the issue, pending a ruling in *White-Smith v. Apollo,* also introduced a new bill that included Smoot's exemption.

Currier had favored the mechanical reproduction right from the beginning, but with many members of the committees still concerned that it would lead to formation of a mechanical music trust, he had concluded that a compromise around a compulsory license, or "universal royalty," was essential. The mechanical manufacturers had already signaled their assent, so pressure needed to be brought to bear on publishers and composers to accept a half loaf. His new bill, which offered them no loaf at all, strengthened his negotiating hand, and the *White-Smith* decision gave him further leverage still.

The joint committees reconvened for a final round of public hearings in March 1908. Currier neither expected nor wanted to hear anything new; he used the occasion to hammer home the need for a compromise on the mechanical right. After Victor Herbert read statements on behalf of the Authors and Composers Copyright League and the American Federation of Musicians, each one larded with tired talking points that the committee members had heard many times before, Currier grilled him on the compulsory license issue:

Rep. Currier. We would like your position well defined about this matter.

Mr. Herbert. I simply want the manufacturer of mechanical instruments to be put in the same position, individually, toward me as the publisher is today.

Rep. Currier. Then we are to understand from you that it is not compensation for your composition that you are asking for, but the exclusive control of your compositions?

Mr. Herbert. The artistic control.

Rep. Currier. . . . It is not compensation that you are looking for, because if that is what you are looking for, you could get that under the percentage royalty.

Mr. Herbert. I am looking for that too.

Currier made it clear that getting both was not an option; that a right to compensation would come at the price of ceding some artistic control through compulsory licensing: "You are prepared to let the bill go to wreck and ruin unless you can have both?" Currier asked. "I want the country to understand who is responsible for the possible failure of this legislation."

Harry Williams, the president of the Words and Music Club, followed Herbert in the witness chair, no doubt impressed by what he had just heard. He told the committees that he did not represent "geniuses," the likes of Herbert and Sousa, whose work would live on after them. "We are men who just write the ordinary popular songs," he went on. "The life of a song is very short, only about one year, and the life of a songwriter is not much longer . . . if he writes one hit in his lifetime, he is pretty fortunate." Williams, whose one hit was "In the Shade of the Old Apple Tree" and who died at forty-two, told the committees that exclusive control would be nice, but as far as his group's membership was concerned, "a royalty would do it."

Burkan received the same message as Victor Herbert. "You should get what you can for the people you represent under this bill," one congressman admonished him. By this time, Herbert was privately telling Burkan the same thing. In the closing minutes of the three-day hearing, during which he had argued at length to a skeptical audience that a compulsory license provision would be unconstitutional, Burkan saw the writing on the wall. Provided that the mechanical interests would agree not to challenge the constitutionality of a mechanical reproduction right subject to compulsory licensing, "I, for one, would advise my people to agree to it. I do not want to oppose anything that is fair and reasonable." Burkan had his fingers crossed—for the remainder of his career he would take every opportunity that came his way to argue for repeal of compulsory licensing, which he considered a blight on his signature legislative achievement.

Once Burkan had capitulated, the tension that had permeated the proceedings for two years suddenly evaporated. Representatives of all the interested parties agreed to stay in Washington to hash out an agreement on a royalty rate. "If you reached an agreement," Currier told them, "it would settle the matter and you would get a bill."

The devil, as always, was in the details. A flurry of meetings in Washington hotels over the next several days yielded no grand bargain. The Words and Music Club and several of the automatic piano player manufacturers, however, did sign a "Compromise Agreement" that was widely disseminated. It provided that mechanical reproduction of musical compositions should "be open to everybody" on payment of a royalty "of two cents for each and every perforated roll, phonograph disc, record or cylinder, music-box cylinder, or other reproducing device." (The two-cent figure had first been suggested, rather in passing, at the December 1906 hearings as an amount, commensurate with the average royalty paid to composers on sheet music, that could be absorbed by manufacturers without raising prices to the consumer.) Crucially, Victor Herbert signed on to the agreement, albeit with the scribbled-in proviso that he believed "composers should get more than two cents."

The music publishers, still divided among themselves on the question of compulsory licensing in principle, much less a paltry two-cent royalty, left Washington without making any concessions. Most of the mechanical instrument makers, who had publicly indicated they would be willing to pay an unspecified "reasonable" royalty, decried two cents as "confiscatory." The holdouts were in danger of marginalizing themselves to the point of irrelevance. For chairmen Currier and Smoot, composers were the real parties in interest. The Words and Music Club was on board. Victor Herbert's signature was on the Compromise Agreement. Nathan Burkan was neutralized. Regardless whether publishers and instrument makers could ever get to yes, the two-cent solution was a fait accompli.

In December 1907, Charles K. Harris, one of the most militant of the Tin Pan Alley publishers, issued an ultimatum to the editors of music trade publications. As the copyright battle entered its final phase, "no lukewarm attitude of neutrality will be tolerated," he warned. "The papers will have to climb down off the fence and indicate upon which side they will line up, whether for the publishers or against them." If it was the latter, he made clear, "it will mean the end to the advertising patronage which has been accorded them by the music makers."

Insofar as Marc A. Blumenberg was concerned, Harris was waving a red cape in front of a bull. Not long after the Musical Courier Company paid Victor Herbert's libel judgment in 1905, it had acquired a bimonthly called the *American Musician and Art Journal,* an odd amalgam of news about brass bands and Tin Pan Alley, supported by many pages of advertisements for band instruments, uniforms, and sheet music. In content and attitude, it was the anti–*Musical Courier.* Blumenberg must have been eager to bring his bellicose editorial sensibility to the new publication. To do that, he made an uncanny hire, choosing songwriter, nose flute inventor, and convicted sheet music counterfeiter Garrett J. Couchois as a staff writer.

Blumenberg and Couchois were strange bedfellows, but in their loathing for Nathan Burkan they found common ground. "Burkan has been my most inveterate enemy," Couchois confided to Blumenberg. "Because of the case Burkan had against me I was locked up for something like seven or eight months." Blumenberg would take a back seat to no one when it came to aggrievement. "Notwithstanding all that," he told Couchois, "I have a more profound hatred of Mr. Burkan than you could possibly have." The two discussed Burkan frequently as they watched his national stature grow through his highly visible role in the copyright debates. They devised a plan to wreak their vengeance and take him down.

Early in the summer of 1908, "egged on by Mr. Blumenberg," Couchois wrote an unsigned editorial for the *American Musician* titled "Some Plain Truths about Copyright." Offered "in the spirit of friendliness"—a sure tell in a Blumenberg publication that mischief was afoot—it undertook to instruct the music publishing trade on the basic principles of copyright. "That such dense ignorance can be so openly displayed by members of a trade whose almost sole assets consist of copyrights is amazing. It has impelled the *American Musician* to enact the role of a kind father who does not spare the rod." The hard "truth" espoused in the piece was that any law containing a mechanical reproduction right would be struck down as unconstitutional, a contention that virtually all the principals in the controversy had abandoned by this time.

When the editorial failed to provoke any response from Burkan, Blumenberg instructed Couchois to use a method he had developed over his long career as a journalist "to smoke people out"—inventing correspondence. In a fake letter to the editor ascribed to an unnamed "popular music publisher," Couchois gave himself the rhetorical opening he needed to attack Burkan directly. The fictitious correspondent cited Burkan's testimony before the joint congressional committees and asked, "Mr. Burkan's opinion must of necessity be given great weight—for is he not recognized as our foremost expert on copyright?"

With that cue, Couchois was off and running. In his "Answer to 'a Popular Music Publisher,'" he disingenuously thanked the writer for calling Burkan's testimony to his attention. He then went on: "It betrays an ignorance so palpable as to make that gentleman's pretensions to knowledge of copyright law bear the aspect of a legal 'four flush.' We can scarcely believe Mr. Burkan was quoted correctly in the Congressional Record." For months thereafter, attacks flowed from Couchois's pen. Couchois portrayed Burkan as deliberately "fleecing" the music publishers, taking their money with full knowledge that the law he was advocating would be struck down as unconstitutional, and called him "a knave" of the "meanest and most pronounced type." He expressed dismay that "any lawyer, much less a lawyer of national reputation," could be advising the Music Publishers Association that a mechanical right would be constitutional, "unless he was deliberately aiming to lead his client astray or was *non compos mentis*."

Burkan wrote a lengthy reply addressed to Blumenberg. It rebutted his constitutional arguments in great detail and addressed the elephant in the room: "It is very apparent that under the pretext of criticizing my views, you have taken advantage of the occasion to gratify your malice, caused no doubt by my humble services in behalf of Victor Herbert in his libel suits against you." Unless *American Musician* retracted the attacks, Burkan said, he would be "compelled, though unwilling, to seek vindication in the courts."

Surely Burkan expected no retraction from Blumenberg. The tone of the editorials only became more mocking. "Is it not time for him to indulge in a little calm introspection to discover if possible which wheel is out of gear?" Burkan's arguments "would have brought discredit to a primary schoolboy's composition, and exhibited lamentable and astonishing ignorance of the whole subject of copyright." Blumenberg, who occasionally interlineated Couchois's drafts, took special delight in adding a cryptic reference to Burkan being an "attorney of obscure and misty origin." The depths of the pair's derangement when it came to Burkan was most evident in a little piece of doggerel they published, adding one stanza at a time, over several weeks. It began:

> There was once a little lawyer,
> Who knew but little law,
> But he made up for the difference
> With his jaw, jaw, jaw.
>
> Now this little four flush lawyer
> Had so buffaloed the trade,
> That he thought his reputation
> Surely made, made, made.

By the time the last installment of this ballad appeared, with the "little lawyer" being unmasked as a fraud ("if your reputation should be built upon a bluff/you're sure to find the sledding pretty goldurned rough"), advertising from music publishers had, as Charles K. Harris predicted, dried up. Subscribers to the *American Musician and Art Journal* must have been surprised to see, when the February 12, 1909, issue arrived, that the publication had been relaunched without fanfare as a show biz rag, the usual portrait of a starchy brass band leader on the cover giving way to the scantily clad "Queen of Vaudeville," Eva Tanguay.

When the 60th Congress returned for a lame-duck session in December 1908, Chairman Currier appointed a subcommittee to draft a final copyright bill, working mostly behind closed doors. Negotiations spilled over into February 1909, when the last two sticking points were resolved. The first was extension of the copyright term. Every draft bill since the Copyright Office's original proposal had provided for a unified term of the life of the author plus some additional years, varying from thirty to fifty. Ultimately, the committee decided to stay with an initial term of twenty-eight years, but doubled the fourteen-year renewal period, for a total copyright life of fifty-six years. This was enough to guarantee that few authors would outlive their copyrights.

The second sticking point was the mechanical right. The die had been cast for a two-cent universal royalty on mechanical reproductions, but details remained to be worked out. In the final version, the compulsory license provision had no retroactive effect and would be triggered only after a composer "permitted or knowingly acquiesced" in the making of an initial mechanical reproduction of a work. From that point, a mechanical license would be available automatically at the two-cent royalty rate to anyone who wanted it. The House committee's report explained that it was seeking to "give to the composer the exclusive right to prohibit the reproduction of his music by mechanical means on the part of anybody if he desired, to secure to him adequate compensation from all reproducers if he did not desire to exercise this exclusive right to prohibit, and to prevent the establishment of a great trade monopoly."

The copyright bill was rushed to the floor and passed by both houses of Congress under suspension of the rules in the closing hours of the 60th Congress. President Roosevelt signed it on March 3, 1909, one of his last official acts before leaving office. The process had not been pretty, but the result was transformative. The Copyright Act of 1909, which was not comprehensively revised until the late 1970s, was the legal framework on which the American entertainment industries of the twentieth century were built.

The music industry was the most conspicuous beneficiary. A common metaphor for the modern music business likens it to a "river of nickels." More than a century later, the compulsory mechanical license (carrying in 2020 a royalty of 9.1 cents per song, an increase far short of the rate of inflation) remains one of the most important tributaries, the legal basis for making and selling "cover" recordings of a song in any material format or digitally. Equally important, in the aftermath of the battle over the 1909 act, the music industry emerged as a powerful force in the politics of copyright, ready to take an aggressive posture in the many battles that lay ahead.

No lawyer in the private sector was more closely associated with these developments than Nathan Burkan. His reputation now spread far beyond Tin Pan Alley. At age thirty-one, he was undisputed dean of the American copyright bar.

There remained one piece of unfinished business for Burkan. In May 1910, he filed his own defamation action against the Musical Courier Company, seeking compensation for the *American Musician and Art Journal*'s long series of attacks on his competence and integrity. The trial, in June 1912, had all the makings of a gala ten-year reunion for the cast of *Herbert v. Musical Courier*. Arthur Palmer tried the case for Burkan and Victor Herbert testified on his behalf, along with a host of prominent character witnesses. Once again, the defense was "justification," resulting in the jurors hearing many days of expert testimony on the constitutional issues surrounding the mechanical right, so that they could make their own determination whether Burkan's "pretensions to knowledge of copyright law" indeed bore aspects of a "legal four-flush."

Even the jury's verdict in Burkan's favor, $5,000, had a familiar ring to it. (Evidence offered in response to the accusation that Burkan had "fleeced" his clients showed that this sum was far more than he had billed for fees and expenses in his four years of work on the copyright act.) The only missing players were Abe Hummel (who had been disbarred and imprisoned in 1907) and Marc A. Blumenberg. A few months earlier, Blumenberg had been indicted by a grand jury in Illinois, along with three of his employees, for criminal libel. The charges arose out of a series of articles on Chicago's Steger & Sons Piano Company that purported to expose fraudulent and oppressive labor practices. Blumenberg sailed for Europe after the indictment came down in January 1912, and he was still there, fighting extradition to Illinois, when Burkan's case was tried.

With Blumenberg absent, Garrett Couchois testified without contradiction to the unrelenting malice that animated the *American Musician* articles. "It took quite a while for me to find out Mr. Blumenberg's real character," Couchois said, but he had come to believe Burkan's case was "a praiseworthy attempt to curtail Blumenberg's pernicious activities."

One of Blumenberg's other lieutenants, William Geppert, was tried on the Illinois libel charge in January 1913. Couchois was the star witness in that case too, testifying that Blumenberg had instructed him to demand $50,000 from Steger with the warning that "if he did not come across, they would immediately turn the batteries of the paper upon him." When Couchois expressed reluctance to participate in a shakedown, Blumenberg assured him the company would have his back: "Matters of this kind are of almost daily occurrence with me. You are not afraid because someone chose to call it blackmail, are you?"

After a three-week trial, Geppert was convicted and sentenced to two years' imprisonment for his role in the Steger affair. Blumenberg, it can be safely surmised, would have received an even harsher sentence. But he died in Paris, still on the lam, just one month later.

PART THREE

Bending the Firmament

CHAPTER 8

Entr'acte

Nathan Burkan's professional life in the 1910s was astonishingly frenetic. His law practice placed him at the geographical and gravitational center of an American entertainment complex that was experiencing unprecedented growth, stimulated by the robust copyright law he had just helped to write and enact. At this point, our narrative must depart from linear chronology. These were the years when, simultaneously, the founding of the American Society of Composers, Authors, and Publishers laid the groundwork for the Great American Songbook, the legitimate theater in America centralized on Times Square and assumed its modern industrial structure, and the studio system that would dominate the movie business for a century began to take shape. Burkan navigated the treacherous shoals of simultaneously representing producers, creators, and performers in each field as they fought over their respective slices of the growing entertainment pie. And there was an added complication: strife between the various media of entertainment as they cannibalized each other's content and audiences.

Burkan's reputation was now international in scope. Copyright reformers around the world sought out his advice. At home, his political capital was compounding at an exponential rate. The Wichita Democratic Club at Madison Avenue and 104th Street became Burkan's political home. Presided over by the Tammany Hall leader for New York's 26th Assembly district, James J. Frawley, the Wichita was part of a network of clubhouses that had become, in journalist Terry Golway's

Burkan, age thirty-six, as a delegate
to the 1915 New York State
constitutional convention. (Courtesy,
Nathan Burkan Jr.)

words, "the physical articulation of Tammany's ad-hoc ideology of service and social welfare." The clubhouse was where "those in need of coal, a meal, a job, or a political favor met with district leaders, who were the public and often highly popular faces of Tammany Hall." Burkan became a trusted aide-de-camp to Frawley. In the summer of 1908, they traveled together to Denver to attend Burkan's first Democratic National Convention. (He would later serve as a delegate to many more.) The two men grew to be close friends.

Burkan was elected a delegate to the New York State constitutional convention that met in Albany through much of the spring and summer of 1915. There he formed lasting political alliances with three sitting state senators on the rise: future governor Alfred E. Smith, future U.S. senator Robert Wagner, and future New York City surrogate James Foley. The four men, each of whom combined a sharp intellect with compassion and political street smarts, constituted a formidable progressive bloc.

As a practicing lawyer in a body dominated by public officeholders, Burkan devoted most of his labors at the convention to arcane matters of court structure and judicial procedure, but he offered some stirring floor oratory on two of the most contentious proposals put before the delegates, both of which took direct aim at his constituency. After the convention initially approved an English literacy requirement for voters, Burkan made a passionate argument for reconsideration:

It is abhorrent to believe that those who toil by the sweat of their brows, who create and improve prosperity . . . shall be disenfranchised because they cannot comply with an irksome test. This proposal aims to penalize an unfortunate class of our population. Illiteracy is not ignorance. It is a sad misfortune. It may be an accident of birth. It may be a lack of opportunity in the case of foreigners because of oppression, denial and discouragement. It is not a crime however, and you have no right to classify illiterates with criminals.

A motion to strike the literacy test carried handily.

William Barnes, a staunchly conservative newspaper editor, offered an amendment that prohibited the legislature from "granting to any person or persons any privilege or immunity not accorded to every other person or persons." It was designed to prevent the legislature from enacting virtually any remedial social welfare laws, and it included explicit prohibitions against laws providing for government payments to individuals "without the rendering of a specific public service therefor," as well as laws "establishing a minimum wage."

One supporter of the Barnes amendment, Judge Alphonso Clearwater of Ulster County, argued that such a provision was necessitated by the post-1880 influx of immigrants from southern Europe, who, unlike earlier immigrants (the "English, Celtic, Scandinavian and Teutonic"), did not "blend in." This "racial degeneration," Clearwater (himself of Dutch and Huguenot descent) argued, had led to the decline of

> that reserve, that Puritanism with its spirit of restraint which tended to the elevation of the citizen, and in its train has come that influx of sensuousness, that receding of religion, that longing for amusement, that greedy craving for joy even with an erotic touch; that grasping for anything which tickles the senses, that flippancy which has introduced the vaudeville on the stage and in daily life, that desire for advantage over one's fellows by . . . special privilege wrung from governmental influence.

Burkan was the first delegate to rise in response. He made no mention of his personal membership in the class that Clearwater had slandered, nor of his professional work for vaudeville and other amusements. He spoke only of his constituents:

> I represent a district of over two hundred thousand people, and this district typifies and represents this so-called undesirable element that has entered this country since 1880. . . . They were brave and adventurous spirits who left the old world behind with courage and hope. . . . This undesirable element from southern Europe is filling a want in this country. They are tilling your soil, clearing the forests, digging your trenches and building your railroads; they are constructing your buildings. They are sober, honest and ambitious.

Burkan went on at some length, reminding the convention of similar warnings that had been sounded against earlier immigrant groups, most particularly the Irish. He concluded on a note of unabashed economic populism. It must have struck most of the burghers in the room as the kind of thinking that they would soon be decrying as Bolshevism, but it undoubtedly played well among the voters who sent Burkan to the convention:

> If there has been a demand for privilege in this country, if there has been a demand for immunity on the part of the working classes, I say the privileged classes are responsible for that condition. . . . They worked these people long hours, took unfair advantage of them, made their lives miserable and unbearable, broke them in spirit and in strength, and the government had to come in and enact laws . . . which do protect certain elements of our citizenship against the greed, cruelty and rapacity of another element.

The Barnes amendment was decisively defeated.

Burkan and his Tammany allies fought unsuccessfully to rescind constitutional provisions that prevented New York City from obtaining representation in the state legislature proportional to its share of the state's population and restricted its home rule powers. "The aspirations of our city are to be the greatest city in the world, to be the leader in finance, in business, industry, art, and science," Burkan told his fellow delegates. Noting that legislators from upstate had been antagonistic to those aspirations, he urged the convention to "give New York City a square deal, give it that equality and fairness of representation that it is entitled to." This fight was lost, and in the end Burkan voted to disapprove the draft constitution due to its "persistent discrimination against the city of New York." In November 1915, voters rejected it in a statewide referendum, with Tammany Hall helping to run up a 250,000-vote margin in New York City alone.

Within weeks of that vote, James Frawley, who had recently purchased an upstate farm, announced his retirement from politics. Burkan won a contested election to replace Frawley as Tammany Hall's leader in the 26th Assembly district, a position that he retained, through party upheavals and partisan gerrymanders, for the rest of his life. In May 1916, hundreds attended a testimonial dinner given by the Wichita Club in honor of its new leader and heard Dudley Field Malone, one of the most progressive voices in Woodrow Wilson's administration, praise Burkan as "a real man and a real Democrat."

By this time, Burkan had moved his law office to the fourteenth floor of the City Investing Building at 165 Broadway. Completed in 1908, at thirty-three stories it was one of Lower Manhattan's earliest skyscrapers and for many years the city's largest office building by square footage. It was a step up from 99 Nassau Street in prestige, amenities, and overhead, making it imperative that the practice grow. After two short-lived attempts to form partnerships with other lawyers, Burkan settled into a business model of hiring associate attorneys to whom he provided exciting professional opportunities but no prospect of partnership.

Among his early hires was Rose Rothenberg, a fellow NYU School of Law graduate and Romanian immigrant, and a rare woman in the New York City bar of the 1910s. Although she left the firm in 1919 to join the Manhattan District Attorney's office, where she became the first woman to prosecute criminal cases in New York State, her relationship with Burkan endured. When New York extended the franchise to women in 1918, Rothenberg became a member of Tammany Hall's executive committee and served as Burkan's co–district leader for two decades.

Like Rothenberg, most of Burkan's associates moved on after a few years. But Charles Schwartz and Louis Frohlich, recent law graduates when Burkan hired them in 1915, made their careers in Burkan's law office, eventually taking over the practice upon Burkan's death in 1936. In 1918, they jointly authored a comprehensive, nine-hundred-page treatise, *The Law of Motion Pictures,* the first book of its kind, which they "affectionately dedicated to Nathan Burkan, to whom we owe our entrance into the field of motion picture and theatrical law." It was a magisterial achievement for two junior lawyers, all the more so because the ground was constantly shifting under their feet as they wrote, thanks in no small part to the restlessness and litigiousness of the Burkan office's marquee motion picture client, Charlie Chaplin.

CHAPTER 9

The Lone Star

Charles Spencer Chaplin was touring the vaudeville circuits of the United States with an English music hall act when the Keystone Film Company offered him an opportunity to appear in moving pictures. He made his first appearance in front of a movie camera wearing his Tramp character's iconic toothbrush moustache, bowler hat, and off-kilter outfit—a pinch too small above the waist, much too large below—in January 1914. The twenty-four-year-old's comic genius was apparent at once.

Under the direction of Mack Sennett, and with such established stars as Mabel Normand and Fatty Arbuckle, Keystone was already a humming comedy factory when Chaplin arrived, churning out a brand of silent comedy that was broad and buffoonish. Chaplin's approach quickly evolved into something more graceful and expressive, still slapstick but not shambolic. In the Keystone style, as biographer David Robinson has explained, bumping into a tree was the gag. "When Chaplin bumped into a tree . . . it was not the collision that was funny, but the fact that he raised his hat to the tree in a reflex gesture of apology."

Within a few months, Chaplin was directing and starring in one- and two-reel comedies (a "reel" being about a thousand feet of film and ten to fifteen minutes of running time) based on his own scenarios, produced at a rate of about one every ten days. Exhibitors could not get enough of them; he was Keystone's hottest attraction. Mischievous, romantic, and resilient, the Tramp exuded universal appeal, confined by no boundaries of age, gender, race, language, or nationality. By the time his one-year, $150-per-week employment contract was about to expire, Chaplin had absorbed all that Keystone could teach him about moviemaking. Its assembly-line ethos could not accommodate the budding artist. Perfunctory discussions of a new contract were followed by an amicable parting, with Chaplin bequeathing Keystone a back catalog of more than thirty short pictures that would "work" (that is, generate profits) for years to come, a movie industry first.

Serving as his own agent and lawyer, Chaplin misplayed the strong hand he was holding. He was too quick to accept when the Essanay Film Manufacturing Company, a Chicago-based firm known mostly for its weekly one-reel "Broncho Billy" westerns, dangled before him a $10,000 signing bonus and salary of $1,250 per week. With memories of youthful penury still fresh, and harboring doubts as to the durability of his success, Chaplin was not ready to speculate on his own profitability. The barebones one-year contract that he signed with Essanay reflected his priorities at the moment: a steady paycheck and the artistic freedom to write, direct, and star in pictures that would be marketed as "Chaplin Brand" comedies.

Chaplin's relationship with Essanay was fraught with frequent renegotiations of financial terms and bickering over production values and costs. Nonetheless, his meteoric rise continued apace. Chaplin's Essanay comedies were artistically and commercially successful. It was at Essanay that Chaplin began to assemble the nucleus of his stock production company, including leading lady Edna Purviance and cameraman Roland Totheroh. And it was during his year at Essanay that Charlie Chaplin broke through as a national and international phenomenon.

Chaplin had gotten into pictures at an opportune time, as the industry, transitioning from infancy to adolescence, was being roiled by creative and economic ferment.

Thomas Edison had received many of the pioneering patents on moving picture technology and was the first to enter the market with equipment and content. As with the talking machine, however, Edison's vision of the new medium's commercial and artistic possibilities proved myopic. His motion picture operation specialized in recording "actualities"—circus or variety acts, hootchy-kootchy dancers, fires being doused—for display to one viewer at a time in fifty-foot fragments (about thirty seconds in duration) on coin-operated peephole "Kinetoscopes." It fell to others to invent and perfect the necessary appurtenances for a vibrant cinematic artform and industry: projection, movie theaters, narrative photoplays, feature-length films, directors, and movie stars.

On January 1, 1909, with thousands of nickelodeon movie screens operating across the country and filmmakers just beginning to master the art of telling stories in silent moving pictures, the Edison Manufacturing Company combined with its closest rival, American Mutoscope and Biograph, to form the Motion Picture Patents Company, commonly known as the "Edison Trust." The Trust announced that it had assembled a pool of "all the patents known by experts . . . to have an important bearing on motion picture and projecting machines."

For several years, the Edison Trust held a near stranglehold on every aspect of the movie business, from production to exhibition. It even locked up the supply of motion picture film through an exclusive contract with Eastman Kodak. It vigorously enforced onerous license restrictions through both legal process and extralegal thuggery. "The Trust sought to standardize the industry, making film into a commodity," writes scholar Peter Decherney. "Producers had to meet a quota. Every reel . . . was sold at the same price like pounds of sugar. Distributors had to buy films sight unseen. Trust members resisted the idea of promoting movie stars or even crediting the actors in films." Among those toiling away anonymously at Biograph during the heyday of the Trust—for paltry wages on low-budget, one-reel pictures—were Mary Pickford, Mack Sennett, Thomas Ince, and D.W. Griffith.

By dint of legal and technical work-arounds, subterfuge, and sheer chutzpah, some independent film manufacturers and distributors survived and even prospered under the nose of the Trust. By the mid-1910s, the Trust's power was withering under the weight of challenges to its patents, a government antitrust action, and its own creative inertia. The independents, who recognized the commercial potential of stars and feature-length story arcs, began raiding the Trust's talent, making Pickford, Ince, Griffith, and Sennett the American cinema's first name-brand artists.

The creative class's window of opportunity was brief. The most forward-thinking and aggressive of the independent moguls, Jesse L. Lasky, Adolph Zukor, William Fox, Samuel Goldwyn, Louis B. Mayer, the brothers Warner—immigrant Jews who in author Neal Gabler's titular phrase would build "an empire of their own"—were already laying the foundation for the studio system, a top-down business paradigm that would make the Edison Trust look like a paper tiger.

In the meantime, though, Charlie Chaplin could write his own ticket. The stars of the Hollywood galaxy had already been moving toward a recognizable alignment when Chaplin arrived on the scene, but his gravitational field unleashed forces that would bend the firmament.

As late as June 1912, when he prepared a detailed curriculum vitae for use during his libel suit against the Musical Courier Company, Nathan Burkan listed no significant clients or cases connected to the movie business. But events were already underway that made it inevitable that he too would soon be getting into pictures in a big way.

Congress was at work on an amendment to the 1909 Copyright Act that would add motion pictures to the list of protected works. Before that, movies were being registered for copyright as collections of photographs, a rickety legal fiction that was serviceable in the days of Edison's actualities but was increasingly unworkable as photoplays became longer and more sophisticated. The 1912 amendment also implemented a Supreme Court ruling, handed down a few months earlier in *Kalem Company v. Harper Brothers,* a case involving an Edison Trust adaptation of the novel *Ben-Hur,* which held that even a silent-movie pantomime can violate the exclusive right to dramatize a literary work. The "visual impression" created by a movie is the same as that of a live performance, wrote Justice Holmes for the court, even if "the machinery is different and more complex." The case represented a conceptual leap forward for a court that had been baffled by player piano rolls just a few years earlier.

It was at about the same time that Adolph Zukor, a onetime furrier who had recently gone into movie exhibition, met with Broadway theater impresario Daniel Frohman at the Lambs Club to discuss a marriage of stage and film. Their vision of putting the biggest stars of the legitimate theater into feature-length movies, re-creating their best-known stage roles, was encapsulated in the tagline "Famous Players in Famous Plays."

No one represented more famous stage players and famous playwrights than Nathan Burkan. He quickly became a force to be reckoned with in the entertainment world's newest frontier, moving pictures.

Famous Players Film Company's first original production, completed in the fall of 1912, was a five-reel *Count of Monte Cristo,* starring James O'Neill, father of playwright Eugene. The elder O'Neill had been playing the role of Edmond Dantès on stage for more than thirty years. Release of the picture was delayed, ultimately for a full year, when Selig Polyscope, an Edison Trust producer out of Chicago, beat Famous Players to the market with its own three-reel version of the story. O'Neill had long claimed to own a common-law copyright on the unpublished dramatization of the Alexandre Dumas novel, which he had performed over five thousand times and which had also served as the scenario for his Famous Players film. When O'Neill filed a copyright infringement suit against the distributor of the Selig picture, General Film Company, Burkan was engaged to defend.

To disprove copying, Burkan prepared a scene-by-scene analysis of the Selig production, highlighting every departure from the dramaturgy of O'Neill's play, however minute, and every common feature that could also be found in the original novel or another adaptation. But Burkan's laborious cross-examination of O'Neill on these points never reached the dramatic climax he was striving for, as the actor exhibited nothing but bemusement and boredom. In a typical exchange, the histrionic lawyer and the monosyllabic actor sparred over a scene in which Dantès receives his commission as captain of the *Pharaon:*

In the Selig picture, Burkan asked, "it is shown in the attic room of Father Dantès, isn't it?"

"I don't remember."

Burkan attempted to jog O'Neill's memory. "Dantès comes in and embraces his father. Morell comes in and then and there hands the paper to Dantès." O'Neill stared back blankly.

Burkan tried a little playacting. "He says, 'Here is your commission,' isn't that so?" Finally catching Burkan's drift, O'Neill concedes that in his play the commission scene is not an interior, but takes place "out in the open" at a betrothal feast, his blasé monotone unmistakably conveying the message that to a man of the theater, such lawyerly distinctions were beneath notice.

Burkan, the trial court found, had demonstrated "industry and skill worthy of a better cause." The Selig film not only used some of the most dramatically consequential incidents and plot devices that were original to O'Neill's stage version, it had also transcribed some of its most famous and original dialogue onto title cards, including O'Neill's trademark line, declaimed while clinging to a rock in the middle of the Mediterranean Sea after he escapes the Château d'If: "The world is mine!"

O'Neill won, but his victory was Pyrrhic—Burkan persuaded an appellate court that the copyright registration that Famous Players received for its film adaptation under the new copyright law divested O'Neill's dramatization of any ongoing protection under the common law. As a result, his damages were limited to the two-month period between the release of the Selig film and the date of the Famous Players copyright registration, and he was no longer able to claim any exclusive right to the play he was so closely associated with.

Vaudeville impresario Jesse L. Lasky's brother-in-law, a glove salesman named Samuel Goldfish, had long been urging him to get into the movie business. Lasky was reluctant. To him, the one- and two-reel moving pictures he had been including in his vaudeville programs were good for nothing but chasing out customers who would otherwise sit through multiple performances of the live acts. The quality of Zukor's features changed his outlook, and one day when Lasky and his creative partner, Cecil B. DeMille, ran into actor Dustin Farnum and playwright Edwin Milton Royle at the Lambs Club, they struck a deal to make a film version of Royle's *The Squaw Man*. The Jesse L. Lasky Feature Play Company was incorporated, with Goldfish as treasurer and general manager and DeMille as "director general." *The Squaw Man* was released within days of Charlie Chaplin's screen debut for Keystone in the winter of 1914. It was an enormous hit.

Lasky's second feature, a comedy called *Brewster's Millions,* ran into trouble with the Board of Censorship in Chicago, which ordered the deletion of scenes ("cutouts") totaling about four minutes. Lasky's distributor for the Midwest, Celebrated Players Film Company, intended to appeal the censor's ruling prior to sending the film to exhibitors. But before it could do so, Sam Goldfish—asserting that "whether the cutouts are made or not is wholly immaterial as they do not in the least effect [sic] the value or attractiveness of the picture"—precipitously terminated Celebrated's distributorship contract. (Lasky and Goldfish had recently befriended Adolph Zukor; they were looking for a pretext to give one of Zukor's affiliated companies the Midwest distribution rights.)

The Lasky Company filed suit in New York to have the contract declared void. Celebrated hired Nathan Burkan to defend. Burkan prevailed upon a federal judge to see an uncensored version of *Brewster's Millions* at a New York theater where, Burkan knew, at least one of the scenes that the Chicago censor ordered deleted was considered important enough to be featured on the promotional materials on display in the lobby. The judge took notice and held that Goldfish had been "too anxious to get matters into a situation where a breach of contract might be forced." He found that it was the Lasky Company, not Celebrated, that was in breach.

The sequence of events that followed makes for a quintessential Burkan tale. Lasky and Goldfish, impressed with Burkan's performance, engaged their erstwhile adversary to represent their company in subsequent cases. After the Lasky Feature Play Company merged with Famous Players in 1916, Adolph Zukor forced Goldfish out, and Lasky's sister, Blanche, divorced Goldfish. When Goldfish tried to renege on his property settlement with Blanche after she remarried, Burkan represented her. *Goldfish v. Goldfish* went all the way to New York's highest court, which ordered Sam to continue making his monthly payments.

Harboring no ill will toward his ex-wife's lawyer, Sam Goldfish "dragooned" Burkan into representing him in his post-Lasky ventures. He even sought out Burkan's advice in disputes with Blanche over custody of their daughter.

Later, Sam Goldwyn (he had adopted as his own surname the portmanteau trademark of the movie studio he founded with Edgar Selwyn after his ouster from Famous Players–Lasky) was trying to hire director Henry King for a project. King, another Burkan client, had previously refused to work with Goldwyn, whom he considered untrustworthy. Burkan arranged for the two men to meet face to face at the Ambassador Hotel, the swank Hollywood social hub that served as Burkan's home base during his twice-yearly trips to the West Coast. As King later told the story,

> Nathan turned to me—this was in Goldwyn's presence—and said, "Look, Henry, this man will carry out to the letter every word there is in a contract he signs. But don't believe anything he tells you or promises you that isn't written."
>
> Sam almost tore the hotel down! "Nate," he cried, "You're my attorney!"
>
> Nathan said, "I'm also Henry's attorney and I'm telling both of you the truth." He wrote the contract in longhand on Ambassador Hotel stationery. That was the contract for *Stella Dallas*.

As a *Film Daily* columnist once quipped, "Nathan Burkan has so many clients, when he starts a court action, he finds the opposing counsel is himself."

The Charlie Chaplin phenomenon that was sweeping the United States in 1915 began as a spontaneous expression of grassroots enthusiasm. Chaplin look-alike contests became staples of small-town holiday celebrations, and Chaplin imitators were busking on the streets of large cities. The now-familiar commercial effluvia of twentieth-century pop culture manias quickly followed. Chaplin merchandise, nearly all of it unauthorized, flooded the market. Charlie Chaplin gag coins (sold for a penny, with an elastic band attached) turned out to be effective nickel slugs, prompting the New York City branch of the Secret Service to ban them.

Tin Pan Alley—a reliable bellwether of pop culture cachet—published dozens of Chaplin-themed songs, many of which were interpolated into vaudeville acts and revues, sometimes performed by whole chorus lines of Charlies. A Kansas newspaper warned its readers that their latest dance craze, in which "the shoulders of the dancers are held stiffly, but the body is rocked slightly from the hips," in imitation of the "ludicrous actions of a movie freak," could be traced back to "an antebellum custom of darkies in the old South." "Any form of expressing Chaplin is what the public wants," reported *Motion Picture Magazine*. "The world has Chaplinitis."

Chaplin, obsessed with mastering his new art, and living frugally within his means in a Los Angeles artist's studio, was paying little attention to the opportunities and perils his growing fame entailed. While Essanay harnessed an income stream from exploiting his name and image, Chaplin largely ignored the collateral merchandising opportunities that came his way. His older half brother Sydney, himself a contract player at Keystone and by the standards of any other family a fine comic actor, stepped in to manage and rationalize Charlie's business affairs, more as partner and alter ego than agent.

As Charlie completed work on his final Essanay picture in January 1916, Syd went to New York to field offers for his brother's future services. Holding court at the Hotel Astor, Syd had filmdom beating a path to his door. *Variety* ran a front-page story headlined "Chaplin's Enormous Offers; Turns Down $500,000 Yearly." The numbers on the table, *Variety* wrote, "seemed almost appalling for one man as salary." Like much of the reporting in the trade papers over the frenzied month that followed, the article was largely based on the self-serving posturing of interested parties. Most concerning to Syd was *Variety*'s parenthetical observation that "whether Chaplin is as 'strong' with the picture fans as he was seems to divide opinion in the trade." Worried that this could stoke Charlie's anxieties and weaken his bargaining resolve, Syd dashed off a telegram to Charlie's secretary, valet, and factotum, Tom Harrington: "Tell Charlie not come east till he hears from me. Tell him to ignore *Variety* article. All wrong. Have some great offers."

Syd believed he had a "big combine" on the hook, and he wanted to seal the deal while his less practical sibling was still pinned down in Hollywood. He dictated language for a telegram that he wanted Charlie to wire back: "This grants Syd Chaplin power to sign any contract on my behalf subject to contract being acceptable to Syd Chaplin and any responsible attorney he may select."

Syd had selected Nathan Burkan. It was Burkan's work for the legitimate theater's leading comedienne and ingenue of the day, Billie Burke, that most likely had captured Syd's attention. Burke had entered the circle of Burkan's theatrical clients by her marriage to another one, Florence Ziegfeld. Burkan negotiated Burke's first two movie contracts, a $10,000–per-week deal for one feature to be directed by Thomas Ince and a flat $150,000 for a twenty-week serial. These were eye-popping numbers in 1915, when the most reliably bankable movie star of the day, Mary Pickford, had just been bumped to $2,000 per week at Famous Players.

The nice round figures in the Billie Burke deals stuck in Syd Chaplin's head. Charlie's asking price would be $10,000 per week, with a $100,000 bonus up front.

Syd believed that he and Burkan could settle matters outside the maelstrom of Charlie's turbulent aura. But the power of attorney he had asked Charlie for never arrived. Instead, Charlie left Los Angeles for New York that very night, intent on taking the temperature of the market for himself.

If Charlie truly feared that his bubble was about to burst, his February 1916 cross-country journey, his first real break from the grind of moviemaking in more than two years, was just what the doctor ordered. At every stop along the way his train was met by throngs of dignitaries and fans. Local papers reported his passage with equal rapture whether he emerged from the train and obliged the crowd with a bit of his famous walk or just slept through the stop in his Pullman berth. "Famous Comedian Dozes Ten Minutes Away When He Might Have Seen Wichita" ran one headline.

Once in New York, he registered at the Plaza Hotel as Charles Spencer and for two weeks mostly stayed out of the public eye while "practically every film manufacturer in the business sought his ear with some kind of a proposition." Syd was still fastened on a proposal from a "big combine" led by Marcus Loew. Loew, the owner of a large chain of movie and vaudeville theaters, was proposing to form a film production company that would ensure his theaters a continuing supply of quality attractions at a time when competitive chains were becoming more vertically integrated. (A few years later, he would solve this problem by purchasing Metro Pictures and Goldwyn Pictures, and hiring Louis B. Mayer to run the merged operation.) Loew was willing to meet Syd's financial terms and to give Charlie an ownership stake in the new company.

Charlie, however, had no interest in partnering with Loew, or with any other mogul who might presume to think he knew something about the creative side of the movie business. He was looking for a hard-nosed financier, someone who would stay out of his way as long as his films were making money. While sightings of Syd and Charlie in the company of Loew fueled rumors that a deal was imminent, by then Charlie was already in thrall to another suitor.

John R. Freuler, the president of the Mutual Film Corporation, was just the type Charlie was looking for. A former real estate broker from Milwaukee, Freuler had gone into film distribution purely as a business proposition; he had no affinity for the artform. He even looked the part of a no-nonsense banker. Terry Ramsaye, then the head of publicity for Mutual and later a pioneering film historian, wrote that Freuler's "imposing height, crowned with white hair and a benignly efficient manner, made his mere mention of a million dollars sound like hard money in the drawer."

Freuler had been monitoring the Chaplin situation for months and was ready to pounce when Charlie arrived in New York. He had calculated the earning potential of a Chaplin two-reeler to the penny. He met Loew's $10,000–per-week salary offer and upped the bonus to $150,000 for twelve pictures over one year. He offered to create a dedicated Chaplin production company that would be capitalized by a syndicate of passive investors. The name of the proposed new entity must have been music to Chaplin's ears: Lone Star. And Freuler closed their handshake deal with a flourish that he knew would impress Chaplin mightily, writing out his personal check for $5,000 as an advance on the bonus.

Freuler and Chaplin agreed that production would begin within four weeks. In that time, capital had to be raised and studio facilities in Hollywood secured. That left only a few days for the lawyers to draw up what Ramsaye called "one of the most ponderous and intricate documents ever evolved for the employment of a motion picture star." Burkan had to devise new language that would guarantee Chaplin an unprecedented level of artistic control, giving legal shape to the not-yet-named and only dimly imagined concept of auteurship. The key provision gave Chaplin

sole charge of the artistic direction connected with the production of such pictures and the general stage management of the scenarios selected for such

purpose. . . . He shall select scenarios, settings, mise-en-scène, and all para-
phernalia necessary for the proper representations of any scenario selected
for production; he shall have the sole supervision, management, charge and
control of and over the production in pictures of the scenarios, the dressing
and make-up of the characters, the adaptation of any scenario so selected,
including the services of a scenario writer, cameraman, casts, the working
force and the cutting of each picture.

Remarkably, the document was silent as to budgetary allowances and
constraints. There must have been far more wiggle room in Freuler's
financial projections than he let on.

The contract was signed without ceremony on February 25, 1916.
After witnessing the signatures, according to Ramsaye, "Nathan Burkan demonstrated his genius by selling his six-dollar fountain pen,
with which the contract was signed, to Freuler for thirty-five dollars."
Burkan said it was the same pen that Billie Burke had used to sign
her first motion picture contract. Freuler, who was planning to sign
more big stars, "deemed that it was time to retire it from such costly
activity."

The following day, Ramsaye staged an elaborate reenactment of the
signing for public consumption. In a fictionalized account that Ramsaye
wrote for Mutual's magazine, *Reel Life,* it was Freuler who handed
Charlie *his* "pet fountain pen, with which all the stars sign." A photograph with Syd peering over the shoulder of Charlie, who looks almost
too young to be legally competent to sign a contract, was published
widely. Mutual began the earn-back on its investment by renting out a
thirty-second print capturing the (reenacted) moment of signing. A
tongue-in-cheek review of this very short subject noted that "a murmur
of disappointment went around the audience when the pictured faded
without a glimpse" of Charlie's paycheck.

Chaplin was somewhat sheepish about his newfound wealth and all
the attention it received. Before February 1916, the off-screen Charlie
Chaplin was so invisible outside of Hollywood, rumors periodically circulated that he had been killed while filming a stunt. He was happy to
be portrayed in the fan magazines as an aesthete whose only respite
from work was playing the violin and cello. His fat contract, he said,
simply "means that I am left free to be just as funny as I dare, to do the
best work that is in me."

Within days, though, the contract was fodder for editorial writers
and preachers across the country. "We have been startled rightly by
Chaplin's salary," a Boston clergyman sermonized. "If he had lived in

(Image digitized by Cineteca di Bologna as part of the Chaplin Project. © Roy Export Company Ltd.)

Puritan times he would have burned as a witch. But he is doing good by provoking laughter and bringing sunshine into souls." When reporters began to question whether the $670,000 figure (the equivalent of more than $10 million in 2020) wasn't just "press agent coinage," Ramsaye circulated facsimile copies, front and back, of Chaplin's cashed paychecks. Freuler patiently explained that it was all hard-nosed business, that Chaplin wasn't being paid all that money for his ability to "inhale spaghetti," but for his power to pull in paying customers to watch him do it. Supply and demand, he said, are "as truly the controlling factors in star prices as in the price of wheat."

In the 1920s and 1930s, it would become a rite of passage for modernist cultural theorists to portray Chaplin as a singular genius who, in Peter Decherney's words, "could work within the capitalist machine of mass production, at the pinnacle of the system, yet remain apart from it." It was an image that Chaplin embraced and cultivated. In 1916, however, Chaplin's struggle to harmonize his art with the demands of commerce was off to an inauspicious start.

CHAPTER 10

Charlie in the Harem

On December 10, 1915, Chaplin completed work on a two-reel comedy for Essanay titled *Charlie Chaplin's Burlesque on Carmen*. It is a unique entry in the Chaplin catalog, his only straight-on parody. His target was not Bizet's opera, which would have been unfamiliar to the great majority of Chaplin's fans, but rather Jesse Lasky's film adaptation of the story, directed by Cecil B. DeMille, which was drawing large audiences even as Chaplin was shooting his send-up. This type of satire was not Chaplin's strong suit—even he conceded the film was not a "world-beater." His Don José (excruciatingly punned as "Darn Hosiery") was essentially the Tramp doing his usual business in the uniform and regalia of a Spanish military officer, an incongruity that was good for some laughs whether the viewer was familiar with the Lasky version or not.

Essanay originally announced a pre-Christmas 1915 release date for the *Burlesque on Carmen*. The holidays came and went with no release, then January, and then February—by far the longest interval yet without a new Chaplin picture.

Essanay was holding *Burlesque on Carmen* back to discourage other bidders for as long as it thought it had a chance to sign Chaplin to a new contract. Once the Mutual deal was announced, Essanay made haste in piggybacking on Mutual's massive publicity blitz. Chaplin had barely begun work at the Lone Star studio in April 1916 when Essanay released *Carmen* as an "Essanay-Chaplin Comedy in four screaming parts." It was twice the length of the final cut that Chaplin had delivered in December.

Essanay's *Burlesque on Carmen* included some of Chaplin's outtakes, but most of the added footage had been shot after he left the studio. In the new scenes, cross-eyed comedian Ben Turpin plays a smuggler, cavorting about on the perimeter of the main action, invisible to Darn Hosiery and Carmen, in what might charitably be described as a contrapuntal subplot. There are occasional nods at continuity—a character booted out of an original scene by a swift kick in the butt from Chaplin tumbles into an interpolated scene with Turpin, who administers another kick or otherwise lamely mimics Chaplin's comic business. To critics, the padding was obvious and tedious. "The literal kicks that might have been figurative hits in two reels," one wrote, "become monotonous in four. The laughter is infrequent, which in a Chaplin subject is really a serious matter."

Commercially speaking, though, Essanay had made an astute move. As a "feature" film it would be expected to command higher rentals than the $25 per day that a Chaplin two-reeler fetched. To meet the enormous pent-up demand, Chaplin-starved exhibitors in some cities bid the price up to more than $2,000 per week, sight unseen. "The disappointment of unsuccessful bidders," one critic deadpanned, "may be mitigated when they see the picture." He was wrong. The public didn't seem to notice or mind its shortcomings. The four-reel *Burlesque on Carmen* was a big hit.

Essanay had given Chaplin the runaround when he asked to screen the *Burlesque on Carmen* before its release. He was relegated to buying a ticket to see it at Clune's Broadway Theater in downtown Los Angeles, where he prepared a scene-by-scene analysis, a painstaking task that must have required multiple viewings. Out of 255 scenes in the four reels, there were 73 that he had no part in creating and another 11 that he had shot but later discarded. The changes, he said, "had the effect of retarding the action of the play, making it monotonous and slow," and leaving the star offscreen for unduly long periods. Advertising it as a "Chaplin comedy," he believed, would irreparably damage his reputation for producing films that were uniformly "excellent to the superlative degree."

At Chaplin's instruction, Burkan filed suit to enjoin distribution and exhibition of Essanay's *Burlesque on Carmen*. It was, said Terry Ramsaye, "the first suit ever filed because a picture is not funny enough."

Ramsaye's jest was more revealing than even he realized. This was a lawsuit in search of a legally cognizable cause of action. It was, and still is, black-letter law—as Schwartz and Frohlich stated in their 1918 treatise—that in an employer-employee relationship the employee "gives up the results of his mental labor in exchange for a stipend" paid by the employer. Essanay's attorneys argued that this general rule applied, that Essanay therefore rightfully owned the copyright to any footage that Chaplin shot while in its employ, and that the company could do with it as it pleased.

Chaplin believed he had protected himself against adulteration of his work by including a provision in the Essanay contract that required his approval before a picture was released under the "Chaplin brand." A near-final draft of the agreement seemingly gave Chaplin that approval right, but a last-minute revision insisted upon by Essanay, and probably not understood by the unlawyered Chaplin, had the effect of limiting it to pictures "other" than those in which Chaplin personally appeared.

With no claim for copyright infringement and only a weak claim for breach of contract, the legal theory behind Chaplin's complaint against Essanay is not easy to discern. Burkan alleged that Essanay had violated Chaplin's "rights as author" by making unauthorized alterations to his work and falsely creating the impression that it was based on a scenario "devised and originated" by Chaplin and "produced, directed, and made under his supervision." This, Burkan went on, created "an unfavorable and disappointing impression on the public and damaged Chaplin's reputation as a motion picture star and as an author and producer of photoplays."

Burkan was implicitly invoking a concept imported from the European continent: the moral right of an author to defend the integrity of a work against alterations that are damaging to an author's honor or reputation. Moral rights, as distinct from any economic rights an author may have under copyright or contract, were not recognized in U.S. law in 1916 (and are recognized only to a very limited extent today), but Burkan was on to something. Courts have from time to time been receptive to arguments of this nature, especially when raised by auteurs who were but small cogs in the massive Hollywood machine. Burkan and Chaplin were just a bit ahead of the times.

Essanay hit back hard against the notion that Chaplin's fame rested on anything other than "his eccentricities and peculiarities as a comedian" or indeed that he had any kind of "reputation as an author or producer of motion pictures." Far from the solitary genius toiling away feverishly on every aspect of the pictures that bore his name—an image cultivated by Chaplin and supported by the great weight of contemporary accounts—the Chaplin described in Essanay's legal papers was an indolent, money-grubbing prima donna. According to Gilbert "Broncho Billy" Anderson (the "Ay" of Ess-and-Ay) and staff director Jesse Robbins, Chaplin's pictures were typical Hollywood collaborative projects;

Chaplin did not write scenarios, he provided only minimal direction to other actors, and he left his work unedited for others to assemble.

Anderson and Robbins were putting the worst possible gloss on a phenomenon that Terry Ramsaye described in wonderment: "Chaplin comedies are not made. They occur." The testimony of George K. Spoor (the "Ess"), however, cannot be so easily dismissed. "His insatiable appetite for large sums of money," Spoor averred, was such that he was constantly discussing other deals "to drive and coerce the Essanay Company into making further large payments of money to him solely for the purpose of preventing him from breaching his contract with Essanay, which he constantly threatened to do." And not even Chaplin could have quarreled with Spoor's assertion that "he refused to work unless he felt like it, and he did not feel like working frequently." The picture Spoor paints has plenty of corroboration. Samuel Goldwyn, a good friend of Chaplin's, wrote that such behavior was the result of a deep-seated need to exert power over others: "Charlie loves power as no one whom I have ever met loves it."

The court did not find it necessary to pass upon Chaplin's artistry or work ethic. On the one hand, it was undisputed that Mutual would pay him his guaranteed compensation of $670,000 regardless whether the Essanay *Burlesque on Carmen* continued to be exhibited. Essanay, on the other hand, showed that it stood to lose at least that much money if the injunction issued. "Whether plaintiff will suffer any damage from the production is problematical," the court stated, "while an injunction is certain to work considerable loss to the defendants." Essanay's clunky four-reel *Burlesque on Carmen* remains in circulation more than a century later, although the unusually detailed notes Chaplin took for his lawsuit made it possible for film preservationist David Shepard, in 1999, to faithfully re-create the original two-reel cut.

Chaplin's films represented only a small fraction of the commerce being transacted in his name, image, and antics during the life of the Mutual contract. Professional Chaplin imitators were appearing onstage in every city. Competition among them was so keen that an ad for one touted, with no conscious irony, that "of all the imitations of Chas. Chaplin, Dedic Velde in 'Chas. Chaplin's Double' stands out alone in his clever and original imitation." The imitators were paying no compensation to the original, and Chaplin was paying no attention to them. Syd Chaplin's brainchild for capturing revenue from marketers and merchandisers— the "Charlie Chaplin Advertising Service Company"—was undercapitalized and lacked the resources needed to compete in what amounted to a worldwide game of whack-a-mole. And now the *Burlesque on Carmen* court ruling gave a green light to opportunists who were eager to cash in on Chaplinitis in the one medium where there had been, up until then, only one Charlie Chaplin: the moving pictures.

The fake Chaplin films first began popping up under the radar, in smaller cities, at second- and third-tier theaters that were thrilled to put the magical name "Chaplin" on their marquees for rentals of as little as $1.50 per day. The first wave included *Charlie the Heart Thief, Charlie in the Trenches,* and *Musketeers of the Slums.* These were apparently crude pastiches of Keystone and Essanay clips, culled from worn-out positive prints that were used to make new negatives, a venerable method of film piracy known as "duping."

The distributors of the spurious pictures avoided publicity that might attract Chaplin's attention. They used direct mail or, occasionally, a classified ad in a trade journal to promote their wares. Local exhibitors were not so circumspect. Their ads and press releases were as conspicuous as they were breezily and willfully misleading. "We have secured Charlie Chaplin's latest gloom killer, entitled *Charlie the Heart Thief,*" one theater announced in August 1916. "This is Charlie's latest production and the funniest the $500,000 comedian has ever appeared in."

After word of the fake Chaplin comedies reached Syd Chaplin's ears, he approached Burkan about taking legal action to suppress them on a contingency-fee basis. Suspecting that any money judgment against the perpetrators would be uncollectible, Burkan prudently declined. Emboldened by Chaplin's inaction, knockoff artists introduced a second generation of fakes which combined old Chaplin clips with new footage that featured Chaplin impersonators. *The Fall of the Rummy-Nuffs,* a comical take on the Russian revolution, had a Tramp-like character called "Chaplinsky." Thumbing their noses at Chaplin, the distributors of *Rummy-Nuffs* booked it into New York City's Crystal Hall theater on Union Square, a well-established Mecca for Chaplin fans with its all-Chaplin-all-the-time booking policy.

In the summer of 1917, the New Apollo Feature Company released *Charlie Chaplin, A Son of the Gods* and *Charlie in the Harem.* Using double exposure to embed authentic Chaplin images into locations and action completely alien to Chaplin's original plot and mise-en-scène, these productions marked a technical leap forward in fakery. New Apollo made the mistake of offering these films to Sid Grauman's Empress Theater in San Francisco, a venue Charlie had played in his vaudeville days. It was apparently Grauman, one of Chaplin's earliest

A lobby poster for a spurious Chaplin film that Burkan described as "vulgar, suggestive, and obscene," 1917. (Exhibit, *Chaplin v. New Apollo Feature Film Company*)

admirers, who prodded Syd Chaplin into opening Charlie's checkbook to put Burkan's office on the trail of the fraudsters.

A Son of the Gods features the Tramp in consort with a bevy of mermaids in Neptune's underwater court. *Charlie in the Harem* is set in Turkey, where the Tramp meets "a couple of harem chickens out for a lark." Disguised in drag as the lovely "Pearl of Persia," he finagles his way into the Sultan's palace, where he enchants both the Sultan and his brood with Charlie Chaplin imitations, only narrowly escaping death when his ruse is discovered. "No more likely situation could be offered this irrepressible comedian than the interior of a Turkish ménage," one theater teased, "and Charlie does the situation full justice."

Posing as an exhibitor's representative, Burkan was able to arrange a screening of the New Apollo films at the Rialto Theater in New York. "The effect created" by the composite scenes, he reported to Syd, "does not do any credit to Charlie." Burkan found the films, on the whole, "vulgar, suggestive, and obscene."

Burkan tracked down the producers of more than a dozen fake Chaplin pictures. "It is a pity that we did not throttle this business at its very inception," he told Syd. "They began to regard this as a perfectly legitimate business." He filed a flurry of lawsuits against the counterfeiters. Again, Chaplin had no claim of ownership to the copyrights in his old clips, so an alternative legal theory was needed. This time Burkan asserted trademark infringement. The trademarks "Charlie Chaplin," "Chaplin Comedy," "Chaplin Production," and other variants, the complaints alleged, had been adopted by Charles Spencer Chaplin to "designate the origin of his productions, and he has employed these names in various forms of advertising to distinguish his productions." They were "universally known and recognized" as such and were therefore "a valuable property right."

The defendants folded rather quickly, each readily giving up the names of others in the distribution chain and, unfortunately for posterity, turning over the offending films for destruction by United States Marshals. By October 1917, Burkan felt that "the principal offenders have been brought to book" and that the publicity from the cases would deter others, but he urged the Chaplins to keep up the effort. He wrote to Syd:

> It will mean a great deal more work to suppress this widespread evil. . . . I have seen quite a number of these fake Chaplins and the spectacles are offensive, debased and degrading. The people who witness these exhibitions leave the theater disgusted. Charlie owes it to himself and his admirers to prevent the further dishonest use of his name, fame, and reputation.

Also of concern to Burkan at this point was the arrival of Billy West on the screen. West had been doing an act called "Is he Charlie Chaplin?" in vaudeville and was considered the best of the imitators. Kay-Bee Pictures was now releasing Billy West two-reelers every other week, filling a vacuum left by the decreasing frequency of genuine Chaplin productions. "We will not miss Chaplin much while Billy West continues to make pictures like this," one exhibitor told a trade journal in October 1917. Burkan was stunned when one of the counterfeiters invited him to his studio and "ran off for my benefit an 'original Chaplin' which did not contain a single original Chaplin scene"—it consisted entirely of duped Billy West clips.

The Chaplins, cash-strapped at the time, were not disposed to invest in waging perpetual war against counterfeiters. Indeed, they balked at paying Burkan's bill for services already rendered. The bill itself is not to be found in Chaplin's otherwise rather exhaustive archives, but it can be safely surmised that it was less than $15,000 for an extensive and effective litigation blitz. Using their Los Angeles–based attorney Arthur Wright as an intermediary, however, the Chaplins complained that they were being gouged. Burkan told Wright that he was fully prepared to drop their mutual client if he was not paid in full: "If my many years of experience, my labor and energy directed to his cause do not entitle me to receive the sum stated in my bill, then I am unwilling to continue to act for Chaplin because I cannot operate my business at a loss." He was unusually candid in his appraisal of the Chaplin brothers. "These men have had no actual business experience, and have never been in any important litigation," he wrote. "Although now engaged in an enterprise yielding hundreds of thousands of dollars annually, they have not the slightest conception of the value of the labor, energy and experience of others." The Chaplins capitulated on the bill, but they remained unwilling to fund the aggressive, ongoing enforcement effort that Burkan was recommending.

Burkan now understood that the extreme thrift for which Chaplin was already becoming legendary would require that he choose his legal battles strategically. He would have to erect a credible "Beware of the Dog" sign without an actual dog to back it up. He and the Chaplins cooked up a new plan to thwart counterfeiters: "The plan is simple," *Motion Picture News* reported. "Chaplin is to be the first motion picture star to follow the universal practice of the brush artist by signing his works as proof of their authenticity." It was not terribly effective, but it was cheap and it appealed to Charlie's artistic vanity. Burkan was gradually learning how to manage a difficult client relationship.

Chaplin applies his authenticating signature to the main title card for *Shoulder Arms*, 1918. (© Roy Export Company Ltd.)

Chaplin later recalled his days at the Lone Star studio as "the happiest period of my career. I was light and unencumbered, twenty-seven years old, with fabulous prospects and a friendly, glamorous world before me." The small facility on Lillian Way in Hollywood was a veritable salon, with literati and aristocrats making regular pilgrimage to witness the Chaplin magic being made. Mutual kept its hands off and John Freuler was indulgent as the increasingly ambitious artist fell into arrears on his one-picture-per-month obligation. Freuler's patience was rewarded with some of the very best of Chaplin's two-reelers—such as *The Pawnshop* and *The Immigrant*—and with profits that exceeded his rosiest projections.

Chaplin's reign as the highest-paid picture star, however, was fleeting. When his deal with Mutual was announced in February 1916, Mary Pickford was working for Famous Players under a verbal contract at $4,000 per week. A few months later, she was Adolph Zukor's partner in the Pickford Film Corporation, earning 50 percent of the profits generated by her productions, with a guaranteed minimum of, not coincidentally, $670,000 per year. In the game of leapfrog being played by filmdom's two biggest stars, it was now Chaplin's turn.

Long before he completed his twelfth and final picture for Mutual, Chaplin had decided he was no longer content to be the world's highest-paid wage slave. In response to an inquiry about his plans, Chaplin wrote that he intended to go into business for himself. "By working for myself," he believed, he "would be unrestricted in the time and cost expended" and could "turn out my greatest pictures and far exceed all my previous efforts." His expectations were perhaps overly optimistic, but his timing was, yet again, propitious. Another turn in the early history of Hollywood was opening a pathway for his ambitions.

Through a series of aggressive and ingenious business moves, Adolph Zukor had attained a level of market power not seen since the heyday of the Edison Trust. The now merged Famous Players–Lasky Corporation, together with a group of thinly veiled affiliates, had signed up every major box office star except Chaplin (most recently having added the dashing and athletic Douglas Fairbanks to their roster). Zukor had also seized control of a leading distribution company, Paramount Pictures, which gave him the leverage to impose a regime of "all or nothing" block booking on exhibitors. Zukor touted his monopoly as a boon to the theater owner, who could decide that "Paramount is the program for his house" and "be taken care of fifty-two weeks in the year for which he pays a flat and settled price."

The benevolence of Zukor's scheme was lost on most exhibitors. In April 1917, twenty-five of the leading first-run theater chains formed the "First National Exhibitors Circuit" with a pledge to "offer its arm of protection to every exhibitor against any manufacturer who tries to use 'steamroller methods.'" First National's plan was to compete directly with Paramount by distributing films made by independent producers on an open booking basis. It would cut out the middlemen, the distribution exchanges that had connected producers with exhibitors since the industry's earliest days, and eliminate their attendant overhead. First National promised stars "more money than they had ever received before" and that their pictures would not be used "as a club to compel the exhibitors to rent an inferior product."

First National could offer Chaplin what he was looking for: distribution and funding for his own independent productions. Mutual sought to preempt a move by offering him a distribution-only arrangement, which, John Freuler told him, "shaved the possible margin to us to the bleeding point": $100,000 per picture for eight two-reelers, along with full ownership of the Lone Star studio facility. "If you still waver and debate with yourself about the offers that others may make," Freuler wrote, "put a big question mark on the wall over your bed. Will it pay? . . . Will you take the certain maximum that we can offer or will you dally with the promises of those who hope but do not know?"

With Mutual's offer in his pocket, Syd Chaplin was soon on a train to New York to meet up with Burkan and find out whether there was hard money standing behind First National's lofty statement of purpose.

CHAPTER 11

The Price of a Good Time

"Everything splendid," Syd Chaplin wired his brother from New York on June 21, 1917. "Burkan is sending contract for you to sign. I have raised the gross another $120,000. You will smile when you read how I did it." In a follow-up letter, Syd detailed his claim to credit for the First National Exhibitors Circuit deal, bragging that he had stood up for Charlie's interests even when "Burkan agreed with them." When it came to wringing every last concession out of a negotiating counterparty, Burkan had learned, the Chaplin brothers were thick as thieves, their joy in prevailing usually far out of proportion to any small, if not entirely hypothetical, advantage they had gained. Charlie loved exerting power over others for its own sake, and both Chaplins were heavily invested in spreading the legend of Syd as business savant. Burkan found it prudent to humor the boys. He was content to let Syd hog the glory and probably even devised opportunities for him to do so.

When word of the deal they had struck with First National first leaked out, the press reported that Chaplin would be earning a million dollars, "the largest salary ever paid to a performer in the history of the amusement world." But this was not an employment contract, and the million-dollar topline figure was not a salary. Rather, Chaplin granted First National an exclusive, worldwide distribution license for his next eight two-reelers, to be delivered at a comparatively leisurely pace over eighteen months, for an initial bonus of $75,000 and then $125,500 per picture. (The odd $500, meant to cover the cost of delivering a second negative for each film, was one of the little chisels Syd was so proud of.) From this sum, Chaplin had to cover all costs of production, not just his own salary. Of far greater import than notionally surpassing the magical million-dollar threshold were several features of the contract insisted upon by Burkan: For the first time, Chaplin would retain the copyright in his productions. First National's exclusive distribution right for each film was limited to five years, after which all rights, the negatives, and all prints reverted to Chaplin's control, where they would still be enriching his progeny more than a century later. First National was prohibited from making any changes at all to the films or using any part of them in other productions.

Chaplin was now an entrepreneur, with all the freedom and all the risks that role entailed. The ultra-perfectionism and whimsical work habits he was known for would now be on his own dime. Even before he returned to Los Angeles, Syd cautioned Charlie—who was in the habit of building sets and then waiting for comic inspiration to strike—that from now on he needed to "decide and know exactly what you are going to do before the sets are ordered."

But Charlie was in no mood for austerity. His wealth still seemed like an apparition. "I had to do something to prove that I had it. So I procured a secretary, a valet, a car, and a chauffeur."

His biggest extravagance proved to be his wisest investment—a five-acre lot at Sunset Boulevard and La Brea Avenue, in a section of Hollywood then mostly covered with citrus groves, where he built the movie studio of his dreams. Eschewing the utilitarian industrial architecture of Hollywood's other film factories, Chaplin's was a nostalgic throwback to the England of his youth. The facades fronting along La Brea, including Chaplin's office and dressing room, were built in the Tudor style. Although later moved fifteen feet to accommodate the widening of La Brea Avenue, they remain to this day a pleasant respite from the resulting traffic and surrounding suburban blight. Inside the gates there were green lawns, fruit-bearing trees, a swimming pool, and a tennis court. "Ye Olde English Village," Chaplin called it. An open-air stage sat unobtrusively on the southern edge of the lot. The Chaplin Studio became a regular stop on Burkan's trips to Los Angeles, where Charlie would greet him with mixed emotions. "I love him, but am afraid of him," Chaplin wrote of Burkan. "His pockets always bulge contracts."

Chaplin's first production at the idyllic complex was *A Dog's Life,* completed on time and on budget in March 1918. A seamless blend of comedy and pathos, David Robinson calls this modest two-reeler "one

Douglas Fairbanks, Chaplin, and Burkan—his pockets bulging
with contracts—at the newly built Chaplin Studio, circa 1918.
(Courtesy, Nathan Burkan Jr.)

of his most perfect films." Immediately after wrapping, at the request of
Treasury secretary William Gibbs McAdoo, Chaplin embarked on a
nearly month-long tour promoting the sale of Liberty Bonds, starting
out with Douglas Fairbanks (who had become his close friend) and
Mary Pickford in the Northeast and then barnstorming through several
southern states on his own.

In New York City, more than twenty thousand turned out for a rally on
Wall Street, but as he left the rostrum Chaplin was greeted by a man serving a new lawsuit on behalf of Essanay seeking damages for alleged
breaches of their 1915 contract. Burkan sought to have the case dismissed,
accusing Essanay of being "ungenerous and unpatriotic" and arguing that
as a British subject acting at the request of the United States government,
Chaplin ought to be granted the same immunity from service of process
accorded to "legislators, voters, and jurors." The court denied Burkan's
plea out of a rather overwrought fear that if it ruled in Chaplin's favor,
"every debtor would be touring the country and asking for exemption
on that ground." Chaplin would soon become more adept at the art of
evading legal process.

Chaplin had endured several years of persistent criticism for doing
pratfalls in baggy pants while other Englishmen his age were going

off to war. It may have been the success of his Liberty Bond tour that freed his mind to conceive a war-themed comedy. *Shoulder Arms,* another commercial and artistic triumph, was released just days before the armistice in November 1918. Syd Chaplin, who was living in a house on the studio grounds, appeared in both *A Dog's Life* and *Shoulder Arms.* One of Chaplin's old English music hall compatriots, Alf Reeves, had moved to the United States and was managing the studio with the patience and good humor that the high-pressure job required. Chaplin was working in a Shangri-La of his own design, surrounded by loyal friends and family. The public's adoration of Chaplin was at its zenith. Critics and the intelligentsia extolled his genius. He was the toast of Hollywood society. A hubris-fueled fall from grace was all but inevitable.

Throughout the production of *Shoulder Arms,* Chaplin was carrying on an affair with sixteen-year-old Mildred Harris. She was already a Hollywood veteran, having played frontier daughters in some of Thomas Ince's earliest westerns. By the time she met Chaplin, Mildred had graduated to adult roles, with her breakthrough star turn coming as a shop girl led astray by a rich boy in a tearjerker with the almost too on-the-nose title *The Price of a Good Time.* Chaplin—in his own mind always the ingenuous victim beset by predators—wrote that they met by chance at a party and that Mildred had pursued him lecherously. It is much more probable that an introduction had been procured through Douglas Fairbanks. A year earlier, the then fifteen-year-old Mildred had traveled to the East Coast to appear in a picture "as Fairbanks' leading lady at the star's personal request." That role never materialized, and Fairbanks was soon engrossed in an extramarital affair with Mary Pickford.

Chaplin married Mildred secretly on October 23, 1918, after learning that she was pregnant. "I had been caught in the mesh of a foolish circumstance which had been wanton and unnecessary," wrote Chaplin, "a union that had no vital basis." It was by all evidence a joyless and loveless marriage. The couple never celebrated their wedding publicly, not even after word of it seeped out and movie theaters throughout the country began booking combined Chaplin-Harris programs and decorating their facades with facsimile wedding invitations. Separately, they were two of Hollywood's most photographed and gossiped-about stars, but public sightings of them as a married couple were virtually nonexistent.

Domestic travail took a toll on Chaplin's creative output. Work on his next two-reeler, the uninspired *Sunnyside,* began after the wedding and dragged on for nearly six months. Whether his creative drought was due to emotional turmoil or merely reluctance to create assets that could be considered community property under California matrimonial law, Chaplin still owed First National six pictures as the eighteen-month term of his contract was drawing to a close in early 1919. "At the rate Charlie is traveling," Syd Chaplin confided to Burkan, "it seems to me that one a year will be his limit." Revenues were not keeping up with the expense of maintaining a studio and a stock company that were idle much of the time. Chaplin was in a deep hole. In a case of his life imitating his art, his Tramp-like first instinct was to dig deeper.

Rumors of an impending merger of Adolph Zukor's Paramount empire and First National were afloat, its ostensible purpose being to put an end to their ruinous bidding wars for top talent. "Some sort of combination between the bigger producers and distributors," Zukor said, "would serve to stabilize conditions and discourage the Bolshevik element in the industry." But as film historian Tino Balio explains, "the addition of hundreds of theaters to Zukor's empire and the dissolution of the most attractive outlet for independent production would spell the end of the star system as it then existed." Chaplin joined with the other members of Hollywood's "Big Four"—Pickford, Fairbanks, and D. W. Griffith—to announce that they were forming their own distribution company and that upon the expiration of their existing contracts they would release their productions exclusively through the new organization: "We think that this step is positively and absolutely necessary," their statement said, "to protect the great motion picture public from threatening combinations and trusts that would force upon them mediocre productions and machine-made entertainment."

As Chaplin understood it, he was participating in an elaborate bluff meant to derail the rumored merger. The feint worked (First National instead went into film production in competition with Zukor and eventually merged with Warner Brothers), but the idea had taken root. On February 5, 1919, papers organizing the United Artists Corporation were drawn up and signed. Chaplin subscribed for shares at $100,000 par value and named Burkan his representative on the board of directors. He was obligated to contribute three two-reel pictures per year for three years to the new venture, beginning no later than September 1920.

Chaplin may have been laboring under the misimpression that he would be free to walk away from his First National contract at the expiration of its eighteen-month term. The same day that the United Artists papers were executed, Syd asked Burkan to confirm this. Burkan firmly disabused him of the notion. First National had waived the eighteen-month deadline but was insistent on getting its eight pictures. It would acquiesce in Chaplin's preference to sacrifice "quantity and speed to quality," but it made clear that any "attendant monetary loss" would be Chaplin's to bear. Charlie would be incurring a significant liability if he failed to deliver, Burkan warned.

Now under contract to two distributors, one of which could call for a $100,000 equity contribution at any time, Charlie was suddenly motivated to complete *Sunnyside* and the balance of his obligation to First National in short order. A trade journal reported in February 1919 that the Chaplin studio had "become the scene of bustling activity." But motivation did not equal inspiration, and to the great chagrin of his new business partners, it would be another four years before Chaplin was at liberty to deliver his first picture to United Artists.

According to Chaplin's autobiography, the pregnancy that led him to marry Mildred Harris was a false alarm. Nonetheless, thirty-eight weeks later, on July 7, 1919, Mildred was delivered of a son, Norman Spencer Chaplin, evidently at full term. The baby lived only three days, a profound tragedy that deeply affected both parents and doubtless hastened the dissolution of an already tenuous marital bond. Mr. Chaplin "was with the baby every minute until he died," one of the household servants later told a reporter. "Since then he hasn't seemed to care and is rarely home."

Sid Grauman took his bereaved friend to Los Angeles's Orpheum Theater to see a new phenom he had discovered: a four-year-old vaudeville hoofer named Jackie Coogan Jr., who was appearing in his father's act and stealing the show nightly. "That kid's immense!" Chaplin was overheard telling Grauman. In Coogan, Chaplin found a way to channel his grief and, just maybe, the means to wriggle out of the contractual entanglements that were engulfing him. Just two weeks after the death of his own infant son, Chaplin announced that he had hired Jackie, whom he called "a born comedian," to be his first true costar. With patience and empathy, Chaplin elicited from the boy one of the most memorable performances ever given by a child actor. Samuel Goldwyn wrote that "possibly Chaplin never shone more brightly in any human relationship than he has in his association with Jackie Coogan."

The Kid, Chaplin hoped and believed, would be his salvation. Production was unusually orderly and linear by Chaplin standards. He knew from the outset that his idea could not be realized in two reels, nor executed on a budget of $125,500, as envisioned under the First National contract. *The Kid* had the makings of a full-length feature with exceptional audience appeal. The story of a dispossessed mother, the child she is separated from, and the resourceful derelict who adopts the waif would be especially resonant in a world still reeling from the Great War. Chaplin would not shortchange his artistic vision for the film, nor would he part with it for anything less than its full commercial value, existing contracts be damned.

Chaplin and Burkan settled on a strategy: they would argue that *The Kid,* as a full-length feature, was outside the scope of the First National contract and could be sold to the highest bidder, possibly United Artists. After several failed attempts to use this threat as leverage to renegotiate the terms of his First National deal, Chaplin interrupted production to dash off another two-reeler, *A Day's Pleasure.* That held First National at bay for a time while he turned his attention to the even more vexing problem of Mildred's claim to 50 percent of his still-unfinished masterpiece as community property.

Chaplin moved back to his bachelor lodgings at the Los Angeles Athletic Club early in 1920, leaving Mildred to fend for herself financially. He evidently believed she would be amenable to a quick trip to Nevada for a speedy and relatively cheap ($25,000) settlement. But Mildred had already resumed her acting career under a contract with Louis B. Mayer that gave her the financial means to wait Chaplin out. When newspapers got wind of the separation in March 1920, Mildred told them: "I shall wait a year to prove to him the kind of woman I am. . . . I don't need Charlie's money nor do I want it. I shall only wait hoping he will come back to me." Her words may have struck the public as a poignant expression of undying love. They were in fact a well-aimed blow to Chaplin's solar plexus.

His frustration boiled over a few weeks later when he encountered Louis B. Mayer at the Alexandria Hotel in Los Angeles and dared the much larger man to remove his glasses. In the fisticuffs that followed, Charlie got much the worst of it. "The whole trouble arose because he has been trying to intimidate Mildred into settling with him for a small amount," Mayer explained. "He threatened her. I did what any man would do to protect a decent woman's reputation." News accounts of the fight noted that Mildred was, at the very hour of the altercation, attending a ball honoring the Prince of Wales.

> When told that her husband had been in a fight with Mayer at the time she was dancing with the future king of England, Mrs. Chaplin showed immediate concern.

"Was he hurt?" she inquired.

When informed that the comedian had stopped a hard right-hand punch with his eye, she bit her lip.

"Oh," was her only spoken comment.

Mildred's sangfroid made her a formidable adversary. Chaplin was taking a drubbing, literally and figuratively. Wisely, if belatedly, he decided to bide his time.

Chaplin completed principal production of *The Kid* on Friday, July 30, 1920. On Monday, August 2, Mildred's lawyers filed suit for divorce in the Los Angeles County Superior Court. Her allegations were hardly the stuff of scandal, but the numerous specific incidents of "surly and selfish" behavior that she detailed certainly constituted, in the aggregate, "mental cruelty" under any reasonable standard. Of more immediate concern to Chaplin, Mildred was seeking an emergency injunction that would prevent him from disposing of the distribution rights for *The Kid*.

Chaplin could not be found for comment. Reporters seeking information about his whereabouts from Burkan's office came up empty-handed; Burkan had left for Europe in early July and was not due back until the end of August. It was later learned that the divorce filing had triggered a contingency plan involving only Chaplin's most trusted employees. Studio manager Alf Reeves awoke cameraman Rollie Totheroh at 3 A.M. and together they packed the raw footage for *The Kid* in coffee tins and wooden crates. The two then met valet Tom Harrington and Chaplin (who was wearing a disguise) at the train station. According to Chaplin, they had 400,000 feet of film and more than two thousand takes still to be edited.

When an intrepid *Los Angeles Times* reporter tracked him down at a Salt Lake City hotel, Chaplin answered the door to his room in "green silk pajamas." His face "brightened up with a spreading smile when he knew that he was cornered." He left Los Angeles, he explained "so I can concentrate on my work without being pestered to death by tenacious lawyers and newspaper men." Chaplin and his entourage were working feverishly to complete *The Kid*. "In one of the bedrooms we laid out the film," he later wrote, "using every piece of furniture, ledges, commodes and drawers."

With his cover now blown, Chaplin gave a more expansive interview to a local paper. He had invested two years and $300,000 in *The Kid*, he said, and "I do not propose to lose the fruits of my efforts. . . . It is a drama of pathos and humor unlike anything I have ever done and it means everything to me." He vowed to "remain here until it is sold and there won't be any divorce until it is sold."

First National responded with a full-page open letter in the trade press. It put the industry on notice that First National "claims and contends that the distribution rights for the world for *The Kid* belong to it" and that it was prepared to "prosecute and defend its rights in the courts of the land to the utmost of its ability." The parade of bidders that Chaplin expected to descend upon Salt Lake City did not materialize.

After about three weeks, Chaplin's entourage repacked the still-unfinished film and headed to New York. Chaplin went immediately to see Burkan to figure out his next legal move, while the others headed to a laboratory in Bayonne, New Jersey, to finish work on the movie. They found that the coffee tins containing the highly inflammable nitrocellulose film, after a cross-country journey in the heat of summer, were on the verge of exploding.

Burkan arranged to host a settlement conference at his office in mid-September. But a story appearing on the front page of the *New York Tribune* the morning of the scheduled meeting threw a monkey wrench into his plan. Mildred had just engaged a former Manhattan prosecutor, Henry Goldsmith, to represent her. They had heard rumors that First National was offering a $500,000 advance for *The Kid,* but that Chaplin was holding out for a million dollars. Goldsmith served notice on First National of Mildred's claim to half of Chaplin's share of any deal, and then he went to the *Tribune* to publicly rattle his sabre.

Unless a settlement was reached at the conference, Goldsmith told the paper, Mildred would immediately apply for a receivership to tie up all of Charlie's property "on the ground that he is a British subject and has threatened to leave America never to return." He went on: "He has stated he was dissatisfied with the laws of this country, because, I suppose, they would not permit him to do exactly as he wished in certain matters. . . . His theories and studies of Bolshevism will be properly exposed when the law begins to take its course."

A charge of Bolshevist sympathies, made against an alien during the Red Scare of 1920, was not to be taken lightly. (The young head of the Justice Department's Intelligence Division, J. Edgar Hoover, who had recently begun to track Hollywood's "parlor Bolsheviki," surely took note.) Burkan relayed Chaplin's riposte through the press: "The Bolsheviki believe in dividing all their property. I don't intend to divide my property with anybody. . . . I am a high-handed capitalist rather than a Bolshevik."

Burkan dismissed the threat of receivership as "bunk" and called Goldsmith's bluff by canceling the meeting. (As a precaution, just in case Goldsmith tried to serve papers, Burkan shipped Chaplin off to a secluded location in the Adirondacks.) "We were planning to let the couple thrash out their little quarrel by themselves," he said, "but my client couldn't think of seeing her after the statements made through her attorney and appearing in this morning's *Tribune*."

Her gambit having failed miserably, Mildred fired Goldsmith and gave a conciliatory newspaper interview: "I hope there will be no further unpleasantries in settling up our unhappy romance." Burkan quickly negotiated a settlement with Mildred's California attorneys, reportedly for about $100,000 cash and property valued at another $100,000. Mildred returned to Los Angeles in early November 1920 to obtain an uncontested divorce decree.

The coast now clear, Chaplin returned to the city and started painting the town red. "Since he arrived in New York, Charlie Chaplin has been ducking process servers like he used to duck custard pies," wrote one gossip columnist. "Charlie has since made up sufficiently with his better half to make the rounds of the Broadway cabarets without being handed a summons." After months of self-imposed exile, scurrying to stay one step ahead of the law, Chaplin was now "being seen almost nightly dining at some Broadway hotel. He is also much about with his attorney, Nathan Burkan, who has introduced the film comedian to almost every official in the Tammany political organization." As Burkan and Chaplin palled around New York City during the fall of 1920, the business relationship they had forged over several years, with Syd Chaplin usually acting as go-between, blossomed into a direct and close personal friendship.

Chaplin states in his autobiography that First National came to him "metaphorically with their hats in their hands" and abjectly capitulated to his demands. There appears to be not a grain of truth in this account. Negotiations were lengthy and arduous, complicated by Chaplin's desire to be released from his remaining obligations to First National, a concession the company refused as a matter of principle and pragmatism.

Chaplin was not negotiating from a position of strength. First National had succeeded in scaring off other potential bidders with the warning that they would be "buying lawsuits." Exhibitors, for whom the arrival of each new Chaplin film had once been like manna from heaven, had already gone a year without a fresh release and were learning to get along without him. An editorial in the *Exhibitors Herald* reflected their mindset: "His action in refusing to deliver pictures he has sold under contract cannot but earn for him the stigma of contract-jumper in the eyes of the trade." It went on: "The case of Mr. Chaplin now reaches an interesting stage, as a once prominent figure in motion pictures seems to be passing over the hill to oblivion—not because he ceased to meet the industry's requirements, but, presumably, because the industry has failed to meet his requirements."

To improve his bargaining position, Chaplin let it be known that he had leased out his studio and hinted that he was prepared to take an extended break, if not retire completely, from filmmaking. After several months of stalemate, Burkan struck a deal with First National on December 3, 1920, that relieved Chaplin of his immediate financial pressures, although it did not win him his freedom. Chaplin received a guarantee of $800,000 against 70 percent of gross rentals of *The Kid* worldwide over six years, at which time all rights would revert to him. Despite its feature length, however, the film would count as only one of the four two-reelers that Chaplin still owed First National under his 1917 contract, and half of the guarantee was to be deferred and paid out in installments as each of the final three films was delivered. Chaplin returned to Los Angeles, after a four-month absence, to reclaim his studio, reassemble his company, and deliver the final cut of *The Kid* to First National on New Year's Eve.

The Kid had its first public showing at the holy of holies of high culture, Carnegie Hall. It was a triumph with audiences and critics, transcending the familiar genres of early cinema. "The picture, besides being his most interesting and versatile to date," the *New York Herald* said, "is also his most human." Comparisons to Dickens were rampant. Gilbert Seldes, no fan of literary pretension in the lively arts, praised *The Kid* for its "moments of unbelievable tension and touches of high imagination," importing to the screen the best aspects of Dickens' prose.

Chaplin had more than come back from the brink; he had surpassed his prior self in popularity, prestige, and power. His future, making feature films at his own production facility for a distributor that he co-owned, was now clearly in focus, but he felt no sense of urgency about getting there. He was ready to relax and smell the roses for a bit. He could even, as David Robinson puts it, "face the strain of having his mother near him." Hannah Chaplin was a schizophrenic and as such was not welcome in the United States under the 1917 Immigration Act. Burkan pulled some strings with a friend at the Department of Justice in Washington to expedite her passage. "The old lady will soon be on her way over," Burkan was assured.

Chaplin decided to return to England for the premiere there of *The Kid,* and to spend a few months soaking up accolades on the Continent. Before sailing from New York in September 1921, he had a quiet dinner at Burkan's apartment with columnist Louella Parsons. He was unusually expansive about his ambitions. "I am eager to bring poetry to the screen such as we have never had. My experiment with *The Kid* taught me there is a limitless field for the expression of poetry through the motion pictures." After dinner he took Burkan to see a Theater Guild production of *Liliom,* the Hungarian play that Rodgers and Hammerstein later adapted as *Carousel.* "I want to see heaven," Chaplin told Parsons. "It has always been one of my favorite subjects."

PART FOUR

Fleeting, Ephemeral, and Fugitive

CHAPTER 12

The Gospel of Performing Rights

In a career filled with ambitious causes and notable achievements, the establishment of the American Society of Composers, Authors, and Publishers (Ascap) was Nathan Burkan's magnum opus, a feat that required the full breadth of his legal knowledge, his political acumen, and his force of will. Just as it is difficult to conceive of the Golden Age of Hollywood as we came to know it without Charlie Chaplin, the success of Ascap was an essential precondition to the creation of what we now celebrate as the Great American Songbook. Remarkably, Burkan was shaping and nurturing both of these cultural dynamos in parallel, during the same short span of years.

Ascap was born in February 1914, just a week or so after Chaplin's first Keystone release hit the theaters. Its story begins in 1897, when Congress granted holders of copyrights in musical compositions the exclusive right to publicly perform them. It was the ultimate joker in the copyright law deck. It had the potential to swamp the revenue obtainable from print and mechanical reproductions of music, but the logistical difficulties inherent in monitoring and collecting royalties, for performances that Burkan aptly described as "ephemeral, fleeting, and fugitive," were daunting. Public musical performances were taking place at virtually every hour of the day in thousands of venues scattered throughout the country. A single musical program might include the works of a dozen or more copyright owners. Any money flow, by well-established, if generally frowned-upon, custom, traveled in the other direction: music publishers paid for plugs; they did not collect a fee for them. Fifteen years after its enactment, the public performance right was languishing in a state of desuetude, a forsaken older stepsibling to the hard-won and vigorously enforced mechanical reproduction right.

A handful of publishers of standard music had made one modest attempt to enforce the public performance right. In response to the practice of school and church choral societies renting their music from libraries rather than buying it outright, the publishers announced that they would grant the right to publicly perform the works only to those who purchased printed copies. Representatives of the choral societies complained to Congress in 1906, prompting Chairman Frank Currier of the House Committee on Patents to muse out loud that perhaps the simplest solution would be to "repeal the statute that was passed nine years ago and put the whole thing back where it was for one hundred years." The 1909 Copyright Act stopped short of repeal, but it did restrict the exclusive right to public performances given "for profit." This proviso, adopted without significant objection from music publishers, was yet another practical barrier to enforcement of performing rights. Its importance would only later become apparent.

In the immediate wake of the 1909 act, one agency stepped forward to take on the challenges of enforcing the public performance right. The French Société des Auteurs, Compositeurs et Éditeurs de Musique (Sacem), founded in 1851, had pioneered the concept of collective rights enforcement—pooling numerous copyrighted works, licensing the entire repertoire for public performance on a blanket basis, and distributing proportional shares of the fees collected to its members. As early as 1904, Sacem had urged American composers to form their own performing rights society, which could enter into a relationship of reciprocity with the French. When that didn't happen, Sacem incorporated its own American branch in November 1910, "for the purpose of protecting copyrights of authors and composers, and to enforce the collection of royalties and remuneration in every necessary way." To manage the American operation, Sacem engaged Ovide Robillard, a French expatriate who had been authorized to practice law in New York under a special act of the state legislature.

Robillard's initial collection efforts were greeted with a mix of puzzlement and annoyance by New York's music community. In France, Sacem's fees were collected by the government; in New York Robillard had to fend for himself. He demanded a five-dollar fee whenever a singer included a number by a Sacem member—say, Claude Debussy or Camille Saint-

Saëns—in a recital program. "Managers of concerts in New York are encountering a curious obstacle to making programs just now," the *Times* reported. The result of "this demand for a sum all out of proportion to value of one song," it predicted, would be "few performances of modern French songs." Pundits could not understand why composers would adopt such a shortsighted course, sacrificing advertising of incalculable value in exchange for a mere pittance. "The attitude of the Society of French Authors is a rather peculiar one," the *Music Trade Review* commented, "as it tends to retard rather than advance the sale and knowledge of their publications." The press, with barely disguised schadenfreude, dutifully reported incidents of performers removing Sacem pieces from concert programs rather than paying the fee, and the resignations of Sacem members who were unhappy with Robillard's methods.

Robillard was unbowed. He went right on preaching the gospel of performing rights with all the zeal that might be expected of a man working on a 50 percent commission. "It is the performing rights that last," he argued. "After a piece of music is published the sale continues for a short time. If the work is liked, it will constantly be performed for many years," so the royalty for performance for profit is "a species of life insurance." The law was clear, he insisted, and the basic justice of Sacem's position was widely recognized. Despite the grumbling, the fees were being paid. He encouraged American popular composers to join Sacem: "If the composers of the ragtime music which is produced so much in Paris were members of this society, they would find out that their rights for performance in Europe would amount to a considerable share of their profits."

As 1911 was coming to an end, Robillard was still being dismissed as something of a crank. "Can you imagine," one New York publisher snickered, "one of the vaudeville or concert hall singers using our songs, and doing two or three turns per day, paying $5 a performance or even $5 per week for the privilege? Huh!"

At that very moment, a new form of entertainment was taking hold in New York. It would prompt some influential players in musical circles to rethink the matter of performing rights. *Variety* called the new craze "midnight vaude." Its promoters preferred the tonier-sounding "cabaret."

Jesse L. Lasky, still two years away from founding his movie studio, introduced the cabaret concept to New York in the spring of 1911 at a theater-restaurant on West 46th Street, the Folies Bergère. The midnight cabaret show, a string of song-and-dance acts, attracted "a hungry and thirsty lot, comprising the classiest crowd of theatergoers night by night that any New York house caters to." But Lasky was a showman, not a food man, and the Folies Bergère, with too few tables to cover its fixed costs, was a short-lived venture. Experienced restaurateurs rushed into the breach. By the middle of 1912, large cabaret-restaurants dotted the Broadway theater district—Café Martin, Churchill's, Rector's, Faust's, Shanley's—and dozens of other restaurants around the city, from basement rathskellers to rooftop gardens, provided cabaret-style entertainment. They offered, in one reporter's words, a "rendezvous for those to whom the witching hour is but the shank of the evening, who, in the dead vast and middle of the night, feel stealing o'er them an unconquerable impulse to eat, drink, dance and see a bit of vaudeville."

Midnight vaude, conceived by Lasky as an after-theater diversion, soon became an all-evening offering that competed directly with nearby legitimate theaters. At Shanley's "Cabaret Extraordinaire," shows began as early as 7 P.M. and ran until the city-enforced closing time of 1 A.M. "Thomas Shanley has the best cabaret show in town and he knows how to run it," *Variety* raved. "The show runs through without any waits over 30 seconds. . . . The cabaret must be hurting theater business. People who would go to theaters in the evening seem to prefer cabaret."

Demand for new acts and new material was intense. Being "caterers rather than impresarios," one writer later observed, "the proprietors developed the practice of taking whatever numbers they liked from current Broadway hits." For composers writing for the legitimate theater, cabaret was a palpable threat. Their curiosity was piqued when Ovide Robillard announced that he had obtained an opinion of eminent legal counsel that cabaret performances were "for profit" under the new copyright law—even though they charged no admission at the door—and that Sacem intended to start collecting royalties for them. Louis A. Hirsch, a French-speaking, twenty-six-year-old wunderkind—a jazz-influenced musical link between Victor Herbert's generation and George Gershwin's—became the first Broadway composer to join Sacem.

A Frenchman collecting fees for Debussy and Saint-Saëns had laid the groundwork for an American performing rights society, and with it a revolution in American popular music.

Back in 1905, George Maxwell, then the manager of the New York branch of British publisher Boosey & Company, had been one of Burkan's complaining witnesses against sheet music counterfeiter Garrett J. Couchois. Maxwell, a Scotsman, went on to become the American agent of the Italian publisher G. Ricordi & Company, and he retained Burkan to represent that company in many legal matters. The Ricordi catalog included much of the best of the Italian operatic repertoire, including the widely performed works of the still very much alive and copyright-vigilant Giacomo Puccini. His arias, popularized by the recordings of Enrico Caruso and others, were mainstays of New York recitals and cabarets. Burkan's clientele in the popular music business was vast, but it was Puccini's U.S. representative who first consulted with him about forming an American performing rights society.

Raymond Hubbell was next. Hubbell had a long and successful career composing for such leading Broadway producers as Florence Ziegfeld, Charles Dillingham, and the Shubert Brothers. His "Poor Butterfly," an homage to Puccini, was a big hit in 1915 and has endured as a jazz standard. He was Burkan's client and friend. When Victor Herbert nominated Burkan for membership in the Lambs Club in 1910, Hubbell provided the second. Upon his retirement in 1937, Hubbell wrote a first-person history of the American Society of Composers, Authors, and Publishers. Although unpublished, burdened with five different title pages, and for long stretches so jargon-laden as to be nearly unreadable, his manuscript is an indispensable and generally reliable resource.

Hubbell writes that, after hearing about what Maxwell and Burkan were up to, he pressed them to share their thinking with a wider circle. As a first step, Burkan deputized Hubbell "to sell the idea to his star client, Victor Herbert, reasoning that it would sound better to Victor coming from a brother composer." Herbert initially rebuffed Hubbell, a reaction Hubbell attributed to an atavistic Irish distrust of Maxwell. Yet once he was in, Herbert was all in. He served loyally as an officer alongside Maxwell and was Ascap's public face and happy warrior for the remainder of his life. So close was Herbert's association with Ascap that most accounts of its origins understandably, if mistakenly, portray Herbert as its founding father.

Hubbell organized a dinner meeting to be held at Lüchow's in October 1913. There were thirty-five RSVPs, but on the rainy night in question only nine (a group recognized ever since as Ascap's founders) showed up. The meager attendance reflected the general lack of enthusiasm for the project in the music community at large. The six writers who were present, including Sacem member Louis A. Hirsch, came entirely from the theatrical, or "production music," side of the business. Besides Maxwell, Jay Witmark was the only publisher to show. Burkan was disheartened by the turnout, but a banquet for thirty-five was already paid for, and at Victor Herbert's urging Burkan walked the group through a translation of Sacem's bylaws and discussed the practicability of adapting its system and structure to the United States.

Thusly fortified, the founders went forth from Lüchow's to proselytize among their peers. "The big laugh in Tin Pan Alley caused by the news that a society was being formed to charge people for playing music slowly changed to a belief that the thing actually might happen," Hubbell recalled. "Along in December and January we had pretty much nearly all the headliners in the music world all het up over the idea." The charter membership roll of ninety-one authors (i.e., lyricists) and composers included such crucial recruits as George M. Cohan, John Philip Sousa, Jerome Kern, and Tin Pan Alley's most recent breakout star, Irving Berlin. The nascent society could credibly claim to represent a musical repertoire commercially essential to nearly any public place of amusement operating in the mid-1910s.

It was Burkan's task to rally music publishers to the cause. Hubbell and the other production writers who made up the core of Ascap's founding nine wanted it to be a writers-only organization. Under their standard contracts, they typically granted publishers only the right to print copies of the full score and individual show tunes. They expressly reserved to themselves all performing rights. The production writers saw no reason to share the new income stream they were anticipating with their publishers.

The typical Tin Pan Alley popular-song contract, however, was different. Songwriters assigned their copyright, including all subsidiary rights, to the publisher outright. Although Burkan had taken the position, late in the debate over the mechanical reproduction right, that publishers hold these copyrights as mere trustees for the authors, the Tin Pan Alley crowd did not see themselves as fiduciaries. They believed that they controlled performing rights absolutely and were deeply skeptical of the prospects for monetizing them. Burkan worried that without the participation of these publishers, the society would be deemed to have no legal basis to license performing rights in the large and important realm of nontheatrical popular music.

Burkan proposed a compromise in which all royalty income, as well as representation on the board of directors of Ascap, would be apportioned one-third to authors, one-third to composers, and one-third to publishers. That split was not particularly attractive to the production songwriters or to the Tin Pan Alley publishers, but, drawing on his deep reservoir of goodwill in the music world, Burkan was able to cajole a critical mass of stakeholders of all stripes to join in the grand experiment.

There was still another preliminary hurdle. Many of the Tin Pan Alley publishers were still routinely paying singers and band leaders for public performances. Lately, some of them had come to believe that cabaret provided especially valuable plugs. "A cabaret show gets three or sometimes four audiences during the night," one publisher told *Variety*. "A number is sung four or five times." It was reported that Tom Shanley did his booking "with the assistance of a music publisher." Payments for these plugs would be an embarrassment, to say the least, when Ascap attempted to turn the tables and collect fees for those very same performances.

Despite their widespread participation in the practice, the Tin Pan Alley publishers generally agreed that paying for plugs was an "evil." ("Evil" here referring to the deleterious effect bidding against each other for plugs had on their bottom lines, as opposed to representing an ethical judgment.) Repeated efforts to stamp out the practice, over many years, had come to naught. But before Ascap tried to solicit its first license, Burkan succeeded in getting the main malefactors to enter into a compact that imposed a moratorium on the evil. The bylaws of the newly formed Music Publishers Board of Trade, with Nathan Burkan as general counsel and offices at the same address as Ascap, provided a $5,000 penalty for any member caught paying for plugs.

The articles of association that Burkan drafted for Ascap stated objectives that were mostly high-minded and beneficent: "to promote reforms in the law respecting literary property," "to promote and foster by all lawful means the interest of composers, authors and publishers of musical works," "to promote friendly intercourse and united action among composers, authors, publishers and producers." Barely noticeable amid these soaring generalities was its true raison d'être: "to grant licenses and collect royalties for the public representation of the works of its members . . . and to allot and distribute such royalties."

The articles addressed in painstaking detail matters of internal governance and the methodology for allocating royalties to members. These provisions would be of mostly academic interest during the seven years that would elapse before Ascap had any net income to distribute. The articles said little about the much more pressing problem of *collecting* royalties from music users, leaving Burkan and Maxwell to write on a blank slate. They were acutely aware that Ascap was challenging a stubborn status quo, and they were anxious to avoid repeating the public relations missteps that had dogged Sacem's New York branch.

Their public statements were measured and reassuring. "The society has not been formed to make a fight upon anyone or to stir up any trouble," Maxwell told the press. Ascap would not be shaking down artists for per-piece fees after they publicly announced their concert programs; Maxwell made it clear that "we shall not burden the musician." Fees would only be sought from the owners of performance venues, and only for use of the entire repertoire on a blanket monthly or yearly basis. By gentlemen's agreement, vaudeville—in recognition of its long-standing symbiotic relationship with the music business—would be left undisturbed. The initial licensing effort would be directed toward the restaurant and hotel cabaret operators who were relative newcomers to show business.

Most important, Maxwell and Burkan envisioned that music fees would be nominal relative to a licensee's other costs of doing business, a nuisance too small to fight over, in exchange for which it would receive the right to use any composition in the Ascap repertoire as often as it wished. "Anyone," Burkan naively predicted, "would pay a small fee for this permission." Ascap would make up for the low price in volume. The real money, Burkan figured, would come not from a few hundred big-city hotels and restaurants to be licensed in the first wave, but from the more than ten thousand motion picture exhibitors already operating throughout the country, with many more certain to follow. The first motion picture palaces employing full orchestras were just then opening, but not even the humblest second-floor nickelodeon would think of showing a "silent" movie without musical accompaniment, even if just an amateur pounding away on an upright piano. With motion picture houses as a revenue base, Burkan expected that Ascap's annual income would very quickly reach into the millions.

Ascap's first officers and directors were elected and the articles of association were approved in a plenary session at the Hotel Claridge in New York on February 13, 1914. "A feature of the meeting at which the organization was perfected was the mingling together on equal terms of the composer of the latest ragtime hit and the composer of the successful opera for mutual protection," read one contemporary account. "It is safe to say that no gathering of composers and publishers was ever held before that was so thoroughly representative of every department and class in the industry." Nathan Burkan, probably the only man in the United States who could have orchestrated such an assembly, was elected general counsel, a position that he or one of his protégés held continuously for the next sixty years.

In 1925, by which time Ascap was successful enough to be the target of a federal antitrust investigation (for the first but not last time), the FBI agent leading the probe reported to his superiors: "It would seem to be true that Mr. Burkan was actuated to a very large extent by a natural sympathy for authors and composers of musical compositions, men and women who for the most part had very little of this world's goods and who individually had no means of enforcing the rights and privileges conferred upon them under the copyright laws of the United States." Raymond Hubbell, who sat on Ascap's board of directors through 1937, writes that Burkan "never received or wanted the fees he was entitled to for his years of service."

Burkan could not, in February 1914, have had any more than the faintest foreboding of the years of struggle that lay ahead.

CHAPTER 13

Shanley's Cabaret Extraordinaire

Starting from scratch, with minimal working capital (only the annual membership fees of $50 from publishers and $10 from writers, totaling less than $2,500), it would take months for Ascap to ramp up even a modest licensing operation. Fees had to be set, legal documents drafted, sales and administrative staff hired and trained, a system for monitoring performances devised. The choice to seek royalties from restaurants and movie houses, where music was incidental to the main fare, made a legal challenge to Ascap's interpretation of the statutory phrase "publicly perform for profit" inevitable. Before that day came, Burkan's plan was to establish performing rights as an ordinary and relatively nominal cost of doing business through a process of polite assertion by Ascap and, he anticipated, no-worse-than-grudging acquiescence by commercial music users.

This process had not even begun when Sacem's general agent in New York, Ovide Robillard, upended Burkan's plans. In June 1914, Sacem's lawyers filed suit on behalf of the John Church Company, a Cincinnati-based standard music publisher, against the Hilliard Hotel Company, owner of the elegant Hotel Vanderbilt on 34th Street and Park Avenue. The orchestra hired to entertain during the stately dinner service there had been playing John Philip Sousa's "From Main to Oregon" march. The Church Company, which had affiliated with Sacem in order to collect Sousa royalties in France, owned the copyright.

This was not the test case Burkan wanted. The complaint named a musician, the orchestra conductor, as a co-defendant. The venue had none of the sizzle of a Times Square cabaret, nor did it compete with Broadway theaters. Ascap had not yet rolled out or priced its product, much less established that hotels like the Vanderbilt had available to them a reasonably convenient and affordable system for licensing performing rights. Burkan feared that the case could prove the adage that bad facts make bad law.

The matter went before Judge E. Henry Lacombe, the same buttoned-up federal jurist who twelve years earlier had fled the courthouse rather than listen to renditions of "It's Up to You, Babe" and "Good Morning, Carrie." The hotel's lawyers argued that because it did not charge for admission to the dining room and added no entertainment charge to the price of a meal, no public performance "for profit" had occurred. Lacombe, who had a reputation for adept handling of complex commercial disputes, made short work of the matter, reasoning that the hotel would not have incurred the expense of employing an orchestra unless it stood to gain some profit thereby, even if indirect. On August 31, 1914, Lacombe issued a preliminary injunction against the Hotel Vanderbilt.

Ascap was not a party to the case, but the legal precedent inured to its benefit. It notified the hotel and restaurant trades that, as of October 1, 1914, unlicensed performances of its repertoire would be prosecuted as copyright infringements.

Ascap's first fee schedule topped out at $15 per month for the largest venues, hardly a confiscatory rate given reports that major cabarets such as Shanley's were spending more than $1,000 each week to put on their shows. A few of the major Times Square cabarets signed on, but the main trade group, the Hotel Men's Association, denounced Ascap as "a hold-up scheme" and declared that they "would not submit to the ultimatum." "When October 1 came in with midnight," the *New York Sun* reported, "the various orchestras in public places folded up their copyrighted music and resorted to old tunes for which the copyrights had long since expired." The first of many Ascap boycotts had begun.

It is impossible to know how things might have played out had Burkan's plan to introduce performance rights licensing incrementally been given a chance to succeed. Perhaps it was inevitable that imposing a charge for something that business owners were accustomed to using for free would trigger a backlash. But Sacem's peremptory resort to the courts certainly hardened resistance to the concept, stirring up strident rhetoric and threats of reprisal grossly disproportionate to the dismal little millage that Ascap was trying to collect. "The assessment has been quickly called the 'ragtime tax' and thus far the levy has been defiantly resisted," one paper reported. It was, of course, no more a "tax" than was a restaurant's cost of procuring roast beef, but the word "tax," as Raymond Hubbell observed, "bites the innards" of the average American. The epithet became a powerful rhetorical weapon that was wielded for many years by Ascap's adversaries.

In the long run, as *Billboard* magazine predicted, it was improbable that "instead of giving the public, who cough up 75 cents for cocktails so willingly, what they undoubtedly desire in the way of popular music, cabarets will keep their orchestras grinding away on 'William Tell,' 'Swanee River,' and 'Old Black Joe.'" Indeed, Ascap's members very quickly discovered that the venues supposedly boycotting their music had never actually stopped using it. This forced Burkan's hand. He hastily filed his first of what would be many hundreds of copyright infringement lawsuits on behalf of Ascap members, choosing the highest-profile offender, Shanley's Cabaret Extraordinaire, which was helping itself to the music of Ascap's hottest member, Irving Berlin.

On advice of counsel, and under protest, Shanley's took an Ascap license pending the outcome of the Hotel Vanderbilt's appeal. Ascap's first lawsuit against Shanley's was quietly dismissed.

When seventy-six members and supporters of Ascap gathered at Lüchow's for the society's first annual dinner in late November 1914, George Maxwell and Nathan Burkan were the guests of honor and principal speakers. Maxwell announced that eighty-five licenses had been issued, at an average monthly fee of $8.23, for a total gross of $700 per month. But he made the extravagant prediction that within a few years one hundred thousand licenses would be in force, mostly to motion picture houses, producing $10 million in annual revenue. Celebrating this modest beginning at one of the relatively few restaurants in New York City licensed to use the Ascap repertoire, the well-liquored guests enjoyed a twelve-course meal to repeated refrains of the public domain "Blue Danube" waltz. "It was decided to confine the musical entertainment to one safe and elderly tune" so that "no jealousies might arise among the composers present." Burkan's remarks emphasized the need for unity and cooperation going forward.

Toastmaster Victor Herbert (in front of mirror) is flanked to his right by President George Maxwell and to his left by General Counsel Nathan Burkan, the guests of honor at Ascap's first annual dinner, November 29, 1914. Burkan's political mentor, James Frawley, is on his left, and Raymond Hubbell is seated third to Burkan's left. (Library of Congress, Victor Herbert Collection)

The license tally had reached 136, still rather short of Maxwell's projection, when the market for performing rights crashed. On February 9, 1915, the federal court of appeals reversed Judge Lacombe's order in the *Hilliard Hotel* case. "The whole case," the appellate court recognized, "turns upon the meaning of the words 'for profit.'" Yet it went on to focus, obtusely, not on whether the hotel profited by offering music, but on whether the guests paid for that music out of their pockets: "It does not make a performance any less gratuitous to an audience because someone pays the musician for rendering it, or because it was a means of attracting custom, or was a part of the operation of the hotel."

The appeals court's ruling was a near-lethal blow to Ascap, a complete repudiation of the legal stance on which it was premised. The organization's viability depended on getting the decision reversed by the United States Supreme Court. But Burkan wanted a better vehicle to bring the issue before the high court, one that he could frame and control from the outset. On April 15, 1915, he commenced the landmark case of *Victor Herbert v. The Shanley Company*.

In nearly every telling of Ascap's origin story, the centerpiece is a fateful night when Victor Herbert happened into Shanley's (in some versions he is accompanied by Puccini) and heard the title number from his

1913 operetta *Sweethearts* performed, without his consent and without compensation being paid to him. This persistent legend is difficult to square with the sworn affidavit that Herbert gave in the lawsuit, which makes no mention of his ever having set foot in Shanley's or personally hearing his song performed there. Burkan chose to target Shanley's because, as a highly visible, free-spending competitor to nearby Broadway theaters, it presented the most favorable factual backdrop for the legal arguments that Burkan wanted to make.

To put the case on a fast track to the Supreme Court, Burkan agreed to have the trial court enter a final, appealable decision without lengthy proceedings, based on a stipulated factual record that consisted primarily of an affidavit sworn by Shanley's manager. He admitted that one of the singers in the cabaret show performed "Sweethearts," but denied that the performance was "for profit" because there was no cover charge for admission to the restaurant, no minimum for food and drink, and the music was "purely incidental to the restaurant business, the price charged for food and service [being] the same without as with the music." Thus packaged, the case was tailor-made to yield a definitive Supreme Court ruling on the meaning of "public performance for profit."

In what appears to be an uncharacteristic loss of resolve, however, Burkan risked clouding the issue. Rather than emphasize the infringement of Herbert's copyright on the song "Sweethearts," his primary argument was that Shanley's use of that one number infringed the copyright on the complete operetta *Sweethearts,* a "dramatico-musical" work under the copyright law. To prove infringement of the dramatico-musical work under the 1909 Copyright Act, it would not matter whether the performance was "for profit" or not. (Dramatico-musical rights, often referred to as "grand rights," permit the staging of musical theater productions and are distinct from the nondramatic performing rights in music, sometimes called "small rights," that are administered by Ascap.) A ruling on this basis would have redounded to the benefit of theatrical composers such as Herbert, and Burkan may have felt duty-bound to make the argument, but it would have left a large swath of Ascap's repertoire, the nonproduction music, unprotected. Once again, Burkan was juggling clients with conflicting interests.

The first stop on the path to the Supreme Court was the courtroom of Learned Hand. Judge Hand had been nominated to the federal bench by President William Howard Taft a few weeks after the passage of the 1909 Copyright Act, and for the next fifty years, sitting as a trial and appellate judge in Manhattan—the country's premier venue for copyright disputes—Hand was the law's most important expositor. He obliged Burkan with a fast decision, rejecting the dramatico-musical argument out of hand and making little effort to hide his displeasure at having to follow binding appellate court precedent on the "for profit" issue: "We now have it, on the authority of *Church Company v. Hilliard,* that a public performance of this kind is not within the statutory copyright" on the individual song. "I was a little unhappy that I had to do what I did," he later told Burkan. "I never had the least doubt about the correctness of Judge Lacombe's original decision."

While Ascap was in legal limbo, it was business as usual along Tin Pan Alley. Most popular publishers, skeptical from the outset about enforcing performing rights, were content to let their memberships in the society lapse. The Board of Trade faded into oblivion. Copyright infringement litigation between music publishers was on the rise. In a speech to the Music Publishers Association, Burkan observed that courts were just beginning to take such cases seriously. "For many years," Burkan said, "a copyright case was a joke in the court and received little attention from either judge or jury." He was undoubtedly recalling Judge Lacombe's disdainful attitude in the "Good Morning, Carrie" case years earlier. Burkan attributed the changing judicial attitude to the heavy volume of copyright cases coming out of the motion picture industry, where the stakes seemed more tangible than the mere copping of a tune. Such cases, Burkan believed, had the effect of "dignifying copyright litigation" in general.

Burkan was on the losing side in several of the early disputes that established the rules of engagement for such cases, rules that are still good law a century later. In 1915, he represented Empire Music in a suit brought by Boosey & Company over an early Al Jolson hit, "Tennessee, I Hear You Calling Me." Boosey claimed that the syncopated Jolson number infringed its copyright on "I Hear You Calling Me," a lamentation sung to a deceased love, which was also a commercial success for the beloved Irish tenor John McCormack.

The judge said that he "had someone, indifferent to the controversy, play both songs for me." He found that the "two compositions are considerably different, both in theme and execution, except the words 'I hear you calling me,' and the music accompanying those words, are practically identical." He went on to hold that in the context of popular music, even such a limited resemblance, if it involved a song's commercial hook, could constitute a copyright infringement: "The main thing that impressed me was the plaintive 'I hear you calling me' in both songs. . . . It has the kind of sentiment in both cases that causes the audiences to listen, applaud, and buy copies in the corridor on the way out of the theater." The decision was, as musician and lawyer Charles Cronin writes, pioneering in its solicitude for "the economic interests of the incipient American music industry."

Leo Feist, a leader on Tin Pan Alley and an Ascap stalwart, published one of the biggest hits of 1915, the anti-interventionist anthem "I Didn't Raise My Boy to Be a Soldier." Its sales had not suffered a bit, indeed were probably boosted, when former president Theodore Roosevelt denounced it as a "menace." Feist hired Burkan to defend a copyright infringement suit brought by a songwriter, Harry Haas, who claimed that the song was a dead ringer for his own composition, "You Will Never Know How Much I Really Cared." The Feist song was composed by one of his employees, Al Piantodosi, who could devise a melody on the piano but, like many other Tin Pan Alley songsmiths, could not write down a note of music.

The case was tried before Judge Learned Hand in the spring of 1916. Hand found that there was "a continuously suggestive melodic parallelism" between the two songs. He conceded the parallels might be musically commonplace—Burkan had argued that the shared themes could also be heard in *HMS Pinafore*—but that "it would be absurd not to regard them as evidence of the most impressive character" when considered in combination with evidence that Piantodosi had heard the Haas song and that he had a reputation for stealing melodies. Piantodosi's own testimony precluded the possibility that his actual source was Gilbert and Sullivan:

Q. Did you ever hear *Pinafore?*

A. I saw it on an electric sign on Broadway one time.

Q. And that is the extent of your knowledge of *Pinafore?*

A. Yes.

Hand's copyright jurisprudence has been highly influential, but in one respect it was quite idiosyncratic. In evaluating the similarities between a copyrighted work and an alleged infringement, it is generally accepted practice to disregard elements that can be found commonly in other preexisting works, on the theory that such elements are not sufficiently "original" to merit copyright protection in the first instance, or, alternatively, on the theory that they are so common they cannot support an inference of copying from any one particular source. Hand saw things differently. If the author of the copyrighted work did not know such preexisting sources, then his work was sufficiently "original" to merit protection from copying even if it was not "novel." And if the alleged infringer did actually use the copyrighted work as his source, it was an infringement even if the same material *could* have been derived from the public domain.

A few years later, in one of the last cases Learned Hand tried before being elevated to the appellate court, Burkan again came out on the short end of the judge's copyright philosophy. Burkan represented Jerome Kern, who stood accused of copying the bass accompaniment from "Dardanella," a huge hit of 1920, and using it to identical effect in "Ka-lu-a," from his 1921 Broadway show *Good Morning, Dearie.*

Burkan attacked the validity of the "Dardanella" copyright on the ground that the bass line could be found in public domain works. Hand rejected the argument, since there was no evidence that the composers of "Dardanella" had in fact copied it from such a source, rather than having hit upon the same musical phrases independently. And although Judge Hand found Kern's denial of deliberate copying credible—Kern, he noted, had "an established place among composers of light opera" and would have no motive to copy—he concluded that "everything registers somewhere in our memories, and no one can tell what may evoke it. I cannot really see how else to account for a similarity which amounts to identity." The theory of "subconscious plagiarism" from the "Dardanella" case is frequently invoked in music copyright cases to this day.

Although Hand had treated the "Dardanella" case, as he did all music cases, with the utmost care and attention, he made it clear that he deemed it a burden on the court: "The controversy is 'a trivial pother,' a mere point of honor, of scarcely more than irritation, involving no substantial interest. Except that it raises an interesting point of law, it would be a waste of time for everyone concerned."

After the court of appeals, as expected, affirmed Judge Hand's ruling in *Herbert v. The Shanley Company* in January 1916, Burkan petitioned the Supreme Court for review. Such review is discretionary, so Burkan had to persuade the court that the case was of "peculiar public interest":

> The more popular a musical composition is, the greater its value to the composer, and correspondingly the greater temptation to appropriate it for cabaret and other similar performances. The decision, therefore, has direct bearing upon the protection of intellectual effort by authors and composers, the fostering of which was the purpose of the constitutional provision.

The Supreme Court agreed to hear the appeals in both *Shanley* and *Hilliard Hotel*. It docketed the cabaret cases for oral argument on Monday, January 8, 1917, but history intervened. A few months earlier, to avert a threatened national railroad strike, Congress had passed an act mandating a standard eight-hour workday for interstate carriers, the first federal labor legislation of its kind. An expedited constitutional challenge to the railroad law was placed "at the head of the call" for that January morning, at which time the court also granted the parties' request for a total of eight hours to make their arguments. For two and a half days, while a closely divided court grilled the opposing teams of lawyers in a courtroom packed with cabinet officers, members of Congress, and reporters, Burkan cooled his heels, waiting to make what would be his first and only Supreme Court argument.

It was late Wednesday afternoon when the cabaret cases were called. The Old Senate Chamber used for the Supreme Court's public sessions, bursting with dignitaries only a short while earlier, had largely emptied out. Raymond Hubbell thought the justices had been too "bored and wearied" by the highly technical railroad case to have much patience left for a show business tiff:

> But the showman in Burkan proved just the counter-irritant needed. Right off the bat he jumped their judgeships from the mathematical atmosphere they had been in to the glamour of metropolitan night-life, with all its dazzle, sparkle and gaiety, music, drama, laughter and revelry. Those nine bodies came to life.

The one wire service reporter who had lingered to observe the argument agreed that the court had "flitted lightly" from the intricacies of railroad labor regulation to the louche pleasures of Broadway cabaret. Burkan had come prepared to press his argument that Shanley's had infringed Herbert's dramatico-musical copyright, rendering the "for profit" issue moot, but Hubbell's intuition was right in one respect: the Court was too weary for such nice technicalities. It was intensely interested in hearing about how Shanley's used its Cabaret Extraordinaire to attract a bustling dinner trade.

Shanley's had engaged a colorful Washington attorney, Levi Cooke, to argue its case. A former newspaperman, Cooke knew how to turn a phrase, but he was too glib and facile by half for a bench that included such luminaries as Oliver Wendell Holmes and Louis Brandeis. He insisted that the words "for profit" did not refer to the purpose for which a performance was offered, but rather to whether it was offered "for free" or not. Any possibility of profit resulting from a "free" cabaret performance was too remote and conjectural to be considered. After all, he argued, "'Sweethearts' may have driven more patrons from the dining room than it lured into it."

Burkan and Hubbell left Washington feeling confident of victory. Back in New York awaiting word from the court, Burkan was spotted in the very belly of the beast, seated at a coveted table for the opening night of the city's most decadent midnight cabaret yet, Florence Ziegfeld's Cocoanut Grove, a tropically themed, glass-enclosed room with views of Central Park atop the Century Theater, where the (presumably licensed) musical entertainment ran until 4 A.M.

The Supreme Court handed down its unanimous ruling, authored by Justice Holmes, just two weeks after the argument. Holmes's reasoning was characteristically concise, penetrating, and pragmatic. "If the rights under the copyright are infringed only by a performance where money is taken at the door, they are very imperfectly protected." It was immaterial that Shanley's attached a price to the food rather than to the music; there was no such thing as a free cabaret performance. "The defendants' performances are not eleemosynary. . . . If music did not pay, it would be given up. If it pays, it pays out of the public's pocket. Whether it pays or not, the purpose of employing it is profit, and that is enough." The opinion was short and sweet enough to be reprinted on a single page and mailed, as Ascap did, many thousands of times, over the course of many years, to every commercial music user in the United States.

"There was jubilation plenty among the writer gang," Hubbell recalled, although "Justice Holmes' use of the word 'eleemosynary' caused more excitement than the decision." When Burkan arrived at the Lambs Club, the center of celebration that night, "he was toasted to the heavens, the compliments that were piled on his always undemonstrative self would have forced a bump of pride into evidence on anyone less unflatterable. His seeming calm in the middle of all our whooping it up was a puzzle."

Burkan had been holding Ascap together with spit and tape for two years as its membership ranks, especially among the publishers, were hemorrhaging. The Supreme Court had removed a legal cloud, but now a weakened and demoralized organization had to address long-deferred practical challenges. Burkan knew he had caught lightning in a bottle in 1914. Doing it again would not be easy.

CHAPTER 14

The Music Tax

While *Herbert v. The Shanley Company* was wending its way to the Supreme Court it was virtually impossible for Ascap to collect license fees, and collecting membership dues was not much easier. The coffers were bare. At the first meeting of the board of directors after the *Shanley* ruling, in the winter of 1917, the treasurer reported that only twenty-four licenses were in force. After Ascap's first general manager had quit in frustration, Burkan placed Julius C. Rosenthal, one of his legal associates and Tammany Hall deputies, in the job. Rosenthal turned out to have just the combination of legal knowledge, business savvy, and determination that the position (which he held until his premature death sixteen years later) required. To expand the society's reach beyond New York, Burkan recruited regional representatives, mostly lawyers, to work on a one-third commission basis throughout the country.

The hoteliers and restaurateurs, by and large, were gracious losers. They quickly came to terms. Within a few months, Ascap had just under one thousand licenses in force (out of an estimated universe of twenty thousand licensable public places of amusement), generating $65,000 in annual income. It was still well short of what was needed to begin distributing money to members, but it was enough to keep the lights on and underwrite the next "play-and-pay campaign," targeting what Burkan had always viewed as the real cash cow: movie exhibitors. Raymond Hubbell was given the honor of being the lead plaintiff in the first test case, brought against a Harlem theater operator for using his tune

"Poor Butterfly" as a musical accompaniment. The courts had no trouble applying the logic of *Shanley* to movie theaters.

Ascap set the annual license fee for theaters at ten cents per seat, about the going rate for a single movie admission at the time. The first audience to fill a theater on New Year's Day could cover the cost of an exhibitor's Ascap license for the year. Burkan anticipated that this nominal sum would meet little resistance. It was another triumph of hope over experience.

The exhibitors at the top of the pecking order were not the problem. The First National Exhibitors Circuit, newly organized by the twenty-five largest and most prestigious chains, was at that very time negotiating with Burkan for Charlie Chaplin's distribution deal; Burkan had little trouble bringing its members under license. For theaters of that class, many of which employed large orchestras and offered elaborate musical interludes between pictures, it was truly a trivial cost of doing business. New York City's grandest movie palace of the day, the Rialto, had more than two thousand seats and paid Ascap only $20 per month. Undoubtedly, the big exhibitors also appreciated that the burden of the "music tax" would fall more heavily on their smaller competitors. First National's Philadelphia franchisee eagerly agreed to serve as Ascap's commissioned collection agent for his territory, although he turned out to be a mite too aggressive. "The only way to treat an exhibitor," he was later quoted as saying, "is to hit him over the head with a club and take his money."

Things got dicier when Burkan turned his attention to independent exhibitors, even in Ascap's hometown. In April 1917, exhibitor organizations in Manhattan, Brooklyn, and the Bronx declared their intention to defy Ascap.

It was absurd to claim, as one expert witness for the exhibitors would testify, that they used music only to "overcome the noise of shuffling feet and coughing." Yet at the smaller houses music was truly incidental to the main attraction—often a single organist or pianist, or even just a mechanical instrument, punctuating the screen action. They had a legitimate beef with the idea that they should pay the same per-seat rate as the glamorous movie palaces. Neither music usage nor profitability was strictly proportional to seating capacity. A dime per seat might have been easier for them to swallow if the big operators were paying a quarter.

Burkan was open to negotiation but found no willing counterparty. The Motion Picture Exhibitors League of America claimed to represent more than six thousand independent exhibitors nationally, but its leader, Lee A. Ochs, was no fan of Nathan Burkan. A few years earlier, Ochs had sued one of Burkan's theatrical clients, Broadway producer A.H. Woods, for fraud. In cross-examining Ochs at that trial, Burkan had led him down a testimonial path that contradicted a crucial element of his fraud case—that he had acted in reliance on Woods's misrepresentations:

Burkan. You didn't take Mr. Woods's word for anything?

Ochs. No sir.

Q. You didn't believe anything that he told you?

A. No sir.

Q. You knew that he was a theatrical man and that such men are not worthy of belief?

A. Absolutely.

Although Ochs won the jury verdict, Burkan prevailed on appeal, the court holding that Ochs's docile admissions sank his cause.

That humiliation was still an open wound in July 1917, when Burkan went to Chicago to explain Ascap's position to hundreds of exhibitors gathered there for the annual convention of the Exhibitors League. Ochs saw to it that Burkan was given a frosty reception. "At the end of Burkan's speech, there was much talk on the part of the members. Some shouted that they were suffering from enough taxation and that it was an imposition at this time to try and put this tax on them."

Ochs appointed a committee to consider the music tax matter and had his personal attorney, Milton Goldsmith, Burkan's opponent in the Woods lawsuit, provide a legal analysis. The committee did not dispute that the rationale of *Shanley* applied fully to movie theaters, nor did it deny that the proposed fee was nominal. Rather, it seems to have been the first body to fix upon a more sophisticated theory that would soon, and for many decades to come, bedevil Ascap: that its large pool of musical copyrights gave it the market power to fix the price of its license at any level it chose, and it was therefore a "combination in restraint of trade" in violation of antitrust law. An individual copyright owner might be free to enforce the performing right on a single number, Goldsmith argued, but collective action "to fix prices and to coerce the users of the sheet music into paying a blanket fee for the privilege of playing *all* the numbers of the society" was quite another thing.

The Exhibitors League adopted a resolution declaring that "the action contemplated by the society strikes at the very vitals of our business and if successful would mean ultimately the absolute ruin of the amusement business as the said society may see fit without legal restraint to increase and make burdensome the license fee and other regulations." Ochs called upon exhibitors to boycott Ascap music, and to contribute $3 per theater to a "Music Tax Fund" to defray the costs of prosecuting an antitrust lawsuit against Ascap and defending individual exhibitors in infringement cases.

Burkan was on the West Coast recruiting Ascap representatives when he received word of the exhibitors' resolution. He announced that his office was preparing to file over one hundred complaints for copyright infringement against unlicensed movie theaters. The Exhibitors League responded, in September 1917, with the first lawsuit to seek the dissolution of Ascap under antitrust law.

Burkan's concern in the late 1910s was not that any court might actually declare Ascap to be an illegal monopoly. His problem was that Ascap had too much competition.

Most of Ascap's publisher-members had resigned during the pendency of *Shanley.* They did not come rushing back into the fold after the Supreme Court ruled. The Music Publishers Board of Trade, which Burkan had cobbled together in 1914 and which had briefly operated as a virtual subsidiary of Ascap, had been superseded by a new organization, the Music Publishers Protective Association. This was an independent trade association managed by a colorful Texan, Edwin Claude Mills. Mills, whose formal education had ended with the seventh grade, had lost a leg in a railroad accident and also survived a bout of yellow fever—contracted while working on construction of the Panama Canal—before opening a vaudeville theater in San Antonio. He came to the attention of the music publishers in New York through his work as a troubleshooter, lobbyist, and dispute mediator for vaudeville trade groups. As a theater man, Mills had no affinity for the concept of performing rights in music and he saw no reason for publishers to sacrifice any of their financial prerogatives for the sake of Ascap, an organization that, so far, had proven itself to be little more than a self-perpetuating lawsuit machine.

While a few members of the Protective Association sat on Ascap's board of directors and were genuinely devoted to the cause, others were actively undermining Ascap's efforts to license movie exhibitors. One sent exhibitors a handy how-to guide advising that they should not feel obliged to meet Ascap's demands, for it is easy enough to evade them, merely by not playing the music which is subject to the ban. Several prominent publishers of New York have not joined the society, among them ourselves, and they do not intend to do so. . . . Any one of their catalogs is large enough to supply even the most progressive orchestra leaders with sufficient material for all purposes.

Movie studios also came to the aid of exhibitors by providing cue sheets for musical accompaniments to their releases that used only "tax-free" music. "The simplest and most effective means of eliminating this rapacious element from the motion picture sphere," said Mutual's music director, "is by ignoring their output and using only non-taxable music." Each week the main trade journals printed long lists of tax-free music.

The Exhibitors League boycott took its toll, leading some songwriters to throw in the towel on Ascap. Harry von Tilzer, Tin Pan Alley's biggest hit-maker before Irving Berlin came along, and also a publisher, submitted his resignation. His calculation was simple: "If I thought it was going to do me any real good, I would have clung to it, but the prospects of deriving any real benefit out of it for a good many years to come (if any at all) are uncertain for the popular publisher, and in the meantime it antagonizes the theaters and musicians who have in the past helped to make all my popular successes." The league's house organ, *Exhibitors Trade Review*, brandished von Tilzer's resignation as proof that its boycott was "bearing fruit."

Even as Ascap's membership ranks sank toward a new low-water mark, a handful of the most prominent and successful publishers on Tin Pan Alley remained steadfast: M. Witmark & Sons; T.B. Harms; Leo Feist; Shapiro, Bernstein & Company; and Waterson, Berlin & Snyder. Together with the operatic music represented by G. Ricordi, it was a repertoire difficult for a movie exhibitor to avoid drawing upon, but not so comprehensive as to give much traction to the claim that Ascap was a "music trust."

Burkan buried the Exhibitors League's antitrust suit in a mountain of counterevidence, most of it coming from the league's own mouthpieces. Its gloating over the success of its boycott of Ascap, and its proven power to drive a wedge between Ascap and its members, suggested that if there was an unlawful conspiracy restraining trade in this sphere, it wasn't Ascap. Burkan ridiculed the exhibitors' assertion that they did not object to paying for copyrighted music, but only to *concerted* action by copyright owners to collect fees:

It should be kept in mind that the right of each composer to enforce his performing right would still continue after their organization was destroyed. ... But the Exhibitors League expects that this right will be reduced to an abstraction, to a shadow and nullity, if the several composers cannot cooperate in making up a fund and in otherwise aiding each other in the enforcement of the right.

By the time the court dismissed the Exhibitors League's antitrust case in April 1918, agreeing with Burkan that an injunction against collective enforcement of performing rights would effectively gut those rights, Goldsmith's legal bills were already approaching ten thousand dollars. The Music Tax Fund, however, had raised less than one thousand dollars, and Lee Ochs's ardor for the fight was dimming. Under his divisive leadership (one trade paper dubbed him the "Little Napoleon of the Steam-Roller"), the Exhibitors League was splintering and on the verge of dissolution. Even Ochs's ill will toward Burkan was abating. New York's highest court had reinstated Ochs's fraud verdict against A. H. Woods, and soon bygones were bygones. Shortly before stepping down as league president in July 1918, Ochs tried, without success, to negotiate a global resolution of the music tax issue with Burkan. Ochs, like many of Burkan's worn-out adversaries, became his client and would remain one for many years thereafter.

With the national organization sidelined, resistance to the music tax devolved into a series of localized skirmishes that followed a predictable pattern. Ascap's representative would send music inspectors to a target city and mail out warning letters to unlicensed theaters. The local exhibitors would adopt a resolution denouncing Ascap. A wave of lawsuits would follow and then, finally, terms of surrender were negotiated before the fight moved on to the next metropolis. It was a grinding war of attrition. "The experience of both music publisher and the exhibitor," *Film Daily* observed, "has not been profitable or pleasant."

As 1920 was drawing to a close, nearly four years after the Supreme Court's ruling in *Shanley* and seven years after Ascap's founding, the millions of dollars in revenues that Burkan had once projected had still not materialized, and the society's litigation expenses were running far higher than expected. Nonetheless, with over three thousand licenses in force, Ascap was operating modestly in the black and its reserves had reached a level where Burkan felt distributions of income to members could, at long last, be contemplated. With the smell of money suddenly in the air, the time was ripe to try to bring recalcitrant tax-free music publishers into the society.

Burkan approached Claude Mills to discuss an arrangement. The deal they negotiated reorganized Ascap to make it a more attractive proposition to music publishers. The articles of association were amended to give publishers 50 percent representation on the board of directors and 50 percent of all distributions, as opposed to the one-third participation provided for in the 1914 articles. Importantly, the new articles required all members to commit for five-year periods, giving the society stability that had been sorely lacking by preventing the ad hoc withdrawal of valuable catalogs at the first signs of trouble. *Variety* went overboard in characterizing this as an agreement to "merge" Ascap and the Music Publishers Protective Association, but that was not without a germ of truth. Nearly all of the Protective Association's popular music publishers joined or rejoined Ascap in 1921, and the major standard music publishers followed suit in 1924.

Burkan believed that by drying up the supply of tax-free music, Ascap would at last be positioned "to carry out the plans which its creators had in mind when it was organized." The deal was a bitter pill for the writers who had founded Ascap and had stuck with it through its early tribulations. They were being asked to forfeit some of their hard-earned share just as the first dividend was about to be paid. Burkan himself, Raymond Hubbell wrote, "had no stomach for it—called it larceny—but what he wanted more than anything else, was a real, thriving, substantial Ascap."

Claude Mills's conversion to the gospel of performing rights was as fervent as it was sudden. Once he brought the publishers in, he held them to a stern code of conduct, fighting their primordial urge to plug songs in unlicensed venues. With wit, roguish charm, an Anglo-Saxon name, and southern manners, Mills became the society's most effective public spokesman. He moved into Ascap's offices and, in 1923, was officially given a salaried position as chairman of Ascap's administrative committee, while continuing as executive director of the Protective Association. Even Raymond Hubbell, the one director who voted against the reorganization plan, eventually conceded that Mills deserved a place on Ascap's Mount Rushmore, right beside Burkan.

In early April 1921, the writer-directors and publisher-directors of the newly reorganized Ascap met separately to perform a delicate and long-deferred task: devising systems of classification for divvying up their respective shares of the first quarterly distribution of $24,000. Class A writers such as Irving Berlin, Jerome Kern, and Victor Herbert, along with such little-remembered cofounders as Raymond Hubbell and Louis Hirsch, were allotted $163 each (about $2,500 in 2020 dollars). Newcomers Ira Gershwin and Vincent Youmans, who collaborated on their first hit that year, were at the other end of the scale, each receiving the minimum of $7.50. George Gershwin, with some notable successes already under his belt, was placed in Class B and received $79. The twenty-eight publishers were divided into six classes, with shares ranging from $740 to $23. The distributions in the first few years, though small, felt like minted money, especially welcome just as the sheet music and mechanical royalties that Ascap's members had long subsisted on began to decline with the arrival of radio broadcasting.

After seven years of struggle, Ascap was a self-sustaining and income-producing organization. It soon had reciprocity agreements with performing rights organizations throughout Europe (even Sacem closed its New York branch and affiliated with Ascap) and "high-class" composers, including Sergei Rachmaninoff and Walter Damrosch, began to join the society. As the 1920s began to roar, Ascap controlled the performing rights to a formidable back catalog of standard and popular music, and to nearly every new hit that came along—by its own reckoning, its members controlled more than 90 percent of the most widely performed music in the United States. It was beginning to look a lot more like something that might plausibly be called a music trust.

When the reorganization plan went into effect on January 1, 1921, Ascap had nearly half of all motion picture houses under license. Then things started to move in reverse. A new trade association, the Motion Picture Theater Owners of America (MPTOA), which arose from the ashes of Lee Ochs's Motion Pictures Exhibitors League, was now carrying the banner of opposition.

The MPTOA was founded in 1920 by a New York City exhibitor, Sydney Cohen, who had made a name for himself the previous year leading a successful push for a state law allowing Sunday movie shows. The music tax was not on Cohen's original agenda for MPTOA. He had organized it to resist Adolph Zukor's plans to expand his vertically integrated empire, already dominant in motion picture production and distribution, into the field of exhibition. Cohen's own theaters held Ascap licenses and he had never been aligned with the music tax resistance. Sensing an opening, Burkan approached Cohen in the hope of negotiating a nationwide truce.

By then, however, Cohen had come to appreciate how deeply hostility to the music tax ran in his membership ranks, especially outside of New York. In his speech at the MPTOA's first convention, he chose to demagogue the issue. Cohen bragged that he had rejected Burkan's overture and had warned him that "we intend to go to Congress with an amendment to the copyright law which would put a stop to this very obnoxious practice."

Egged on by Cohen's rhetoric and pledges of financial support, local chapters of the organization encouraged their members to defy Ascap. His patience exhausted, Burkan prepared for a renewed wave of litigation against movie exhibitors. At Claude Mills's behest, he stayed his hand while Ascap ran full-page warning messages in all the major picture business trade journals for five consecutive weeks in the spring of 1921. "I urged patience, and another sincere try at showing the exhibitor what it was all about," Mills later rued. "The exhibitors met this effort with defiance of the law, contumely, and epithet."

Shortly after the last of the warning ads ran, Burkan commenced a shock-and-awe litigation campaign. Twenty cases in Kansas, fifty in North Carolina, and more than sixty in the Philadelphia area alone.

Burkan's feud with Cohen became unusually personal and nasty. He authorized Mills to state publicly that "Sydney Cohen's checks in payment of the fees for his theaters are among the ones most promptly received by the society." Mills gave a facsimile of one such check to a trade publication, which published it alongside the observation that "despite the fact that he has urged exhibitors all over the country to fight the music tax with all the means at their power, Cohen himself has never refused to pay the tax, and has never volunteered to make a test of the copyright law by permitting himself to be made a defendant in a music tax case." The accusation of hypocrisy struck a chord. When Cohen visited Philadelphia a few weeks later, the chapter president warned him that "it would be more pleasant for him" if he didn't mention the music issue, "inasmuch as our boys had been martyrs and had been induced to defy the music tax people and stand the suits at his suggestion."

Cohen had, with a nudge from Burkan, painted himself into a corner. To save face with his members, he had to terminate his own Ascap licenses. Burkan then slapped him with twenty-two separate copyright infringement lawsuits. Not since Marc A. Blumenberg died in exile ten years earlier had Burkan nursed a grudge with such obvious and wicked glee.

Feeling intense pressure to show some results, in December 1922 Cohen brought the exhibitors' grievances against Ascap to the Federal Trade Commission (FTC) and to Attorney General Harry Daugherty. With its pooling of so many desirable copyrights, the theater owners argued, Ascap possessed the ability to impose monopoly prices, to "take every dollar away from the public that they cared to." They complained bitterly that Ascap publisher-members would importune them for plugs, even provide complimentary sheet music, only to have Ascap "turn around and sue us for back taxes in a very short time." Ascap's inspectors, they claimed, would readily perjure themselves to prove up a copyright infringement: "They notified us that on a western serial picture our pianist played 'It's a Long Way to Tipperary.' What's to prevent them from swearing that we played 'The Holy City' in a Lloyd comedy?"

The FTC declined to intercede, finding that a claim for royalties, made in apparent good faith, was not "an unfair method of competition," because the parties were not in competition with each other and there was nothing unfair about the "assertion of a supposed legal right which is fully determinable by the Courts." But at the Department of Justice, unfettered by the FTC's narrow statutory mandate, the complaints were turned over to acting director of its Bureau of Investigation, J. Edgar Hoover, who launched a full field investigation.

Tin Pan Alley, before the coming of Ascap, would not have been out of place in Dickens's London or Hugo's Paris, an industrial slum populated by rapacious publishers and oppressed artists who lived precariously and often died penniless. Ascap aspired to make songwriting a respectable profession for a family man or woman. To long-suffering artists, it held out the promise that they would not go broke in their old age, nor be buried in unmarked graves. A significant portion of Ascap's revenue went to providing income to no-longer-productive old-timers (who were assigned to special "permanent" classifications with fixed distributions for life) and to the relief of their widows and orphans. The pace of upward mobility was steady but slow. As late as 1924, Burkan said he knew of only two songwriters who owned their own home and automobile.

If the Ascap of the early 1920s was, as its detractors claimed, a shakedown racket, a music trust, it was a ludicrously inept and inefficient one. Although its musical repertoire was large and ubiquitous, Ascap's rock-bottom pricing guaranteed that its share of the American entertainment dollar would, at best, amount to only a small fraction of a penny. Its costs for detecting infringements and taking violators to court, to obtain damages that rarely exceeded the statutory minimum of $250, further eroded the financial equation. Burkan—who believed from the beginning that a regime of voluntary, near-universal compliance with performing rights licensing was the key to Ascap's long-term success—made it a practice to bring lawsuits only after a prolonged, graduated sequence of warnings, and then to let malefactors off the hook, even after judgment was entered against them, if they agreed to take a license and pay fees going forward. Only about a third of Ascap's gross income was being distributed to members in the early 1920s.

A bootlegging operation so benign, so smalltime, wouldn't have attracted the Prohibition Bureau's attention. Nonetheless, Ascap soon found itself under serious scrutiny and fighting for its survival in all three branches of the national government.

CHAPTER 15

The Ether Toy

The Bureau of Navigation, under the purview of Secretary of Commerce Herbert Hoover, granted the first thirty-one radio broadcast licenses in 1921 and several hundred more in 1922. Some were granted to manufacturers of radio equipment, others to newspapers, hotels, department stores, and other commercial enterprises interested in exploiting the unprecedented reach of radio to promote their primary lines of business. There was not yet any proven, practical way to monetize broadcasting services directly. But a rapt and ready audience was already listening in. By the middle of 1923, an estimated 2.25 million radio receiving sets were in use in the United States. The newest home entertainment accoutrement, the "ether toy," had arrived with startling swiftness.

From the very beginning, music, including the latest popular hits, filled a large percentage of airtime, as much as 80–90 percent. On Tin Pan Alley, it was widely feared that radios would displace pianos and phonographs in many homes. And the conventional wisdom among publishers was that while radio could provide "the greatest plug ever," with instant exposure of a song to an audience of millions, the incessant repetition of a number on radio reduced sheet music and record sales in the long run. In contrast to the leisurely dissemination of a song across the country by vaudevillians carefully selected and coached by the publishers, in circuits that might take a year or two to complete and which would leave a lingering demand for sheet music and records in their wake, the ready availability of amateur performances of dubious quality at the turn of a radio dial could be hazardous to a song's health. "Do we hear Jolson, Belle Baker, Eddie Cantor, Will Rogers?" Claude Mills asked rhetorically in 1924, naming future radio stars who, at the time, were prohibited by their theatrical contracts from performing on the air. "No, we hear Tillie Blatz, who has just graduated from some singing school, and this, that, or the other amateur individual or organization." When broadcasters insisted that Ascap's members should be grateful for the free advertising they were providing, the heartfelt answer was "please don't do us any favors."

In March 1922, *Variety* reported that Nathan Burkan was preparing a legal opinion for Ascap. "He will interpret the law as to whether the broadcasting of music through the ether is considered a public performance for profit. Meantime, the music men are permitting the radio fad to develop." In fact, Ascap's leaders had already concluded that radio was no passing fad. They were determined not to let another new entertainment medium ingrain a habit of exploiting copyrighted music for free while cannibalizing its members' other sources of revenue. Burkan remembered well how arduous the battle to secure the mechanical reproduction right had been. "On this radio matter," he said, "we are profiting from our experience. We are not going to get into a situation where courts may say 'You slept on your rights.'"

Burkan rendered a formal opinion that broadcast of music by commercial entities, whether it was to promote the sale of radio receivers or to generate goodwill for other enterprises, constituted public performances for profit under the 1909 Copyright Act and *Herbert v. The Shanley Company*. In May 1922, Ascap sent every broadcast licenseholder in the United States a copy of Justice Holmes's opinion, under cover of a disingenuously saccharine circular signed by general manager J. C. Rosenthal but undoubtedly coauthored by Burkan and Mills:

> Due to the unprecedented rapid development of "Radio" in its popular aspects, a situation has been created wherein authors, composers, and publishers, as copyright proprietors, are deprived of revenue and rights, through the infringement of their copyrights. . . . Apparently in the very rapidity of this development the proprietors of broadcasting stations have in good faith overlooked the rights of these parties.

The circular continued: "The position of the composers, authors and publishers to 'Radio' is not a hostile or unfriendly one. They realize the great potential service which it may render to the whole people, and they would not be disposed, even if they could, to hamper or retard its fullest development and service." The tone was diplomatic, bordering on unctuous; the underlying threat was clear.

Among the recipients was David Sarnoff, who had recently been promoted to general manager at the Radio Corporation of America, a cooperative venture of General Electric, Westinghouse, American Telephone and Telegraph, and Western Electric, the major patent holders in radio telephony. All five entities were ramping up to service a growing market for transmission and receiving equipment, as well as operating their own broadcast stations. Even to Sarnoff's "lay mind," he wrote, the *Shanley* opinion seemed "rather sweeping." His legal counsel advised him that there was no material distinction between cabarets and radio: "We render our broadcasting services to increase the sale of our receiving sets. That we do obtain an indirect profit is shown by the tremendous increase in orders that pour in as a result."

Representatives of the "Big Five" met with Burkan and Mills in the fall of 1922, in two conferences that were fully transcribed and widely circulated. The discussions stand out in the early annals of Ascap for their candor, absence of bluster, and overall sobriety. These broadcasters conceded that their use of music constituted public performance for profit, but argued that Ascap should not impose additional costs on them as long as the most fundamental question in the economics of radio broadcasting—"Who is to pay the bills?"—remained unanswered.

Internally, Ascap was struggling to settle on a yardstick for assessing a license fee. Burkan and Mills proposed a fee scale that started at $5 per day for the smallest stations. The Big Five's counteroffer was to pay nothing. The willingness they expressed to do without the Ascap repertoire, if the alternative was to pay for it, was completely sincere.

With the industry's leaders holding firm, Burkan and Mills capitulated. For the next several years, Ascap offered experimental licenses for fees of a few hundred dollars per year, provided stations acknowledged the society's rights in the form of an on-air announcement that songs from the Ascap repertoire were being broadcast "by special arrangement."

Even on those easy terms, the experimental licenses had only about three dozen takers out of more than five hundred commercial broadcast stations, yielding a paltry $16,500 in annual revenue. J. C. Rosenthal warned Ascap publishers not to pursue plugs from the unlicensed stations:

The radio plug may be the biggest plug in the world . . . but with the goal in sight of securing from this source within a few months enough money to double our present rate of dividends, it seems short sighted and foolish to throw the chance away for some little temporary advantage. One member isn't going to sit by and be idle when he sees another member broadcast. Either all should do it or none; for the present none should.

Ascap struggled to keep its troops in line. In early 1924, one of Ascap's most long-standing members, the publishing firm of Waterson, Berlin & Snyder, submitted a letter of resignation, complaining that "the majority of the large publishers are resorting to subterfuge in order to have their numbers broadcasted over unlicensed broadcasting stations." (Although the firm retained his name, Irving Berlin, a lifelong Ascap loyalist, had left it some five years earlier to form his own self-named publishing company.) Invoking the five-year commitments that Burkan had insisted on back in 1921 to prevent just such a situation, Ascap treated the Waterson resignation as a legal nullity.

Eugene F. McDonald was David Sarnoff's counterpart at the Zenith Radio Corporation. While Sarnoff was just temporizing, putting off a financial obligation that he knew would eventually come due, McDonald would give Ascap no quarter at all. He operated his radio station not to sell Zenith radios, he rather dubiously claimed, but "simply because I have got that fever, the thrill of broadcasting. I love it." In April 1923, he brought together sixty broadcasters from twelve states at Chicago's Drake Hotel, where they organized the National Association of Broadcasters (NAB) and girded for a battle with the music trust. They would, their communiqué avowed, "pay no heed to the protests of Ascap, now or at any future time."

Burkan filed the first lawsuit to test the radio question against Bamberger's Department Store, which operated a station in Newark, New Jersey. Bamberger's argued that because "everything it broadcasts is broadcasted without charge or cost to radio listeners, there is no performance publicly for profit." The court readily dispensed with that argument under *Shanley:*

> If the development or enlargement of the business of the department store was completely out of the minds of the promoters of this broadcasting enterprise, is it reasonable to believe that the slogan, "L. Bamberger & Company, One of America's Great Stores, Newark, N.J.," would be announced to all listeners one, two, three, four, five, or six times a day?

Bamberger's was an independent broadcaster, affiliated with neither the Big Five nor the NAB. Ascap's victory over Bamberger's packed little punch as far as the vast majority of broadcasters were concerned. Burkan followed up by bringing suits against a member of the NAB, American Automobile Accessories, which made car radios and broadcasted as the Crosley Radio Corporation of Cincinnati, and against General Electric, one of the Big Five, which operated a station out of Schenectady. With little reason to believe the results would be any different, the NAB petitioned Congress for relief.

The NAB had clout on Capitol Hill. Senator Clarence Dill of Washington State agreed to sponsor a narrow bill that would amend the 1909 Copyright Act to specifically exclude radio play of music from liability for copyright infringement. NAB member stations put Senator Dill on the air to drum up public support for "free radio music." No law or regulation required that the opposition be given equal time, or for that matter, any time at all. At the outset of hearings before the Senate Committee on Patents in April 1924, Senator Dill announced that "more telegrams have come in here on this bill than have ever come on any bill, except that for the declaration of war in 1917." It was one of the earliest demonstrations of the political power of mass media.

Piggybacking on the NAB's public relations coup, the Motion Picture Theater Owners Association succeeded in getting a hearing scheduled before the House Committee on Patents for its preferred copyright amendment, which would allow *any* purchaser of printed music to perform it publicly without liability. To the chagrin of the NAB, which hoped to position radio as a unique situation, the hearings before the two committees in April and May of 1924, respectively, became free-for-alls in which every commercial music user group piled on in the hope of administering a fatal blow to Ascap.

The first day of the Senate hearing was given over to the proponents of the Dill Bill. All that was missing was a fife and drum corps, so shamelessly did the NAB's witnesses wrap themselves in the flag. Radio provided therapy for bedridden soldiers, brought news of the outside world to polar explorers, and relieved the suffering of shut-ins and invalids of all kinds. It was a public service provided for free to the listeners, with no prospect of financial reward to the broadcaster, they claimed. "Just the moment they put obvious advertising on the air," Eugene McDonald predicted, "that station would be killed . . . there would be nobody listening."

The final witness for the NAB was its lawyer, Charles H. Tuttle. Tuttle was the very model of a white-shoe Wall Street lawyer. A future United States attorney for Manhattan, Franklin Roosevelt's Republican opponent in his 1930 race for reelection as governor of New York, and a devout Episcopal vestryman, Tuttle employed a speaking style that was declamatory and imperious. The official record of the House committee hearing held a few weeks later captures one member, perhaps sotto voce, referring to him as "King Tut."

In a carefully choreographed move on the day before the hearings began, Tuttle had filed a federal antitrust lawsuit against Ascap on behalf of Waterson, Berlin & Snyder, complaining that the society's refusal to honor the company's withdrawal was an unlawful restraint of trade. Tuttle read the committee a letter from Henry Waterson, who stated that his firm was seeking to leave Ascap because he was "not in sympathy" with its efforts to license broadcasting stations, hotels, and moving picture theaters, "agencies which we believe to be of distinct value to us in advertising our products." This was rather at odds with the reason for the withdrawal that Waterson had given to Ascap. There can be little doubt that both the lawsuit and the letter, which was read over the air on its member stations, had been ginned up by the NAB.

Tuttle laid out for the committee the gist of his antitrust theory, which stood for many years as the most nuanced analysis of the issue:

> They have the ability to fix the price and they exercise it. They have the ability to punish any recalcitrant member and they exercise it, and they have the ability to say to anybody, "You shall not put out a single piece of copyrighted music unless you buy from us wholesale," and they exercise that. I do not know what are the other indices of illegal monopoly. They are all there.

He implored the committee not to be taken in by the modest fees Ascap had imposed up to that point. "We are in the same position as the mouse who accepts the friendship of the cat's paw," Tuttle said, "there will come a time when playing with us ceases, and mastication begins."

The NAB witnesses were followed by Sydney Cohen speaking on behalf of the motion picture exhibitors. The performance right, he argued, was "now being perverted into a legal blackjack in levying tribute upon the theater owners of the country."

A recess in the hearings gave Burkan just over a week to marshal his forces before it was Ascap's turn. He recalled that during the battles over the mechanical reproduction right much of the hard work of persuading legislators had occurred over friendly libations in the Capitol's "Inner Sanctum." Prohibition now made things a little trickier. Fortuitously, a few months earlier, Ziegfeld Follies lyricist Gene Buck, a colorful showman's showman, had succeeded the staid and stolid George Maxwell as president of Ascap. Burkan asked Buck to put on a show.

More than thirty members of Ascap made the trip to Washington, led of course by Victor Herbert. On the night before the Senate hearings resumed, they gave a concert for three hundred members of both houses of Congress at the National Press Club. Herbert played old Irish airs on the cello, John Philip Sousa told stories, Raymond Hubbell played "Poor Butterfly," and Irving Berlin sang his then-current hits "What'll I Do?" and "Lazy." The highlight of the evening for the mostly older audience was a performance by two of Tin Pan Alley's originals, Charles K. Harris and Harry von Tilzer (who had resigned from the society in 1917, but rejoined in time to share in the first distributions in 1921). The duo had the senators and representatives tearfully singing along with their sentimental ballads from the turn of the century, "After the Ball" and "Wait 'Till the Sun Shines, Nellie." The appearance of these beloved old-timers—long past their productive primes and now living off the residual income that performance rights provided—was a more eloquent response to the portrayals of Ascap as a masticating, predatory beast, a blackjack-wielding thug, than any words that its witnesses could utter in the hearing room the next day. Raymond Hubbell, who attended many congressional hearings over the next thirteen years, believed that the goodwill Ascap won that night at the National Press Club permanently "smothered" such slanders.

The next morning, Ascap's main witnesses—the formidable troika of Buck, Mills, and Burkan—were confident and unapologetic. Speaking with the authority of a man who made his living with his pen only, Buck argued that if the Dill Bill passed, "there are not going to be many song writers in this country, for you are taking away initiative; you are going to take the one thing that makes a fellow sit down day and night and try to concoct a thought and try to create something."

When it was his turn to testify, Mills responded to the NAB's patriotic smarm with withering sarcasm:

We think that radio is the greatest contribution that science has ever made to man, that it will bring about a universal language, that it will make wars impossible, that it will make the farmer happy, and that in general it will render the greatest service to humankind of anything that has ever been conceived.

Ascap's delegation to Senate hearings on the "Dill Free Radio Music Bill," April 1924. Gene Buck is third from right, front row, between Victor Herbert and John Philip Sousa; E. Claude Mills is on far left, second row; Burkan, on Mills's left, seems, as usual, the most careworn of the group. (Courtesy, Ascap)

Songwriters were entitled to wave the flag too, Mills reminded the senators. "One of our men wrote a song called 'Over There,' and to the inspiration of that tune were sold more Liberty Bonds than all the perfervid oratory in the war-time period." Mills was armed with facts and figures about the profitability of the movie and radio industries, eight- and nine-figure numbers that dwarfed Ascap's modest distributions ($56,000 divided among 326 members in the first quarter of 1924). He questioned why songwriters should not have the right to "share fairly and equitably and decently" in the profits that others were reaping from the use of their works.

Burkan gave an impassioned account, riveting in its firsthand detail, of Ascap's origins and the ten years of organized and implacable opposition it had faced, first from cabarets, then movie exhibitors, then radio. "It is a pathetic history," Burkan said. "There was much quibbling, all sorts of delays and technicalities, all sorts of obstructions to deny the right you gave these men." He responded directly to Tuttle's antitrust theory with much the same argument he had made against the movie exhibitors six years earlier: "And why do they call us a monopoly? Because they know the individual composer is helpless. Deprive him of the organized and cooperative rights of his fellow composers, and his rights are nullified."

Tuttle was given an opportunity to rebut Burkan, and at that point things turned ugly. Tuttle lashed out at Burkan for using "police court" tactics, a remark that may have been meaningless to most in the hearing room, but among members of the New York City Bar with memories of the era of Howe & Hummel, it was an unforgivable slur.

Then Tuttle played the New York Jew card. Arguing that Ascap wielded the power to suppress the music of nonmembers, he asked the congressmen to imagine a songwriter, "an American-born and -bred boy whose ancestors dated back several generations in this country," who had written a song "drawn from the depths of his soul." A radio man agrees to broadcast his song, "and there was suddenly opened to him as an audience the whole people of the United States." But our hero's dreams are thwarted by dark forces:

> He saw a chance to take care of his wife and children by making a reputation for himself, and they were all ready to hear that song go out on the air that night. But, lo and behold, from Forty-fifth Street in New York City there goes out the long warning finger: You do not play that man's independent music.

An undercurrent of anti-Semitism can be found in many anti-Ascap screeds of the era. Only three years earlier, Henry Ford's *Dearborn Independent* had excoriated "the moron music of the Yiddish popular song trust" for "spreading degenerate ideas." Sydney Cohen, who ought to have known better, accused Ascap of using "Shylock tactics." In invoking the stereotype of the long-fingered, puppet-master Jew, Tuttle was trafficking in a not uncommon form of bigotry.

Neither the Senate nor the House committee reported out a music copyright bill in the 68th Congress. The momentum that the NAB had gathered by the start of the hearings dissipated for a number of reasons, the expert stagecraft of Ascap's counterattack being only one.

The law of legislative inertia was working in Ascap's favor. Congress was loath to take any action while there were proceedings pending before the other branches that might render the question moot. The Department of Justice still had an open investigation. "If we are an illegal combination, then the Department of Justice can easily ascertain that fact and put us out of business very quickly," Burkan told the House committee. "It is one of the functions of the Department of Justice to squelch monopolies." In this regard, Tuttle's decision to file a private antitrust action on behalf of Henry Waterson ("the Judas Iscariot of the music business," Gene Buck called him) probably backfired, because it gave Congress another reason not to act.

While the hearings were in progress, a federal court in Cincinnati had ruled in the Crosley Radio case that a performance rendered in a broadcasting studio and transmitted to the public over the airwaves did not qualify as a public performance. "In order to constitute a public performance in the sense in which we think Congress intended the words, it is absolutely essential that there be an assemblage of persons—an audience congregated for the purpose of hearing that which transpires at the place of amusement." It was a surprising win for the broadcasters. But with Ascap promising an appeal, it seemed likely the Supreme Court would eventually be weighing in on the issue. All the more reason for Congress to stay its hand.

Burkan and Ascap had succeeded in preserving the status quo, but a few weeks after the hearings concluded they suffered a devastating blow on another front. On May 26, 1924, after lunching for the last time at the Lambs Club, bantering with friends over his favorite dish of Irish bacon and eggs, Victor Herbert collapsed while climbing the stairs of his doctor's home, dead of a ruptured aorta at the age of sixty-five. Although he had been in creative decline for several years, at his death it could still reasonably be said that "the whole country was whistling, singing, and dancing to his tunes."

In his merger of elements of nineteenth-century European operetta with American burlesque and vaudeville, Herbert had forged a crucial link in the evolution of the twentieth-century musical comedy. But time was overtaking him even as he cranked out his final score for the *Ziegfeld Follies of 1924*. Few of Herbert's songs can be classified as standards, and his theatrical works are rarely revived today. The librettos, bemusing even to the original audiences, have only grown hoarier with age. His Cello Concerto No. 2 receives an occasional performance, but otherwise his concert works have disappeared from the repertory.

Herbert's reputation today rests in large part on his nonmusical legacy—his tireless advocacy of the rights of songwriters, side by side with the much younger man he anointed to lead the crusade, Nathan Burkan. Speaking, at the 1927 unveiling of a bust of Victor Herbert that stands near the Central Park bandshell—a gift to New York City from

Ascap—then-Mayor James J. Walker offered a fitting epitaph: "Herbert would have been a great man even without his music."

It did not take long for Eugene McDonald's prophecy that advertising would be radio's death knell to be proven wrong. By 1925, many stations were very profitably selling time to advertisers, using a "toll" broadcasting model in which advertisers bought blocks of time to present sponsored programming that they produced. So novel was the concept, Burkan's description of it for the court in the Waterson antitrust suit had to be clinically precise: "The radio broadcaster renders entertainments varied unexpectedly from time to time with talks on where and when to buy commodities and commending such commodities. This advertising is paid for, yet those who listen do so mainly in expectation of more entertainment to follow."

With the arrival of sponsored programming, a direct source of profit for broadcasters, Claude Mills declared that, as far as Ascap was concerned, radio's "experimental period" was over. The society was further emboldened when a federal appeals court in Ohio reversed the adverse ruling in the Crosley Radio case, holding that a performance "is no less public because the listeners are unable to communicate with one another, or are not assembled within an enclosure, or gathered together in some open stadium or park or other public place." The court could not ignore the fundamental fact that "radio broadcasting is intended to, and in fact does, reach a very much larger number of the public at the moment of the rendition than any other medium of performance." A broadcast performance is public even if it is mostly enjoyed in private.

Ascap sent out license renewals that doubled or tripled broadcasters' base licensing fees, with additional charges of $20 for every hour of sponsored programming. For the larger stations, it meant an increase from a few hundred dollars a year to as much as a few hundred dollars a day.

After the Supreme Court declined to review the Crosley Radio case, the broadcasters returned to Congress with a new tack. Copyright owners, they now conceded, should receive compensation for broadcast performances of their music, but the logical way to provide it would be to extend the compulsory mechanical licensing provisions of the 1909 Copyright Act by analogy, requiring copyright holders to offer licenses to broadcasters at royalty rates set by Congress. Senator Dill dutifully introduced a bill to implement this new approach, explaining that "a wise man changes his mind, and the man who does not change his mind has no mind to change. I think the whole situation has changed in the radio world." In April 1926, a by now familiar cast of characters from Ascap and the NAB reconvened for joint Senate-House committee hearings on the new Dill Bill.

The draft bill had a blank space where the royalty rate per song would go. A much humbler Charles Tuttle told the committees, "we are here in the position of persons who wish to tender to an impartial body representing the public a blank check." But Ascap would not be baited into a public negotiation of a fixed royalty rate. Claude Mills, never one to mince words, scoffed that Tuttle's blank check was drawn against "the Bank of Bunk."

The 1909 mechanical reproduction compromise that created the compulsory license, with its stingy two-cents-per-song royalty established by Congress, had long rankled Burkan, who regretted having acquiesced in it. "I am ashamed of it and ashamed of having had anything to do with it," he confessed to Congress on another occasion. In the years since its enactment, he had handled numerous cases arising from nonpayment of the royalty by record and piano roll makers. "Our bitter experience with crooked, irresponsible, and 'fly-by-night' phonograph record and roll manufacturers," Burkan told the committees during the 1926 hearings, "has made us sadder but wiser men."

Burkan attacked the proposed legislation with a full-throated appeal to economic populism, challenging the broadcasters to produce their books and records for inspection:

> You are going to be staggered at the profits this industry has made in the last year. They have taken in $600,000,000 directly and indirectly from the operation of radio. They say that 90 percent is due to what we have created; all they have paid us is $113,000, and they begrudge us even that amount.

The NAB stations had, once again, broadcast appeals to the public, asking them to write their congressmen in support of the new Dill Bill, lest they risk losing the free entertainment they had come to expect. Again Congress was deluged with letters. Pointing out that Ascap had been refused time to make a rebuttal, even though it had offered to pay the broadcasters their established rates for advertising, Burkan put a chilling spin on the NAB's propaganda campaign:

> Assume for a minute that the right to use the mails of America were to be put in the hands of one group for the purpose of fostering and promoting legislation, what do you suppose that group could do? Don't you suppose they

could undermine the Constitution? They could overthrow the Government. They could make, seat and unseat men. And isn't it high time for Congress to do something to take away from these men an instrument that they are not competent to handle?

Looking directly at Senator Dill, Burkan warned: "While today they are supporting your bill, tomorrow they may oppose your candidacy, and you will have no way of retaliating."

"Radio in Show Business" was *Variety*'s front-page banner headline on November 10, 1926. David Sarnoff's Radio Corporation of America was preparing to launch the first nationwide radio hook-ups, the National Broadcasting Company's "Red" and "Blue" networks, with top-drawer professional talent and advertising revenues conservatively projected to be $15 million in the first year. There was no longer any question who was going to pay the bills for broadcasting. For NBC, a few thousand dollars per station for access to the whole of the Ascap repertoire was an acceptable cost of doing business. It made little sense, after all, for sponsors like Eveready Batteries to shell out $100 per minute to put Eddie Cantor on the air if he couldn't sing his hits "If You Knew Susie" or "Makin' Whoopee!"

The 69th Congress took no action on the Dill compulsory licensing bill. Just a few weeks before NBC's premiere, Senator Dill publicly expressed his hope that the NAB and Ascap would negotiate a resolution that would obviate the need for legislation. Over the next five years, broadcasters hashed out their differences with Ascap privately, one license at a time; by 1931, Ascap was collecting nearly $1 million per year from radio.

Nineteen twenty-six was a banner year for Ascap all around. The tide of resistance from movie exhibitors finally began to ebb. Waterson, Berlin & Snyder abandoned its private antitrust suit and rejoined the society. For several years, Burkan had been giving the agent conducting the Justice Department's antitrust investigation, John A. Brann, unfettered access to Ascap personnel and documents. Brann's report to Director Hoover debunked, point by point, every charge of overreaching, extortion, and perjury that had been leveled against the society. Brann lavished praise upon Ascap's unpaid officers, concluding they were "actuated solely by a desire to help the underdog, the little fellow." Shortly thereafter, Brann retired from the government and became the head of Ascap's radio division, one of the first of many government overseers of the music industry to pass through the revolving door to a more lucrative post on the inside.

The federal antitrust investigation was closed in July 1926, when Assistant Attorney General William Donovan approved a finding that licensing intangible rights to put on musical performances which were "entirely local in character" did not touch on interstate "trade or commerce," and therefore was not subject to federal antitrust scrutiny. Donovan noted that licensing to broadcasters might stand on a different footing than licensing to theaters, hotels, and dance halls, but he deferred that issue to another day. (That day would come when a Democratic administration took over the government in 1933.)

Five years of relative peace allowed Ascap to lower its overhead from 65 percent to below 25 percent of revenues and to increase its annual distribution of income to members from about $320,000 in 1925 to over $1.3 million in 1931, with the largest writers' shares quadrupling from $1,300 to $5,200 ($85,000 in 2020 dollars). It was during those years that a new generation of composers, including Harold Arlen, Cole Porter, Hoagy Carmichael, and Richard Rodgers, received their first Ascap distributions. Ascap relocated its offices to the newly constructed Paramount Building on Times Square, taking the entire twenty-fifth floor. Ironically, the Paramount was built on the former site of Shanley's Restaurant, which Prohibition had bankrupted in 1923.

Performing rights were now well on their way to becoming the popular songwriter's most important source of income. The music publishers of Tin Pan Alley were no longer popular music's unchallenged gatekeepers. Soon they would be relegated to being, as one of them, Edward B. Marks, put it, merely "a kind of authors' agents, placing the product and collecting for its use."

Ascap's success revolutionized not only the business of popular music, it sparked a revolution in popular music itself. The standards of the Great American Songbook are products of this new business paradigm. Songwriters were no longer subsistence pieceworkers prized solely for their conformity to established rules, or for their ability to crank out knockoffs of the latest hit or to cater to the latest dance craze. The rising generation of songwriters was writing first and foremost for the professional performer, not the home musician. They were artists, free to make demands on the public, instead of kowtowing to its established preferences.

With its institutional future reasonably secure for the first time, Ascap and its general counsel could turn their energies to the next big thing, a development that would destroy the last remnants of Tin Pan Alley as the entertainment world had long known it. It was "along about this time," Hubbell writes, "that we began to hear about a thing called 'talking pictures.'"

PART FIVE

Chief Justice of Celluloidia

CHAPTER 16

The Silent Screen

After nearly two decades practicing law in Manhattan's downtown financial, political, and judicial center, in 1919 Burkan moved his office to the Times Square neighborhood where all phases of New York's entertainment industry had become firmly ensconced. The Hotel Astor on Broadway at 44th Street, a popular gathering place for show people, replaced Lüchow's as the hub of Burkan's professional life. (Although August Lüchow, when he died in 1923, left his "friend and legal advisor" a bequest worth $2 million in 2020 dollars.) The Witmark publishing house, the offices of Ascap, the Lambs Club, and the headquarters of United Artists were all short strolls from Burkan's new office at 1451 Broadway. Burkan was, as *Variety* observed, taking part in a general uptown migration of the theatrical bar. Although their show business clients "would as soon (and did formerly) travel downtown to their former Park Row or Broadway locations, they have had to defer to the fact that the inconvenience of being removed even that little ten minutes' subway distance from the Main Alley was detrimental mutually."

Burkan's mother died in February 1919, a late casualty of the Spanish flu pandemic. His younger brothers Benjamin and David went off on their own. Burkan, at age forty, was living a gentleman bachelor's life in a bay-windowed apartment on Central Park North with only his valet, Hideyeshi Nagayama. He stabled a horse in the park and rose every day at 5 A.M. to ride. Burkan's social life was a constant swirl of political, business, and charitable banquets, with no known romantic attachments.

Burkan's services were by then as widely sought in the movie business as in the music world. *Photoplay* dubbed him the "Chief Justice of Celluloidia." As it explained: "If there is any lawyer in the theatrical or photoplay business who has ever occupied so unique a position as Nathan Burkan, we'd like to know it." His roster of clients included, in addition to the Chaplin brothers, many other major figures of the silent era: actors Theda Bara, Mae Murray, and Thomas Meighan; directors Thomas Ince, King Vidor, Cecil B. DeMille, and Henry King; producers Samuel Goldwyn and William Randolph Hearst—among dozens of others.

Of the motion picture matters Burkan was handling at the outset of the Jazz Age, only one could compete with the saga of Charlie Chaplin and *The Kid* for the general public's attention: the case of Jewel Carmen versus the William Fox Film Corporation.

Jewel Carmen, a winsome blonde, played the ingenue in four Douglas Fairbanks movies produced by the Triangle Film Corporation in 1916, for which she was paid $50 a week. William Fox, who had just begun to produce films on the West Coast, offered the nineteen-year-old a one-year contract at $100 per week. The contract identified Jewel as a minor and was signed on her behalf by her mother. In July 1917, Jewel was called into the production manager's office at Fox's Hollywood studio and given a contract extension to sign. The terms were one-sided. For an additional $25 per week, the contract gave Fox a series of options to extend Jewel's services, six months at a time, for four years. Her salary would escalate with each extension but topped out at $250. Some dates were left blank. Jewel signed the document on her own behalf in Hollywood. (Fox's lawyers had advised that, under California law, the age of majority was eighteen.) Several weeks later, at the company's New York office, Jewel picked up a copy of the contract, which had the blanks filled in and was countersigned by William Fox.

Fox was grooming Jewel Carmen for stardom. The Fox publicity apparatus arranged fan magazine photospreads, gave her a tagline—"the girl who photographs like a million dollars"—and concocted a myth that she had been discovered at a soda fountain by a director who was impressed by how she "ate a plate of ice cream so toothsomely." Up to that point, Fox had been known for featuring actresses of the dark seductress type, like Theda Bara, for whom the term "vamp" was first popularized. Jewel, in contrast, was dainty and fair. Louella Parsons described her as Fox's Snow White, "a lily as it were in a bed of flaming poppies."

Jewel came to believe that Fox was taking advantage of her. "I was underpaid and by virtue of my experience and ability as a screen actress, I was entitled to the advantages, privileges, and courtesies usually enjoyed by star screen actresses, none of which were accorded me." In March 1918, Jewel entered into a two-year contract with Frank A. Keeney, a vaudeville producer who was just then entering the picture business, at a salary to start at $450 per week and rise to $550. Under New York law, which Jewel's lawyer believed governed her agreement with Fox, she would have the option to disavow any contracts she made before the age of twenty-one. On July 15, 1918, the first Monday after her twenty-first birthday, Jewel notified Fox that she was voiding her contract. Frank Keeney announced that he would be releasing eight "big pretentious" Jewel Carmen pictures over the next year.

William Fox, "a fighter by nature and a paranoid by experience," as described by film historian Neal Gabler, was determined to make of Jewel an object lesson for any other star who might even think of contract jumping. Although his lawyers argued that Jewel's contract was governed by California law and therefore not voidable by her, the outcome of a suit against her for breach, hinging on a close "choice of law" question, would have been uncertain at best. So instead of suing Jewel, Fox played a bank shot. He threatened to sue Keeney to enjoin the release of any picture starring Jewel, but at the same time offered to indemnify Keeney for any liability he might incur from repudiating his contract with Jewel. Keeney decided he could not take the risk of investing large sums in a Jewel Carmen picture only to have it get tied up in litigation. Jewel found herself out of work and effectively blacklisted in the industry.

Burkan was the obvious choice to represent Jewel in her dispute with Fox. The Fox studio was barely three years old, but Burkan had already faced off against it in several cases. He knew that William Fox was not one to back down from a fight and that the battle would be long and drawn out. He probably did not, however, foresee it lasting nine years.

In October 1918, Burkan filed an action in federal court seeking a declaration that Jewel's contract with Fox was void, an injunction preventing Fox from further "interfering or intermeddling" with her livelihood as a motion picture actress, and damages for inducing Keeney to breach Jewel's contract. Burkan immediately moved for a preliminary injunction to protect Jewel while the case was pending.

The judges of the federal district court in Manhattan seemed to understand the power dynamics of the situation. They came down firmly on Jewel's side. In granting the motion for preliminary injunction in December 1918, one judge observed that "if the defendants believe themselves to have been the victims of a contract jumper, their remedy lies in the courts and not in harassing the plaintiff by threatening suits that are not brought, by indemnification agreements, nor even by the teaching of lessons to recalcitrant stars." After a short bench trial in June 1919, a second judge decided all issues in Jewel's favor, made the injunction against interference permanent, declared the Fox contract void, and awarded Jewel $43,500 in damages, the full value of her contract with Keeney.

Jewel was just beginning to resume her career when Fox's appeal was heard in November 1920. Fox's lawyers now framed the case not as a technical choice between New York and California law, but as a morality play in which Jewel was a fraudster who had abused her presumed status as a minor "to place herself on the auction block, make as many contracts as she could, and break all except that of the highest bidder." The court of appeals adopted that view of the matter. Even if Jewel was within her legal rights in rescinding her contract with Fox, the court found it morally reprehensible: "Her action in repudiating her pledged word was misconduct of which no person of honor and conscience would have been guilty. That no action could be brought against her at law because of what she did does not alter the moral character of her act."

The court of appeals reversed the lower court's ruling on the basis of the somewhat arcane distinction between "law" and "equity." Because Jewel was seeking forms of relief, an injunction and a declaration of her legal rights, which are considered "equitable" in nature, the court of appeals believed it was not bound to apply the law strictly, if that would result in an injustice. "One who comes into equity," the court said, invoking a maxim dating from medieval times, "must come with clean hands, and her hands are not clean." The court's righteous umbrage and hectoring tone are difficult to understand as the product of anything other than reflexive misogyny and a prudish revulsion for Jewel's chosen profession.

Even Fox's attorneys, however, conceded that Jewel was not without further recourse. The court had ruled that she was not entitled to relief from a court of equity, but she could still sue Fox in an action "at law" for damages for wrongful interference with her contract with Keeney and be entitled to a trial by jury. In June 1921, Burkan instituted such a case in the New York state court. During the four years that would pass before that case came to trial, Jewel Carmen's career was back in limbo.

Copyright law does not protect titles, but in the movie industry they are coin of the realm. Burkan had pioneered the use of the common law of unfair competition to protect titles when he represented Richard Outcault, the creator of the *Buster Brown* comic strip, in a suit to enjoin a theatrical production from using that title. If it could be shown that the public had come to associate a distinctive title with a particular work, the court held, it would enjoin others from using that or a confusingly similar title, essentially treating the title as a trademark. Burkan employed that standard on behalf of some early film producers to prevent their competitors from using such unremarkable titles as *The Rosary* and *The Come-Back*, even on films that bore no other similarity to the originals whatsoever.

In the spring of 1922, Sam Goldwyn was preparing to release a film based on William Gillette's well-known stage play *Sherlock Holmes*, starring John Barrymore. First produced in New York in 1899, with Gillette in the title role, the play used only three main characters— Holmes, Watson, and Moriarty—and one incident found in Sir Arthur Conan Doyle's stories; it was otherwise Gillette's original creation. It had been tremendously successful, with frequent revivals and tours.

Preceding Goldwyn's *Sherlock Holmes* into theaters by several months was a British-produced serial, consisting of fifteen two-reel shorts, each one faithfully dramatizing a single Conan Doyle story and bearing the title of that story, such as "The Red-Headed League" or "The Priory School." Goldwyn asked Burkan to stop the American distributor of the serial from advertising it under the umbrella title *The Adventures of Sherlock Holmes*. Although movie title litigation was by then something of a cottage industry in Burkan's office, which was well equipped to seek judicial action on an expedited basis in such matters, this case had some obvious weaknesses. Burkan did not rush it into court. Instead, he took it to Will Hays's office.

If Burkan was the chief justice of celluloidia, Will Hays was the czar. When the major studios organized the Motion Picture Producers and Distributors Association early in 1922, they chose Hays, President Warren G. Harding's highly efficient postmaster general and political savant, to lead it. His broad charge included rehabilitating the industry's public image in the wake of a spate of scandals (most notably the infamous Fatty Arbuckle manslaughter case), fighting the encroachment of government regulation, and mediating intra-industry disputes. Burkan thought that Hays, brand new to the picture business and an employee of the major studios, would instinctively side with a big-budget domestic production over a cheap import and bring some of the moral suasion he was known for to bear on the matter.

The Saturday morning meeting did not go well. Hays proved to be less partisan and less forceful than Burkan had hoped. Hays would eventually turn his organization into an efficient out-of-court dispute-resolution apparatus, but in May 1922 he was still too green to put his foot down. Fresh from a career in Indiana Republican politics, Hays probably had no idea who Burkan was. If the legal precedents Burkan was citing, and boasting of having established, were so strong, Hays suggested, he ought simply to lay them out to his opponent, who would surely want to do what the law required.

Burkan filed suit shortly thereafter. In support of a motion for preliminary injunction, he submitted affidavits from a who's who of the era's theatrical producers—Lee Shubert, Abraham Erlanger, A. H. Woods—each attesting that Gillette's play "is one of the great landmarks of the American theater and has a popularity and celebrity unique in the annals of the stage." The public, accordingly, would associate the words "Sherlock Holmes" uniquely with it.

The court was not persuaded. *Sherlock Holmes* the play was no *Hamlet.* Sherlock Holmes the name was associated principally with the Arthur Conan Doyle character (it had already entered the language in such phrases as "you're a regular Sherlock Holmes") and not with any particular dramatization of the stories. Nor was it likely anyone interested in seeing a feature-movie adaptation of the famous Gillette play would be confused by a two-reeler bearing the title of a single Conan Doyle story.

His trademark theory thus rejected, Burkan turned to an alternative argument based on contract. Goldwyn, who had purchased the film rights to *Sherlock Holmes* from Gillette and Charles Frohman, the original Broadway producer of the play, claimed that Conan Doyle had granted them an *exclusive* dramatization right. Gillette so testified but had no documentation to prove his exclusivity. Charles Frohman was not available to testify—he had died in the sinking of the *Lusitania* in 1915. Burkan had one last card to play. Sir Arthur Conan Doyle was in New York to give lectures on spiritualism at Carnegie Hall. On April 12, 1923, Burkan went to the author's suite at the Biltmore Hotel to take his deposition.

He found Sir Arthur in an expansive mood and genuinely desirous of being helpful. Conan Doyle had been very happy to be receiving his royalties on Gillette's play over the years and was most pleased and pleasantly surprised to receive a $6,000 check for his share of what Goldwyn had paid for the film rights. But his testimony destroyed Burkan's case.

It all began, Conan Doyle explained, when Gillette and Frohman had paid him a visit at his home in England in 1898:

> It was chatty. We were smoking, having a cup of coffee and talking. It wasn't a formal matter at all. Frohman started out as a general proposition that "Sherlock Holmes" might be a popular feature on the stage and that Gillette said he thought he could throw it into shape which would suit him as an actor, and I, on my part, said I would be delighted if he could do so—that I couldn't do it myself. That was about the gist of it.

Conan Doyle gave Gillette artistic carte blanche. When Gillette sent him a cable asking if he could give Holmes a love interest, Conan Doyle cabled back: "You can marry him, murder him, or do what you like with him." Conan Doyle was aware that many of his readers thought Sherlock Holmes was real, but despite his own belief in sprites and fairies, he was not interested in indulging their fantasies.

At some point, Conan Doyle recalled, an arrangement where he, Frohman, and Gillette would be equal partners in the dramatization was spelled out in correspondence. But Sir Arthur couldn't provide copies. His agent at the time "committed suicide under very painful circumstances. His letters and papers were found scattered all about." Then Conan Doyle was asked flat out: "So far as you can recall, in your talk with Frohman and Gillette, was the word 'exclusive right' or any similar word used?"

"No, the question of exclusion did not come at all," he answered emphatically. "The proof of that is I did dramatize 'The Speckled Band,' and Mr. Gillette had no grievance at all." Conan Doyle believed that Gillette was justified in his position that the words "Sherlock Holmes" standing alone had come to be associated exclusively with his play, but the British producer of the serial was entitled to use the longer "The Adventures of Sherlock Holmes."

Burkan persuaded Goldwyn to drop the case and to pay court costs to his opponents.

As 1922 was ending, Charlie Chaplin had still not completed his obligations under the eighteen-month, eight-picture contract he had signed with First National back in June 1917, nor had he even begun working off his nine-pictures-in-three-years commitment to United Artists, signed in February 1919. But "the Chief," as studio manager Alf Reeves called Charlie, had an idea.

He was finishing work at the Chaplin Studio on an excellent four-reel comedy called *The Pilgrim*. He would offer it to First National in lieu of the final two-reeler he owed them, provided that First National would agree to special terms. Chaplin asked for an additional $400,000 in advance against a favorable split of the profits, comparable to the deal they had struck on *The Kid* two years earlier. Otherwise, Chaplin would deliver *The Pilgrim* to United Artists and give First National a dashed-off two-reeler, *The Professor*, in accordance with the terms of the original 1917 contract. *The Professor* was a project that Chaplin had abandoned several years earlier, after filming only one scene, which he now padded with outtakes from *Shoulder Arms* and *Sunnyside*. "Before delivery of either," Reeves wrote in a note to Syd Chaplin summarizing the plan, "Mr. Burkan and yourself will see that they sign full release of Chief of all his contractual obligations."

Burkan had found his previous negotiations with First National on Chaplin's behalf arduous. With so much accumulated ill will, implementing the Chief's plan would not be easy. He obtained a counterproposal from First National. "Cannot entertain proposition," Chaplin cabled back. He agreed to a few minor concessions but otherwise insisted "contract must be the same as my last feature . . . These are my final terms." Burkan came back with another counter from First National. "Proposition ridiculous," Chaplin responded. At Chaplin's suggestion, a First National executive went out to Hollywood to screen *The Pilgrim*, but he "failed to offer suitable conditions for production of special four-reel feature," an angry Chaplin reported back to Burkan. He instructed Burkan to "deliver two-reeler *Professor* in accordance with contract."

Burkan stalled and somehow kept the lines of communication open, and early in 1923 a deal was struck for *The Pilgrim*, on terms falling well short of Chaplin's original demand but including the crucial acknowledgment that he had "fully and faithfully performed each and every term" of his First National contract. (*The Professor* never saw the light of day.) Chaplin was finally free to begin working for United Artists.

It was not a moment too soon. Chaplin's partners—Pickford, Fairbanks, and Griffith—were learning that independence had its drawbacks. UA, unlike Paramount or First National, could not provide capital to finance their productions, which slowed down their output. And

The first annual meeting of the United Artists Corporation, April 1919. From left to right: Dennis F. O'Brien, Hiram Abrams, Albert H. T. Banzhaf, Mary Pickford, W. G. McAdoo, Syd Chaplin, D. W. Griffith, Douglas Fairbanks, Oscar A. Price, John Fairbanks, and Nathan Burkan. (Mary Pickford Papers, Margaret Herrick Library, Academy of Motion Picture Arts and Sciences)

with no films at all in the pipeline from Chaplin, the company simply could not earn enough to meet its overhead. As its deficits mounted, UA was forced to look to outsiders for content, forming various subsidiaries so that the prestige of the "United Artists" name would not be tarnished by product that did not measure up to the standards of the Big Four.

Chaplin wasn't pulling his weight during UA's troubled infancy, yet he had no compunction about weighing in on any proposals to rescue the foundering company that he considered to be inconsistent with its noble purpose. It was a difficult position for Burkan, his proxy on the board of directors, who once complained to a reporter "Funny, I have to read the papers to learn what's going on" with UA. Early in 1923, Pickford and Fairbanks devised a plan to set up a subsidiary, Associated Authors, as a production company for three well-known screenwriters, which would release its films through UA. To provide financing, the bank required personal guarantees from the shareholders. When Chaplin balked at participating, Burkan stepped up to sign the papers himself.

When the venture folded after just three pictures, Burkan only narrowly escaped personal liability for a share of the resulting loss.

Chaplin's first release for UA did not do anything to endear himself to his partners or to alleviate the company's financial woes. In the four years since he had signed his UA contract, he had lost interest in making two-reel comedies. *A Woman of Paris* was a full-length drama, a star vehicle for Edna Purviance in which Chaplin did not even appear, much less provide the star presence the company had been counting on. By early 1924, the dissolution of UA seemed imminent. Sharks were circling the waters. Chaplin had a new comedy feature in the works, *The Gold Rush,* but it was clear that UA was never going to get the kind of productivity from him that its original projections had assumed. D. W. Griffith was withdrawing from the company altogether. To save UA, Pickford and Fairbanks proposed to bring in another star of their magnitude, actress Norma Talmadge, and equally if not more importantly, her husband, the producer Joseph Schenck. Schenck had the connections and business reputation needed to attract significant new financing, new producers, and new stars to the company.

The parties worked out the broad outlines of a reorganization plan in a series of meetings at the Pickford-Fairbanks Studio in Hollywood during late October 1924. The fly in the ointment was Chaplin. "Charlie Chaplin has not entered into the spirit of the merger with any great enthusiasm," one of the trade papers reported, "and it is said he held up negotiations for days to see where he figures in the deal." He argued that UA "should be a closed corporation without taking in either outside money or other film stars." Chaplin would not commit to anything until Burkan, who was tied down in New York until election day, could get to the West Coast. (Having served two weeks during the preceding summer as a delegate to the Democratic National Convention, which went to 103 ballots, and himself appearing on the November ballot as a presidential elector, Burkan was determined to see the campaign of fellow New York attorney John W. Davis through to its conclusion.) When Burkan arrived in Los Angeles for what the press had been led to believe would be the ironing out of a few details and a signing ceremony, things "did not pass with the smoothness and precision anticipated . . . there are those on the 'inside' who claim that it is simply a matter of a toss of the coin whether the project will culminate in a fizzle."

The agreement that was signed on November 22, 1924, included many concessions to Chaplin. Schenck was named chairman of the board and given authority to bring in outside money and content, but subject to limitations that preserved UA's independence and cachet. (Schenck's first two acquisitions were old Chaplin friends, Gloria Swanson and Sam Goldwyn.) Chaplin was relieved of his original obligation to contribute nine two-reelers. He now committed to deliver five feature-length pictures by the beginning of 1929, a rate of one per year. He was given the option to withdraw his future pictures from foreign distribution by UA if in his "sole and absolute judgment" foreign receipts for *The Gold Rush* were not satisfactory. It is a testament to Chaplin's unique prestige and to Burkan's diplomacy that so negligible a contributor to UA's bottom line, one deeply in default on his obligations to his partners, could still exercise so much sway.

Chaplin delivered only two pictures to UA by 1929, *The Gold Rush* and *The Circus,* and a third, *City Lights,* not until 1932. All were gems, giving him more than enough currency to maintain his self-appointed role as the conscience of United Artists, the keeper of the spirit of 1919. When Schenck, late in 1925, attempted to merge UA with Metro-Goldwyn-Mayer, where his brother Nicholas was a top executive, it was Chaplin who scotched the deal. Although some suspected that his old grudge against Louis B. Mayer was really the issue, Chaplin complained loudly in the press that he did not want to be associated with a "trust" that would foist inferior product on exhibitors. As if on cue, UA was deluged with telegrams from exhibitors opposing the merger on the same grounds, forcing the Schencks to abandon the deal. It was later rumored that the bulk of the protest letters came from members of the New York Theater Owners Chamber of Commerce, where Nathan Burkan was general counsel.

Jewel Carmen's state court action for damages against the Fox Film Corporation came to trial in April 1925, seven years after the events at issue. Burkan had already obtained several significant pretrial legal rulings in her favor. Most importantly, New York law, under which the age of majority was twenty-one, would apply. The studio would not be permitted to defend on the ground that it believed in good faith, albeit erroneously, that its contract with Jewel was governed by California law and therefore valid. If Jewel could prove she was under the age of twenty-one when she signed her 1917 Fox contract—that her date of birth was, as she claimed, July 13, 1897— and that Fox had in fact induced Frank Keeney to repudiate his contract with Jewel, she would prevail. Unfortunately, by this time Fox had unearthed some problematic information from Jewel's past. It turns out this was not the first time that her age was the central issue in a court proceeding.

Jewel was born Florence Lavina Quick, in Tillamook County, Oregon, "near the post office in Blaine." Her father, Amos, an itinerant carpenter, and mother, Minerva, were barely literate. Minerva gave birth to Florence, whom the family called "Vina," at home, with a neighbor serving as midwife. Tillamook County did not begin keeping birth records until 1905.

Minerva left her husband and moved to Los Angeles with Vina and three of her other eight children in 1911. Vina almost immediately began supporting the family with motion picture and other work, using the name Evelyn Quick and casually lying about her age to get jobs.

In April 1913, Vina was arrested for prostitution. She claimed that she was under sixteen, which would make her not a prostitute, but a victim of statutory rape. A prominent local auto dealer was charged with contributing to the "dependency" of a minor. In response to a defense subpoena for records of her daughter's birth, Minerva produced a family Bible in which Amos had written, in ink on the flyleaf, the birthdates of the eight Quick children, including an entry "Lavina Vina Quick borned [sic] July 13, 1897." The "7," however, was written in pencil, superimposed over a "5" written in the original ink. If 1895 was the correct year of her birth, then Vina was over sixteen, the age of consent, when she transacted with the auto dealer in 1913, and she was over twenty-one, the age of majority, when she signed her contract with Fox in 1917.

The auto dealer's trial ended in a hung jury, with two jurors reportedly holding out against conviction because they disbelieved the complaining witness's claim to having been underage. After an interval of a few years, the actress known as Evelyn Quick reemerged in the movie business as Jewel Carmen.

The Quick family Bible had disappeared long before 1925, but much of the four-day jury trial was devoted to Fox's efforts to use testimony about the long-lost book to once again discredit Jewel's claimed birthdate. Transcripts from the auto dealer's trial were read, participants in that trial, including the judge, testified, and Jewel and her parents were cross-examined at length. The testimony of Amos and Minerva—who were unable to remember anything, or state anything positively, other than the 1897 date of Vina's birth—was maddeningly obtuse. How was it, Amos was asked, that of his eight children, it was only Vina's year of birth he remembered without referring to the Bible?

> "Well the only way I know is incidents happen that I know of. Florence Lavina; I was in California at that time. I remember that."
>
> "Could it have been 1898 or 1896 or 1895?"
>
> "Could have been, but it wasn't."
>
> "How is that year 1897 fixed in your mind so firmly?"
>
> "Because I was in California at that time."

Burkan objected repeatedly to all references to the family Bible, but to no avail. The presiding judge, John M. Tierney, was intensely interested in hearing about it. As his later charge to the jury showed, Justice Tierney harbored a nostalgic fascination with the American frontier and the pioneer spirit:

> Now gentlemen, the parents of this plaintiff were wanderers over the United States of America in its western parts. They were typical of the people who blazed the trail of civilization across the plains of the American continent. opening up sources of wealth for those who followed them. . . .
>
> When the children of these pathfinders were born, they had not the advantage of luxurious lying in hospitals, or skilled physicians in their accouchements, but in their travail had only the kindly and sympathetic aid of their women neighbors. . . .
>
> Their records were crudely made and not with meticulous care like is done in our hospitals when they have the benefit of those skilled to help women bring into the world children, which is the function of every good woman.

Justice Tierney also had trouble hiding his distaste for William Fox. Burkan's cross-examination of Fox exposed numerous inconsistencies in Fox's testimony and established that Fox had misled Keeney about the facts surrounding the signing of Jewel's contract. Burkan, by this time in his career, had developed a reputation as a fierce and relentless cross-examiner. Fox, however, seemed entirely unperturbed, never losing his supercilious smirk. The damage Fox was doing to his own case might have been lost on the jurors, so unflappable was his demeanor. The judge stepped in:

> *The Court.* This amuses you?
>
> *Fox.* It does not, your Honor, I am trying to be as truthful as I know how.
>
> *The Court.* But you smile so frequently, I wonder whether it is a matter of amusement to you.

Counsel. I object to that remark on the part of your Honor.

The Court. This witness had twice testified to failure of memory, and his attitude, Counselor, and smiling over a situation like this, incites my wonder to ascertain whether or not he regards it as a serious matter.

Burkan's closing argument was not transcribed. It could hardly have been more grandiloquent or persuasive than were Justice Tierney's instructions to the jury, which all but directed a verdict for Jewel:

Bring to your minds this whole situation. This plaintiff coming as a child from the plains of Oregon after her father had disappeared from the view of his family—this miner, who was going about perhaps seeking to get wealth out of the soil and disappointed in every one of his wanderings. [Amos, the reader may recall, was a carpenter.]

This girl got to California and engaged in the occupation, if it may be called that, of portraying scenes in moving pictures. . . . Would she repudiate contracts with corporations like those owned by Fox if she were in fact 21 years old or over, thus incurring the animosity of this influential man? . . .

I am not asking you to accept this as my conclusion. I am drawing a picture for your view.

The jury returned a verdict for the full amount of the Keeney contract plus seven years' interest, for a total of nearly $60,000. Another two years passed before Fox's appeals were exhausted. "Who says lawyers are heartless?" *Film Daily* asked when it was over. "Nathan Burkan represented Jewel Carmen in her suit against Fox without compensation, and the case has been dragging since 1917." If Burkan had taken a fee, he would, in all fairness, have had to share it with Justice Tierney.

Jewel made only one more movie before retiring from the screen at the age of thirty. William Fox remained Burkan's loyal foe, one of the few permanent enemies Burkan ever made.

Shortly after the Jewel Carmen trial, Burkan left for his now-annual summer trip in Europe, where, it was reported, he would "take the cure" at Karlsbad. A stress-filled work life, several nights a week gorging on catered banquets, and a fondness for Hamburger à la Lüchow (beef and veal kidney fat), with Bavarian weinkraut, were catching up with Burkan at the age of forty-six.

CHAPTER 17

The Jazz Singer

The RMS *Majestic,* sailing from Southampton, England, was met with more than the usual degree of commotion when it arrived in New York on August 25, 1926. The celebrity-filled passenger manifest was topped by Mary Pickford and Douglas Fairbanks, who were returning from a five-month sojourn in Europe. "Mr. Fairbanks and Miss Pickford were almost carried off their feet by the rush of admirers eager to get their autographs. . . . Inspection of passengers' baggage had to be suspended while the pier police cleared a space for business." MGM director Rex Ingram, screen ingenue Constance Talmadge, and the young British actor Leslie Howard also drew gawkers. Movie theater magnate Jules Mastbaum was bringing home forty Rodin sculptures destined for a museum dedicated to the artist that he was building in Philadelphia. Jeddu Krishnamurti, an Indian mystic of beatific demeanor and suspect intentions, "heralded as a new Messiah" by theosophists, assured the curious reporters who swarmed around him: "I come to reform and not to tear down."

It would have been easy to overlook an unassuming, middle-aged lawyer in all the hubbub, but a reporter from *Film Daily* spotted Nathan Burkan and buttonholed him for an interview. Burkan had sailed for Europe eight weeks earlier in the company of Broadway star Al Jolson and his second wife, former Ziegfeld girl Ethel Delmar. After helping the Jolsons procure a quick and quiet Paris divorce, Burkan had made his annual rounds of Great Britain and the Continent, mixing business and pleasure. Burkan offered the reporter his observation that "agitation against American pictures" was on the rise throughout Europe and that further restrictions and quotas on imports of American films were likely. He urged the domestic film industry to step up and "set aside a certain percentage of revenue to produce abroad, and to distribute those pictures in the United States." He proudly pointed out that United Artists "has distributed one foreign picture to every six American. Others should act in accord."

When the *Majestic* was a little more than a day's steaming distance from New York, Burkan received a radiogram containing news that stunned the floating film colony—the death of screen idol Rudolph Valentino. Reporters scrambled to get expressions of grief from Doug, Mary, and the other disembarking movie folk. No one, however, was asked to comment on a recent event of far greater significance in the annals of celluloidia. On August 5, 1926, Warner Brothers had given the first demonstration of its Vitaphone sound synchronization technology, to an invite-only audience of press and VIPs, at the Warner Theater in New York. The Vitaphone program opened to the public the following night and had been playing to sold-out houses ever since. "Amazing Invention Coupling Sound with Screen Images Stirs Audiences," blared a headline in the *New York Times*.

The Vitaphone program included a short introductory speech by Will Hays, instrumental performances by illustrious musicians, arias sung by Metropolitan Opera stars spanning the vocal spectrum, and the New York Philharmonic playing the *Tannhäuser* overture. The feature was *Don Juan,* a silent film starring John Barrymore, for which an orchestral score and some sound effects had been recorded and synchronized. "Vitaphone" was a Latin-Greek compound for "living sound," but "no single word," the *Times* effused, "is quite adequate to suggest the amazing triumph which man has at last achieved in making pictures talk naturally, sing enthrallingly, and play all manner of instruments as skillfully as if the living beings were present instead of their shadows." That first program reflected Sam Warner's vision for Vitaphone, not as a means of replicating the legitimate theater with actors speaking dialogue, but to bring the experience of the big-city movie palace, with its pit orchestra and high-class live "presentation acts," to the "smallest hamlets." Talking pictures "do not intrigue us personally," one commentator wrote. "It is our conviction that motion pictures belong to the art of pantomime. Vitaphone will serve exhibitors and audiences in small towns where the capacity of the theaters will not permit a large, expensive orchestra."

Vitaphone was very much on Burkan's mind when he arrived in New York. After clearing customs, he was whisked away from Pier 50 by Ascap general manager J. C. Rosenthal. The score to *Don Juan* included several copyrighted Ascap numbers. A few days earlier, Rosenthal had told the press that Ascap fully intended to take action, the exact nature of the steps to be decided upon when Burkan returned. Burkan and Rosenthal headed straight to Ascap's offices to start figuring out what Vitaphone meant for composers, authors, and publishers.

That same day, Al Jolson, who had returned to New York a week earlier, was signing a contract to appear in a Vitaphone short. "You are to enact before the camera and record for us one number of approximately seventeen minutes duration, to include one or more of your well-known songs and a certain amount of monologue," the letter agreement provided. It was a sweet little deal for Jolie. He was to be paid $25,000 for four days of work at the Manhattan Opera House, which Sam Warner had retrofitted to serve as the world's first soundstage.

News of Jolson's signing hit the newspapers the next day. It was a matter of considerable concern to Burkan for two reasons. First, Jolson's well-known songs were all Ascap repertoire. And second, Burkan was still busy cleaning up the mess left in the wake of Jolson's first, disastrous foray into the world of motion pictures.

Al Jolson had been the headliner at the Shubert Brothers' Winter Garden Theater since the day it opened in 1911, appearing in free-form extravaganzas that were built to showcase his talents and could be varied from night to night to indulge his whims. He alternated long New York seasons with exhausting national road tours. He was, hands down, the most valuable plug a song could have. (He would often insist on co-authorship credit, called a "cut-in," for songs he popularized, and he accumulated enough of them that by 1928 his Ascap distributions were equal to those of Irving Berlin and George Gershwin.) To the millions who later listened to Jolson on records, over the radio, or at the movies, his gift for putting over some of the best popular songs of his day was obvious and undeniable. In his prime, though, it was universally agreed that it was on the Broadway stage that he earned his billing as "The World's Greatest Entertainer." "Jolson is driven by a power beyond himself," wrote Gilbert Seldes. "I cannot help thinking of him as a genius."

Those stage performances—and the film appearances that give us some little sense of his on-stage energy, physicality, and magnetism—were almost all done in blackface. It is not simply a matter of archaic stage makeup. Jolson's blackface alter ego was an amalgam of vile racial stereotypes—a strutting, lazy, bug-eyed, malapropping, wisecracking man-child. He held fast to a simple piece of advice that J.J. Shubert had given him early in his career, when Jolson was apt to take liberties with the archetype: "You must not lose sight of the fact that you are playing the character of a nigger."

Jolson did not even come by blackface honestly, as so many others did, by performing in the highly ritualized minstrel shows that were once important and somewhat dignified, if ultimately repellant, staples of American popular culture. Burnt cork was just a comedic mask that Jolson had glommed on to when he was floundering as a comedian in vaudeville. To Gilbert Seldes, though, the blackface was "absurd" and "so little negroid" it did nothing to detract from his admiration of Jolson. Much of the intelligentsia shared that outlook.

It would be easy to dismiss Jolson in retrospect as merely a vulgar comedian and a "mammy singer," but to do so would be to overlook his profound influence on the great generation of songwriters that wrote for him, and on the singers that emulated him.

As early as 1914, while he was on a national tour in *The Honeymoon Express,* Selig Polyscope had approached Jolson about appearing in pictures. J.J. Shubert, however, refused to allow his star attraction, whom he had just signed to a five-year contract, to be cheapened in this way: "Under no consideration have your picture taken for moving pictures. They advertise you all over for ten cents. It is all right for the dead ones but not for live ones."

With the wear and tear of stage work and frequent touring taking its toll on his voice and his psyche, in the early 1920s Jolson began to think seriously of getting into pictures. And he was thinking big. He wanted to be directed by D.W. Griffith in what he thought would be the perfect showcase for him, an adaptation of a short story by Samson Raphaelson called "The Day of Atonement." It was about a cantor's son who leaves his orthodox family to enter show business, but returns to chant Kol Nidre, the central prayer of Yom Kippur, while his father is on his deathbed. Jolson, whose orthodox rabbi father had never acknowledged his achievements, could readily identify with the lead character. Raphaelson said his story was inspired by Jolson, whose singing reminded him of synagogue cantillation.

Anthony Paul Kelly, a young playwright who had written film scenarios for D.W. Griffith, obtained a six-month option on the film rights to "The Day of Atonement" and pitched the project to Griffith on Jolson's behalf. When Griffith balked at the idea of doing a Jewish melodrama with a blackface comedian, Kelly found a story more in keeping with both Griffith's and Jolson's specialties. "Mammy's Boy" was about a black servant, Uncle Eph, framed for a murder committed by "cullud" bootleggers, and a young writer who dons blackface to penetrate the bootlegging ring and exonerate Uncle Eph. Griffith, who had "long nursed the idea that this generation is ready for a new Uncle Tom," agreed to do the picture. Kelly bought the film rights for $1,500 and prepared a screen scenario.

Jolson asked Burkan, who at the time was representing him in a plagiarism case involving the lyrics to "April Showers," to draw up a contract for the Griffith picture. Jolson still hadn't signed the document when production began at Griffith's Mamaroneck, New York, studio in late June 1923. He was acutely aware that many other stage stars had laid big eggs in pictures and he wanted a contractual right to veto release of the movie if he was unhappy with it. That was not a clause Griffith could possibly agree to, so Jolson stalled in order to keep his options open for as long as possible. Griffith, in the meantime, hired a cast, built sets, and started shooting without a signed contract from his lead player.

"I was delighted with his work," Griffith said. "We had taken a number of preliminary shots, first in white face to study costuming schemes and then in black face to get Mr. Jolson set as to character mood—to settle whether he would be a flashy, sporty, 'cullud pusson or just a shabby darky." The *New York Clipper* reported that "everything seemed to go according to schedule until the black face stage comedian got the first glimpse of himself on a big screen in the 'natural.' . . . The sight of this was more than Al could stand. He felt he was ruined." The next day, instead of reporting to the studio, Jolson went to the racetrack. The day after that, he sailed for Europe.

Griffith calculated his out-of-pocket losses, resulting from what he sarcastically called Jolson's "retirement," to be $72,000. "But most broken-hearted of all," *Variety* reported, "is Anthony Paul Kelly, who devoted more than 18 months of his time bringing Griffith and Jolson together." Both Kelly and Griffith sued Jolson to recover damages; their cases would still be a nagging problem for Jolson and Burkan when, in 1926, Jolson was ready to give the movies another shot.

Burkan's twenty-five years of zealous and effective advocacy on behalf of music copyright holders now paid a most welcome and unexpected dividend. Unlike record and piano roll manufacturers, cabaret owners, movie exhibitors, and broadcasters, Warner Brothers never advanced the notion that the music it wanted to use in Vitaphone films should be available for free as a quid pro quo for the plug. Nor did it ever threaten to boycott copyrighted music if that was the only alternative to paying for it. Burkan had succeeded in establishing a fundamental understanding in the entertainment world that royalty-bearing music was a good value proposition and a normal cost of doing business. It remained to be determined how much movie makers would pay and to whom they would pay it.

The Vitaphone technology used sixteen-inch lacquered discs to record and play back sound, one disc per reel of film. They were essentially large phonograph records. An obvious analogy suggested itself. Warner Brothers would have been very happy to treat this as another form of mechanical reproduction, entitling it to compulsory licenses on payment of two cents per song per copy. Even under its most optimistic projections, Warner would never have reason to order more than about a thousand copies of each Vitaphone disc.

At that time, the Music Publishers Protective Association was serving as the clearinghouse for nearly all compulsory mechanical licenses issued under the 1909 Copyright Act. Record manufacturers simply sent a notice of their intent to use a number to Claude Mills, in his capacity as trustee for the publishers, and the license was issued in due course. But when Vitaphone Corporation (the joint venture of Warner Brothers, Western Electric, and American Telephone and Telegraph that developed and licensed the technology) tried to invoke this process for the copyrighted numbers in the *Don Juan* score, Mills objected. Synchronizing music with pictures that were to be projected to audiences that might aggregate in the millions went far beyond mere reproduction on a mechanical device meant for the private home entertainment of individuals, and was clearly, in Mills's view, outside the contemplation of the two-cents compulsory licensing rate.

Meanwhile, back at Ascap headquarters, an emergency meeting of the board was convened. Burkan opined that recording music on Vitaphone discs did not constitute the giving of a public performance that came within the society's purview. Provided a theater using the discs was licensed for public performance—and the few theaters initially being wired for Vitaphone were —Ascap could not ask for more. Gene Buck, concerned that songwriters were going to be frozen out, argued that with respect to this "new right," Ascap "could handle the industry's interests in the same manner that it had the performing right, thus insuring everybody equality and a square division of the rewards."

Not interested in equality and square division, the publishers declined to put this new right—the "synchronization" right—under Ascap's aegis. In September 1926, Claude Mills, acting on behalf of the Music Publishers Protective Association, made the first blanket deal for motion picture synchronization rights, with Vitaphone Corporation agreeing to pay $104,000 for the use of the music of the association's members for one year. Mills would distribute this fee to members based on actual usage of their music, and the publishers would in turn pay writers in accordance with their contracts. Ascap received a consolation prize: the synchronization licenses required that the Vitaphone pictures be exhibited only at Ascap-licensed theaters. Mills was, after all, an officer of Ascap too.

This was a first. Music providers, on the one hand, and a group of music users, on the other, without the intervention of Congress or the courts, had grappled with a new technology, recognized an implied right in the interstices of the Copyright Act and together created a reasonably functional mechanism for licensing it.

Jolson filmed his Vitaphone short, *A Plantation Act,* during the first week of September 1926. Appearing in blackface and costumed as a sharecropper, he sings three well-chosen hits on a single painted set before a single camera. It is a rather static visual presentation, with none of the choreography Jolson was known for on stage, but he is in fine voice and intersperses the songs with some of his famous patter, including his catchphrase "you ain't heard nothin' yet." With Vitaphone still a novelty, it would make for a striking screen debut. Warner Brothers intended to include it on a program with its second Vitaphone feature, a Sydney Chaplin comedy called *The Better 'Ole,* which was due to be released in October 1926.

Burkan was most anxious to get the long-delayed trials in the D. W. Griffith and Anthony Paul Kelly cases over with before the whole world saw that Al Jolson's fear of the silver screen had been unfounded. *A Plantation Act* would premiere on October 7. The Griffith case was placed on the federal district court calendar in New York for September 14, with the Kelly case to follow immediately in the New York state supreme court. It was a tight window. Jolson, whose last big Shubert Brothers show, *Big Boy,* began a six-week engagement in Boston on September 13, would have to commute between the two cities in order to be present at the trials.

Griffith's studio had completed the Jolson project with another director, star, and title (*His Darker Self*), and released it to indifferent success.

When his case came to trial, Griffith sought total damages of $572,000, which included lost profits. In support, Griffith offered his expert opinion that Jolson was destined for big success in films. Griffith and Burkan, of course, knew each other well from United Artists, but there was no love lost between the two men. Burkan's cross-examination was mocking and laced with sarcasm, making Griffith look foolish. "Everybody at Trial Gets a Laugh, Except D. W." was one headline. Griffith repeatedly lashed out at Burkan, insisting that he had started production without a signed contract, against the advice of his staff, only after Burkan had told him and Jolson to "shake hands and go ahead with the picture" while the contract was being drawn. "I thought you had more brains than some of my associates, Mr. Burkan," rued Griffith.

Burkan took the stand as a witness for the defense. (It is another one of those head-scratchers for contemporary lawyers—acting as both a material witness and an advocate before the same jury is generally forbidden under the ethical rules of the profession.) Burkan denied ever telling Griffith to go ahead with production on the basis of a handshake. He testified that he had been with Jolson when Griffith screened the test shots. Jolson, Burkan testified, turned to him and said: "That's rotten, I'm not a screen star."

Jolson joked and mugged his way through his testimony. "You say that when you saw the first test you decided that you were terrible and rotten?" Burkan asked. "Just let it go at rotten," was Jolson's answer. He put on a convincing act. He did not come across as a contract-jumper; rather, he seemed to have genuinely feared that a failure in pictures would ruin his career. To drive that point home, Burkan ventured onto somewhat hazardous territory with an artfully worded question:

"Have you ever appeared upon the screen as a screen actor?"

"No sir, not yet."

The jury gave Griffith a verdict of only $2,600, evidently its estimate of the cost of making Jolson's screen tests. Burkan was beaming when the verdict was read and he personally thanked each juror, "his face suffused with a broad smile." Griffith, for his part, accepted the verdict as a "moral victory."

The Kelly case was called for trial on October 6. Kelly was claiming damages of $250,000, his estimate of the value of the services that he had provided to Jolson. There was no written contract, signed or unsigned, but Kelly testified that "Al Jolson promised to put me on

Broadway in a Rolls Royce and pelt me with pearls" if Kelly could get him a movie deal with Griffith.

Midway through the trial, Burkan filled in for Jolson (who was still appearing nightly in Boston) at the gala New York premiere of *The Better 'Ole* and a program of short subjects. Jolson's Vitaphone turn was the evening's highlight. "The golden voice of Jolson," wrote one critic, "made the hearts of his listeners beat faster." Robert E. Sherwood, playwright, movie critic, and sardonic Algonquin Roundtable wit, was effusive in his review of the program:

> Mr. Jolson is no less than sensational. His expressive face and his thrilling voice—even his urgent gasps—reproduce perfectly. When he had finished, I applauded vehemently, actually believing that he might be persuaded to come back and sign again if I clapped hard enough. That shows how effective the Vitaphone is.

Jolson's big screen success that night was problematic for the defense that Burkan was putting on in court by day. Jolson, down from Boston, took the stand and preposterously explained that D. W. Griffith had "hypnotized me into believing I was good on the screen," which "actually caused me to forget how bum I was." Burkan was relieved to escape from that courtroom with a hung jury.

Griffith was not amused. When he heard about Jolson's success in *A Plantation Act,* he had his lawyers request a new trial on the grounds that the jury had been misled by Jolson's testimony that he had "not yet" appeared "upon the screen as a screen actor." In response, Burkan submitted an affidavit from the father of Vitaphone, Sam Warner, who explained at length his view that Vitaphone was intended to simulate live musical performances and had nothing to do with "acting." He engaged Jolson only for his singing: "I knew Jolson was not a motion picture actor and I would not have him on the screen as a motion picture actor if he offered his services for nothing." Warner and his brothers would, very soon, have occasion to reconsider that judgment.

Appearing on the same Vitaphone program as *A Plantation Act* was a comedic monologue by George Jessel called *At Peace with the World.* Jessel, a young vaudevillian, was on the cusp of stage and screen stardom. His first feature under a three-year contract with Warner Brothers, a silent comedy called *Private Izzy Murphy,* was about to be released. Jessel's Vitaphone debut was well received, if somewhat overshadowed by Jolson's.

A year earlier, Jessel had made a splash on Broadway in the role of Jack Robin, the Jolson-like character in Samson Raphaelson's stage adaptation of "The Day of Atonement"—retitled *The Jazz Singer*. Warner Brothers purchased the screen rights to the story for $50,000, with the intention of adapting it for the silent screen, giving it a Vitaphone score, and having Jessel recreate his Broadway role. Production was to begin in Hollywood in May 1927. As Warner Brothers developed the screen scenario, the story was given a new epilogue. Raphaelson's play ended with Jack Robin stepping into his dying father's pulpit on Yom Kippur, rejecting the siren call of show business. The Warner scenario added a final scene in which Jack Robin's apostasy is complete—he is seen performing on a Broadway stage, his widowed mother in the audience.

Only a few weeks before production was scheduled to begin, Warner Brothers made a fateful decision: "Jessel's singing in a synagogue and in a Broadway theater will be Vitaphoned." Vitaphone would not simply provide background music; it would for the first time be integrated into the action, the "diegesis," of a narrative film, if only to the limited extent of "reproducing vocal numbers and their accompaniments" in a story about a singer.

This came as news to Jessel, who felt that he was entitled to additional compensation if he was going to sing as well as act. In early May, as elaborate preparations were being made to equip Warner's Hollywood studio for synchronized sound, Jessel arrived in Los Angeles still holding out for more money. Jolson was also in town for a two-week engagement in *Big Boy*, to be followed by a four-week San Francisco run. Jessel and Jolson, who had known each other for years, spent some time together palling around Los Angeles, but Jolson did not say anything about a change in plans for *The Jazz Singer*.

Unbeknownst to Jessel, back in New York Nathan Burkan was negotiating with Sam and Harry Warner for a deal to give Jolson the role he had long wanted to play in the movies. (Indeed, to keep Jessel off the scent until it was a fait accompli, Burkan signed the contract in New York using Jolson's power of attorney.) The agreement called for Jolson to perform five songs in addition to chanting Kol Nidre for Vitaphone. Of particular importance after the D. W. Griffith affair, the contract gave Jolson the right, "at any time," to screen rushes and hear playbacks of his songs, and to be present for "cutting, assembling and titling."

Overall, though, Burkan did not drive a hard bargain. Jolson's compensation was $75,000 (plus $2,500 to cover Burkan's fee), with no profit participation. "When this chance to portray a role which so vitally concerns me and my people was offered," Jolson told reporters, "I felt that it was only right to accept gladly. I have no present intention of ever appearing in another movie, feeling that *The Jazz Singer* will be my only living document."

Blindsided by Jolson's treachery—he learned about it from the newspapers—Jessel was furious. He was, almost certainly, the source of an "explanation" for the star-switch that first surfaced even before Jolson arrived on the soundstage and that persists to this day. As reported in *Billboard*:

> An explanation of the mystery as to why Warner Brothers substituted Al Jolson for George Jessel as the star of the film version of *The Jazz Singer* has come to light and is going the rounds here. The story is that, thru Nathan Burkan, New York attorney, $1,000,000 was turned over to the Warners on condition that Jolson appear on the screen. . . . The Warners were enabled to make the picture without a cent of their own money being involved.

Warner Brothers was a public company, with Goldman Sachs financing behind it. For a project that was increasingly emphasizing music as it was being developed, Warner got Jolson, the outstanding popular singer of his generation and the inspiration for the story, rather cheap. Casting Jolson in place of George Jessel made perfect sense as a financial and artistic proposition. There is no need to posit the intervention of a shadowy million-dollar bagman, except perhaps as a salve to Jessel's bruised ego.

The success of *The Jazz Singer* changed the trajectories of Jolson's career, of the movie industry, and of the music business. In May 1928, with the audience for *The Jazz Singer* still growing as more theaters were wired for sound, and a follow-up, *The Singing Fool,* already in production, Jolson sent Burkan a multifilm contract to review:

> My Dear Nat,
> The terms under which Warner Brothers want to sign me are all perfectly agreeable to me. . . . Kindly draw up a contract accordingly and I will more than appreciate your cooperation with the Warners as they have been perfectly wonderful to me and I want to sign with them and no one else.
> Will appreciate if you speed this contract up as we want to make a general big announcement through the trade papers etc.
> Sorry you can't be here to enjoy the wonderful sunshine.
>
> Your loving son,
> Al

Jolson went on to make six more films for Warner Brothers over a ten-year period, but his motion picture legacy would be almost exactly the same today if he had stopped at two. *The Singing Fool* made even more extensive use of Vitaphone than *The Jazz Singer,* was an even bigger hit, and was an even bigger impetus to the development of the movie musical. *The Singing Fool* introduced a new song, "Sonny Boy," written especially for the film by the team of Ray Henderson, Buddy DeSylva, and Lew Brown. It was a smashing success, demonstrating previously unimagined commercial synergies that could be obtained by combining music with moving pictures. "The picture biz is a life-saver for the music men," *Variety* observed. "The screen has given them phenomenal hits at a minimum of exploitation cost." The studios raced to improve sound technology and to create the first all-singing, all-dancing movie musicals.

The making of *The Singing Fool* also revealed the legal snags that stood in the way of the full flowering of the movie musical as a genre. The 1926 Vitaphone synchronization rights agreement had been superseded in 1927 by a similar, five-year agreement between the Music Publishers Protective Association and Electrical Research Products, Inc. (known as ERPI), a newly formed Western Electric subsidiary that was now licensing Vitaphone and other sound technology to all the major Hollywood studios. (A boycott by other studios had forced Warner Brothers out of the partnership.) The limitations of the arrangement soon became apparent to Warner. Jolson wanted to use one of his signature songs, "Keep Smiling at Trouble," but he had to make a personal plea for permission to Max Dreyfus, the head of T. B. Harms, which had opted out of the ERPI arrangement. Louis Silvers, Warner's musical director, used a tune from Victor Herbert's operetta *The Red Mill* in the score. Although M. Witmark & Sons had partially joined in the ERPI deal, the contract by its terms specifically excluded production music, for which the studio had to separately negotiate rights.

The nickels and dimes for these non-ERPI music rights came out of the studio's pocket, and the hassle of chasing them down disrupted tight production schedules. Even "Sonny Boy," written to order for *The Singing Fool,* ran into trouble when Warner released the film in England, where the local publisher, unaffiliated with ERPI, objected and demanded royalties. "This certainly is a darn shame," one Warner executive commiserated with another, "this song was written especially for our picture and to allow ourselves to be held up for such a terrific amount in England makes me feel more certain that we should have some tie-in on the songs that appear in our pictures."

Tie-ins between movie studios and music publishers became quite the rage. Warner Brothers, in particular, went on a shopping spree for music catalogs. In January 1929, it purchased M. Witmark & Sons, lock, stock, and barrel. It must have been bittersweet for Burkan to see a client of such long standing swallowed up, but the transaction left his old and dear friends the Witmarks set for life, and he had the satisfaction of knowing that he had created much of the value that constituted the company's principal assets, its copyrights. Within a few months, Warner had also purchased T. B. Harms, Jerome H. Remick & Co., and several other publishers. Warner rolled all of its acquisitions into the "Music Publishers Holding Corporation," the forerunner of today's vast and powerful Warner Music Group. Having spent some $10 million to acquire a large portion of Tin Pan Alley's legacy, Warner Brothers created the *Looney Tunes* and *Merrie Melodies* animation series for the purpose of promoting and exploiting its burgeoning music catalog.

Other studios followed Warner's lead. MGM acquired the Robbins Music Company, which had been the leading provider of synchronization music under the ERPI deal, and Leo Feist's company, another long-time Burkan client. By the mid-1930s, only a few of the old-line Tin Pan Alley publishers remained independent. "Tin Pan Alley is rapidly changing its colorful tune," wrote one reporter. "The Wall Street blues are being heard. . . . Even as it hums, it knows its happy-go-lucky days are over."

To ensure the flow of new material, the studios put songwriters on staff. "Tin Pan Alley Goes West en Masse" was one headline. Jack Yellen and Milton Ager were writing "Happy Days Are Here Again" at MGM; DeSylva, Henderson, and Brown were at Fox; even Irving Berlin was writing Mammy songs for Jolson at Warner. Long accustomed to being freelancers, songwriters learned the joys of a steady paycheck—as much as $2,000 per week—but also the drudgery of a nine-to-five workday. "There is not much left of Tin Pan Alley except memories," wrote columnist O. O. McIntyre. In Hollywood, the once swashbuckling songwriter "punches the clock."

By going into the publishing business, the studios not only secured a ready supply of music for synchronization, they also reaped profits from sheet music sales, compulsory mechanical licenses, and public performance royalties. The question, posed by *Photoplay* in the fall of 1929, "Which has absorbed which? Is the motion picture industry a subsidiary of the music publishing business or have film producers gone into the business of making songs?" practically answered itself. The Tin Pan

Alley business paradigm, which had thrived and adapted since the 1890s, experienced an extinction-level event when synchronized sound arrived.

The rush to sound had initially been a boon for Ascap; theaters that wanted to show movies with ERPI technology were required to take licenses. But now that Hollywood was scooping up its members, Burkan could foresee another crisis on the not-distant horizon. The publishers that were being bought up by the studios had five-year commitments to Ascap that would expire at the end of 1930. What then? Studios, *Variety* predicted, "will inevitably create their pictures free of any copyrights but those they control themselves." When that came about, what would stop them from offering their movies "music tax free" as an inducement to exhibitors? What would prevent a publisher with the resources of a major movie studio behind it from leaving Ascap altogether and collecting performance fees on its own? *Variety* suggested that it was all leading to the "ultimate disintegration of the American Society of Composers, Authors, and Publishers."

PART SIX

Twenty Days in January 1927

CHAPTER 18

Rumrunners

Few years resonate as deeply in the history of American popular culture as 1927. It was the year of Charles Lindbergh's transatlantic flight, the Jack Dempsey–Gene Tunney "long count" heavyweight bout, Babe Ruth's majestic sixty-homer season, and the premieres of *The Jazz Singer* and *Show Boat*. That memorable year began with national attention focused on two legal dramas playing out in New York City. Nathan Burkan was at center stage in both.

On the first business day of 1927, Frank Costello went on trial at the federal courthouse in lower Manhattan. Born Francesco Castiglia in Calabria, the toe of the Italian peninsula, he had arrived in New York in 1895. He took an Irish name and a Jewish wife and brought multiculturalism to the Sicilian mafia.

Costello stood accused with seventeen others of conspiring to operate a $25 million liquor smuggling ring in violation of the National Prohibition Act. Their rum-running racket, the government told jurors, was executed "with all the careful attention to detail of a modern American corporation." It was a harbinger of the scale, ambition, and audacity that would characterize the city's organized crime syndicates for decades to come. The trial of the politically savvy and (relatively) violence-averse Costello offered New Yorkers one of their first glimpses of an archetypal mid-twentieth-century mob boss.

Costello's operation controlled a sizable portion of the seafaring traffic on both sides of Rum Row, an imaginary line just beyond the United

States' territorial waters running parallel to the Eastern Seaboard, especially along the segment that extended from Long Island Sound to Cape May. Liquor-laden ships of foreign registry, sailing from the French enclave of St. Pierre-et-Miquelon—an accommodating, low-duty hub off the coast of Newfoundland—dropped anchor there every day, offloading their cargo to a ragtag armada of smaller vessels that carried out the much dicier task of surreptitiously bringing the goods to shore. Through his straw men and corporate shells, Costello owned several twin- and tri-masted schooners that made the St. Pierre–to–Rum Row round-trip, and a fleet of faster, more maneuverable boats for the final leg of the journey to Montauk and other landing points. Once on land, the liquor could be diluted, adulterated, and mislabeled before reaching consumers.

Rum Row also did a thriving retail trade. Costello's "home office," at a respectable Lexington Avenue address, radioed the schooner crews seemingly random multidigit numbers in lieu of buyer names. These were matched against the serial numbers of dollar bills tendered by customer contact boats before a prepaid order changed hands. This protocol obviated the need for either party to the transaction to carry large quantities of cash that could attract pirates, or for documents that could prove incriminating in the unlikely event of interdiction by the authorities.

In this way, Costello and his compatriots slaked the thirst of the more discerning palates of the northeastern megalopolis, those for whom bathtub gin and drugstore nostrums would not suffice. During the five halcyon years that followed passage of the Prohibition Act in 1919, running rum was easy money. But in 1925 the territorial waters of the United States were extended by treaty to one hour's steaming distance (on average twelve miles as opposed to the previous three), making the trip from Rum Row to shore longer and riskier. And the Coolidge administration—up until then notably stingy in providing the materiel needed for credible enforcement of the dry laws at sea—approved a large increase in Coast Guard personnel and put twenty mothballed World War I–era navy destroyers at their disposal.

The newly commissioned men were poorly paid and the conditions of their service were atrocious, making them as susceptible to bribery as the land-based cops and prohibition officers Costello had already bought off. "Working for thirty-six dollars a month plus room and board," Daniel Okrent writes in his history of Prohibition, they "found it difficult (if not pointless) to remain incorruptible." For pitiably small gratuities paid in liquor and cash, Coast Guardsmen would not only look the other way as illegal liquor crossed the waters, they would provide enthusiastic assistance. They would ferry rum boat crewmen, guide boats that wandered off course or into dangerous shoals, feed misinformation to the crews of the destroyers, and take liquor ashore themselves, firing light ordnance when necessary to create the illusion that they were chasing rum, not running it. On at least one occasion, a Coast Guard patrol boat captured, looted, and sank a rum schooner that had refused to "do business" with Costello. The crew split the proceeds from sale of the booty.

Nine Coast Guardsmen had been indicted along with the Costello gang. Six had pleaded guilty and were cooperating with the government.

Largely ignoring the substance of the prosecution's overwhelmingly inculpatory evidence, Costello's legal team, led by Nathan Burkan, relentlessly attacked the government's investigatory methods and the character of the "rats" it was putting on the witness stand, contributing an important chapter to the playbook that mob lawyers would employ ever after. But it was a tack that, in this case, could easily have backfired if not implemented with a deft touch. The government's witnesses, rum crewmen and Coast Guardsmen-turned-informers, were not hardened criminal types whose testimony would necessarily beggar belief. They were rather ordinary schnooks, trapped in the vortex of Prohibition, a legal regime that rendered nearly everyone, or at least someone they knew, a lawbreaker.

William Newman, for one, portrayed himself as having been a law-abiding dental prosthetist until the conspirators, who appreciated the virtue of sobriety—at least when it came to their crewmen—recruited him to supervise cargo on the Costello schooner *Vincent A. White*. Press accounts agree that Burkan gave Newman an exquisitely difficult time on cross-examination. He coaxed Newman into admitting that, by the time he had been approached by Costello's men, it was already common knowledge around his hometown of Freeport, Long Island, that he was devoting far more time to running liquor in his own boat than to fabricating dentures and bridgework. But Newman's twelve peers on the jury were probably satisfied with his explanation: "Everybody down at Freeport was doing it, so I decided that I'd take a chance."

Burkan was now forty-eight years old. Full face, the odd juxtaposition of his bulbous prizefighter's nose on an otherwise avuncular face was all the more pronounced under a fully receded hairline. In profile, his head was pointed high in the rear, somehow reminiscent of an Ottoman vizier. Three-piece Savile Row suits, high-end accessories, and the bellicose demeanor of "an angel of vengeance" leveled the playing field when he, of immigrant stock and public-school pedigree, squared off in the court-room against Ivy-educated Brahmins. (In this case his opponent, a much younger and impossibly well credentialed prosecutor named William Stevenson, was a Rhodes Scholar and Olympic gold medalist to boot.) "Does *everybody* at Freeport run booze?" Burkan asked, seething with an expertly faked high dudgeon, and not much caring how the witness would answer a question posed only for its theatrical effect.

"Well—a good majority of the people do."

Rattled by Burkan's bluster and sarcasm, Newman prattled on. He volunteered that after the Costello gang had stiffed him on his wages, he had written to the Prohibition Bureau in Washington and offered to serve his country as an informer. Now, Newman swore, he was willing to rat out his best friends—even his own brother—in his capacity as an undercover agent in the employ of Mr. A. Bruce Bielaski. Burkan, a reporter noted, "seemed greatly interested" at the mention of that name.

Burkan had occasionally helped a client out of a minor criminal scrape, but he had little experience in major felony trials. In 1926, however, he had defended Charles Duell, a movie producer, against charges that he had committed perjury during an earlier civil suit against the actress Lillian Gish. The jury deadlocked on Duell's guilt, freeing if not quite exonerating him, and the trade press gave Burkan's performance boffo reviews. "His skill at cross-examination was a revelation," *Variety* gushed, "and he unfailingly brought out hidden points from witnesses for the prosecution. . . . That Burkan will be sought for other criminal defense actions is certain."

One would not imagine that Frank Costello retained Burkan based on his notices in *Variety*. The introduction was probably made by mutual acquaintances in Tammany Hall, where Costello had many customers and benefactors—not for nothing would he become known as the "Prime Minister of the Underworld." For Burkan, the case offered a chance to advance the ambitions of an old friend and political mentor, Alfred E. Smith, who had just been sworn in for his fourth term as governor of New York and was planning a run for the presidency in 1928. If an Irish-Catholic "wet" was to have a shot at the nomination of a national Democratic Party deeply divided by Prohibition, much less win the White House, the public face of Prohibition would have to be conspicuously bloodied. A highly publicized trial of rumrunners provided a perfect opportunity to administer the blow.

Burkan drew first blood when a former Coast Guard patrol boat captain, Nicholas Brown, took the stand. Brown, it appeared from his own testimony and that of several of his crewmen, was a bad egg—a brawler and a drunk who ended many of his Coast Guard service days prostrate and unconscious, sometimes on his own vessel but often aboard the very rum boats his cutter was assigned to surveil. He testified about one night when the crew of a patrol boat he commanded smuggled 350 cases of liquor ashore. Brown admitted to sampling the wares. "I got drunk," he confessed, "but I did not pass out until I reached the buoy at Montauk Point."

On cross-examination Burkan elicited an even more harrowing tale from Brown. After he had been indicted with Costello and the other conspirators in January 1926, and while he was free on bail, federal agents had seized and imprisoned him aboard the Coast Guard cutter *Seneca,* manacling his arms and legs to a stanchion in its dark hold, where temperatures dipped below zero. "The hatches were battened down and the air was foul. They fed me on rotten meat and water and never told me why I had been seized."

"Was the *Seneca* a prison ship?" Burkan asked. "No, sir," answered Brown; "she was worse than that."

After a week of this torture, Brown's captors relayed an offer to him. If he was ready to confess, he would be released. "I was almost crazy from pain and cold. I was out of my head," Brown testified. "They took me to the office of A. Bruce Bielaski and I said I would plead guilty to these charges." Although he declined Bielaski's offer of a position as an undercover agent, Brown was allowed to go free. The story of Brown's captivity made headlines nationally, the *Chicago Tribune* taking top honors with "Cold Storage Treatment for Dry Law Witness."

In the official history of the Federal Bureau of Investigation, Alexander Bruce Bielaski is recognized as its second director, although during his tenure (1912–1919) neither the FBI nor the position of director existed as such. World War I, with its attendant outbreak of Germanophobia, was a watershed event for Bielaski, as he assumed the role of the nation's top domestic spy hunter. His job was to cull the actual subversive threats from the millions of spurious reports of, as the *New Yorker* put it, "poison in every pretzel and a time-fuse in every dachshund's tail." By all accounts, Bielaski was particularly innovative in his use of undercover investigative techniques.

After the war, Bielaski had gone into private law practice, his name resurfacing in the news only once, in 1922, when he "escaped" from kidnappers in Mexico. With his well-earned reputation for subterfuge, Bielaski was never able to shake widespread suspicions that he had staged his own abduction.

Assistant Secretary of the Treasury Lincoln Andrews, head of the Prohibition Bureau, brought Bielaski back into government service in 1925, giving him the opaque title of "personal representative" and a budget of $250,000 to fund a secret Prohibition enforcement operation under cover of a Wall Street law practice. The signal success of this operation was busting two parallel, interdependent rum rings known as "The Combine," one run by Costello and the other by William "Big Bill" Dwyer, the founding owner of the New York Rangers hockey team, who had been convicted in July 1926. But in the months following the Dwyer trial, Bielaski's reputation had taken a considerable hit under the unremitting bombardment of Congressman Fiorello H. LaGuardia of Manhattan.

Just as the Costello trial was beginning, LaGuardia took to the floor of the House of Representatives to denounce Prohibition enforcement in New York City as corrupt and incompetent, and Bielaski's undercover force as a "vast system of espionage and blackmail." It had emerged that Bielaski used government funds to set up a Manhattan speakeasy as a honey trap for bootleggers. Replete with waiters outfitted in Brooks Brothers vests and bartenders in alpaca coats, the "Bridge Whist Club," LaGuardia charged, "served hundreds of customers a day right over the bar in the good old-fashioned manner." He demanded that the Justice Department prosecute Bielaski for "as clear and perfect a case of conspiracy to violate the prohibition law as ever came to the attention of any District Attorney anywhere, any time."

Burkan was no political ally of the reform-minded Republican LaGuardia—an implacable antagonist of Tammany Hall—but in opposition to Prohibition they made common cause. Bielaski was a bogeyman useful to them both. Burkan availed himself of every opportunity during the Costello trial to invoke Bielaski's name, prompting Judge Francis Winslow to remind him that "Mr. Bielaski is not on trial in this case." "I think he will be," Burkan replied defiantly, "before this case is ended."

The court admonished the jury to disregard Burkan's "highly improper" remark. But with LaGuardia publicly flogging Bielaski in the newspapers almost every day, the court took the extraordinary step of sequestering the jury under twenty-four-hour supervision by federal marshals for the remainder of the trial. Veteran court observers could not remember the last time a New York jury had been locked down in the middle of a trial.

The jury had enjoyed only one night at the Hotel McAlpin at the government's expense when Frederick C. Pitts took the witness stand. Pitts testified that he had been hired by Costello personally to operate one of his speedboats, but that Costello failed to pay him as promised. Pitts gave him an ultimatum: pay $2,400 in back wages owed, or he was going to the feds. Costello refused, and Pitts was soon on Bielaski's payroll.

On Burkan's cross-examination Pitts admitted that he had taken the Costello job while under a threat of being imprisoned for abandonment of his wife. He was on the horns of a dilemma, facing a choice "of going to state's prison or to the federal prison," Pitts explained wryly, so he chose federal prison. "Have you served any time yet in federal prison?" Burkan asked. "No," Pitts conceded, because "I have been working for Mr. Bielaski." Burkan pressed further, forcing Pitts to admit that he was actually a "double double-crosser." When Mrs. Pitts was once again on the verge of having him imprisoned for nonsupport, Pitts went to Costello's attorneys with a new proposition—for $4,800 he would leave the country and never testify for the government.

"So, you offered to sell out Bielaski for $4,800?" Burkan bellowed.

"Well, if you want to put it that way."

The government immediately moved for revocation of bail. Pitts was whisked straight from the courthouse to the Manhattan Tombs.

It was a vignette many a defense lawyer dreams of, but Burkan had no time to savor his coup. It was shunted to the inside pages of the next day's newspapers by a superseding force of overwhelming magnitude. For at that very moment another client was en route from Los Angeles to see Burkan, bringing with him explosive troubles and luggage packed, reputedly, with more than two million dollars in cash and government securities.

CHAPTER 19

The Bindlestiff

Charlie Chaplin married Lillita Louise MacMurray, sixteen years old and four months pregnant, in the hardscrabble railroad depot of Empalme, Mexico, on November 25, 1924. Lillita had grown up near the Chaplin Studio in Hollywood, and at the age of twelve she had a small role in *The Kid*. Chaplin promoted her to leading lady for *The Gold Rush*, renamed her Lita Grey, seduced and impregnated her, and then, in light of her family way, recast her role with Georgia Hale. That the circumstances of these nuptials were legally fraught, if not obvious on the face of the matter, was evidenced by the presence of Chaplin's New York lawyer, Nathan Burkan, in the small wedding party. Locals, as puzzled as they were star-struck, told reporters who belatedly arrived on the scene that the groom had abandoned his bride after the daybreak civil ceremony and spent the rest of the day shark fishing with a Mexican guide.

Just over two tumultuous years later, Lita left Chaplin's Beverly Hills mansion for the last time, taking with her Charles Jr. and a second child, Sydney, conceived during a brief interval of connubial peace that followed the birth of the first son. On January 10, 1927, after six weeks of fruitless financial negotiations, Lita sued for divorce. Her complaint told a tale as old as time: Chaplin had married her to avoid facing prosecution for statutory rape, and then subjected her to humiliation, cruelty, and intimidation calculated to end in divorce, but only at such time and on such terms and conditions as suited him.

This pattern of abuse began on the train trip back from Mexico, where Lita overheard Chaplin telling his entourage, "Well, boys, this is better than the penitentiary; but it won't last long." When they arrived home he said to Lita, "I'll make you so damn sick of me that you won't want to live with me." Chaplin berated her for refusing to have an abortion, "as many other women had done for him"; demanded that she perform "acts and things for the gratification of his abnormal, unnatural, perverted and degenerate sexual desires"; and regaled her with details of "his personal experience with five prominent moving picture women involving such practices." Throughout their marriage, the complaint alleged, Chaplin "openly associated with other women," including "a certain prominent moving picture actress."

Lita's lawyers had left only one bargaining chip on the table for future negotiations: the names of the "certain prominent moving picture actress" with whom Chaplin regularly kept company and the five starlets with whom he had boasted of sharing unnatural congress.

In later years, by then comfortably settled into the role of a Chaplin ex-wife, Lita was embarrassed by her lawyers' rhetorical excesses and disavowed the more puritanical fulminations contained in the divorce papers. But she never recanted the allegations of neglect, mental cruelty, or adultery, which, without embellishment, constituted ample grounds for a bill of divorcement.

The Los Angeles divorce court appointed temporary receivers to take control of Chaplin's assets, personal and corporate. Bank accounts and safe deposit boxes were frozen, and guards were posted at the mansion and at the Chaplin Studio. Chaplin's work-in-progress, *The Circus*, had been in production there for months and was nearly complete, but the receivers found virtually no motion picture–making apparatus on the premises. Chaplin had suspended production a few days after Lita's departure from their home and ordered his cameraman, Roland Totheroh, to smuggle all footage out of California. By now, Totheroh had a name for this drill—he called it "Eluding Charlie's Wives."

With its blend of lurid specificity and Victorian delicacy, Lita Grey's divorce petition was a sensation. The county clerk had to remove it from the public files as a crowd control measure. Enterprising pamphleteers were hawking "Charlie Chaplin's Divorce Case (Uncensored)" for 25 cents and doing a brisk business. Newspapers took full advantage of their legal privilege to report the contents of this official court document. "Bestial Acts Charged" was one midwestern headline.

Self-appointed guardians of public morality called for boycotts and bans of Chaplin films. It was speculated that Chaplin would have to throw himself on the mercy of Will Hays to avoid the fate of his one-time Keystone Studios costar Fatty Arbuckle, whose career had been destroyed by the sex and manslaughter scandal that had prompted Hays's appointment.

Chaplin had left Los Angeles by train before the divorce papers were filed, conveniently rendering himself unavailable for comment or service of process. The only voice speaking publicly in his defense was that of Nathan Burkan. Lita's complaint "was a lot of nonsense," he insisted. "The wedding was a happy affair for both of them. I was the best man, I was on the train with them. It was obvious that the two of them were very much in love."

"That's Charlie's story," snarked one reporter after interviewing Burkan, "and he's going to stick to it." Burkan also let slip that settlement negotiations had ended with Chaplin offering $500,000 and Lita demanding $1 million.

The public relations pummeling was already in its third day when Chaplin finally surfaced in Chicago. Reporters staking out Dearborn Station, the eastern terminus of the Atchison, Topeka, and Santa Fe Railroad, spotted a "dejected and disconsolate figure ambling down the train shed" accompanied only by his diminutive valet, Toraichi Kono—a tableau that might have been staged in a modern-dress production of *Don Quixote*. Chaplin politely waved off reporters' questions: "It's just simply too terrible for words." He volunteered only that he was headed to New York, for reasons that were at once enigmatic and vaguely ominous: "I'm going there to write the concluding chapters to a story of my life, which is now appearing in a New York magazine."

In a perceptive analysis of Chaplin's failings as a husband, journalist Adela Rogers St. Johns wrote that, to him, other people simply did not exist "in the ordinary sense. Yet when he finds a human brain that has something to give, or a human character that is new and worth studying, he grabs it like an octopus. He may bring home a tramp, a great psychiatrist, a colored washwoman, an English duchess, and spend hour upon hour talking with them." Jim Tully, a boxer and itinerant roustabout-turned-writer, was one such specimen in Chaplin's collection.

A few years earlier, Tully was a newly celebrated but still financially challenged literary lion, dubbed the "hobo poet" for his autobiographical depictions of life on the bum in his first novel, *Emmett Lawler*. One night he found himself at a swank dinner where Chaplin was the guest of honor, a gathering for which Tully was underfinanced, underdressed, and undercultured. Chaplin—sensing in Tully a kindred soul, a fellow "bindlestiff" adrift in an uncomprehending world—immediately set him at ease. Some months afterward, one of that evening's hosts, the director Paul Bern, sent an urgent telegram to Chaplin requesting that he make time to see Tully. "He is frightfully depressed and says a talk with you will restore his confidence," wrote Bern. "You may be saving his life and, anyway, this is one of those obligations which go with your great achievements."

Chaplin took Tully under his wing, giving him an ill-defined day job at the Chaplin Studio. One observer of their interactions thought Tully's duties consisted "wholly in discussing political movements with Chaplin." Tully spent eighteen eventful months with Chaplin during the production of *The Gold Rush,* doing some publicity and ghostwriting, but also finding time to complete his second novel and compile detailed notes for a biography of his boss. Tully and Chaplin had their inevitable falling out, possibly over a line in Tully's 1926 Hollywood spoof, *Jarnegan,* that compared Chaplin to the "illiterate and vain" title character. They feuded for many years after. Noting that Tully came from a long line of ditchdiggers, Chaplin once gibed that "what his forebears did with a shovel, Jim strives to do with a pen."

The first installment of "Charlie: His Real-Life Story," by Jim Tully, appeared in the January 1927 issue of the *Pictorial Review,* a magazine that existed primarily to disseminate the dress patterns of its corporate parent, the American Fashion Company. Tully's article recounted the deprivations of Chaplin's childhood and the pluck with which he overcame his humble beginnings. It portrayed Chaplin as a deeply serious thinker whose comedy masked a pervasive melancholy, a son deeply devoted to his beloved but troubled mother, a man profoundly appreciative of the role children had played in his success, and a lover of dogs and horses. Tully could not have done much better by Chaplin were he still on his payroll.

Chaplin had not objected when Tully informed him of his plans. But on January 7, just before Chaplin left Los Angeles, Burkan signed off on legal papers that sought to enjoin publication of further installments and $500,000 in damages. The legal basis of the action was not, as widely misreported at the time, defamation. Rather, Chaplin claimed a violation of a New York State "right-of-privacy" statute, which prohibited the use of an individual's name for advertising purposes without written consent. (It was the same statute Burkan had used, nearly twenty-five years earlier, to prevent Zonophone from selling records credited to an ersatz "Victor Herbert's Band.") *Pictorial Review,* so Burkan's theory went, violated this prohibition by advertising that it was running the life story of a man identified as "Charlie Chaplin" without his consent.

As Burkan's office was filing the *Pictorial Review* complaint, attorneys for James Joyce were drawing up an action based on the same statute to enjoin a middlebrow pornographer named Samuel Roth from publishing bowdlerized excerpts of *Ulysses,* which at the time had no copyright protection in the United States. Joyce's legal theory—that identifying him as the author without his consent violated the right-of-privacy law—was a stretch; Chaplin's case was downright frivolous. The statute had never been employed to prevent the editorial use of a public figure's name or likeness in news reporting. Indeed, years earlier, Burkan had been the losing attorney in a key precedent in which the court had refused to enjoin use of a person's name in "truthful" statements of fact on matters of legitimate public interest.

Why such a tendentious, aggressive response to a feel-good profile in a politely decorous ladies' magazine? Tully's tenure in Chaplin's entourage had coincided with the courtship of Lita Grey and he had been one of the few around Chaplin with the courage to express reservations about her abilities, openly dismissing her as simply the boss's plaything du jour. He had chafed at being tasked, first, with persuading the press that Chaplin had discovered a major new talent, and then with covering up her delicate condition until a decent interval after the wedding had passed. Now he was in a position to dish some dirt just as the marriage was disintegrating.

But *Pictorial Review* was not a likely platform for salacious material, and Tully's low regard for Lita was already a matter of record. Chaplin's representatives had been given advance copies of the first three installments, all of them perfectly hagiographic. Perhaps, as the magazine's editor charitably suggested, Chaplin's reaction could be ascribed to the "eccentricities of genius." Or, just possibly, the lawsuit was a handy pretext for Chaplin's sudden departure from the state of California. Perish the thought that Charlie Chaplin, with Lita's aggressive matrimonial lawyers nipping at his heels, had just decided to take a powder.

After spending a night in a Chicago hotel, Chaplin and his valet boarded the Twentieth Century Limited at LaSalle Street Station, accompanied by a contingent of reporters hungry for a scoop and prepared to shadow Chaplin all the way to New York to get it.

Chaplin was reticent at first, deferring any comment on his legal predicament until he could confer with his lawyer in New York. To pass time he entertained the press corps with a detailed synopsis of *The Circus,* illustrating the action with energetic pantomime. He spoke of his children, but only superficially—the eighteen-month-old was "very musical," the nine-month-old "more serious"—in no way dispelling the perception that he was no more than a remote presence in their lives. He said that his main concern was that Lita's accusations would sully the children's names, a strikingly off-key note in what was otherwise a disciplined performance.

But late that night Chaplin invited two friendly, pliable reporters—Austin O'Malley and James Doherty—to his compartment. Six hours later, they emerged with a first draft of Chaplin's side of the story. "The desire to tell someone his troubles was overpowering," Doherty wrote. "Four days of agony he had endured since publication of his wife's allegations. Four days of suppression of emotion, with only Kono, his Jap valet, for a sympathizer and confidant. It was too much."

Over a game of cards, Chaplin told the two reporters that he planned to make his story into a movie in which he would portray himself. He demonstrated his creative process in real time, spinning off ideas, reworking them, and starting again, mixing fact and fiction, with no regard for continuity and evidently forgetting that he would not be doing the final edit.

Chaplin improvised a scenario that followed a template familiar to his fans—a little fellow, pure of heart, falls for an unattainable beauty. In this telling, he loved Lita "purely, deeply, devotedly." He was blissfully happy as he exchanged vows in a Mexican magistrate's "rude cabin." "A ray of sunlight penetrated through a tiny window which was crossed by four wooden bars," Chaplin recalled. "The shadow of the cross was thrown full on my breast, and I gasped, wondering at its significance." It was only later, after the babies were born, that Lita declared she "got no kick" out of being married to him and began running around with other men whom Chaplin, obligingly, named for the reporters.

Then he blocked out a darker version of the story. Lita had threatened, "You've got to marry me or we'll go to the district attorney." She told Chaplin that she considered marrying the father of her unborn child a sacrifice, for she was in love with another. A financial settlement was discussed and agreed upon, but Lita backed away. A brief thaw in

Lita's attitude after Charles Jr. was born was only a "pretense." She spent lavishly on herself and spread vicious slanders that Charlie was a degenerate. "Like many fool men, I loved her more when she wronged me, and I am afraid I still love her."

Doherty thought Chaplin, in that Pullman berth, "seemed like one seeking solace in a confessional." But he had confessed to nothing more than being a besotted romantic, manipulated and played for a fool by Lita's mother, whom he accused of continually putting her "big, well-developed girl" in the path of a helpless naïf, exploiting his desperate yearning for fatherhood. "Both mother and daughter think mostly of sex," Chaplin added gallantly, whereas he had "reached the age where sex was incidental." He was thirty-seven, Lita was eighteen.

By the time the card game broke up, it was Friday morning and the train was nearing New York. Chaplin briefly considered getting off at Croton-Harmon and taking a car into New York City to avoid the scrum of reporters and photographers that awaited him at Grand Central Terminal. His traveling companions persuaded him that any such evasion would only make the journalistic beast, which he would encounter sooner or later, more surly.

When he alighted at Grand Central just before 10 A.M., rain from Park Avenue grates dripped onto Chaplin's pearl gray hat and full-length astra-khan-collared coat. "Melpomene, the muse of tragedy, stalked the trail of the prince of all the clowns as he strode haltingly toward the outer air," one reporter rhapsodized. Dozens of flashbulbs went off when Chaplin was greeted by Arthur Kelly of United Artists' New York office. A police escort guided Chaplin, Kono, and Kelly to the Vanderbilt Avenue taxi stand, through a "half-antagonistic, half-ribald" crowd of several hundred. He was hungry, Chaplin told reporters. He might go dine at the Ritz, or maybe at Child's (where the buckwheat pancakes were a favorite of his). He would then go meet with Mr. Burkan, stop by United Artists, and spend the night at the Ambassador Hotel.

But the reporters lost his trail. They would not find Chaplin at any of these places, and Burkan, they could readily ascertain, was tied up in court all day. It was as if the world's most recognizable man had "vanished into some burrow with his solitaire deck and his Atlantic Monthly and his hand baggage and his Japanese valet."

The ostensible purpose of Chaplin's trip to New York, assisting with the prosecution of *Chaplin v. Pictorial Review Company,* was already a moot point. Burkan had appeared before federal judge Thomas Thacher early that morning to argue for a preliminary injunction. Lawyers for the magazine gleefully pointed out that Tully's article was the only good publicity Chaplin was getting and he ought to be grateful for it. Judge Thacher posed a hypothetical: Would President Coolidge have a cause of action under the New York right-of-privacy law against a magazine that published articles about him without his consent? Burkan had to concede that, under his theory of the case, the president could enjoin such publications.

Burkan's argument, as lawyers would say, "proved too much." Although Judge Thacher reserved issuing his ruling, he plainly telegraphed that it would go against Chaplin. The hearing concluded in time for Burkan to hurry back to Judge Winslow's courtroom, where the government put several more severely compromised former Coast Guardsmen on the stand in *U.S. v. Costello* and then rested its case. Court adjourned for the weekend and Burkan headed home to unwind after a day that would have tested any lawyer's stamina.

His day, as it turned out, was just beginning to get interesting. A high-maintenance house guest awaited him.

CHAPTER 20

New York's Spotlight Lawyer

Chaplin had taken refuge in Burkan's luxurious Fifth Avenue penthouse. On the fourteenth floor of a newly constructed building at the corner of 95th Street, the apartment overlooked the Central Park reservoir and had unobstructed views of the developing Manhattan skyline. It was tastefully decorated with furniture and objects Burkan had purchased on his European travels. Over the course of their friendship, Burkan had come to share many of Chaplin's tastes and proclivities, including his preference for Japanese manservants. Chaplin and his valet could make themselves right at home.

Accounts of Chaplin's wee hours interview aboard the Twentieth Century Limited had not yet made the New York papers. When he arrived home, Burkan was not aware that Chaplin had already disobeyed his advice to be circumspect in public comments about Lita. In the quiet of Burkan's apartment, Chaplin seemed to be in full possession of his formidable powers of personal magnetism. Burkan decided to invite some reporters and photographers up to meet Chaplin on this friendly turf.

As the men and women of the press filed in, Chaplin tried to stay in the background, sinking low into a deep armchair while Burkan briefed the reporters on his legal "strategy." He intended to disprove every one of Lita's allegations and countersue for the anguish she had inflicted on poor Charlie. But the reporters, especially the "feminine among the scribes," pelted Chaplin with questions far more probing and personal than any he had fielded from his card-playing companions en route to

New York. At first his answers were measured and rueful, but he became increasingly bitter, combative, and creepy as the interview wore on. Did he still love Lita? "I couldn't. Cruelty kills love." What about the five actresses? "Do I like five women? You bet I do. I like fifty women."

One reporter asked Chaplin why he married such young girls. He conceded that they did not offer the kind of intellectual companionship he craved, yet they had a certain "primitive, instinctively healthy outlook on life" that appealed to him. It was more of a "parental feeling," he said, "you can have the same companionship and love for them as for your children." Then, without further prompting, he blurted out: "I am completely crushed by the accusations of this viperous vixen!"

After the reporters left his apartment around 9:30, Burkan and Arthur Kelly tried to get Chaplin's mind off his troubles by taking him to catch the second act of *George White's Scandals,* a bawdy Broadway revue. Afterward, to work off some of Chaplin's nervous energy, they walked the more than fifty blocks from Times Square back to Burkan's apartment. The early editions of the Saturday papers were waiting for them. For the first time, a complete record of Chaplin's Twentieth Century Limited monologues appeared in print. Only then did Burkan fully realize that the great mime had already said way too much.

The following morning, Saturday, Burkan appeared at the New York offices of United Artists, where an even larger gathering of reporters was waiting for a promised formal press conference with Chaplin. Burkan announced that Chaplin was exhausted and could not see anyone. After their long walk the night before, Chaplin had still been too agitated to sleep. At some point he collapsed, and a "nerve specialist," Dr. Gustav Tieck, was called. Chaplin was an artist of fragile temperament, Burkan said, and "the lies that have been broadcast from the West Coast would put a Gene Tunney in bed."

Burkan was vague about the exact nature of Chaplin's indisposition, and over the next few days, as he and Dr. Tieck tag-teamed the press with a stream of medical bulletins, the diagnosis remained nebulous—"nervous prostration," "exhaustion," "highly unstrung," "hysteria," "melancholia." Rumors of a suicide watch were alternately stoked and then scotched. The only thing they made crystal clear was that Chaplin's condition did not allow him to speak publicly. To enforce the quarantine, Burkan stationed guards in the lobby of his building and had his telephone temporarily disconnected. Much of the resulting reportage was alarmingly credulous, accepting as fact that Chaplin had suffered a nervous breakdown—"Chaplin Takes Gravely Ill, Kept to Bed" was the headline in the *New York American*. Other coverage was more cynical. The *New York Sun* provided the most clear-eyed assessment of the situation: "Chaplin Hides in Lawyer's Home and Is Ordered to Quit Talking."

A weekend spent nursing Charlie Chaplin and ministering to the press did not handicap Burkan's defense of Frank Costello and company. On Sunday, with Chaplin purportedly confined to the guest bedroom, a dozen lawyers—Burkan, his associates, and the rest of the Costello defense team—met in the living room to map out their case-in-chief and closing arguments. Monday morning, after putting just a few character witnesses on the stand, Burkan rested his case and arguments began.

Burkan's was a stem-winder, a scathing denouncement of A. Bruce Bielaski as "a mysterious and invisible power who employs bribe takers, rum runners, and pirates; a menace to the free institutions of this country." He went on to ask rhetorically:

> Why wasn't Bielaski called here to explain his methods of investigating rum running? Why was Fred Pitts, who admitted on the stand that he was a blackmailer, promoted to be an "under-cover" agent? ... It is a sad day when the government has to pay dirty money to men who would stoop as low as that for it ... Either they promised to weave their stories the way Bielaski wanted them to, or they were threatened with a dungeon.

Accounts differ as to whether Burkan whispered or shouted his peroration: "The depraved character of the witnesses and the foul use of money in this case by the government make it an insult to your intelligence to have to pass judgment upon it."

The jurors deliberated from late afternoon to nearly midnight before returning to the Hotel McAlpin without having reached a verdict.

Meanwhile, back in Los Angeles, after hearing testimony from Lita Grey—"modishly dressed, but with less elegance than many of the shop girls and society women who composed the audience"—Judge Walter Guerin of the Superior Court ordered Chaplin to pay Lita $4,000 per month temporary alimony and child support. With two installments already due, as well as attorneys' fees and certain other costs, Chaplin's bill, payable immediately, was over $14,000.

With the voluble Chaplin out of the public eye, his retinue rallied on his behalf, in court and out, with more disciplined messaging. They sought to avert the public's gaze away from Lita's shocking allegations and toward the extravagance of her financial demands (the temporary alimony she was awarded was nearly $55,000 a month in 2020 dollars); away from Chaplin's peccadilloes and caddish behavior and toward the priceless joy that his fragile gifts had brought to millions. They called upon the public to separate the art from the artist and not to allow a passing scandal to derail the career of an irreplaceable genius. Gavin McNab, the Chaplin Studio's West Coast attorney, likened the alimony hearing to a "screening of the second *Gold Rush*," adding that "the only thing they failed to ask for is an order that Chaplin get out of bed and complete *The Circus.*"

Drawing on Chaplin's unmatched cache of goodwill, their dissembling worked. Editorials appeared decrying the very scandal-mongering that some of the same papers had indulged in just days before, and urging the public not to rush to judgment. Enlightened women's groups expressed at least qualified support for Chaplin. Far from being boycotted, Chaplin's old pictures enjoyed a small surge in business. Letters to the editor portrayed Lita as an ingrate for refusing the $50 weekly checks Charlie was generously sending and urged her—an eighteen-year-old with two babies—to get a job.

During breaks in *United States v. Costello*, Burkan fed reporters acrid, off-the-cuff commentary on *Chaplin v. Chaplin.* His remarks were widely reported and drew a sharp on-the-record retort from Judge Guerin, who took umbrage at Burkan's insinuation that, in allowing Lita to pursue corporate assets and authorizing the receivers to crack Chaplin's safes, the court itself was party to a "cheap publicity stunt." The judge warned that if Burkan intended to come to Los Angeles to appear as counsel for Chaplin, as he was promising to do, "there would be due me and the courts in this county an apology."

No such apology was forthcoming. Another legal development out of Los Angeles was causing Burkan more consternation than the divorce proceeding. The Internal Revenue Service, evidently prompted by rumors that Chaplin was preparing to leave the country, filed tax liens totaling more than a million dollars against his personal and corporate property, covering claims for six years' back taxes. But there was a silver lining in this new cloud hanging over Chaplin: the IRS liens had priority over any claims of Mrs. Chaplin and prevented the receivers from seizing Charlie's assets.

Nearly twenty-four hours after beginning their deliberations, the *Costello* jury, "haggard and worn," informed the court it had reached a verdict of acquittal for eight of the defendants—Coast Guardsmen and other minor players—but were deadlocked 6–6 on Costello and the other leaders of the ring. Uncharacteristically, Burkan did not provide any quotes for attribution, but his hand can be discerned in press reports which gave the outcome the precise spin he desired: "A complete loss for the government and a direct thrust at the methods of prohibition enforcement employed by A. Bruce Bielaski." The headline in the *Daily News* was "Rum Jurors Repudiate Bielaski." One juror told reporters that "we'd have held out until doomsday before we'd have convicted anyone on evidence such as the government offered in this case."

Congressman LaGuardia piled on. In a letter to Treasury secretary Andrew Mellon he stated that he was "reliably informed that the jury disagreed solely on account of the character of the government's witnesses" and called for the dismantling of the "vicious" undercover operation, which had proved "conducive of blackmail, oppression and abuse of law." Within weeks, after a reorganization of the Treasury Department substantially reduced the budget for undercover Prohibition enforcement, Bielaski retired permanently to the private sector.

Frank Costello's bail was immediately reduced to $5,000, and he was never retried on the rum-running charges. On December 1, 1933, nearly seven years after the mistrial and just four days before the 21st Amendment repealing Prohibition was ratified, the indictment was dismissed. By then Costello had transformed himself into a slot machine kingpin, and the biggest threat to his empire was the newly elected mayor of New York, Fiorello LaGuardia, for whom gambling was a distinctly disfavored form of vice.

Burkan was justifiably proud of his role in exposing some of the more pernicious side effects of Prohibition. In June 1933, he had the satisfaction of serving as a delegate to the New York State constitutional convention that voted to ratify the 21st Amendment.

While Burkan was waiting for the jury to come back with the Costello verdict, a representative of the Charles Chaplin Film Corporation had gone to the Times Square branch of the Bowery and East River National Bank to withdraw the company's entire balance of $500,000 in cash. Fifteen minutes later, Secret Service agents appeared at the same bank, attempting to place an IRS lien on the just-closed account. Burkan moved quickly to dissuade anyone from jumping to any untoward conclusion that Chaplin was trying to thwart either his wife or Uncle Sam. Money had been moved to New York, he falsely assured reporters, as part of a plan to complete production of *The Circus* there—a plan that

Chaplin, on the mend from the "nervous breakdown" that he had suffered a week earlier, meets the press under Burkan's watchful eye, January 22, 1927. (Queens Borough Public Library Archives, New York Herald–Tribune Photo Morgue Collection)

supposedly predated Chaplin's marital woes—and funds had now been withdrawn to meet payroll. It is improbable that Chaplin ever seriously considered completing *The Circus* anywhere but the Chaplin Studio in Los Angeles, as he eventually did, but Burkan and Chaplin kept up for months the ruse that the actor might never return to Los Angeles, at one point spreading a rumor that they were shopping around for studio space in the Bronx.

When he arrived home after the Costello verdict, Burkan was met by IRS agents who were eager to question the bedridden taxpayer. Marathon discussions that began that night and continued for several days resulted in an arrangement that satisfied the government and maximized Chaplin's leverage in the divorce proceeding. He was permitted to post a bond that freed up his assets in New York, while the government's liens on his California property—i.e., the assets that were within the reach of the divorce court and the receivers—were left in place pending completion of a more extensive audit of the tax years in dispute. Lita's pleas for help from the commissioner of Internal Revenue fell on deaf ears. She was left holding an uncollectible temporary alimony order.

The time was right to reintroduce Chaplin to his public. Burkan unveiled a chastened, more physically and philosophically presentable Chaplin to thirty reporters and photographers at a Saturday afternoon press conference in his apartment, just one week after Chaplin's purported nervous breakdown. Chaplin was soft-spoken and terse. He thanked the public for suspending judgment and expressed no rancor toward Lita or her family, letting Burkan answer the most difficult questions. The Tramp had once again dodged a falling anvil. He could dust off his bowler hat and waddle off to the horizon with his dignity, and his career, intact. An ugly divorce that started out looking like a rout had become a long war of attrition, and Chaplin settled in for a long encampment at his lawyer's Fifth Avenue penthouse. Time, Burkan knew, was on his client's side.

During those twenty days in January 1927, Burkan had successfully juggled the legal crises of Frank Costello and Charlie Chaplin and dispatched the forces of public sanctimony in the full glare of national attention. Syndicated columnist Grant Dixon dubbed him "New York's Spotlight Lawyer." It was a sobriquet twenty-five years in the making, and one that Burkan would retain for the rest of his life.

Chaplin idled in New York for seven months—plenty of time to sit for an oil portrait by the British painter Cathleen Mann, the Marchioness of Queensbury, which Chaplin gave to Burkan as a thank-you gift. The two men were seen out and about together frequently—at Burkan's usual rounds of political and industry banquets, at opening nights, at Yankee Stadium for a Jack Dempsey–Jack Sharkey heavyweight bout. And the two took advantage of Chaplin's extended stay to tend to one other piece of unfinished legal business, a long-delayed jury trial in the case of *Loeb v. Chaplin.*

Leo Loeb was a Marine stationed at Fort Mifflin in Philadelphia in the spring of 1918, when he conceived an idea for a wartime comedy. Charlie Chaplin, he thought, would be just the man to execute it. He mailed a three-page synopsis of the story, which he called "The Rookie," to the Chaplin Studio. On April 23, it came back with a polite rejection letter from a studio employee, who stated that Mr. Chaplin felt it would be inappropriate to do a burlesque of the military during wartime. A little over a month later, however, Chaplin began production of *Shoulder Arms.*

After the war, Loeb, then working as a disinfectant salesman, filed a lawsuit claiming that *Shoulder Arms* was based on his scenario and that he was entitled to be compensated for his contribution to the acclaimed and profitable film. The sequence of incidents and plot devices in Chaplin's picture were indeed broadly similar to Loeb's story outline—a drill scene, a trench scene, a bunk scene, a sentry mission, an unlikely heroic feat, a spy mission, and so on. Loeb's theory of the case, that Chaplin had used his scenario as a framework, to which Chaplin applied his unique genius for gags and comic business, was not implausible. The timing and wording of the rejection letter were, at the very least, curious. Loeb's legal theory was not copyright infringement, but rather that Chaplin had been unjustly enriched.

The case came to trial before a jury in May 1927. Chaplin would be the star witness in his own defense. The old United States Courthouse and Post Office across from City Hall in lower Manhattan had seen its share of celebrity trials, but this one was special. "Work in the courthouse was virtually suspended with Chaplin's arrival. Stenographers, clerks, doormen and other attaches stormed the courtroom and deputy marshals had to form riot lines to keep the crowds from breaking in the doors."

Chaplin was plainly nervous as he took the stand. "Are you at perfect ease?" Burkan asked him.

"No."

"Now, calm yourself down and get to perfect composure."

Chaplin assumed his characteristic sitting pose, with one leg crooked underneath his posterior. He firmly denied ever having seen Loeb's scenario. He explained that he had been touring military bases in the South on the Liberty Bond campaign in April 1918 when the document passed through his studio. It was his experience on the tour that changed his attitude toward making a war comedy. "I had been to many cantonments. I could see the possibility of giving a humorous angle of the war." Inspiration for the various incidents came from numerous sources that were all around him during the war. "I don't think anybody who is sensitive could possibly miss the feeling of the war or what it would suggest in the way of creative work."

Chaplin gave Loeb's excellent attorney, Mortimer Hays, an opening to exploit. Asked by Burkan how he started the process of making a motion picture, Chaplin answered, "I have just a general conception of a framework, a structure, an attitude, and that framework is a flimsy structure upon which I can hang my individual bits of business." Indeed, if he wrote his framework down, Chaplin said, he might be able to fit it "on my cuff." Loeb had conceded that his scenario of a few hundred words was only a barebones framework, but now Chaplin was admitting that he required nothing more than that to get started creatively.

On cross-examination, Hays handed Chaplin a copy of the Loeb scenario to read. "I cannot see without my glasses," Chaplin said. The reporter for the Associated Press describes the business that followed, none of which is captured in the official court record:

> Chaplin scrutinized the paper with expressions of exaggerated concentration which brought gales of laughter. He shrugged with a pathetic gesture of frustration and the spectators rocked in their seats. . . . Nathan Burkan, the comedian's lawyer, handed up his own glasses, and Chaplin tried them on his nose and then stared blankly at the paper. His expression and pantomime of his inability to see brought more laughter, in which the judge joined. He leaned over the bench and proffered Chaplin the judicial spectacles. The actor took them with a bow, tried them frontwards, backwards, as a monocle with the extra glass riding over one ear, and then as a magnifying glass.
>
> "I can read," he cried with a happy smile, and the crowd cheered.

Once the hilarity had subsided, Hays recovered nicely: "Do you see three pages of fairly close-written typing?"

"Yes."

"And is that not more than you would write down on your cuff?"

After nearly eight hours of deliberations, the jury reported that it was deadlocked. The court declared a mistrial. Reporters learned that the jury's vote was 10–2 in favor of Loeb, with the majority inclined to award Loeb the full $50,000 he was seeking. That news was eye-opening for Burkan. When the case was retried in November 1927, Chaplin was three thousand miles away from the courtroom. Burkan simply read Chaplin's prior testimony to the jury, without the funny business. With Chaplin in absentia, that second jury returned a verdict in his favor.

The Chaplins' divorce action continued to be hotly contested in the Los Angeles Superior Court and in the press through the spring and summer of 1927. In his answering papers, Chaplin accused Lita of "extreme cruelty" (although the specifics of the charge read like the whining of a jilted teenager), demanded custody of the children (he had detectives tailing Lita to get dirt on her), and suggested that the community property to be divided totaled only about $270,000. Lita's lawyers continued to pursue discovery of Chaplin's earnings and hidden assets. Her public settlement demands remained well north of $1 million.

Chaplin resisted intense pressure from his business associates to settle. United Artists chairman Joseph Schenck, who was awaiting delivery

Lita Grey Chaplin poses after the final divorce hearing, August 22, 1927. (© Roy Export Company Ltd.)

of *The Circus*, already a year behind schedule, was getting increasingly impatient. Subpoenaed by Lita to appear at a temporary alimony hearing, Schenck testified that while Chaplin, when he worked, was the highest-paid person in the motion picture business, he worked only when inspired. Time meant nothing to Chaplin. "We'd lose our bankroll if we had to pay him a salary." Consequently, Schenck said, his future income was entirely unpredictable.

Trial of the divorce action was scheduled for August 22, 1927. Burkan headed west several weeks in advance of the trial to participate in last-ditch settlement discussions. Chaplin followed in mid-August. Still unwilling to venture into Los Angeles, Chaplin met with Burkan up the coast in Monterey, where Burkan informed him of Lita's final demand: a $625,000 property settlement, full custody of the children, and a $200,000 trust fund for the boys. The divorce would be granted on routine grounds of neglect and cruelty, with all salacious allegations dropped. Chaplin had little choice but to agree. If the case went to trial, Lita's evidence of his boorishness and hidden wealth would result in a judgment devastating to his wallet and reputation. Even with the settlement, *Variety* estimated, the whole debacle would cost Chaplin upward of $2 million when various court costs, fees paid to "two of the most expensive legal minds in the country" (Burkan and Gavin McNab), and the costs of delayed production were figured in.

Lita Grey liked to repeat a mythical version of how the settlement came about. In this account, she went to see Marion Davies, mistress of William Randolph Hearst, an occasional Burkan client, and told her that she would be identified at trial as the "certain prominent motion picture actress" mentioned in the divorce complaint:

> The story goes that Charlie summoned Nathan Burkan to Los Angeles, a distance of 3,000 miles from New York, and met him at the train station. They went to a coffee shop and Charlie asked, "Nate, what shall I do?" Burkan answered in a single word—"settle"—and took the very next train back east.

It is unlikely that revelation of an affair with Marion Davies was a significant concern of Chaplin's; rumors of it had been rife in Hollywood for several years. But Lita was right that it was a short meeting. Chaplin left Monterey after one day and headed for Los Angeles to get the Chaplin Studio out of mothballs and finish production of *The Circus*. The settlement was approved by Judge Guerin, with only "a few sensation-hunters" attending the perfunctory final hearing, where, according to the *New York Times,* Lita's "pale and lifeless" testimony was "finished in record time."

PART SEVEN

The Naked City

CHAPTER 21

Love's Undertaker

"Despite his reputation of being the hardest boiled bachelor along Broadway," Nathan Burkan, 49, "has succumbed at last to the whizzing love darts of Cupid." More than one hundred guests, invited to "a reception" of unspecified occasion, gathered at Burkan's penthouse on Saturday night, October 8, 1927, and witnessed his surprise wedding to a tall, pretty twenty-nine-year-old department store buyer, Marienne Alexander. Among the guests were Al Jolson, fresh from the opening of *The Jazz Singer* two nights earlier, Joseph Schenck and Norma Talmadge, Gene Buck, Jay Witmark, and Burkan's three brothers and their wives. Charlie Chaplin, who had only recently vacated the guest bedroom, telephoned his congratulations from Hollywood.

Details of the couple's courtship were not made available to the press. Burkan's social doings and travels had been well chronicled in the trade and daily papers for years, but he had never been connected in print with Marienne or, for that matter, any other woman. Of their plans, reporters were able to divine only that "following an extended honeymoon, they will refit Burkan's 5th Ave. apartment, and build a palatial country home in Great Neck, Long Island." The 8,000-square-foot Tudor mansion with formal gardens, at the very tip of the Kings Point Peninsula (F. Scott Fitzgerald's "West Egg"), was ready for occupancy in time for the birth of their only child, Nathan Jr., in May 1931.

Hollywood gossip columnist Louella Parsons, who knew the Burkans well, wrote that "for years, Burkan was cynical on the subject of marriage, having seen so many matrimonial ventures go on the rocks. He once laughingly referred to himself as 'love's undertaker.'" (Parsons liked Burkan's offhand remark so much, she later appropriated that moniker for herself.) "But when he finally did choose a wife," Parsons went on, "he made a singularly successful choice. His life with Mrs. Burkan was extremely happy."

Burkan's attitude toward marriage was born of long experience fighting the battles of the sexes in the courts. New York divorce practice in that era was no game of tiddlywinks. There was only one cognizable basis for granting a divorce: adultery. Property distribution, alimony, and custody issues were all subject to moral evaluations, often leaving a woman whose conduct was not entirely beyond reproach with—to use a favorite Yiddishism of Burkan's—bubkes, nothing.

Within days of returning from his honeymoon at the Greenbrier in White Sulphur Springs, West Virginia, Burkan found himself back in the thick of other people's marital woes. George Leary was a prosperous dredging contractor and dry-dock builder. His wife, Julia, a patron of Catholic charities, was made a papal countess by Benedict XV in 1907. Julia had sued for divorce a few weeks earlier, naming a certain telephone operator as the current object of her husband's affections. The immediate trigger for her action, however, was the "shock and pain" of learning that her husband of twenty-seven years had been arrested by Prohibition agents after they found a still on the premises of an upstate electric utility in which he owned an interest. Burkan got back to New York just in time to represent Julia at a hearing on temporary alimony.

In the course of examining George Leary about his assets, Burkan asked, with a touch of sarcasm, if his electric company wasn't also involved in the manufacture of alcohol. Leary "leapt to his feet and advanced on Mr. Burkan." But when he loomed over the lawyer, Leary put his hands in his pockets and said, "I am not going to strike you." Retaking the witness stand, Leary continued to fume: "I just wanted to look him in the eyes and see if he would say it." Having identified a sore subject, Burkan went right back to it. Leary's lawyer, Vincent Leibell, interjected: "Your tactics are a disgrace to the profession. When the papers were filed in this case the first thing you did was show them to reporters. Reporters try all of your divorce actions," Leibell sniffed. "You and your matrimonial cases."

With that, the hearing went off the rails. For the remainder of the four hours, Burkan and Leibell argued over which one of them exercised the "most taste and tact" in divorce cases. It was an unseemly and intemperate display by two highly regarded lawyers, both of whom would later be considered by President Franklin Roosevelt for a federal judgeship. (Leibell was nominated after Burkan's death.)

Matrimonial cases brought out the worst in otherwise good people. Trying a case in the press—an offense that Burkan was most certainly guilty of—was hardly the worst of it. The headlines that follow are from the New York City tabloids that thrived for years on the titillating chum that Burkan regularly fed them.

"JELLY MAGNATE TELLS HOW TO DISCARD WIFE QUIETLY"

There was the strange case of Orator Francis Woodward, the playboy heir to a $30 million Jell-O fortune. For nearly two years, Orator had been living in a $2,000-a-month suite at the Sherry-Netherland Hotel in New York City, while his estranged wife, Persis, was living in Paris with their two children. In January 1929, Orator and his lawyer, Herbert C. Smythe, hatched an audacious plan to bring the marriage to a quick and, they hoped, inexpensive end.

Orator first took a lease on a furnished house in suburban Nyack, New York, and then filed a divorce complaint against Persis in the Rockland County court, a venue that Burkan called "a Mecca for wealthy and distressed gentlemen who want to get rid of their wives." Certainly, it had a reputation for being a quicker and quieter divorce venue than Manhattan. The complaint accused Persis of infidelity with six men—in Paris, in Italy, on the Riviera—specifically naming one Russian dance instructor and one Parisian "gigolo."

Orator and Smythe then left for France, where they orchestrated an abduction of the Woodward children as they were leaving school one afternoon. (Under French law, Orator, as the father, was entitled to do so. Indeed, he was assisted by the Prefecture of Police.) Orator immediately headed back to New York with the children; Smythe stayed behind to serve the Rockland County divorce papers on Persis and to gather witnesses against her. Orator was, for the moment, holding all the cards. A reporter he spoke to while crossing the Atlantic on the *Île de France* thought Orator "looked more or less pleased with himself, as he cast a deprecatory glance at a pile of English newspapers recounting 'sensational kidnapping by millionaire father.'"

Persis had a fine lawyer in New York to look out for her interests: Dudley Field Malone. Malone, a progressive politician and one of

Clarence Darrow's co-counsel in the Scopes Monkey Trial of 1925, specialized in divorce and had an office in Paris. Before sailing to France to retrieve Mrs. Woodward, Malone brought Burkan, an old friend and political ally, into the case as his co-counsel. After conferring on strategy, the two lawyers told reporters that they viewed the kidnapping as "an obvious attempt to put up a bluff and get a cheap settlement. Mr. Woodward has started something and we'll finish it."

Burkan filed a writ of habeas corpus in the state supreme court in Manhattan, seeking an order compelling Orator to turn the children over on the ground that he was an unfit guardian. The habeas petition—compiled with the help of private detective James McIntyre, known in the press as the "society sleuth"—detailed Orator's lengthy history of drunkenness and physical abusiveness toward Persis. It went on to allege that he suffered from delusions of grandeur, believing that he was "some sort of potentate," and that "one of his favorite amusements is to make his daughter salaam in his presence."

Orator's strange behavior was attributed to his infatuation with a mysterious Turkish "princess," Fatima Ala, with whom he consorted when in Europe. "She has thick black hair and a certain voluptuous walk that attracts attention everywhere," the affidavit of Orator's mother-in-law stated. "I have been informed she is not really a member of the Turkish nobility. Her father was a rug peddler." McIntyre's operatives told reporters that Fatima was actually "short and fat and has warts."

> But there is one thing the sleuths won't gainsay, and that is the princess' ability to interpret the oriental dances. While peeping through a transom, three of them piped Fatima doing the dance of the seven veils for the edification of Woodward. Each undulation of the dancer's diaphragm was greeted by the food king with vociferous applause.

After seeing reports of the case in the Paris newspapers, Fatima Ala issued a statement in which she asserted that her dancing ability was limited to "conventional ballroom steps." She offered to bring her family Koran to New York to substantiate her claim to nobility. "Furthermore, she protests that her description as being swarthy and possessing warts is uncomplimentary and untrue."

Burkan sent private eye McIntyre to meet the *Île de France* at the pier and serve the writ of habeas corpus. But Orator was able to evade service with the help of the crew, who spirited him and the children from the bowels of the ship via a lower-level gangplank. All McIntyre found was a note that Orator had left in his cabin: "To all reporters, greetings. We have enjoyed the *Île de France* and have had a nice trip. I have nothing further to say." A few days later, McIntyre's operatives found and served Orator in Nyack.

Reports that Orator had been accompanied by "seventeen gigolos" who would attest to Mrs. Woodward's infidelity proved unfounded. But several days later his attorney, Smythe, returned from Europe with two French women, two Russian men, and a Dutchman who reportedly would "tell of Paris parties and love rodeos on the Riviera in which sleek gigolos and dancing masters are said to have played Romeo for Mrs. Woodward." Private detectives hired by Orator kept the witnesses under constant guard to prevent reporters from speaking to them.

At a hearing on the writ of habeas corpus in Manhattan, Orator's lawyers contended that the court lacked jurisdiction to decide the custody issue in light of his prior divorce filing in Rockland County. Burkan argued that Orator's residency in Nyack was a sham and that his legal action there should be disregarded. Burkan grilled Orator on his sudden urge to live in the country. It turned out that he had slept in Nyack only once, and that was an afternoon nap. The court determined that it had jurisdiction but deferred further action until Persis arrived back in New York.

Burkan sent word to Persis that there was no need to rush back from Paris. His detectives had learned that Smythe was having trouble keeping his witnesses corralled. One of the Russian men died of delirium tremens on Ellis Island; one of the French women met the love of her life and disappeared, and the other became homesick:

> But the detectives convoying the foreigners had their greatest trouble with two other men, a Russian and a Dutchman.
>
> Otar Berk Tugai of Moscow insisted on a $25-a-day suite at the Ritz and caviar for breakfast, served in bed. He gave Woodward's sleuths nervous prostration by disappearing for three days and coming back to the hotel, almost out of his mind from the effects of synthetic vodka.
>
> Tugai also became temperamental and objected to the Dutch witness, Dirk Pen, stopping at the same hotel. The two met in the lobby and before an amused crowd called each other *cochon* and *canaille* in the language they both understood, French.

Within days of Mrs. Woodward's return to New York, the couple reached a settlement. Orator got his wished-for termination of the marriage, but it did not come cheap. He paid Persis $1 million and established trust funds of $750,000 for each child. It was, the press declared, a "sweeping victory" for Persis and "a new high price for millionaires who fail in efforts to break the bonds of matrimony." For a few weeks' work, Burkan and Malone split a $100,000 fee, which was also paid by Orator. Big paydays like that, often subsidized by men of great wealth and poor judgment, made it possible for Burkan to sustain his long-running, unremunerative crusades for Ascap, Jewel Carmen, and other causes dear to his heart.

"PEEPER PULLS A PIP ON PULLMAN"

Nayfack v. Nayfack had just the right mix of sex, celebrity, and pathos to attract and hold the attention of the 1920s tabloid press. Dentist Jules Nayfack, nephew of movie magnates Joseph and Nicholas Schenck, met and married Emily Nord, a dance instructor, in 1922. The Nayfacks and Schencks had opposed the match. "I realize how much you are in love and how unjust it seems to have us all opposed," Uncle Joe told Jules. "I want you to remember my prophecy: In two years you will wish you hadn't married her and you will be most unhappy. But it won't be so easy to get rid of her."

After the birth of a son, Joseph Nicholas, Emily began to spend time at her old dance school, where she met and teamed up with an Argentinian dancer billed as "Don Sebastian." With financial support from Jules, who was borrowing heavily from his family, the dance team of Sebastian and Nord tangoed and fandangoed in second-rate cabarets and vaudeville houses across the United States and Europe for the next three years, billing themselves as the next Vernon and Irene Castle. The act never earned enough from its bookings to cover expenses.

Jules repeatedly pleaded with Emily to return home, but she and Sebastian were remarkably adept at manipulating him. Sebastian wrote him from Los Angeles, where, over Jules's objection, they had gone for an engagement:

> Dear Friend Jules,
> If we make good here in Ambassador we will get in movies and if we do that means your troubles are over. I hope you will forgive me just once and wish for our success as our success means your success too. . . .
> Don't listen to everybody who talk to you lowdown filth, just trust.

Emily wrote: "Don't be discouraged. You have a son to be proud of and that's more than your Uncles Joe and Nick have with all their money. Take care of Sonny boy."

"I had deluded myself with the thought that my wife was neglecting our child because she was obsessed with a fascination for the stage, which I thought could be cured," Jules later explained. "I did not nourish the belief that it was a desire for Don Sebastian." When Jules finally abandoned all hope, he took his family's advice and hired Nathan Burkan to secure a divorce and custody of his son. It would not be enough for Jules to show that he and the child had largely been abandoned; he would also have to produce evidence of his own cuckolding by Sebastian. Burkan put the most dependable private detective he knew, Benjamin Kerin, on the case.

"Broadway Benny," as he was called, was the antithesis of the dashing private eye of noir fiction. Short, gap-toothed, and averse to drama and conflict, he was nonetheless a consummate professional to whom Burkan entrusted many difficult assignments that did not require derring-do or the debonair touch of a "society sleuth." Kerin knew how to get incriminating evidence on an errant spouse that would hold up in court. He adhered to a strict policy of never raiding a love nest without at least three witnesses in tow.

Kerin caught up with Emily and Sebastian in Pittsburgh. On the evening of October 2, 1927, he traveled back to New York on the same Pullman sleeper car as his subjects, who had reserved the upper and lower berths of the same compartment. At 1 A.M., Kerin saw Sebastian buttoning the curtain of the upper berth, leaving the light on to make it appear occupied, and "letting himself into the lower berth backwards, looking up and down the aisle as he did so." Kerin summoned three members of the train crew, unbuttoned the curtain, lit a match, and beheld the couple, if not in flagrante delicto, at very least in a compromising pose.

At the jury trial the following spring, all four witnesses testified. "While there was some discrepancy as to what Sebastian wore," the *Daily News* reported, "all the witnesses agreed he was not dressed for a blizzard. Kerin said the female member of the dancing team of Sebastian and Nord had on a white nightgown and a look of indignation." As he pulled Sebastian out of the berth, Kerin noted that he was buttoning his trousers. The couple insisted they had been discussing their just-completed engagement in Pittsburgh, that their state of partial dress was due to it being a hot evening, and that the curtain was buttoned and the lights were off to hide that Emily was smoking. Burkan, in an affidavit that he drafted for Jules, responded with withering sarcasm:

In their modesty and propriety, they proceeded to discuss between one and two o'clock in the morning, in the dark and curtained Pullman berth, the engagement which they had just concluded. They had before them many hours of tedious travel by train. What more opportune time could they find for their conversation than under these conditions, when they both were hot and so terribly fatigued?

Sebastian had been so effective at gaslighting Jules over the years, he seemed genuinely perplexed at being cast as a homewrecker. In a pretrial affidavit he wrote: "For Dr. Nayfack to cast such aspersions upon my own good character and reputation after all the years of our friendship during which he so implicitly trusted me is the saddest event of my life. I cannot and will not believe that these are the acts and utterances of Dr. Nayfack! It cannot be and it is not he!" Sebastian reduced the courtroom to peals of laughter by insisting that "I was dancing with Mrs. Nayfack at Dr. Nayfack's request and for his own good. It was really as a favor to the doctor that I took on his wife as my partner."

Although the case was effectively over once Sebastian had testified, Burkan did not let up in his cross-examination of Emily:

> Like a picador baiting a bull, Nathan Burkan, the doctor's legal light, plagued the fair dancer with excerpts from her husband's letters, begging her to return to him and Sonny.
>
> Tears coursed down the pallid cheeks of the tormented mother. She clutched her handkerchief in her hand and tugged frantically at her sleeve, in agony at the prospect of losing Sonny if Dr. Nayfack prevails in his action.
>
> But amid the glamour of the theater, behind the bright footlights, she preferred her career to being at home with her child and yearning husband, she admitted.

The jury came back with a verdict for Jules. The presiding judge, John Tierney—who three years earlier had instructed Jewel Carmen's jury that it is the "function of every good woman" to bring children into the world—was well pleased. "I do not see how the jury could have rendered any other verdict," he commented. "When the child grows to manhood, he will realize that his mother is the woman this jury has characterized her to be." Then he turned to Burkan: "This Don Sebastian is a menace to all decent society. As an officer of the court, get him out of this country if you can." Reporters noted that Emily showed no signs of grief or perturbation; one overheard her saying of Jules, "At least I got rid of that millstone around my neck."

"MA'MSELLE TRÈS POLITE, SHE SAYS"

The "heart balm" torts—alienation of affections, seduction (procuring intercourse by deceit), criminal conversation (adultery with the spouse of another), and breach of promise to marry—all had long lineages in the common law. During Burkan's career, such cases were meal tickets for many lawyers and for the tabloid press, but this may have been an instance of too much of a good thing. The intense and sensational coverage these cases received was believed to encourage spurious claims and create undue pressure to settle them, giving rise to what was known as the "heart balm racket." In the mid-1930s, a national movement to abolish these ancient causes of action took hold with unusual speed.

Although there were some proto-feminist arguments for abolishing the heart balm torts as tending to infantilize women and limit their freedom of association, the opposition was largely driven by the belief that men were being victimized. The New York legislature declared that these torts had been "subjected to grave abuses," caused "extreme annoyance, embarrassment, humiliation and pecuniary damage to many persons wholly innocent and free of any wrongdoing," and were "exercised by unscrupulous persons for their unjust enrichment." The heart balm torts were abolished in New York effective May 28, 1935.

At the very moment the legislature was acting, Burkan was defending Arthur Loew, the forty-five-year-old son of Marcus Loew and a Metro-Goldwyn-Mayer executive, in one of the last seduction cases ever to go to trial in New York. The press savored this farewell to a much-loved story genre, utterly beguiled by the coquettish plaintiff, Colette François, a "petite Parisian ma'mselle " of twenty-two.

Five years earlier, Colette had sailed with her mother from New York to Marseille on the SS *France,* a ship so opulent that it was known as the "Versailles of the Atlantic." Loew was also on board, on his way first to Naples and later to a conference of MGM executives in Paris. Loew danced with Colette several times during the voyage, including the night before he disembarked at Naples, when he asked for Colette's address and phone number in Paris, so they could meet there to discuss prospects for her going into motion pictures. She went to Loew's cabin the following morning and wrote out her contact information for him.

Through an interpreter, Colette testified that after arriving home she received a call from Loew and made an "appointment" to see him the next day at the Hotel Majestic, where he was staying in Paris. Her attorney, Bernard Sandler, who represented many plaintiffs in heart balm cases, interrupted:

Sandler (to the interpreter). Didn't she use the word "rendezvous"?

Interpreter. Yes. I call that "appointment" in French.

Sandler. I think the word "rendezvous" might be a little more romantic than "appointment."

The Court. The difficulty with you is you are a Bohemian, not a Frenchman.

Sandler. Please proceed.

Colette (through the interpreter). He made a rendezvous with me for the next day.

Burkan. I move to strike out "rendezvous," it calls for a conclusion.

The Court (to the interpreter). You repeated the French word.

Interpreter. I said it to please Mr. Sandler.

The Court. You are here to interpret, not to please anyone. Repeat the word in English.

On the pretext of leaving her house for a music lesson, Colette went off to her appointment with Loew. She was ushered up to his suite, where Loew, who spoke French fluently, told her she should do a screen test to see if she was suitable for pictures. He asked her to turn so he could see her profile. ("As she told of these events," one paper reported, "Colette's profile, with its retroussé nose, under a rakish beige hat, presented an agreeable view to the businessman jury.") Loew put on music, danced with Colette, and served her cognac, the first liquor she ever had. He invited her into the next room, where he forced her onto the bed and removed her clothes. The next thing she remembered was waking up in bed next to him. A daughter was born nine months later. Arthur Loew was the only man she had known sexually.

Liquor and the use of force were not mentioned in Colette's pretrial filings, which alleged seduction, not assault, and Burkan was evidently taken by surprise. He subjected Colette to a protracted, raking cross-examination calculated to show that she was Loew's willing sexual partner. Colette stood her ground against Burkan's battering ram of questions:

Burkan. Please tell the jury why you walked into the man's cabin and sat down and wrote out your name and address?

Colette. Because I am honest with people, when they ask me for something, I comply with their request. . . .

Q. And you gave to a man who was a total stranger a piece of paper containing your name, address, and telephone number?

A. No, he was not a stranger to me. I had been introduced to him, I had danced with him. . . .

Q. Why didn't you tell your mother or father that there was an American gentleman that made you a proposal to put you in motion pictures and wanted you to come to his hotel to talk the matter over?

A. I knew my father and mother were French bourgeois and they wouldn't allow me to enter the moving pictures. . . .

Q. You told the Court and jury that you were grossly betrayed and outraged and you didn't want to let anybody know that this dreadful thing had happened to you on this occasion; is that your testimony?

A. Well, I was afraid. I didn't know what people would say about it.

Undoubtedly, Burkan thought this line of attack would resonate with an all-male jury, but courtroom observers thought the jurors' sympathies were with Colette. After she left the witness stand, the judge called a recess and met with the attorneys in his chambers. Rumors of settlement spread through the courthouse. A family friend told reporters that Colette had rejected an offer of $5,000 as insulting, saying, "Phoo-ey, give that to the fund for abandoned babies."

When the judge and lawyers reemerged, both sides abruptly rested, even though witnesses for the plaintiff were still waiting to testify. The court curtly announced that it was dismissing the case for insufficient evidence Burkan denied there had been any settlement. Sandler said he couldn't comment. But reporters couldn't help noticing that, despite what seemed on the surface to be a complete defeat, Colette was all smiles, and that she shook hands warmly with Loew.

What took place in chambers can be surmised from comments the judge made to reporters later. He thought each side had a problem. On the one hand, Colette's account did not quite meet the technical requirements for the tort of seduction, the theory on which the case was pleaded. On the other hand, he thought she had told a completely credible story of assault and was inclined to let the case go to the jury on that basis. The outright dismissal of the case in open court allowed Loew to save face while making a cash settlement behind the scenes.

Reporters asked the opposing attorneys for their views on the abolition of the heart balm torts. Burkan, who had in the past disparaged heart balm plaintiffs as "houris of the hist," called it a "marvelous" development, but warned that men "must watch their step just the same. Women now will be bringing assault cases." Sandler said the repeal was "a vicious law," and worried that "now the offspring of the idle rich are free to ravish the poor man's daughters."

The press learned that Loew had given Colette a $5,000 down payment on a $30,000 settlement (over $500,000 in 2020 dollars), plus her legal fees. Reporters gathered at the pier to bid her "adieu" before she sailed for France the next day. "Colette reached up and kissed her lawyer when reporters asked her if the agreement was satisfactory. 'Mais oui,' she said as she gave her lawyer a box of candy."

CHAPTER 22

Nightstick Censorship

After a twenty-year apprenticeship at the entry levels of New York's theater hierarchy—burlesque, vaudeville, revues—Mae West achieved success on the legitimate Broadway stage in 1928. Playing the title role in *Diamond Lil,* a Bowery melodrama that she also wrote, West perfected the shimmying, campy, sexpot persona that would make her a top Hollywood star of the 1930s. *Diamond Lil* introduced West's famous come-hither line, "Why don't you drop in and see me some time," and showcased her inimitable way with a bawdy song, in this case "Frankie and Johnny." "Diamond Lil is a scarlet woman," the *Times* critic wrote. "As played by Miss West she is a pretty credible and interesting figure. She is a good actress is Miss West even though her playwriting is a bit thick."

West had just finished a Monday night performance of *Diamond Lil,* on October 1, 1928, when two policemen knocked on her dressing room door and placed her under arrest. Two blocks away, a large squadron of cops had just carried out a raid at the conclusion of the opening-night performance of another play authored by West. When she got to the precinct station, West and fifty-four members of the cast of *The Pleasure Man,* some still in costume and makeup, were charged with indecency under New York's Stage Regulation Act of 1927. After commotion and merriment worthy of a cast party, they were each released on $500 bail.

The Pleasure Man juxtaposed the conventions of a backstage show with the story of a rakish actor who uses and discards numerous women before getting his comeuppance. The theatrical setting was a handy pretext for having a troupe representing assorted types from West's professional past—song-and-dance acts, acrobats, and female impersonators—on hand to do their shtick and provide comic relief from the maudlin central plot. In the third act, as the flamboyant female impersonators are throwing a raucous party for the traveling vaudevillians who have descended upon a quiet midwestern town, they learn that the title character has died from complications of an unspecified surgery performed on him by a stage crew member, the brother of one of his conquests. At the play's denouement, as the police take him away, the perpetrator explains: "I didn't think he would die. . . . I wanted him to live—in pain—and in shame—and to know that he could never again use people for his rotten pleasure."

West insisted that her play was a cautionary tale, "the true picture of a man who was weak and who forgot the wise law of moderation . . . who came to no good at the end. Many young men could learn a lesson from the play." New York theater critics who had seen the play were unanimous in panning it. "Smeared from beginning to end with such filth as cannot possibly be described in print, such filth as turns one's stomach even to remember," was a typical appraisal.

After the raid, West's manager was sent to track down Nathan Burkan, an avowed opponent of censorship. He was at the State Democratic Convention in Rochester, where, at almost the same moment as the arrests, a deal had been brokered to nominate Franklin D. Roosevelt to succeed presidential nominee Al Smith as New York's governor. By the next morning, Burkan was back in New York City, where he obtained a temporary injunction against further police interference with *The Pleasure Man,* just in time for the second performance to proceed as scheduled that night. In the meantime, Burkan promised the judge, he would negotiate revisions to the play with the district attorney.

To Burkan's surprise, Manhattan district attorney Joab Banton, following instructions from Mayor James J. Walker, refused to talk. "This is a community of liberal people and the Mayor is liberal and always has been and will be a patron of the theater," Walker said in a statement to the press. "But anything so offensive to the decency and morality of the citizens of this community cannot continue in this town while I am Mayor."

The Wednesday matinee performance of *The Pleasure Man* was in progress when an appellate court vacated the temporary injunction against interference. Police ordered the curtain down at the beginning of the third act. Burkan advised West and the producers that it would be "foolhardy" not to close the show. *The Pleasure Man* had a run of only two and two-thirds standing-room-only performances.

Governor Smith and Mayor Walker were vigorous crusaders against Prohibition, but when it came to another great moral crusade of the 1920s, stage censorship, they saw no political percentage in opposing the movement to stamp out smut. John S. Sumner, the leader of the New York Society for the Suppression of Vice, wielded political clout grossly disproportionate to the actual level of public support for his cause. Between 1921 and 1924 he led five separate "crusades" to clean up the New York stage. By 1925 he had to concede that his crusades had accomplished nothing but "the advertisement and prolonged runs of a few bad plays." Indeed, he suspected that many complaints were being ginned up by producers "inspired by the motive of causing morbid public interest in certain shows which were previously on the verge of failing for lack of patronage."

A New York stage regulation law dating from 1909 made it a misdemeanor to present "any obscene, indecent, immoral or impure" play "which would tend to the corruption of the morals of youth or others." Prosecutions under that statute, Sumner believed, took too long, were too prone to fail on technicalities, and when successful resulted in penalties that were insufficient to deter further violations. In 1925, Sumner convinced District Attorney Banton to try a different approach, the "Citizen Play Jury." Under an agreement reached between Banton's office, Actors' Equity, and the Producing Managers Association, complaints of indecency were reviewed by a panel of twelve citizens, randomly selected from a pool of several hundred theatergoers. Producers were bound to carry out any edict supported by at least nine jurors, ranging from revisions to closing the show. The proceedings were kept confidential until a decision was announced, so as to avoid giving a box office boost to the shows under review.

Sumner quickly became disillusioned with his own brainchild. Those who volunteered to sit on Citizen Play Juries were too open-minded. He was particularly incensed when, in the spring of 1926, a jury that included such luminaries as architect Raymond Hood and economist Alvin Johnson gave a clean bill to Mae West's first Broadway production, titled *SEX*, in which she played "a prostitute who is more or less

true to the British navy and the paramour of a crook and a blackmailer."
Sumner pressured Walker and Banton to resume criminal prosecutions,
and he lobbied the state legislature to beef up the stage regulation law.

In February 1927, Banton announced that he was abolishing the
Citizen Play Juries and would resume bringing criminal prosecutions
against indecent plays, promising there "will not be more than a week's
delay between the indictment and trial." Banton said that there would
be no retroactive prosecution of plays already passed upon by a Play
Jury, but less than a week later he caved to further pressure and charged
West and the rest of the cast of *SEX*, which had already been running
for nearly a year, with indecency. West was convicted and served ten
days in a workhouse on Welfare Island. She turned that incarceration
into a publicity bonanza.

On April 5, 1927, the same day that West was convicted, Governor
Smith signed a new Stage Regulation Act, popularly known as the
"Wales Padlock Law." Unlike the earlier statute, it specifically allowed
for prosecution if any part of a play was deemed indecent, even if the
play as a whole was not, and also specifically made it a crime to depict
or deal with "the subject of sex degeneracy or sex perversion." In addition to a prison term of up to a year for each violation, the Wales law
provided for the closing of the offending theater for up to a year.

The Pleasure Man would be the new law's first test. After the police
raid, a grand jury indicted a total of fifty-seven defendants (the play's
director and producer, as well as West and the cast) on two counts of
violating the Wales law and one count of creating a public nuisance.
The district attorney made it clear that he would seek the maximum
sentence of one year on each count for Mae West.

Virtually every editorial page in the city cheered on this latest campaign to clean up the theater, but some notes of caution were sounded.
Even a meritorious prosecution, one paper observed, "invites all sorts
of narrow-minded bigots to suspect and investigate and bowdlerize
and suppress such serious or good-natured treatment of sex as has a
perfect right to exist in 1928," with the result that "all the legitimate
advance in freedom of subject and language on the stage suffers a setback."

Burkan, who had fought many battles against film and stage censorship, shared this view, and he was especially concerned with giving the
police the power to shut down a play on nothing more than their own
opinion as to what constituted indecency, as happened with *The Pleasure Man*. He was determined to do more than win an acquittal for West.

He wanted to prove that what he called "nightstick censorship" could only result in a total fiasco.

The People of the State of New York v. Mae West came to trial in the Manhattan Court of General Sessions on St. Patrick's Day 1930. The assistant district attorney prosecuting the case, James Wallace, complained that in the year and a half since the raid, Burkan "has made more motions in this court than any of Miss West's actors have on the stage." (Among other things, Burkan had asked for a change of venue, arguing that pervasive pretrial publicity guaranteed that a trial in Manhattan would amount to a "Roman holiday.") Burkan continued his filibuster as the trial began. Three days of preliminaries passed before the first testimony was taken.

The court had summoned a venire panel of seventy-five men, all of them professionals and business owners, from which a "blue ribbon" jury of twelve would be selected. Burkan objected that it was undemocratic to limit the jury to members of the "privileged class." "Why can't a jury of laborers and artisans decide this case rather than a jury of the intelligentsia? We are entitled to have this case tried by the kind of people who went to see the play." Judge Amadeo Bertini overruled Burkan's objection.

Burkan questioned each prospective juror closely. Did they belong to any anti-vice organizations, or had they donated money to them? Were they theatergoers? Had they seen any of Mae West's plays? Did they harbor any prejudice against actors or theater people? Did they know John S. Sumner, who had been seen lurking about the courtroom? Did they agree that men portraying women on stage were simply "character actors, making a living as you and I must make a living"? Through his questions, Burkan introduced an important theme of his case, that female impersonation was a venerable tradition in the theater, in no way a badge or depiction of male degeneracy. He asked prospective jurors if they were familiar with well-known drag performers such as Julian Eltinge or Bert Savoy. To jog their memories, Burkan imitated Savoy's famous catchphrase, "You don't know the half of it, dearie," in a "piping falsetto."

Burkan and West were satisfied with the jury that resulted. Three members had seen West in *Diamond Lil* and found nothing objectionable about it; one even praised it lavishly. Two said they attended varsity musicals at their alma maters in which men played female roles. Wallace, for his part, believed that he had excluded anyone who opposed

Mae West draws a crowd as she and Burkan leave court after first
day of jury selection, March 17, 1930. *(New York Evening
Graphic)*

censorship in principle or was skeptical of police testimony, and he was
confident that the jury would find that *The Pleasure Man* was no innocent drag show, but a thinly disguised homage to male homosexuality,
the work of the "foulest-minded pervert."

After the last juror was seated, Burkan moved to strike one phrase
that appeared repeatedly in the prosecution's bill of particulars: ". . .
giving every appearance of being a male degenerate by actions and
voice." "It is no crime—as yet," he argued, "for a man to be effeminate
and have a falsetto voice." The motion was denied.

The prosecution did not have the script for *The Pleasure Man* or any
recording of the performance to show the jury. A mere synopsis of its
plot, even a verbatim repetition of its dialogue, would not necessarily be
inconsistent with Burkan's defense theory that the play was a wholesome entertainment with a powerful moral lesson about the wages of

sin. It thus fell to the police officers who saw the show to prove that, in live performance with all its attendant stage business, *The Pleasure Man* was a bacchanal of perversion and degeneracy. Burkan promised that "if they insist on bringing in filth, I'll make this one of the filthiest cases ever heard."

"The court room will be treated to unusual maneuvers on the part of big burly cops, who will be somewhat embarrassed, to say the least," the *New York Sun* teased in its trial preview. Indeed, the proceeding was nothing short of Monty Python–esque. Captain James J. Coy, who had once done a bit of acting himself, carried most of the load for the prosecution. Coy (a name that might well have been bestowed on him had this been an Oscar Wilde play) had watched the opening-night performance with a police stenographer, whom he would nudge with his elbow when he wanted something taken down. He testified to about a dozen individual examples of indecency in the form of dirty dialogue and song lyrics, as well as a two-man acrobatic stunt in which a larger man (Lenzen) in baggy pants balances a smaller man (Selig) on his hands. As described in the District Attorney's court papers, the two men tumble in a manner that allows Selig's head and shoulders to disappear inside Lenzen's prop trousers, bringing "Selig's head to a point approximately where Lenzen's private parts would be located," with Selig "moving his head about in the vicinity of Lenzen's private parts." But most of all, Coy objected to the mincing, fanny-poking, whoopsing, and yoo-hooing of effeminate men in ladies' clothing.

"Once Coy got going," the *Daily News* reported, "the spectators began to wring the blushes out of their hair." Coy whooped and snakedanced and spoke in falsetto to demonstrate for the jury what he had witnessed at the theater. His mince, in particular, delighted the courtroom spectators:

> He put his left hand on his hip, and his right fingertips up to his shoulder and he walked in front of the witness chair.
> "That," he said positively, "is how they walked on the stage of this show. Very effeminate."

In contrast, Captain Coy opined, the famous Julian Eltinge stage walk was not objectionable because he did not put his hand on his hip. Coy also found it very concerning that one of the female impersonators in the play sewed lampshades during scenes set backstage.

Coy had an unfortunate propensity for malapropisms. The prosecutors had wanted to make some hay from an exchange in which one female impersonator asks, "Did you ever have a platonic love affair?" and another responds, "Yes, but then his wife found out." Coy testified that the phrase used was "chronic love affair," rendering the dialogue, if not innocent, then at least incomprehensible, which was just as good for the defense.

Burkan tormented poor Coy for hours on cross-examination. "You 'whoop' pretty well, now let us hear you sing. Give us a couple verses of 'I Am Queen of the Beaches' as you heard it sung in the show." Coy had testified that the last word of the title phrase was slurred to rhyme with "ditches," not "peaches." Coy demurred: "I don't know the woids. I don't even know the foist voise." Coy's memory failed him again and again when pressed for details. At length, Burkan forced him to concede that on direct examination he had not been testifying from his own memory of the show, but from his recent study of the stenographer's notes. "Isn't it true that your recollections [on the stand] were better than they were fifteen minutes after you saw the play?" Coy admitted that was so.

As his last witness, Assistant District Attorney Wallace offered a vice squad detective to testify as an expert on the argot of the New York City homosexual, who could explain to the jury the nefarious coded messages embedded in *The Pleasure Man*'s dialogue, stage business, and song lyrics.

"You have had a lot of experience as a police officer with male degenerates, have you not?" Wallace asked.

"Yes, for seven years."

"You know their manners, their slang, and the words they use that have double meaning?"

"I know all the woids."

Burkan cut Wallace off right there. "If the questionable phrases are in common use, why explain them to the jury? If they are not, who are they going to harm?" Wallace argued that the testimony was critical to the state's case, that "the jury has a right to consider that these words have a hidden, special meaning."

The testimony was indeed crucial to Wallace's case. The jury would be instructed that, under the Wales law, it was not enough to find that the play contained matter that was coarse, vulgar, or repulsive; to convict they would have to find matter that actually depicted or described same-sex relations in a manner "which tended to arouse sexually degenerate desires or appetites." West's allusions to homosexual acts needed to be decoded.

Burkan had the better of the evidentiary argument. Self-proclaimed police experts, he pointed out, could

> place a double, dire, sinister and objectionable meaning to words and lines that had been innocently conceived by the author, innocently spoken by the actors, and innocently understood by the jury. Words sung by children at Sunday School and whole lines of Shakespeare may be legally adjudged indecent if such testimony is introduced.

Burkan was swimming against a strong tide of homophobia. As one reporter paraphrased his argument, "Nathan Burkan saw no reason why a detective who patrolled Broadway with a butterfly net instead of a nightstick should be allowed to testify on the peculiarities of sweet-voiced, eccentric behaviorists whose antics have baffled even students of morbid psychology." That is probably the way Judge Bertini heard it too. After considering the issue overnight, he allowed the state's "sexpert," Sergeant Terence Harvey, to testify. Harvey explained to the uninitiated what the line "I perform on my knees" really meant. Likewise, the word "horse" in the lyric "Officer, let me pat your horse, isn't it coarse, my, hasn't it grown since June." And the word "moon" in the lyric "Get out and get under the moon."

Burkan put seven cast members on the stand in the defense case-in-chief. They testified that the police had misunderstood dialogue and omitted important context. ("I perform on my knees," they insisted, was followed by the innocent explanation, "I'm a Mammy singer.") The actor who played the pleasure man professed surprise to be learning for the first time that his stage death was caused by a botched castration. One cast member sang the offending songs with clasped hands and such exaggerated choirboy earnestness that "Miss West, at counsel table, covered her mouth with her black handkerchief to hide her laughter.") The German acrobatic team of William Selig (all four feet of him) and Herman Lenzen reenacted their famous trouser stunt, which they said they had been doing for years in vaudeville.

> The jury retired while the two acrobats modestly hid behind the jury box and arrayed themselves in their trick garments. Court attaches summoned the jury back and the twelve gentlemen ranged themselves in a semi-circle. Lenzen balanced Selig and then went into their fall. It was all over in a minute, and everybody seemed mildly surprised that the act was so tame. Even the prosecutor looked as if he had expected more.

When Captain Coy retook the stand in rebuttal, one juror rose to ask him, "Why didn't you take the trousers to the station house when you made the arrest?"

Burkan rested his case without putting Mae West on the stand. His two-and-a-half-hour closing was an unrelenting attack on "nightstick censorship and perjured police testimony." Who were the police to decide that scenes of men sewing lampshades were unfit for the theater? "Why, I know a policeman who makes beaded bags in his spare time."

"The police officers," he shouted, "went deliberately to this theater to get Mae West and they got her. Coy sat down later and deliberately framed the testimony he gave in court." He went on: "This case proves that the power of censorship should be taken away from the likes of Captain J. J. Coy. I wouldn't hang a dog on this police testimony."

"The test is whether the show presented to the eye and ear is naturally calculated to excite in the spectator impure imagination," Judge Bertini instructed the jury. "Such a purpose is really more dangerous to the public morals than any mere vulgar exhibition of nudity. The latter may arouse impure thoughts, but it is more apt to incite disgust. The greater danger lies in the appeal to the imagination."

One newspaper, commenting on Judge Bertini's decision to allow expert testimony on double entendres, lamented that "no longer can the new spring moon be used as a symbol of young love, and made to rhyme with 'spoon' and 'June' by our best lyricists." And perhaps, by that standard, writers of legal history should no longer state that a jury was hung. Let us say, rather, that after ten hours of deliberation the jury in *The People v. Mae West* could not reach a verdict. Wallace immediately signaled that there would be no retrial: "In view of the expense to which the state has been put, it may be just as well to let it go and consider that we have done our duty."

The first test of the Wales Padlock Law had produced general agreement on at least one thing: the law was an abject failure. Judge Bertini called for creation of a state board of censorship made up of "broad-gauged and intelligent men." In addition to "the inherent impossibility of producing in court a show as it was seen on the stage," he pointed out that a prosecution like *The People v. Mae West* is self-defeating: "By the trial itself, millions of people find out all about the play. The trial spreads filth and obscenity throughout the country. You've increased its audience so materially that more harm is done to society in an effort to enforce the law than if no effort were made at all."

Burkan met with a reporter from the *New York Post* to expound on his views about nightstick censorship. "The Police Department has no place in this situation. They might just as well claim the right to regulate the Stock Exchange under the gambling statutes." The trial showed that policemen lacked the expertise to distinguish between old vaudeville gags "dug out of mothballs" and something that could actually corrupt anyone's morals. It was unfair to make producers "kowtow" to their arbitrary edicts.

Initial reports of the jury's split had varied from 8–4 for acquittal to 7–5 for conviction. Two weeks later, however, eleven members of the jury sent a letter to Governor Franklin Roosevelt, echoing Judge Bertini's call for some form of preproduction censorship. An enterprising reporter tracked down the one non-signing juror, a maker of children's clothing in Greenwich Village, who told him, "I was the one who held out for a not guilty verdict against the other eleven, and I want it to be known." His views on nightstick censorship tracked Burkan's: "I don't want theaters put in the same class as speakeasies, where they can be shaken down by the cops." Nor could he endorse the idea of a board of censorship. That "would give a lot of jobs to some bum politicians."

Prosecutions under the Wales Padlock Law were rare after *The Pleasure Man* case, but it remained on the books until a general revision of the New York Penal Code was enacted in 1967. As for Mae West, Burkan "guaranteed" that "any show she writes in the future will not be a cause of public discussion." Urban legend has it that Burkan's fee for the case bankrupted West. Burkan did have to sue the actress to collect the $9,000 balance on a fixed fee of $14,500 that was still outstanding when the prosecution was dropped, but the outcome and the publicity West received was worth many times that amount.

West moved on to Hollywood, where she had a brief run as the top female box office draw, until her frank treatment of human sexuality collided with Will Hays's 1934 Motion Picture Production Code. "Mae West, the box-office champ in 1933," writes critic David Denby, "was replaced, in 1934, by Shirley Temple, and was thereafter tamed and marginalized."

CHAPTER 23

The Big Bankroll and the Little Flower

Arnold Rothstein, high-stakes gambler and reputed fixer of the 1919 World Series, was a fount of liquidity for the major profit centers of Jazz Age New York's underworld: bootlegging, fencing, labor racketeering, narcotics trafficking, loan sharking. He would gladly extend credit to borrowers on the right side of the law as well, sometimes on very easy terms, especially if a short-term loan could compromise a man with law enforcement responsibilities for the long run. Of all Rothstein's nicknames, "the Big Bankroll" was the most apt.

On the evening of November 4, 1928, Rothstein went to the Park Central Hotel to meet with someone about a disputed poker debt. After the discussion ended with a single .38 caliber gunshot wound to his abdomen, Rothstein somehow dragged himself from a third-floor room to the street-level service entrance, where he collapsed before being transported by the police to nearby Polyclinic Hospital. Still conscious and coherent, he wouldn't name his assailant, but he asked a police officer to call his lawyer, state assemblyman Maurice Cantor.

By the time Cantor was able to get inside his client's hospital room the next afternoon, Rothstein was in extremis. The two nurses who had been caring for him for the previous eight hours, the only other people in the room, observed that Rothstein was no longer capable of rational thought, that his speech had "no sense to it at all." Cantor took a ten-page, single-spaced legal document out of his pocket.

"Arnold, this is your will. The will you spoke about this morning. It is just as you told me this morning. I put in everything you told me. You know this is your will, Arnold."

Rothstein's eyes opened a slit and he feebly repeated the word "will."

"Whose will?" one of the nurses asked him.

"My will."

Cantor placed a pen in Rothstein's flaccid left hand, guided it to the signature line, and traced out an X. Cantor then asked the nurses to sign as witnesses to the mark. They initially refused, but eventually relented—"in order to get him out of the room," they said. Rothstein died the following morning, November 6, 1928, as voters were going to the polls to elect Herbert Hoover president and Franklin Roosevelt governor of New York. Rothstein's bets on those outcomes would be good for winnings of $1.7 million, assuming they could be collected.

The deathbed will named Cantor and two of Rothstein's business associates as executors, and bequeathed to them a significant share of the estate, believed to be worth at least $3 million. The will provided for ten years of income to Rothstein's estranged wife Caroline, but also made provision for his final showgirl mistress, Inez Norton. His parents and sister received nothing. Rothstein's father, Abraham, with the support of Caroline and other family members, filed a challenge to the deathbed will in the Surrogate's Court of the County of New York, and asked for the appointment of temporary administrators to manage the estate until the will contest was resolved.

In the early twentieth century, an era of smaller government and higher rates of mortality, Manhattan's surrogates, quasi-judicial elected officials, were among the city's most prominent public figures. They administered estates and trusts worth hundreds of millions of dollars each year and dispensed valuable patronage, in the form of guardianships and other fiduciary appointments, from an imposing Beaux Arts courthouse on Chambers Street (in more recent years also a shooting location for television's *Law and Order*). In the 1920s, Tammany Hall placed two of its most scholarly, honest, and dedicated public servants—James A. Foley and John P. O'Brien—on the court, both of whom discharged their duties honorably while providing a steady stream of lucre to Tammany-connected lawyers and businessmen.

Surrogate O'Brien decided to appoint, as temporary administrators of the Rothstein estate, one person from each side of the will contest, along with a third neutral party. He suggested that they engage Nathan

Burkan, a lawyer whom they could all trust, to oversee the herculean task of inventorying and preserving Rothstein's far-flung and often hidden assets, and collecting his debts, legitimate or otherwise. A fortnight had passed since Rothstein's demise and the crooked house of cards that he had built was already teetering on the brink of collapse.

James J. Walker was sent from central casting to be the mayor of Jazz Age New York. One contemporary journalist wrote that "Beau James," as he was called, "symbolized his period as perhaps no other man could. His virtues were those of the time: open-handedness, amiability, wit, tolerance, a certain careless sympathy for the inarticulate underdog. His vices were equally contemporary. He was glib, vain, prodigal, luxury-loving and amazingly indifferent to the rules of common honesty." Walker was long associated with the reform-minded wing of Tammany, and his administration had some notable achievements in improving public health, advancing racial equality, and building public works. His personal failings were, for most of his constituents, easily overlooked, if not actually a source of almost daily amusement and begrudging admiration

Burkan had backed Walker's bid to unseat an incumbent Democratic mayor, John F. Hylan, in 1925. Burkan organized one of the signal events of Walker's successful primary campaign—a noontime parade of movie stars in "200 gayly decorated automobiles, starting from Fifty-eighth Street and proceeding down Seventh Avenue to the Hotel Astor, accompanied by showers of confetti thrown from hundreds of office windows along the route." The contrast with Mayor Hylan's colorless, austere image could not have been starker, a foreshadowing of the ambience of a Walker administration. Burkan remained in Walker's kitchen cabinet of informal advisors throughout the mayor's tenure in office.

When Mayor Walker got word that Rothstein had been shot, his first thought was "That means trouble from here on in." He knew that if the extent of Rothstein's political influence became known, it could be a mortal blow to his political career and to the entire Tammany Hall machine. "When Rothstein's safe deposit boxes are opened there will be a lot of suicides," one of Rothstein's former attorneys told reporters. "Go put that in your papers."

It quickly became apparent that the authorities were in no hurry to solve the murder or to expose Rothstein's business affairs to daylight. "The Rothstein case, they have concluded, was just a passing fad, like mahjongg or numerology," the Daily News remarked. "There is sentiment blaming Arny for his lack of tact in getting shot." Newspapers were soon putting nouns like "investigation" and "hunt" in scare quotes when it came to the Rothstein case.

> For years to come students of the social and criminal life of New York will be amazed to read that in the year 1928 A.D. no deathbed watch was kept by the police, and no effort was made by the police or prosecutor to find and impound the private papers of a notorious and murdered man, who was known to be the director of innumerable underworld activities.

Immediately upon his engagement as counsel to the estate, Burkan went to Rothstein's apartment at Fifth Avenue and 73rd Street, where Caroline had been living alone for some months. He was accompanied by an assistant district attorney and two assistant United States attorneys. He had in his hands a court order authorizing him to inspect the contents of a safe. The posse was surprised to find two steel file cabinets which had been moved to the apartment from Rothstein's office as he lay dying. District Attorney Banton announced that the cabinets were "the richest prize we have won in many a day. There are more than 60,000 notations in the files." (That prize, of course, had been available for the taking for two weeks.) Burkan had the file cabinets moved to a bank vault for safekeeping. Banton anticipated that it would take three weeks for his assistants to thoroughly review the records.

But the next day, in one of the more supine derelictions of duty that reporters on the New York crime beat had ever witnessed, Banton pulled his men off the document review. "The task," Banton said, "is too dreary. I have complete confidence that Nathan Burkan will tell me if anything of a criminal nature is found. I wish I had a few men around here like Mr. Burkan." When it came to light a few weeks later that there were significant gaps in the Rothstein files—the B, C, G, M, Mc, and T folders had all gone missing—eyebrows were raised. It was widely assumed that the missing documents included promissory notes from public officials connected with Tammany Hall.

Banton tamped down the controversy and criticism of his office by indicting two men for Rothstein's murder in December 1928. But as the 1929 New York City mayoral campaign was getting into full swing the following fall, one of the defendants was still at large (having disappeared after questioning by the police), and the other had still not been brought to trial. The Republican candidate seeking to unseat Mayor Walker, Congressman Fiorello LaGuardia, thought the mishandling of the Rothstein case could be a potent issue.

By then Rothstein's files, after first being impounded by the district attorney for the use of his grand jury in the homicide case, had been turned over to the office of the United States attorney, Charles H. Tuttle, who was investigating Rothstein's connections to narcotics trafficking. Tuttle, a Republican with his own ambitions for elective office, was an old nemesis of Burkan from his days in private practice representing the National Association of Broadcasters against Ascap. Referring to information that was almost certainly leaked to him by Tuttle's office, LaGuardia wrote an open letter to District Attorney Banton a few weeks before the mayoral election:

> Among the files and papers of Arnold Rothstein there were several little black books which contained memoranda of his personal accounts, particularly money handed out, given, and loaned by him. The several little black books are not now in the files in the custody of officials. They are in the possession, I am informed, of Mr. Nathan Burkan, a Tammany district leader.
>
> May I therefore suggest that you make public the contents of these little black books? Whether or not you care to follow the clues which I gave you, for goodness' sake do something!

The "little black books" were a red herring. It all sounded suspicious, but those books had been of no interest to law enforcement. Burkan issued a heated reply to LaGuardia: "The statement of LaGuardia is the strategy of a desperate man who is willing to attack reputations in order to make headway." But LaGuardia's cleverly framed innuendo revived reporters' flagging interest in the question of Rothstein's relationship with Tammany Hall. Within hours, Mayor Walker and Tammany Hall leader John Curry publicly denied any Tammany-Rothstein connection. District Attorney Banton issued a statement asserting that "no notes or any documents compromising politicians or public men were to be found in the Rothstein files."

Now that he had the attention of the press, the next day LaGuardia dropped the juicier nugget of information that had been leaked to him. Whoever it was that purged the Rothstein files, it turned out, had missed one thing: a copy of a friendly letter from Arnold Rothstein to a Bronx County magistrate judge, Albert Vitale, forwarding a check for $20,000, lent at 7 percent interest. "Judge Vitale is at this very moment actively campaigning for Mayor Walker and has announced the formation of an Italian-American committee to support the Mayor," LaGuardia declared with an air of triumph. "I now ask Mayor Walker either to repudiate or support Judge Vitale."

By this time, Burkan was wrapping up his duties with respect to the Rothstein estate. The contest over Rothstein's deathbed will had been settled in the spring of 1929. It was withdrawn in favor of an earlier will, one far more favorable to the widow and family. Permanent administrators of the estate were designated. As they closed their books, Burkan and the temporary administrators reported that they had gathered property with a net value of nearly $2 million, a notable accomplishment given the deliberately opaque nature of Rothstein's affairs. From a business perspective, however, it was not a successful engagement for Burkan. The fee he requested, $75,000, was reduced by Surrogate Foley to $57,500, and Burkan never saw a penny of even that reduced amount. (Burkan's heirs eventually settled the claim for $3,500, after ten years of Dickensian legal diddling had left the once-flush Rothstein estate insolvent.)

An undeserved black mark against his reputation was about all Burkan had to show for his troubles. LaGuardia's innuendos took on a life of their own. Latter-day Rothstein biographers have taken it as a given that Burkan's job had been to "keep any incriminating documents from seeing the light of day, anything that might embarrass Tammany and its friends." There is, however, almost no possibility that Burkan did that. With his well-deserved and carefully tended reputation for moral rectitude, he was the last person Tammany Hall would deputize to carry out any such felonious act. His brief custody of the Rothstein records was, in any event, legal, not physical. The unfriendly eyes of U.S. Attorney Tuttle were looking over his shoulder from the outset. The only time a purge of incriminating documents could have occurred was during the two weeks that the steel file cabinets had been left unsecured in Rothstein's apartment and, as Burkan pointed out to reporters, "had probably been visited and inspected by employees from Rothstein's offices."

The Rothstein-Vitale loan disclosure lit a fuse that would, in the fullness of time, lead to the end of Walker's mayoralty and the advent of LaGuardia's, although not in 1929. Walker was reelected that year, defeating LaGuardia by a large margin. But shortly after the election, Judge Vitale received more unflattering attention when it came to light that he had been the guest of honor at a testimonial dinner attended by many known criminals.

Under the judicial discipline procedures of the time, the New York County Bar Association investigated Vitale and petitioned the courts for his removal from the bench. The petition strongly intimated that the

Rothstein "loan" was actually a gratuity, given in appreciation of Vitale's dismissal of criminal charges against a Rothstein associate, and possibly other services rendered. No direct quid pro quo was proven, but Vitale was removed from the bench on grounds of negligence in accepting something of value from a known underworld figure. The Vitale case led the court system to begin a wide-ranging investigation of the city's magistrate courts, which handled much of the criminal caseload. A distinguished lawyer with a long-standing grudge against Tammany Hall, Samuel Seabury, was put in charge.

Seabury's investigation was so effective in exposing a market where justice was bought and sold that the Republican-controlled New York State legislature created a committee to investigate corruption throughout New York City government. It put Seabury in charge of the investigation and gave him the resources to do the job well. The magistrate investigation "brought down the avalanche," wrote journalist Milton MacKaye. "Tammany had taken the town too carelessly, and the public wanted it back." By May 1932, the Seabury investigation had worked its way to the top. Mayor Walker was summoned to give public testimony about his personal finances.

Burkan accompanied Walker to the Seabury hearing not as his attorney, but as his friend. He looked on helplessly as Walker was filleted by Seabury's surgical questioning. The focus of the hearing was on nearly one million dollars that was mysteriously deposited into the accounts of a clerk employed by Walker's former law firm over the course of the mayor's first five years in office. Walker at first tried to deflect suspicions with his characteristic wit: "I hope he proves it is mine, I will try to collect it." Gradually, though, he realized the predicament he was in. The committee was not, as originally advertised, just interested in recommending legislation to address corruption. "It looks as if someone is seeking my political life. Is this an inquiry or a preliminary to a political inquest?" Walker asked with growing apprehension.

On September 1, 1932, Mayor Walker, facing removal from office by Governor Roosevelt, his perfidy no longer deniable by even his most ardent supporters, resigned. Another Tammany ally of Burkan's, Surrogate John P. O'Brien, won a special election to serve out Walker's unexpired term.

On November 8, 1932, forty-two of forty-eight states delivered their electoral votes to Franklin Delano Roosevelt, a resounding 472-to-59 landslide that unseated incumbent president Herbert Hoover. Two months later, New York's forty-seven presidential electors, including Nathan Burkan representing the 19th congressional district, gathered in Albany to cast their formal votes in the so-called Electoral College. On Roosevelt's inauguration day, March 4, 1933, Burkan issued a statement offering his congratulations to the country for its new leadership. "I feel that Mr. Roosevelt's liberal views and his genius for statecraft will bring us out of the depths of the depression and will guide us into a new era of peace and prosperity." For Democrats like Burkan, it was a sweet restoration to national power after twelve long years in the political wilderness.

In New York City, however, Tammany Hall was losing its stranglehold on power in the wake of Jimmy Walker's resignation and the Seabury investigation. Just a few days after Roosevelt's swearing in, Burkan gave an interview to the *New York Post* in which he offered a ringing defense of Tammany Hall, trying to align it in public perception with Roosevelt's advocacy for the "forgotten man." "Is anyone else willing to champion the cause of the little man?" he asked. "Our schools are grinding out thousands of boys and girls in whom the spirit of ambition has been awakened. But these young people have no contacts with the influential. So they will come to us, there is no one else to help them." He insisted that Tammany's hold on power depended not just on doling out turkey dinners and other favors to the poor, but in its message. "Real leadership is a thing of ideas. Did Hitler give the Germans turkey dinners? No, he gave them thought." Corruption, Burkan conceded, existed in certain corners of Tammany, but he blamed that on the indifference and neglect of men of training and experience. "Men of the type I mention do not want to bear the travail, the pangs, the agony of politics. They criticize, they complain, but they refuse to go into the game seriously."

The *Post*'s interviewer did not doubt Burkan's personal integrity or the sincerity of the views he expressed regarding Tammany Hall. He concluded, however, that Burkan's "courtroom defenses of his clients have been more successful."

In November 1933, Mayor O'Brien lost his bid for reelection by a landslide to Fiorello LaGuardia, who was running on a Republican-Fusion ticket. In the waning days of the year, the lame duck O'Brien appointed Burkan to serve as chairman of the Triborough Bridge Authority.

Plans for a Y-shaped span that would connect Manhattan, the Bronx, and Queens had been on the boards for nearly twenty years. Some preliminary construction had been done, but work had long been stalled due to lack of funding. President Roosevelt's New Deal gave the project a jumpstart in the form of a $35 million loan commitment from the federal Public Works Administration. Construction was expected to employ eighteen thousand at the depth of the Great Depression.

In the spring of 1933, the state legislature created the three-man Triborough Bridge Authority to oversee construction and operation of the bridge. It was to be an independent body, but the mayor of New York City was granted the power to appoint its members. When Mayor O'Brien's initial appointee to the chairmanship resigned in November due to illness, Burkan accepted the unpaid post, "at the sacrifice of a lucrative law practice," he said, "to put thousands of men to work and for that reason only."

The incoming mayor was more than mildly chagrined at being saddled with this fait accompli. LaGuardia's anglicized nickname, "the Little Flower," belied his razor-sharp elbows. LaGuardia was intent on making the city's most important public works project an exemplar of the sort of good government he had promised during his campaign. Before his inauguration, he had his aides audit the Authority's expenditure of the first $100,000 tranche of federal funds. Their report disparaged Burkan and his two fellow O'Brien appointees on the Authority as "Democrats who have not been identified conspicuously with efforts to clean up the city." Within days of taking office, the LaGuardia administration had leveled charges of malfeasance, inefficiency, and incompetence against Burkan's two colleagues, resulting in two vacancies for the new mayor to fill. (The matters complained of—a kickback on an office lease, and payments of excessive salaries and fees—predated Burkan's appointment as chairman.) When he heard that Burkan was telling friends that he expected to be next on the chopping block, LaGuardia quipped: "I am always glad to get suggestions from Mr. Burkan, and this one will receive the Mayor's serious consideration."

LaGuardia sent Burkan a letter demanding that all further Authority communications to the federal government be transmitted through the mayor's office. "We are going to build a bridge, and not patronage," LaGuardia vowed. "We are going to erect a structure of stone and steel. That word is spelled 'steel,' and not 'steal.'" Burkan deeply resented LaGuardia's "unwarranted, despicable and low accusations." Did the Mayor really think that "men who undertake work of this patriotic nature should be called thieves by others to suit political exigencies."

LaGuardia never attempted to remove Burkan from the Authority; he preferred to keep him around as a convenient scapegoat for anything that went wrong. The mayor was content to control a majority of the three-man board, especially since he was able to fill one of the seats with Robert Moses. Moses was already serving as president of the Long Island State Park Commission, as chairman of the State Council of Parks, and as New York City parks commissioner. The pattern of Moses—the subject of Robert Caro's classic biography *The Power Broker*—acquiring new unelected posts while never relinquishing the old ones would continue over the course of his career, during which he supervised construction of thirty-five highways, thirteen bridges, two world's fairs, Jones Beach State Park, and Lincoln Center.

Immediately upon taking his seat, Moses became the de facto chief executive officer of the Triborough Bridge Authority, leaving Burkan with no actual power to go with the title of chairman. Only when trouble was brewing did Moses recede into the background and let Chairman Burkan, the Tammany Hall holdover, take the incoming flak. At one point, the steel workers union and the steelmakers trade association complained that the Authority had purchased about $19,000 worth of German steel to meet a specialized engineering requirement. Moses left it to Burkan to explain to the public that the German bid had come in so far below those of domestic steelmakers that, under regulations governing the use of federal funds for the bridge, the Authority had no choice but to award the contract to them. Secretary of the Interior Harold Ickes, who oversaw the Public Works Administration, turned the ire of the American steel industry back on Burkan: "Mr. Burkan has all the authority in the world to hold the contract up. He's merely trying to pass the buck." "That's fine," an exasperated Burkan told reporters; "if the Authority can ignore Public Works Administration regulations, that is splendid."

LaGuardia had been in the hospital during the German steel dust-up, but when it was over, he couldn't resist doing a little grandstanding, with Burkan as his foil. He released an open letter:

> My Dear Nathan,
> I have patiently and quietly watched, and listened to, from the sideline the controversy over imported material for the Triborough Bridge.
> I have reached the conclusion that the controversy has ended in a draw, to wit: nobody wants the damned steel. Therefore, just tell the contractor to furnish American-made material with the job. That's all. . . .
> Verstehen Sie? (Do you understand?)

The mayor added a postscript: "The only commodity we can import from Hitlerland now is hatred, and we don't want any in our country."

PART EIGHT

Modern Times

CHAPTER 24

New Deal Days

On June 16, 1933, President Roosevelt signed into law the National Industrial Recovery Act, one of the cornerstones of his New Deal. The act sought to implement nothing less than a fundamental reordering of the American economy through the promulgation of enforceable codes of fair competition in more than five hundred industries. The codes would regulate wages, hours, and working conditions, establish collective bargaining, and eliminate cutthroat forms of competition. One of the associates in Nathan Burkan's law office, Sol A. Rosenblatt, was appointed a divisional administrator of the National Recovery Administration (NRA) with responsibility for the "amusement" industries, including motion pictures.

A thirty-two-year-old graduate of Harvard College and Harvard Law School, Rosenblatt was one of the most powerful behind-the-scenes figures in the entertainment universe for the next two years, earning him the shorthand "Rosy" from *Variety*'s ever-economical headline writers. Although his appointment came about as a result of his personal relationship with General Hugh S. Johnson, the head of the NRA, his eight years in the Burkan office qualified him eminently on the merits. Burkan had demonstrated his high regard for Rosenblatt by allowing him to argue a case for the firm before the U.S. Supreme Court when he was just five years out of law school.

The task of drafting codes of fair competition was left to the participants in each industry. For motion pictures, that meant that Will Hays's

Motion Picture Producers and Distributors Association would be the dominant force. In the Recovery Act's relaxation of antitrust rules and its emphasis on reducing costs of production, the big studio moguls saw an opportunity to address some of their most irksome problems, such as high star salaries and competition from independent producers, distributors, and exhibitors. As one cultural historian has written, "they used the making of the code to attempt to cement and further the advantages they enjoyed while offering little to other interests in the film industry."

The writing of the Code of Fair Competition for the Motion Picture Industry was complex and contentious. The initial draft, largely the work of the "Big Eight" studios that composed the core of the Hays organization, was greeted with brickbats. The Academy of Motion Picture Arts and Sciences stepped forward to lobby on behalf of its five "talent groups"—actors, technicians, directors, writers, and producers—in the negotiations that ensued. The Academy asked Burkan, who had been elected its first "special" member at its formation in 1927, to represent its members' interests before the NRA.

In those days the Academy was a threadbare operation, highly dependent on the patronage of the big studios for its survival. Consequently, Burkan's advocacy was tightly constrained. (He was also, at the same time, serving as a director of two of the Big Eight, United Artists and Columbia, and representing a third, MGM, in a major copyright lawsuit.) The tepid brief that he filed on behalf of the Academy, and his testimony at public hearings conducted by Rosenblatt in mid-September 1933, failed to address the major concerns raised by the Academy's constituents. The actors, who objected to provisions of the proposed code that would put a cap on salaries and limit their freedom to negotiate with competing producers, were particularly angered by the Academy's obeisance to the big studios. Within weeks, hundreds of actors had resigned from the Academy and joined the newly formed Screen Actors Guild. Eddie Cantor, the new group's president, explained that "we just want to be 100% represented in an organization not subsidized by any one."

Cantor went to see President Roosevelt in Warm Springs, Georgia, to make the actors' case to him personally. He must have been persuasive. In his executive order of November 27, 1933, approving the Motion Picture Code, Roosevelt suspended enforcement of the provisions regarding salaries and negotiations pending further study of the issues. (Rosenblatt eventually concluded that "as a matter of principle, no salary is too high or excessive if the picture produced by the individual receiving the salary meets with unusual public favor," and he recommended that the suspension be made permanent.)

By the end of 1933, the Academy of Motion Picture Arts and Sciences had $301 in the bank, and its signature event—an annual dinner to award gold statuettes for meritorious achievement in its various branches—very nearly had to be canceled in 1934.

It does not appear that Burkan had much further involvement with the NRA, except to serve as a convenient target for some of its most vociferous critics. In the spring of 1934, Senator Gerald P. Nye of North Dakota, one of Roosevelt's fiercest opponents, took to the floor of the Senate to attack the Motion Picture Code, calling it "one of the most iniquitous of all codes, an agreement under which small independent interests are being annihilated and the public forced to pay higher prices for entertainment deteriorating in quality." Senator Nye endorsed a theory of the Motion Picture Code's origins that held great currency among the smaller players in the business:

> Mr. Rosenblatt went directly from his association with Nathan Burkan to his association with General Johnson and to the place of supreme designator of what the Movie Trust could and could not do.
>
> Did Mr. Burkan, intimate associate of Will Hays, movie czar, actually pull the strings from behind the scenes as Rosenblatt wielded the hammer which was to destroy the living-making power of many honest American citizens? He threw the gates wide open, told the trust to do as it pleased, gave them everything it wanted.

A year later, as the Industrial Recovery Act was coming up for reauthorization, the Senate Finance Committee investigated charges of "injustice, oppression, and favoritism in the administration of the codes." Representatives of independent exhibitor groups came to air their complaints, still harboring the belief that Burkan was the villain of the whole piece. "Prior to the time that Burkan became active in the matter, Rosenblatt was most considerate of the exhibitor representatives and repeatedly assured them that the code would remedy many of the outstanding abuses in the industry," one witness testified. "When Burkan became active there was a noticeable change in the attitude of Rosenblatt." Their belief was not based on Burkan and Rosenblatt's former professional connection, they claimed, "but rather on the extraordinary privileges granted and deference shown to Burkan by Rosenblatt during the discussions."

Rosenblatt was succinct in responding to these accusations, which he justifiably took as a personal affront: "The innuendos made with respect to the participation of Mr. Nathan Burkan are unequivocally erroneous. Mr. Burkan had no more to do with the draftsmanship of the Motion Picture Code approved by the President than did any of the Pages of the Senate."

The Finance Committee never issued a report. Just a few weeks after the hearings concluded, the Supreme Court struck down the Recovery Act as an unconstitutional exercise of Congress's power to regulate interstate commerce and an improper delegation of legislative authority. The decision, *A.L.A. Schechter Poultry v. U.S.,* one of the most impactful in the history of the Supreme Court, led to invalidation of much of Roosevelt's original New Deal legislation and eventually to his court-packing plan. It also rendered speculation as to the true authorship of the now-defunct Motion Picture Code moot.

The early years of the Roosevelt administration were a golden age for the law office of Nathan Burkan. Burkan was leasing the entire twenty-fifth floor of the newly constructed Continental Building at Broadway and 41st Street. Although the interior design was basic—framed mementos of his famous clients and cases served as the main form of decoration— the view north overlooked such Times Square landmarks as the Paramount Building, the Hotel Astor, and the Capitol Theater. It was a spectacular panorama of Burkan's professional domain.

It is not at all certain that a young Nathan Burkan, coming out of City College and NYU School of Law, could have landed a job as an associate in the Burkan law office of the 1930s. In addition to his longtime associates Charles Schwartz and Louis Frohlich, both entering the prime of their legal careers, the firm had an outstanding cadre of younger attorneys. Herman Finkelstein had joined the firm in 1928, after serving as an editor of the *Yale Law Journal* and as law clerk to two distinguished federal appellate judges, Learned Hand and Thomas Swan. Finkelstein was, in fact, the first law clerk ever to be hired by judges at that level of the federal judiciary, with Hand and Swan paying his salary out of their own pockets.

When Sol Rosenblatt left the firm in 1933 to join the NRA, Arthur Schwartz took his place. Schwartz had graduated first in his class at Columbia Law School, served as editor-in-chief of its law review, and had turned down a clerkship with Supreme Court justice Harlan Fiske Stone to become a federal prosecutor in Manhattan, where he began a long political apprenticeship under Thomas E. Dewey.

James Murray, the "house goy," was a relative of William Randolph
Hearst. A handsome socialite, he was a regular guest at the Hearst Ranch
(no one, he would tell you, called it San Simeon) and he was married to
an actress who had appeared in several Charlie Chaplin movies. Adelaide
Burkan Bodow, the daughter of Burkan's younger brother Benjamin,
joined the firm after graduating from NYU School of Law in 1935.

Burkan was a demanding boss, not pompous but somewhat gruff and
aloof. The associates would never become his partners or his social bud-
dies. The attraction of the job was the opportunity to work on cutting-
edge legal matters for a glamorous and high-powered clientele in a
culture of meritocracy. "If Burkan liked a person and had confidence in
him," Sol Rosenblatt later recalled, "there was nothing he would not do
for him."

More than forty years later, a journalist named Barbara Goldsmith
spoke with some of the old associates about those heady, formative
years in Burkan's office. They described to her an atmosphere "that was
light years removed from the propriety of a Wall Street firm."

> Burkan's establishment was a seat-of-the-pants operation, full of élan, excite-
> ment and disorganization. Doors were almost always left open and if a law-
> yer had a bright idea, he simply dashed around to see an associate. One
> lawyer who worked for Nathan Burkan recalled finding the key to winning
> a multimillion-dollar suit while conversing with an associate in front of the
> men's room urinals.

Burkan's work ethic set a pace that the younger lawyers struggled to
match. Finkelstein joked that "whenever he raised his fork to take the
first bite of dinner" the phone would ring with Burkan on the line to
discuss a legal matter. When Burkan was working out of a suite at the
Ambassador Hotel in Los Angeles, as he did at least twice a year, the
calls might come in the middle of the night. According to Adelaide
Bodow, her uncle packed stacks of work-related papers in a duffel bag
so that he could keep up with his reading while on the road. Burkan, she
said, was the confidant and friend of his famous clients, but "he was not
at all like them."

When he was in New York, Burkan would call each associate into his
office first thing in the morning to discuss their cases. Legal papers on
his desk would be "sprawled in untidy profusion. Shreds of toilet paper
served as markers for the relevant passages." Louis Nizer, who had met
Burkan while working for the New York Film Board of Trade as a
young lawyer in the early 1930s, wrote that Burkan was "fond of long

walks and would compel friends to accompany him at the most unexpected times." Nizer described Burkan as a "fresh air fiend," whose
office was "always frozen."

One of the biggest Broadway hits of 1930 was a melodrama titled *Dishonored Lady,* cowritten by Edward Sheldon and Margaret Ayers
Barnes, which opened shortly after the stock market crash. Based
loosely on published accounts of a sensational 1857 Scottish murder
trial of a young woman named Madelaine Smith, the basic plotline of
Dishonored Lady is easily summarized. The heroine, renamed Madelaine Cary, a libidinous young lady of some social standing, has a liai-
son with an alluring man of exotic foreign origins and lower station.
When she attempts to end the affair and marry a more suitable mate,
her former lover will not let go. The rake threatens to expose their
affair. Madelaine acquiesces in a night of passionate lovemaking, after
which she poisons him. When questioned on suspicion of murder, she
provides a false alibi, that she was with a third man the entire night in
question. She is acquitted of murder, but her reputation is ruined—
hence the title.

MGM's head of production and "Boy Wonder," Irving Thalberg,
was interested in obtaining the motion picture rights to *Dishonored
Lady,* which he thought would be a perfect vehicle for Greta Garbo.
The discussions advanced to the point where a contract for $30,000
was drawn, but the deal was never completed because the Motion Pictures Producers and Distributors Association deemed the play unsuitable and imposed a ban on its adaptation for motion pictures. Thalberg
attempted to convince Will Hays that Garbo's unique personality could
render palatable stories that "with any other actress would not have
been acceptable to the public." Hays was unmoved. Several months
later, Thalberg purchased the film rights to an English novel, *Letty Lynton,* also based on the Madelaine Smith case, which he saw as a vehicle
for another rising MGM star, Joan Crawford, because it had a happier
ending than *Dishonored Lady.*

The creative team behind MGM's *Letty Lynton,* released in 1932,
had all seen or read *Dishonored Lady.* The film's dialogue is entirely
original, but its basic characters and incidents more closely track those
of the play than of the novel it was supposedly adapted from, with only
such departures as were necessary to get the project past Will Hays and
state censorship boards. Letty is portrayed as an innocent led astray.
The sexual nature of her affair is left ambiguous; indeed, the movie

begins with the ending of the affair. She makes a clean break with her lover, never even pretending to still desire him (she goes to see him again only to try to retrieve incriminating letters in his possession). She does not plot to murder him; the poison that he mistakenly takes was meant for herself. Letty never lies during the inquest into the rake's death—the false alibi is volunteered by her fiancé. Whereas Madelaine Cary is shunned and despised after her acquittal in the play, Letty Lynton marries her true love and seems destined to live happily ever after.

Sheldon and Barnes sued MGM for infringement of their copyright on *Dishonored Lady.* MGM engaged Nathan Burkan to defend. Two decades earlier, in *O'Neill v. General Film Company,* Burkan had parsed the various versions of *The Count of Monte Cristo* with what the court described as "industry and skill worthy of a better cause." In the case of *Letty Lynton,* Burkan thought that he had found that better cause. This was not simply a case where a filmmaker drew upon disparate versions of a fictional tale, some that happened to be under copyright and some not. Here the ultimate source material was historical fact. And the similarities that MGM's dramatization bore to other fictional works drawing upon the same facts, especially *Dishonored Lady,* Burkan believed, were elements so common to the romantic melodrama genre as to be scènes à faire, common literary property available to all. The plaintiffs, Burkan argued, "seek to recover on a theory which is unsound, unsafe, and which would be revolutionary in our present law—a theory which would impose on the public domain restrictions and limitations that would entirely subvert the intent of Congress and the spirit of our Constitution."

Sheldon v. MGM was assigned to federal judge John M. Woolsey, a highly literate if somewhat idiosyncratic jurist. He conducted the two-day bench trial over a weekend in April 1933 at the New York County Bar Association's headquarters. After posttrial briefs were filed, Woolsey summoned the lawyers to his summer home in Petersham, Massachusetts, for two days of oral arguments. Very shortly thereafter, Woolsey was assigned the landmark First Amendment obscenity case that arose out of the Customs Service's seizure of James Joyce's *Ulysses.* As a result, the *New York Times* reported, the judge "will pass a good deal of his vacation" reading *Ulysses.* With one of the twentieth century's most notoriously difficult novels on his desk and the press of other business, Woolsey was not able to immerse himself in *Sheldon v. MGM* and issue his ruling until he got back to Petersham for the summer of 1934.

Woolsey ultimately saw the case Burkan's way. He did not simply compare the two works as would an ordinary audience member, but rather assumed "a more Olympian viewpoint" that encompassed their common source material. He did not find it astonishing that

> the basic plot, after passing through the medium of the minds of two sets of modern writers, showed that coefficients of refraction substantially alike had been in operation on it, and that the results differed mainly in so far as the two sets of minds differed in their literary skill in dealing with the dramatic situation inherent in the common subject-matter.

Only *Dishonored Lady*'s individualized literary embellishments of the historical record were protected by copyright, and Woolsey found none of these were used in the film *Letty Lynton*.

Sheldon and Barnes took an appeal. Their case was heard by a three-judge panel that included Learned Hand. Burkan could not have been pleased with this draw. Burkan had assembled a voluminous evidentiary record showing that the similarities between *Dishonored Lady* and *Letty Lynton* in character and action were all commonplace dramatic tropes. But if Hand approached this case the same way he had approached the "I Didn't Raise My Boy to Be a Soldier" and "Dardanella" music plagiarism cases that Burkan had tried before him many years earlier, he could be expected to ignore all such evidence if he believed that MGM's actual source was the copyrighted play.

Hand's summaries of the works in question show more than a passing familiarity with the dramatic and linguistic conventions of the bodice-ripper. He recounts the major plot points with both lawyerly precision and mischievous winks. "At once he falls to wooing her," he says of the first encounter between Madelaine Cary and her forbidden lover. "He finds her facile and the curtain falls in season." When Madelaine returns to administer the poison, "her animal ardors are once more aroused and drag her, unwillingly and protesting, from her purpose. The play must therefore wait for an hour or more until, relieved of her passion, she . . . puts the strychnine in his coffee."

Once he gets down to legal business, Hand finds, at a granular level of detail, numerous uncanny parallels between *Dishonored Lady* and *Letty Lynton*, too many to be explained as resulting from anything but copying. Nor did Hand, in contrast to Woolsey, find it significant that such details—a dying man reaching for a telephone, a family history of waywardness, a sex alibi—could be found in countless other works. He concludes:

The dramatic significance of the scenes we have recited is the same, almost to the letter. True, much of the picture owes nothing to the play. . . it is enough that substantial parts were lifted; no plagiarist can excuse the wrong by showing how much of his work he did not pirate. We cannot avoid the conviction that, if the picture was not an infringement of the play, there can be none short of taking the dialogue.

Burkan petitioned the Supreme Court for review, arguing that Hand's opinion had created uncertainty in an area of the law "of the utmost importance to authors and dramatists, and to a great industry, international in scope." He included a list of dozens of well-known motion pictures adapted from public domain works and historical materials, and showed that much of that source material had already been adapted for stage and screen multiple times before. Seventeen movie studios joined in a friend-of-the-court brief that asked whether, in light of the *Letty Lynton* precedent, "a later adaptor must forsake everything that he has learned or seen and embark upon an adaptation that will be free of the most ordinary ideas and most elementary stage business, merely because they were present in previous adaptations?"

The Supreme Court declined to review the case. The market for adaptations did not experience so much as a hiccup. *Letty Lynton*, however, has been out of circulation ever since Judge Hand's appellate ruling came down in January 1936.

Alfred Cleveland Blumenthal—"Blumey" (or "Blumie") to all who knew him—sought out and received lots of press during the darkest days of the Depression. His business and social exploits were closely chronicled in the dailies, and in early 1933 he scored a two-part profile in the *New Yorker*. "If his name does not spring at you from the front page now, it leaps at you from the theater, movie, real estate, or financial section," Alva Johnston wrote. "Some of the New York papers are gradually being reduced to Blumenthal house organs."

Blumey had started out in California real estate. He came east in the mid-1920s and made a fortune brokering William Fox's acquisition of several large theater chains, at a time when rival movie studios were frantically bidding up prices. He became Fox's partner in a real estate subsidiary, his all-purpose business guru, and practically a member of the Fox family. Then Fox's grip on his empire started to slip away in the wake of the crash of 1929—in part due to the failure of his $50 million bid to acquire Loew's Incorporated, parent of MGM, which Blumey had negotiated. One night, Fox woke up with a start. Upton Sinclair told the story in a biography that he wrote with Fox's assistance:

> His wife asked him what was the matter, and he told her that he had just dreamed that Blumey had double-crossed him. She told him to go back to bed. "All the others that you have faith in may double-cross you, but never Blumey." She looked upon Blumey as if he were her son.

Blumey was, in fact, double-crossing Fox at that very moment. He had made a deal to assist Wall Street financiers who were plotting to wrest control of the Fox studio from its founder, in exchange for forgiveness of a seven-figure debt that Blumey owed the company and a $500,000 commission on the sale of Fox's stock. "God will strike you dead for what you have done to me," Fox told Blumey when the scales fell from his eyes. Like many others who ended up on the wrong side of William Fox, Blumey hired Nathan Burkan to handle the litigation that ensued.

Before long, he had entrusted Burkan with all his legal affairs and become a close friend. Blumey and his wife, a former Ziegfeld girl named Peggy Fears, were known for their extravagant entertaining. Mr. and Mrs. Burkan became regular guests at the film screenings Blumey gave at his estate in suburban Larchmont and at lavish parties he threw at his favorite Manhattan haunt, the Central Park Casino.

Blumey was a choice client to have in the bleak years that followed the crash of 1929. He was a rare pool of liquidity in a sea of red ink, with ready cash that made him a player on Broadway and at City Hall. He was, wrote Johnston, "the premier of Jimmy Walker's nocturnal cabinet," the Mayor's "chief stooge" and "chief counselor." Indeed, the Seabury investigation had looked into whether Blumey was the source of the funny money that had brought Walker down. Just as he had escaped unscathed from the wreckage of William Fox, Blumey walked away from the fallen Jimmy Walker smelling like a rose.

Elfin in stature and puckish in demeanor (Walker called him "Junior"), Blumey loved to surround himself with celebrities and leggy beauties. In 1933 he was frequently being linked in the tabloids with a vivacious young widow, Gloria Morgan Vanderbilt. In June, gossip columnist Ed Sullivan, an inveterate stoker of marital strife, reported that "when A. C. Blumenthal sails for England, Gloria Vanderbilt will be on the same tub." A few days later, he reported that reaction to his previous item had been immediate. "Peggy Fears, sobbing wildly, called Blumenthal. And now he may call off his trip." (As we shall see, he did not.) In December,

Gloria and Blumey were photographed together celebrating the repeal of Prohibition at the Central Park Casino. Peggy Fears was there too, the caption in the *Daily News* noted, but Blumey was "squiring" Gloria.

One day, in the summer of 1933, Blumey brought Gloria to Nathan Burkan's office to get his advice with respect to a most distressing family conflict.

CHAPTER 25

Gloria

A.C. Blumenthal was in many ways an archetypal Nathan Burkan client—a brash, up-by-his-bootstraps money magnet. Gloria Morgan Vanderbilt—a stammering, dispossessed blue blood and socialite—was something altogether different. She belonged to a world totally foreign to Burkan's experience. But the story she told when Blumey brought her to Burkan's office struck a chord, and her case became a final, heartbreaking crusade for him.

The three daughters of Harry Hays Morgan and Laura Kilpatrick Morgan—Consuelo, the eldest, and the twins Thelma and Gloria—had been darlings of the society pages ever since the end of the Great War, their beauty and antics inspiring prose so purple it can be exhausting to read a hundred years later. Even a note on the betrothal of the one Morgan son, Harry, congratulated him on taking "a bride whose pulchritude, 'tis said, puts in the shade even the oft-sung physical gifts" of his "heavenly" sisters.

The twins, born in Lucerne in 1905 and raised mostly in Brussels, where their father was a long-serving diplomat, were especially photogenic and lively. Their pictures were first splashed across American newspapers in 1916 when, as impish, curly-haired eleven-year-olds, they wintered in New York with their mother. From the time they returned to the United States three years later to complete their educations at a convent school in New York, their arrivals and departures, their debuts and costume balls, their cameo roles in motion pictures, and very soon their marriages, were avidly reported.

The Morgans' distinguished lineage and residencies in foreign capitals allowed them to endow their daughters with cosmopolitan social graces, though not with conspicuous wealth. Marrying well was an imperative. Laura Morgan became widely known for being "one of the cleverest matchmaking mammas society has ever seen. Never has any single woman engineered more pretty but undowered daughters into such gilded unions."

"The marriages of the Morgan girls," one reporter observed, "are always very romantic and interesting and show a tendency to be brief." Consuelo's first marriage, at eighteen to a French count, a scion of a noble and wealthy family, lasted two years. She was soon remarried to Benjamin Thaw Jr., "the most popular young man in the immensely wealthy Thaw family of Pittsburgh." Thelma, at age sixteen, eloped with James Vail Converse, grandson of the founder of AT&T. That marriage dissolved after a year, and Thelma Morgan Converse went on to become the Viscountess Furness, wife of one of the wealthiest men in Britain, Marmaduke Furness, whom she divorced in 1933.

Gloria, at age eighteen in 1923, married Reginald C. Vanderbilt, great-grandson of the railroad baron Cornelius. Reggie, who was forty-two, divorced, and had a daughter Gloria's age, was the very model of an international sportsman and bon vivant. "If horses, yachts, automobiles and other luxuries of that sort can make a woman happy, Gloria Morgan can have all of her dreams fulfilled," one newspaper predicted. A daughter, Gloria Laura Morgan Vanderbilt (hereinafter, "Little Gloria"), was born to the couple on February 20, 1924. Eighteen months later, Reggie was dead of cirrhosis of the liver.

Few men have been as lionized in life or eulogized in death for their sheer profligacy quite like Reggie was. "Reginald C. Vanderbilt Dies; Millions Employed in Gaiety by Sportsman Extraordinary" was the headline on one front-page obituary. Newspaper readers were fascinated by the details of his financial life as they became public through the probate of his will. He had lived off the income of a spendthrift trust fund established by his father. At Reggie's death, under the terms of the trust, the corpus was distributed not to his widow, but to his children. His "residuary" estate—everything he owned outside the trust, including homes in Manhattan and Newport—went to his surviving spouse.

Little Gloria, newspapers realized instantly, was now one of the richest toddlers in the world. "Only a dimpled, playful baby of 19 months, already she commands all the power and luxury that $3,000,000 can create." Another year passed before it became widely known that Reggie's residuary estate was insolvent. Only by exercising her common-law right of "dower" was Gloria able to keep about $100,000 realized from the sale of the houses out of the hands of her late husband's creditors.

Under New York domestic relations law, the Surrogate's Court had authority to appoint a guardian for Little Gloria's property. Not yet twenty-one herself, and completely unschooled in stocks and bonds, Gloria was ineligible and unwilling to serve. At her request, Surrogate James A. Foley appointed Wall Street lawyer George Wickersham as guardian. Wickersham, who had served as attorney general under President William Howard Taft, was a friend of the Morgan family whom Gloria knew as "Uncle George." He turned most of the actual work of the guardianship over to a younger lawyer in his office, an expert in trusts and estates, Thomas Gilchrist, who was eventually named co-guardian.

Surrogate Foley sympathized with the young widow's financial predicament (reform of the law of dower, which left many widows in near penury, was a pet cause of his). He devised a solution that seemed eminently sensible. He granted a yearly allowance of $48,000 ($675,000 in 2020 dollars, less than half the income that Little Gloria's wealth, conservatively invested, was earning) for the "support, maintenance, and education" of the child. This statement of purpose tracked the verbiage of New York's guardianship statute, but it was a fiction—Foley understood that it would be the family's only income and would be used to maintain both the mother and child in a manner befitting American aristocrats. The press, though, ran with the idea that this was the child's personal budget, making Little Gloria, at $4,000 per month, the "World's Most Expensive Baby."

No longer comfortably ensconced in New York society, Gloria moved back to her native Europe with her daughter, promising Surrogate Foley that they would return when Little Gloria was ready to begin school. Gloria's own inheritance was quickly depleted in establishing a new household in Paris and supporting her increasingly needy parents. Little Gloria's allowance, however, sufficed to maintain a large, servant-filled house in Paris, to allow the Vanderbilt ménage to spend summers in Biarritz, and, in Gloria's words, to "keep up appearances and maintain a social position of the high standard set by the Vanderbilt family, name and tradition." Gloria provided an annual accounting of her expenditures.

After reviewing the 1927 report, Surrogate Foley remarked that Gloria was "living at a pretty extravagant rate."

As Gloria resumed her social life, she delegated her daughter's care to her now-divorced mother, Laura Morgan, whom the girl called "Naney," and her ever-present nurse, Emma "Dodo" Keislich. Never having known her father, and her mother but a "beautiful stranger glimpsed only fleetingly," Little Gloria came to view her primary caregivers as "Mother Dodo and Father Naney." The two women could not have been more devoted to the little girl. Nor could they have been more officious, meddling, and conniving. They exhibited the symptoms of a classic folie à deux, in their case a shared delusion that the mother—who stood to inherit Little Gloria's fortune if she died before the age of twenty-one—would kill the child, or at least let her die of neglect, if left to her own devices. Naney and Dodo's hostility toward Gloria spread like a malignancy to the servants and, as she grew a bit older, to Little Gloria too. "Naney and Dodo's feelings toward her became my own," Little Gloria wrote in her old age, "and my fear would only grow in later years."

In 1927, Gloria was engaged to a Bavarian hereditary prince, Gottfried zu Hohenlohe. The young man would not be coming into his inheritance for many years; in the meantime, he was a member of the ranks of penniless European nobles. Laura Morgan saw him not as a suitable mate for Gloria, but as a probable coconspirator. "She objected to my marrying Mrs. Vanderbilt on the ground that I had no fortune to speak of, and she accused me of wanting to murder the child," Prince Hohenlohe later testified. "These accusations were brought up perhaps a hundred times . . . that was a theme song of hers."

Unbeknownst to Gloria, her mother took her concerns to Wickersham. A letter from Thomas Gilchrist soon arrived in Paris. Surrogate Foley, he wanted to let Gloria know, had stated that "the allowance was extremely generous and he requested me to advise you that it would be dramatically reduced if at any time he should receive credible information that any part of the infant's income was being used, as he put it, to 'finance a second marriage.'" Gloria called off the engagement. (Hohenlohe later married Princess Margarita of Greece and Denmark, the sister of Philip Mountbatten, future consort to Queen Elizabeth II.)

After breaking off the engagement, Gloria began to travel more frequently, often leaving Little Gloria and her caregivers behind. She began to summer in Cannes while sending Little Gloria and Dodo to the Alps. She went to England frequently, where her twin sister Thelma Furness had become the mistress of Edward, Prince of Wales, giving Gloria entrée to a rather exclusive social circle. She was befriended by the Marquis of Milford-Haven, a cousin of King George V, and became the constant companion of his exotic Russian marchioness, Nada. When Gloria brought her daughter along on one English sojourn, she housed the girl and her caregivers five hours away from the Furness country estate where Gloria was staying.

Gloria managed to put off her promised return to the United States until March 1932, after she had received a warning from Wickersham that unless she arranged "to bring the child to this country to be educated, we would have difficulty in getting the allowance continued at anything like the same sum which is now being granted." After leasing a brownstone on East 72nd Street, not far from the school where Little Gloria would enroll in the fall, and attending to Little Gloria during a ten-day hospitalization for a tonsillectomy, Gloria returned to Europe for the summer of 1932, ostensibly to "close the Paris house." It was then that Gloria's formidable sister-in-law entered the picture.

Gertrude Vanderbilt Whitney, Reggie's older sister, led two parallel but equally prominent lives. She was reigning matriarch of two of America's wealthiest clans, the Vanderbilts and the Whitneys, an imposing doyenne presiding over New York society and dispensing philanthropy from her palatial Fifth Avenue mansion and her country estate on Long Island, Wheatley Hills. She was also an accomplished sculptress, a libertine spirit, and the patron of an international colony of bohemians that orbited around her Paris studio and her recently opened Whitney Museum of American Art in Greenwich Village.

Gertrude had barely known Little Gloria before 1932. But after the child had her tonsillectomy that spring, Gertrude offered to let her convalesce at Wheatley Hills, where she would be surrounded by eight hundred rolling acres, horses, and playmates—the eight Whitney grandchildren who lived on the family compound. Gloria, eager to get back to Europe for the summer, gratefully accepted Gertrude's offer of hospitality. Nurse Keislich moved in with Little Gloria. Laura Morgan, who had also moved to New York, was a frequent visitor. Their pathological anxieties remained ever-present parts of the girl's life.

When Gloria returned from Europe, Gertrude convinced her that Little Gloria—who had arrived at Wheatley Hills pale, underweight, and nervous—was doing so well in the country that she should stay on at Wheatley Hills for a few more months and enroll in a nearby school for the fall term. At Gertrude's suggestion, Gloria put her daughter in the care of a new pediatrician, William St. Lawrence, whose medical ideas now seem rather quaint, if not downright quacky. Dr. St. Lawrence treated Little Gloria for chronic constipation with a diet high in calories, carbohydrates, and fat. He prescribed a daily routine of sixteen hours of sleep, no more than three hours of school, and two hours of afternoon rest. He permitted her no exercise other than riding a horse for twenty minutes, twice per week.

At Christmas 1932, Gertrude and Dr. St. Lawrence persuaded Gloria to leave her daughter on Long Island, where she was doing well at school and moving her bowels regularly, for the remainder of the school year. Gloria's visits to see her daughter at Wheatley Hills became more sporadic and shorter. She made several trips back to Europe. When in New York, she took in its pleasures in the company of a show business and café society crowd, attracting a good deal of press attention. Inevitably, the overseers of her daughter's property took note. "Your prolonged absence from this country, coupled with your daughter's continued residence with Mrs. Whitney," Gilchrist wrote Gloria in March 1933, "creates a troublesome situation." The financial screws were tightened. Instead of getting $4,000 per month, few questions asked, as she had for seven years, Gilchrist now gave Gloria $750 per month, paid her servants' wages directly (ensuring that their loyalties were in the right place), and paid her other household bills, which he closely scrutinized for some connection to Little Gloria's maintenance.

Gloria found herself on the horns of a dilemma. Dr. St. Lawrence continued to urge her to leave Little Gloria at Wheatley Hills; Gilchrist penalized her financially for doing so. When Gloria raised the idea of renting a house near the Whitney compound, where she could stay with her daughter, Gilchrist shot the suggestion down, telling Gloria the surrogate would not pay for a country house with the 72nd Street brownstone already on a four-year lease.

That's when Blumey took Gloria by the hand to see his lawyer.

Burkan had represented his share of beautiful women in distress. If not thoroughly bedazzled by Gloria's charms, he was at least partially blinded by sympathy for her plight. Her style of child-rearing, distant and heavily dependent on servants, was common among the upper crust. Even the merely nouveau riche Nathan and Marienne Burkan were raising their two-year-old son by what Nathan Jr. would later describe as "remote control." A peripatetic, nocturnal lifestyle such as Gloria's was not incompatible with contemporary standards of parental care.

Burkan's view of the matter was also colored by the gnawing feeling that, despite his achievements at the highest levels of the legal profession, among the Whitneys and Vanderbilts of the world he was looked down upon as a Jewish shyster representing disreputable clients. He was, perhaps, a little too eager for an occasion to take them on.

Gloria's problem, at that stage, seemed relatively straightforward of solution. Burkan saw no reason why, as the natural guardian of her daughter's "person," as opposed to her property, she could not simply assert her right to custody. He advised her that no one had any legal standing to prevent her from taking Little Gloria home, and warned her that she must resist any further blandishments Gertrude might offer to leave Little Gloria with her. "Possession is nine-tenths of the law," Burkan told Gloria.

Gloria tried to follow Burkan's advice, literally snatching Little Gloria at Grand Central Terminal when she returned from a summer vacation at Newport in September 1933. But she soon succumbed to suasion from Dr. St. Lawrence, who told her, "Just a few more months there, little mother, I know your heart is breaking." Notably, the attitude of the guardians and Surrogate Foley had taken a turn in the months since Gloria began keeping frequent company with Blumey, a married Jewish man. Rather than holding discontinuance of the allowance over her head, Wickersham now assured Gloria in writing that "this being the advice of a competent physician, I think you are thoroughly justified to send her to Long Island for the coming season. I understand that Mrs. Whitney has offered to take the child for the winter, without adding to her living expenses. This will relieve you of any criticism in that regard."

The status quo continued until the spring of 1934, when Alice Vanderbilt, mother of Reggie and Gertrude, died. The dowager had been fond of Gloria and left her $100,000. This modest bequest (Little Gloria, in contrast, received another $750,000 in Vanderbilt trust money on Alice's death) gave Gloria the resources to take a more aggressive legal posture. Burkan filed a petition with the Surrogate's Court in June 1934 to have Gloria formally named legal guardian of her daughter's person and a co-guardian of her property. Publicly, he was careful not to criticize Wickersham and Gilchrist, saying only that he believed Gloria should have equal standing before the surrogate. It appears, however, that he had concluded that the guardians had been co-opted in some way by Gertrude and could no longer be trusted.

Burkan believed that Surrogate Foley, his friend and political ally dating back at least to the 1915 New York constitutional convention, would grant these measures routinely. But lawyers for Laura Morgan and Gertrude Whitney, apparently put on alert by the guardians (thus confirming Burkan's suspicions about them), appeared in the case to oppose the petition. They intimated that their grounds for the opposition would be Gloria's "unfitness." It was an ill-defined standard under New York law, where courts had held that "the right of a surviving parent to the custody of his child is absolute provided such parent be a fit person." In the case of a widowed mother, Burkan told Gloria, he thought those opposing her guardianship would be required to prove that she was "immoral or amoral or a prostitute."

Rumors of a brewing custody battle over Little Gloria began appearing in the press. "Mrs. Vanderbilt's continued friendship with A. C. Blumenthal and the constantly recurring reports of her betrothal to the real estate and theatrical magnate have done nothing to endear her to her in-laws," one society page writer noted. Her sources were saying that Gertrude was fighting "to insure the rearing of her brother's child as far removed from Broadway influences as possible." But the principals in the controversy were being careful in their public statements. A reporter asked Gloria whether she believed "somebody is desirous of keeping Little Gloria away from you permanently?" "That is what I am trying to find out," she answered. "There are so many things about this that I don't understand."

It was Surrogate Foley's standard practice to try to amicably "adjust" all family controversies. The Vanderbilts, it was said, had always succeeded in laundering their dirty linen out of court. With an air of misplaced optimism, Foley scheduled a settlement conference to be held in his private chambers.

"No less than three women, representing outstanding American families," one paper reported, "will be represented tomorrow by a formidable array of fourteen lawyers in Surrogate's Court to battle for possession of the child." None of those three women would be present, nor would the now ten-year-old girl whose future was at issue. The matter was in the hands of the lawyers, all men, who converged on the Surrogate's Courthouse on the morning of July 26, 1934.

Behind the scenes, Gertrude's family lawyer and fixer, Frank Crocker, was calling the shots for the Whitney side. He had assembled a high-powered legal team for Laura Morgan and Gertrude Whitney. First chair was John Godfrey Saxe, the general counsel of Columbia University and a member of the board of the Metropolitan Museum of Art. He was also a political ally of Surrogate Foley, having headed a commission that a few years earlier had carried out Foley's desire to modernize New York estate law, including the law of dower (a reform that came too late, alas, to benefit Gloria).

Burkan appeared with Louis Frohlich and James Murray. "It did not escape the attention of society that Nathan Burkan, who is representing Mrs. Vanderbilt in the present legal entanglement, has been Mr. Blumenthal's representative in the courts." The patricians that Burkan and his associates faced across the table that day did not seem at all like the types who did their legal work in the men's room.

In that dark-paneled conference room, away from the glare of the press, the Whitney legal team gave Burkan his first taste of what was in store for Gloria, and for himself, if they insisted on the path of confrontation. There is no stenographic record, but we know that Saxe told Burkan that he "had something" on him that would result in his disbarment. "I told him where he came off," Burkan later said. "They were going to disbar me because I put up a fight, because this boy from the tenements said he didn't care anything about the Whitneys." The Vanderbilt-Whitney family fight became highly personal for Burkan that day, his better judgment sometimes compromised by class resentment.

By late August, after several more meetings, including one with Gloria and Gertrude at Foley's home, the attorneys believed they had an agreement regarding Little Gloria's custody. All that remained was for them to draft a form of order for the surrogate's signature. "For some unknown reason, or because of some disagreement, the nature of which was never disclosed to the surrogate, the decree of compromise was not submitted," Surrogate Foley later wrote. "Had this settlement been completed, unwholesome and salacious notoriety, with its inevitable injury to the child, would have been avoided." It had been agreed that Little Gloria would remain with Gertrude for another year, with Gloria getting custody for one month. The breakdown occurred over what would happen at the end of the year. Gloria understood that her petition for guardianship would be granted and Little Gloria returned to her custody "absolutely and unequivocally, without any reservations or restrictions"; Gertrude understood that Surrogate Foley would simply revisit the issue at the end of the year.

The matter was still up in the air in mid-September, when Little Gloria went into New York to spend a week with her mother before the start of the new school year.

On September 21, 1934, Burkan was basking in the success of a charitable endeavor to which he had devoted much of his energy over the summer. The night before, at Yankee Stadium, he had hosted a benefit "Night of Stars" to raise funds to support Jewish refugees from Nazi Germany, where Hitler had declared himself Führer a few weeks earlier. "The Jew in Germany today is a sad and tragic figure," Burkan said in announcing plans for the program over the CBS radio network. "He finds himself in sorrow, desolation, distress and destitution, with his means of earning a livelihood markedly curtailed. . . . To hold out a beacon light of hope and courage to this stricken people is our mission."

Before a crowd of thirty-five thousand, from a stage set up on the infield, Burkan gave some introductory remarks and then turned the night over to the remarkable array of talent he had recruited. The eclectic program included Jack Benny, Bill "Bojangles" Robinson, and Leopold Stokowski conducting "an orchestra of 1000." As a fundraiser it was a smashing success; as entertainment it suffered from excess. The reporter covering the event for the *Times* had to leave early to meet his deadline: "As midnight approached less than half the program had been completed. . . . Even George M. Cohan, who wrote a special song for the occasion, still had to go on."

A phone call from Gloria Morgan Vanderbilt late that Friday afternoon spoiled Burkan's celebration. Little Gloria, she explained, had been spending the last few days of summer vacation at her house in the city and had not been due to return to Gertrude's until Sunday. Accounts vary as to exactly what triggered the events of that day. It appears that Gloria had arranged to rent a house near Wheatley Hills and had just informed her servants that they would all be moving there. Under the ruse of taking Little Gloria to Central Park to roller-skate and feed the pigeons, nurse Keislich and Gloria's chauffeur spirited the child to Gertrude's Greenwich Village studio. When Gloria caught up with them later, at the Fifth Avenue Whitney mansion, she found Little Gloria surrounded by medical personnel and in a state of hysteria. Little Gloria ran at the sight of her mother, screaming, "Don't let her hurt me! I hate her, I hate her! Don't let her take me!" No one would contradict Gloria's later testimony that her daughter had never behaved this way around her before, but Gloria could not take her home in that state.

Gloria told Burkan that she wanted to take immediate legal action to regain permanent custody. She was convinced that Little Gloria's mind was being poisoned against her. "To permit the child to remain under the same influences and in the same surroundings for one more year," she later said, "would have meant that I would no longer have a child."

Burkan advised her there was one legal avenue available to wrest Little Gloria from Gertrude's clutches. A writ of habeas corpus would require her sister-in-law to justify her continued "detention" of Little Gloria before a judge in open court. Although he believed the law was on Gloria's side, Burkan was reluctant to take this route. It would mean taking the matter out of the relatively benign and predictable hands of Surrogate Foley and rolling the dice on a new judge in the state Supreme Court. And it would mean all-out warfare with well-heeled and well-armed adversaries. But Gloria was insistent. Burkan had a writ served on Gertrude the next day.

Gloria had been warned repeatedly, by Burkan and others, that a court battle would soil the reputations of everyone involved. The warnings did not seem to take. On Monday, as news of the weekend's events was spreading, Gloria was spotted by one society reporter lunching with Blumey at one of café society's favorite watering holes, the Colony, "looking as happy and serenely confident as if the court fight were over instead of just beginning."

"Anyway, everyone loves a good family row," the dishy item concluded, "and is looking forward to a swell three-cornered court battle between Mrs. Vanderbilt, Mrs. Whitney, and Mrs. Harry Morgan."

Justice John F. Carew scheduled an initial conference on Gloria's writ of habeas corpus for Friday, September 28, 1934. Large crowds and newsreel cameras gathered outside the classical temple–like façade of the New York County Courthouse on Foley Square. The atmosphere was reminiscent of a heavyweight title bout, but with the combatants wearing silver fox stoles and Princess Marina hats, arriving in chauffeured Rolls Royces, their cornermen decked out in three-piece suits and fedoras. As required by the writ, Gertrude brought Little Gloria to court. The girl walked in briskly in her tweed coat and was seen leaving the courthouse with a doll in her arms. Reporters noted she looked "pale and frightened."

This proceeding would take place behind closed doors in Carew's chambers, but while the parties waited to be ushered in, reporters in the corridor watched as Little Gloria icily ignored her mother: "The little girl, having black bobbed hair and wearing a tan coat, hat, shoes and socks, did not glance at her mother or greet her as they waited the arrival of Justice Carew." In full public view, "the glittering world of glamorous Mrs. Gloria Morgan Vanderbilt reeled and crumbled."

The assignment of the matter to Justice Carew was unlucky for Gloria. After serving eight terms in the U.S. House of Representatives,

Carew had been appointed to the bench by Governor Roosevelt in 1929. He lacked Surrogate Foley's expertise in custody matters and was, for a politician, rather uncomfortable in the public spotlight. He was a devout Catholic, and his views on matters of religion and sexual morality were inflexible. In a speech he gave in 1930, when already serving as a judge, he called for men in public life to fight "the tide of irreligion" and denounced "free speech on the fundamental matters of sexual morality" as un-American and anti-Christian.

The previous day, Gertrude's legal team had filed opposition papers that included an affidavit by Laura Morgan attesting to her daughter's unfitness. Mrs. Morgan averred that during their years in Paris, "my daughter paid absolutely no attention to Little Gloria. She devoted herself exclusively to her own gay pleasures. Usually she slept until one or two in the afternoon and from that time until the early hours of the following morning she was at cocktail parties, dinners and night clubs. . . . Little Gloria was like a poor orphan," she added, "she was not wanted." The affidavit concluded with a foreboding bit of paraleipsis: "I do not consider that it would be for Little Gloria's best interests for me to go further into the unpleasant details about my daughter's life and associations."

After a short conference, Carew directed the parties to return the following Monday, October 1, to begin presenting their evidence in open court. He put the burden of proof on the Whitney side and said it would take the most compelling evidence of Gloria's unfitness as a mother for him to deny her custody of her own daughter. In the meantime, though, Little Gloria would stay where she was.

Blue Bloods Meet the Hoi Polloi

With accusations of kidnapping and debauchery in the air before the first line of testimony was taken in court, the Little Gloria Vanderbilt case exploded into the national headlines. Justice Carew's courtroom was overflowing with reporters hungry for a scandalous exposé of the high and mighty that would appeal to Depression-era readers. They would not be disappointed.

Frank Crocker had brought in yet another pedigreed lawyer to try the case. Herbert C. Smythe was the quintessence of courtroom smoothness. His understated, aristocratic manner disguised a mastery of every sharp practice that a savvy litigator could get away with. "Tall, ruddy, immaculately dressed, Smythe examines witnesses quietly. . . . For the most part, he is taciturn." In courtroom demeanor, the reporter for United Press observed, Burkan and Smythe were "as far apart as Broadway and Park Avenue." These opposites had crossed paths before in a high-profile custody dispute—it was Smythe who had masterminded the "liberation" of Jell-O heir Orator Woodward's children in Paris a few years earlier.

Smythe's first witness was Little Gloria's nurse, Emma "Dodo" Keislich. Keislich used her moment of national attention to vent ten years' worth of spleen. Every question Smythe asked elicited a stream of opprobrium directed toward Gloria. Often, she did not even wait for a question. "It discredits a witness when she seems to be too eager to volunteer too much," Carew warned her. "It shows a partisan spirit which discounts her testimony severely." As the reporter from the *Daily News*, Julia McCarthy, the most trenchant of all the scribes covering the trial, summarized the nurse's testimony, it "painted her former employer as a lazy, loose, erotic woman—addicted to books and pictures treating of sadism and other forms of abnormal sex behavior, indifferent to rats and vermin that swarmed in her home and cruel to her child."

The testimony that was ultimately most damaging to Gloria in Judge Carew's eyes was on the matter of her daughter's religious training. According to Keislich, who kneaded her rosary beads as she testified, Gloria had declared that she did not want her daughter brought up in the Catholic religion of her "fanatic" grandmother.

"Was that the word she used?'" Carew asked.

Keislich confirmed that it was. The nurse testified that she had taught Little Gloria Catholic prayers and took her to mass three times a month. "You won't take offense if I tell you that you should go every Sunday," Carew gently reproached her.

By the time Smythe concluded his direct examination, the fundamental asymmetry of the battle was apparent to Burkan. Although his opponents bore the burden of proof, they would only have to make a few damning allegations of immorality and neglect stick —allegations that were easier to make than to rebut. The other side knew far more about Gloria's past than did Burkan. They had her mother on their side; they had her hostile household servants.

Burkan's cross-examinations would have to be relentless; he would need to bury damaging testimony in a fog of details, inconsistencies, and equivocations, and to wear down adverse witnesses until they made a helpful admission or two. And he was so in the dark, he would have to break the cardinal rule of cross-examination by asking questions he did not know the answer to. It was a blunderbuss approach that could easily backfire.

Keislich's penchant for exaggeration and her combative attitude, refusing to concede even the most self-evident facts, made her relatively easy prey for Burkan. With a rapid-fire barrage of questions, Burkan exposed her as the miserable, querulous biddy she was. Caring for a child of tremendous wealth, she tried to explain, was for her a source of great anxiety: "Wealth brings greed; money brings greed. They are avid for that money even from a baby lamb, an innocent child. It would not make any difference to them, their greed for her money. That was my affair."

Burkan asked Keislich if she was willing to take instructions from Gloria pertaining to the child:

    Keislich. Certainly, if they are good ones. She is the mother of the child. If
    she behaves herself. . . .

    Burkan. Are you to pass upon the instructions that this mother gives you as
    to whether they are good, bad, or indifferent for this child? Are you the
    one to judge?

    A. No, the law should protect her. The law should judge, she should be in
    the hands of the law until she is 21, the law or some very severe lawyers
    to watch everything she does. To watch her, to guard her, every move she
    makes, her money, her life.

Burkan had made his point. Carew wondered out loud whether "she
was an influence that would destroy any possible affection that this
child had for its mother," and whether her services shouldn't be dispensed with. ("Of course, it is very necessary for them to get rid of me,"
Keislich chimed in.) The nurse had sealed her own doom as Little
Gloria's caretaker, but her allegations of neglect, immoral conduct, and
irreligion would be amplified and corroborated by others.

Burkan's lengthy, grating cross-examinations of Smythe's witnesses
became a familiar feature of the trial. Burkan, one reporter wrote,

    is a dynamo of energy on cross-examination. . . . He barks out his questions,
    stands impatiently when replies are tardy. Mild sarcasm is a weapon he fre-
    quently employs. . . . Rapidly he changes from one mode of questioning to
    another, suddenly dropping a point almost established. Later he will score
    with another question that may catch the witness unawares.

When Smythe complained about Burkan's treatment of his witnesses,
Justice Carew dryly observed: "He is a forcible gentleman. He has quite
a lot of energy. He does not tire very easily." Near the end of her many
hours of cross-examination, Laura Morgan wailed: "I did not know
that I was going to be called to go through this Calvary on earth!"
    The risks inherent in Burkan's approach were revealed to the whole
world when Smythe called a surprise witness. Maria Caillot had been
Gloria's personal maid from 1928 to mid-1933. A petite French bru-
nette, she described in heavily accented English, as Julia McCarthy
reported,

    the Paris that Mrs. Gloria Morgan Vanderbilt knew—where three jazz bands
    in relays tooted all night for a handful of guests in the drawing-room while
    rats scurried about below; where the boudoir of her cold, ancient dwelling
    held seven hot modern books, and where the sun rose merely to mark a
    party's end.

She could recall the title of one of Gloria's bed table books: *The Beautiful Flagellants of New York*. Caillot introduced the name A.C. Blumenthal into the case, testifying that he became a daily visitor to Gloria's New York home in 1933. She also testified that Gloria had rushed back to Europe after Little Gloria's tonsillectomy in 1932 not to "close the Paris house," but to summer in Cannes with the Marchioness Nada Milford-Haven.

Burkan chipped away at her testimony on cross, but then walked into a trap that Smythe had set. After getting Caillot to concede that the Marchioness Milford-Haven was "a fine decent lovely lady," Burkan turned to Gloria and Nada's summer holiday in Cannes. Caillot conceded that she had not seen Gloria running around there with any men. That would have been a fine note on which to end that line of questioning, but Burkan continued: "You saw nothing improper in her conduct the entire two months, isn't that true?"

"Yes, I remember something, it seems to me very funny."

Barely looking up from his notes, Burkan asked Caillot what it was that she had found so amusing. Serving breakfast one morning, she said, she found Mrs. Vanderbilt in bed reading the newspaper. "And there was Lady Milford-Haven beside the bed with her arm around Mrs. Vanderbilt's neck, kissing her just like a lover."

Recalling that exchange a few years later, after attending Burkan's funeral, Gloria thought that "his face in death looked no more stricken and still than it had at this moment."

Burkan had fallen for one of the oldest courtroom tricks in the book, and he knew it instantly. There was no doubt on Gloria's side of the courtroom that Smythe had coached Caillot to blurt this story out on cross-examination. Doing it that way magnified its dramatic impact and allowed Gertrude and her lawyers to distance themselves from unseemly mud-slinging. Burkan instinctively tried to recover by highlighting the other side's gamesmanship: "So you told Mr. Smythe about this and he forgot to ask you when he was questioning you before?"

Smythe played innocent. He didn't forget, he said. "I tried to keep away from that kind of thing."

It was a bracing moment for Burkan; all at once he could apprehend the lengths to which Gertrude Whitney was prepared to have her proxies go to win, and how little he really knew about what embarrassments lay ahead.

Carew gaveled the courtroom to order and had it cleared of press and spectators. He decided to close further proceedings to the public and placed a gag order on the parties and counsel. Reporters would from now on have to rely on bowdlerized summaries of the testimony read out twice daily by Justice Carew, and on the "warfare in haughty pantomime" they could observe through two small panes of glass in the courtroom doors.

A three-day recess in the trial gave Burkan a chance to regroup. Burkan finished his cross-examination of Maria Caillot behind closed doors, getting her to retreat from some of her more salacious allegations. The summary that Carew provided to the press contained little in the way of accurate information about what transpired, but plenty of discouraging clues about the judge's thinking: "Mr. Burkan gave her a long cross-examination on that incident, and I am sure he feels he diluted it somewhat; while the opposing counsel undoubtedly feels he did not. I don't think Burkan got it to the point where the incident was just a friendly greeting. The maid stuck to her story."

Laura Morgan then took the stand to reiterate her accusations of hedonism and neglect. Her performance was positively operatic. She dabbed her eyes frequently with a handkerchief, heaved with sobs of self-pity, and clutched a crucifix to her bosom. "It is not my daughter's fault," she said. "But she has not been born with a maternal instinct. She was indifferent to the child." As she had in her affidavit of unfitness, Laura Morgan attempted to leave the question of Gloria's morals to the realm of innuendo, as something she expressly did not wish to be asked about.

Carew insisted, however, that she testify regarding a certain late-night Biarritz bedroom encounter between Gloria and Prince Hohenlohe that, according to Nurse Keislich, both women had witnessed. What she described was a rather chaste scene—Gloria and the prince were both clothed and seemed to be having an argument, not making love—but nonetheless it was clearly beyond the pale for Justice Carew.

On cross-examination, Burkan pounced: "Didn't you hate this man before the time you say you saw him in your daughter's bedroom?"

"Why certainly," Mrs. Morgan admitted. "He wanted to adopt my granddaughter, he wanted her to change her name, he wanted to bring her up as a German, he wanted to discipline her according to his own ways, and he was to handle the money of the baby . . . and not the lawyers, yes."

"And from that time on, you began to do everything within your power to stop the marriage, isn't that true madam?"

"Wouldn't you have done it with you own granddaughter if he was trying to get her money? She is an innocent child, and all that stands between her money and this . . . " The judge didn't allow her to finish the thought.

To Gloria, her mother's outburst revealed the "essence" of the whole case, "all of its motives and cross-purposes." But it did not seem to have much impact on Justice Carew, who told the press only that Gertrude's account of the Hohenlohe incident added "nothing new." What seemed to impress Carew most about Laura Morgan's testimony was her great emotion "when she told of having her grandchild Gloria baptized a Roman Catholic, although her daughter was opposed to it."

As the second week of trial came to an end, Justice Carew told reporters that the testimony of Gloria's butler, Charles Zaug, and chauffeur, Thomas Beasley, had been a bust for Mrs. Whitney. Beasley had driven Mrs. Vanderbilt to many restaurants, cabarets, and theaters, but her escorts were "men who were obviously and unquestionably respectable." Zaug, Carew said, had testified that Gloria's parties were quiet affairs and that the guests were all "perfect ladies and perfect gentlemen." When asked about Maria Caillot's claim that Gloria often drank before breakfast, Zaug could recall only serving her and a guest "one drink, one morning."

Reporters asked Justice Carew who was said to have been with Mrs. Vanderbilt when she had her morning nip.

He smiled and answered: "A lady."

The *Times*, which had been relying implicitly on Justice Carew's daily summaries, went all in on this account with the headline: "Servant Defends Mrs. Vanderbilt."

The tabloids, however, smelled a story, and by the weekend they had it. The chauffeur Beasley had testified to dropping Gloria off late at night at the homes of married men, including but not limited to Blumey. The butler Zaug had testified that Gloria and her prebreakfast drinking companion, her old school friend Helen Thomas, had both been completely naked. He also testified that Caillot had shown him a book in Gloria's bedroom that he was too embarrassed to describe:

The Court. Were those pictures of naked women?

Zaug. Yes sir.

Q. You are over 21. You don't need to be ashamed to tell us what you know. Tell us what it is.

A. They were naked.

Q. You don't think you can shock me. Tell us what it was all about. Don't leave me to drag it out of you. I don't want to hear it, but I have got to.

A. They were Sisters . . . and they were feeling young girls.

Q. How do you know they were Sisters if they were naked?

A. Some of them were Sisters. But the young girls, they were naked.

If there were any reason to doubt that Smythe would have introduced evidence of Gloria's bisexuality, even if Burkan had not blundered into it with Caillot, Zaug's testimony should lay that to rest. Too much blame has been laid at Burkan's feet for having, admittedly, asked the French maid "one question too many."

Reporters confronted Carew in his chambers. "Instead of Ivory Soap, how about telling us what Mrs. Vanderbilt and Helen Thomas were doing when the butler caught them nude and drunk at 6 in the morning?" Carew ordered the reporters out. "One of the reporters began: 'May we ask—.' The justice's fist smote his desk. 'Not a word,' he shouted."

Burkan's frustration over the leaking of the servants' testimony, obviously by the Whitney team, was compounded by the realization that the mounting evidence of his client's "morbid affection" for women and her assignations with married men was narrowing his options. His comments to the press reeked of desperation. Zaug's story, he said, was a figment of Gertrude Whitney's "nude conscious" mind: "In fighting to retain custody, Mrs. Whitney attributed to the mother ideas with which she herself was most familiar. In her Greenwich Village studio, she often has nudes of both sexes." He vowed that Gertrude would soon be getting a taste of her own medicine.

Reinforcements began to arrive from Europe. Reporters welcomed the ship carrying Thelma, Viscountess Furness, whom they identified as one of the favorite "hostesses" of the Prince of Wales, although she had in fact been displaced some months earlier in his affections by another American divorcée, Wallis Simpson. Harry Morgan accompanied his sister. They were followed by Prince Hohenlohe and his wife, both of whom had come to vouch for Gloria's good character and motherly love. American reporters were impressed by this display of Old World urbanity and grace.

Also arriving in New York that day was Theobald Mathew, a British solicitor closely associated with the royal family, who was sent by the Marchioness Milford-Haven to protect her interests. His secret mission was to keep the entire House of Windsor out of the range of mud splatter. It was soon clear why King George V and Queen Mary thought so highly of him.

"Blue Bloods Meet the Hoi Polloi" was the caption on this October 17, 1934, photograph. Over lunch at one of his courthouse district haunts, Burkan (2) confers with Gloria Morgan Vanderbilt (3), Prince Gottfried zu Hohenlohe (5), Princess Margarita (1), Harry Morgan (4), and Thelma, Viscountess Furness (6). (Manuscripts and Archives Division, New York Public Library, Astor, Lenox, and Tilden Foundations)

Mathew requested a private meeting with Burkan, who was eager to host the "King's solicitor" and hear what assistance Nada Milford-Haven could provide to Gloria. The meeting, held over dinner at Burkan's Great Neck mansion, did not go as Burkan had hoped. It turned out that Mathew had already met separately with Gertrude's lawyers, who had given him a very detailed list of damaging evidence they were still holding in their back pockets. He communicated their proposition to Burkan: Gertrude would not introduce any evidence of additional indiscretions, if Gloria would refrain from exhuming Gertrude's skeletons. Burkan had little choice but to accept.

The peephole testimony thus came to an end. Smythe began putting on the professionals who supported Gertrude, most importantly Little Gloria's pediatrician, William St. Lawrence.

Dr. St. Lawrence came off as a self-congratulatory ass, a self-proclaimed miracle worker inordinately proud of having cured a stubborn case of constipation in a preadolescent. (It is impossible to tell from the eighty-five-year-old transcript whether Smythe's response to the doctor's graphic description of the girl's bowel movements—"I think we can pass all that"—was an intended pun or not.) On cross-examination, St. Lawrence conceded that Gloria had come to him many times over the two years he was treating Little Gloria, and that each time he had urged her to leave the girl at Wheatley Hills, even after he had concluded as early as September 1933 that she was "in excellent condition." Burkan had him read the notes he made during his initial meeting with Nurse Keislich: "God awful nurse," Dr. St. Lawrence had written. "A terrible person for Gloria. She hovers over her like a hen and makes the child self-centered, introspective, and neurasthenic. See Mrs. Whitney about chucking nurse."

All that remained of the Whitney case-in-chief was the testimony of Gertrude and, finally, Little Gloria herself. Gertrude took the high road, generally speaking well of Gloria and finding little fault with her mothering, other than the infrequency of her visits with Little Gloria since she had been at Wheatley Hills. She conceded that the girl had shown no antagonism to her mother prior to the events of the past summer; at worst she had been indifferent. When they kissed, it was perfunctory, like "French generals." On cross-examination, Burkan sparred with her over whether Little Gloria's current attitude wasn't just a fear of leaving Wheatley Hills, where she was being indulged with ponies, puppies, and other goodies, as opposed to actual antipathy toward her mother. Burkan made little headway on this or any other issue. He had never before faced off in any courtroom against quite so imposing a battle-ax. Throughout, Gertrude regarded him with what one reporter watching through the windowpane described as "the cool distant look of an affronted aristocrat."

The subject of Gertrude's past being off-limits, Burkan mounted an attack on the moral character of her art studio and museum, suggesting that both were filled with smut and pornography. It was the only topic on which he succeeded in getting under Gertrude's skin. At one point, reporters watching through the courtroom door saw Burkan hand her what appeared to be a photo of a nude sculpture. "The question accompanying this action seemed to arouse the witness' temper. She threshed her arms and shouted a reply in which the word 'art' was plainly audible to those outside." The erstwhile defender of Mae West and crusader against censorship had been reduced to feigning moral outrage over nudity. Carew, a genuine prude, pointed out the obvious: "Looking at a picture of a naked woman up in the Metropolitan Museum of Art is a very different thing from sitting in a room and having it in your lap and taking it to bed with you."

Elaborate precautions were taken to bring Little Gloria into the courthouse unseen and unphotographed. Carew tried to disguise Little

Gloria's testimony as a friendly chat with a kindly old man, with only himself, the two lead lawyers, and a stenographer present. (Gloria chose not to attend.) Frank Crocker had been drilling Little Gloria for this moment for some time. She understood "that if I was to remain with Auntie Ger, the law required that I appear in court to meet Justice Carew and tell him in my own words why I didn't want to live with my mother." Crocker rehearsed her answers to a fare-thee-well, coaching her to emphasize how much she had moved around with her mother and how little attention she had received from her.

Little Gloria did not flub her lines. Carew tried to lead her into admitting some affection for her mother. She was adamant that she feared and hated her mother, and that she always had, though her reasons seemed rather vague. But what nobody thought to rehearse with Little Gloria were her prayers, or how to do the sign of the cross. Justice Carew was appalled by her lack of religious training.

Burkan tried various tacks to show that Little Gloria's ill feelings toward her mother were recent and the result of undue influence. He needed to get her off the script that Crocker had written for her. He went through a large pile of affectionate letters she had written to her mother. "Did you hate your mother then?" he asked her repeatedly. "Yes," she answered, saying she wrote them out of fear. Was she lying when she wrote them? "Yes." An adult would have been shamed into giving Burkan at least some small concessions. Little Gloria stood her ground. Hadn't her mother given her a dog? "He was getting quite old, and then he died." Hadn't she knitted her a sweater? "The sweater was too small. It was about up to here (indicating)."

Then Burkan showed Little Gloria a letter she had written thanking her mother for the sweater. Pointing to the postscript of the letter, which the veteran trial lawyer had evidently overlooked, the ten-year-old, spontaneously and unrehearsed, administered a coup de grâce:

Little Gloria. And look! She doesn't even tell me where she is.

Burkan. "P.S. Where are you now?"

A. Yes.

Q. She didn't even tell you where she was?

A. No.

If, as Justice Carew had told Burkan just before Little Gloria's testimony, "the case is still on the lap of the Gods, as far as I am concerned," that was surely no longer the case when she was excused.

Carew briefed reporters after Little Gloria's interview. By this point, Carew had repeatedly demonstrated his disdain for the press and for the public's right to be informed. Newspapers that should have known better credulously repeated his account: "The child made it plain she did not dislike her mother. . . . She simply and positively did not want to be taken away from Mrs. Whitney." Her prayers were "letter perfect."

After four agonizing weeks, the time came for Gloria to put on her case. It was already obvious to Burkan that he would not prevail with Carew. He and his team were in the unenviable position of having to come to court every day to laboriously build a record for appeal.

Burkan did not have a lot to work with. He put on Gloria's siblings, he put on some loyal servants (though they were mostly short-tenured), he put on some of those with whom Gloria had been accused of unwholesome friendships (though not Blumey, Nada Milford-Haven, or Helen Thomas). Prince Hohenlohe's courtly demeanor and candor seemed to impress the judge, but Carew made it clear that he had no truck with idle European nobility. Listening to Harry Morgan give a long litany of titled grandees whose presence graced Gloria's home in Paris, Carew lost patience. He didn't care if "the Duke of Boloney" had paid a call. "The names do not appeal to me at all. This was a little American girl, the less she has to do with the people who bore these names, the better off it might be for her."

The judge frequently reminded the lawyers on both sides that "things don't always look the same up here as they do down there." Indeed, the views he expressed from the bench often caught the combatants off guard. Burkan fought hard to introduce evidence that Maria Caillot, an unmarried lady, had a miscarriage while working for Gloria. Carew thought it reflected badly on Gloria that she kept the maid in service. Similarly, Burkan thought it worth introducing evidence that Gloria had rarely laid a hand on her daughter in discipline, only to learn that Carew was a "spare the rod, spoil the child" man. Neither side had come prepared to deal with Carew's rigid views on religious training. It was a pox on both houses. Only Burkan personally escaped blame. After Little Gloria's testimony, Carew had ranted that "the child's spiritual and religious education has been very, very sadly neglected." When Burkan tried to respond, the judge snapped: "I don't expect you to teach the child the sign of the cross."

That is the closest thing to an explicit acknowledgment of Burkan's Jewishness to be found in the trial record. But the snide and disdainful attitude of the Whitney witnesses and lawyers, even "the help," shines through. They all treated Burkan as a loathsome interloper. "We are not all liars. We are not your sort, we are not your kind," Nurse Keislich blurted out when Burkan deigned to express skepticism about her testimony. Moments later, Burkan tried to hand her an exhibit:

Burkan. Don't shrink from me.

Keislich. Don't touch me.

Q. Now, Madam, this is not Mrs. Whitney's home. We are in a court room. . . . If you won't shrink, I am going to show you a letter.

A. Put it down.

Q. I haven't got the needles. But I am liable to get it if I stick too close to you. . . . Don't look at me.

A. I am not anxious to look at you.

Carew grew increasingly dyspeptic as the trial was winding down. He knew that public sentiment had generally been with Gloria and that the ruling he would be announcing was not going to be popular. When a woman appeared at his chambers with a petition, signed by three hundred mothers, calling for him to restore custody to Gloria, he refused to accept it and warned that if she insisted on leaving it, he would "make her eat it with catsup."

Carew's press briefings, which had been steeped in outright fictions from the start, descended further into bizarre fabulism. After a session in which Burkan had introduced photographs of risqué pieces from the Whitney art collection, Carew told reporters the exhibits included one etching of "sportive nudes playing leapfrog" while "gentlemen in top hats gaze on admiringly," and that the arguments of counsel had veered into a "lively classical debate" on Homer's *Odyssey* and Milton's *Paradise Lost*. As strange as his public utterances were becoming as the trial dragged into its second month, it should be said that Judge Carew's courtroom rulings remained generally fair and even-keeled, even as his patience understandably wore thin.

Burkan put off Gloria's testimony to almost the very end. She had lately been making only brief appearances in the courtroom, always attended by a trained nurse. The press was told she suffered from a fluttery heart. ("That's the first I ever heard of any heart trouble," Laura Morgan responded scornfully. "She could always dance all night.") Burkan made the best of the situation, telling reporters, "If she has to be carried in on a litter by fourteen nurses, she's not going to the let the Whitneys get away with this." Marienne Burkan, only a few years older than Gloria, began coming to court to lend moral support.

When Gloria took the stand, she was an effective witness. "With a catch in her voice and her eyes brimming with tears," *Daily News* reporter Julia McCarthy wrote, Gloria "defended her rights and reputation in a hearing so interlaced with suppressed emotion that even Justice John F. Carew was profoundly affected." Guided by Burkan's well-crafted direct examination, illustrated by many photographs and letters, she was able to tell her story of a loving mother-daughter relationship, and she was forceful in her denials of the charges of immoral conduct.

Gloria largely maintained a steely poise during Herbert Smythe's multiday cross-examination, but the holes in her story were easily exposed. Her travel itinerary was damning. Smythe confronted her with press clippings that documented her glamorous social swirl, beginning in the days she claimed to have been in deep mourning for Reggie in 1926.

More damaging was Gloria's behavior since Little Gloria had gone to stay at Wheatley Hills. Smythe examined Gloria at great length about her relationship with Blumey, in particular their sailing to Europe "on the same tub" in June 1933, which Gloria claimed was happenstance. Smythe showed that they had made their travel arrangements through the same agent, that they both had their names removed from the published passenger list, and that although Gloria's stateroom was some distance from Blumey's suite, Gloria's maid stayed in a cabin connected to it. Gloria protested too much:

> *Smythe.* How did it happen that your maid had a stateroom adjoining and connecting with Mr. Blumenthal's?
>
> *Gloria.* That is purely an accident Mr. Smythe. You don't think for one single moment—I know the insinuation you are trying to make—considering my friendship with Mr. Blumenthal, that I would park my maid in the cabin next door so she could listen to everything that went on?
>
> *Q.* No, but it did give access to Mr. Blumenthal's room?
>
> *A.* You mean to insinuate that I went through my maid's room into Mr. Blumenthal's room. Really you are Machiavellian in thinking things up.

While she was in Europe during the spring of 1934, Gloria learned that Gilchrist had found a short-term subtenant for the 72nd Street brownstone. Smythe introduced into evidence an urgent radiogram that Gloria sent Gilchrist: "HAVE HANNAH REMOVE ALL PERSONAL

EFFECTS AND BOOKS FROM MY ROOM STOP." Why, Smythe asked, only the books in her bedroom?

Most effective of all, however, was Smythe's cross on Gloria's limited contact with her daughter at Wheatley Hills. He forced Gloria to admit that she did not know the names of her daughter's teachers or playmates, the grade she was in, or the names of any books she had read. Gloria had not attended any school functions. One question Smythe asked was still lingering in the air long after Gloria stepped down from the witness stand: "Did you spend one percent of all the days of the year with the child?"

When the testimony ended after nearly seven weeks, Carew immediately announced, "I will not send this child back to the life that it lived from the time that its father died until it came to New York and was delivered to Mrs. Whitney." He stated that he did not approve of Gloria's conduct with relation to her daughter, "and I will limit it to that, because I don't want to pass upon certain aspects of the case unless I have to." He believed, however, that Gloria should "have such access to the child as will not interfere with the present life of the child" and he would allow her an opportunity to "win back the respect and affection of the child." Carew asked Smythe and Burkan to try to work out the details of an arrangement that would effectuate his intent.

Burkan saw no possibility of such a resolution. Gloria would not agree to anything other than full custody, subject to whatever conditions the court cared to impose. Short of that, his instructions were to appeal the ruling to New York's highest court. He could not engage in any discussions that might be construed as acquiescence in the court's ruling and undermine his arguments on appeal.

"You will insist you are licked, won't you?" Carew asked Burkan. "I'm afraid so," Burkan responded. "I have put everything that is in me into this case."

"Counselor," Carew said:

> There was never a man that worked harder or threw more of the center of his soul into a case than you did in this. And that is not flattery, and that is not said for the purpose of consoling you. I know that the very core of your heart and soul went into this case.

Carew asked the lawyers to return the next day to resume the discussion. In the meantime, he dictated a curt statement for the press: "Mr. Justice Carew has decided that the child, Gloria Vanderbilt, is not to have for the future the life that it had from the death of its father up till June 1932." Reporters asked Carew for an explanation of what his ruling meant. "It was designed to keep you from finding out what it meant," he told them. "This is absolutely my last word in this case. I am never going to talk to you again."

The next day the lawyers returned to Carew's chambers to hash out the terms of a decree. Burkan's mouth was effectively sealed by Gloria's intent to appeal, although Carew gave him a chance to make a statement off the record. The key points that emerged were that Gloria would be made a ward of the court, with Gertrude as legal custodian and Gloria having her daughter on weekends and for the month of July and Christmas Day each year. Gloria was required to maintain residence within thirty miles of Wheatley Hills, and neither she nor Gertrude could take Little Gloria out of the state of New York. Carew ordered Gertrude to hire a live-in Roman Catholic governess who would see to Little Gloria's religious observance and training. As for Emma Keislich, the discussion was brief. "The nurse goes?" Carew asked. "The nurse goes," Smythe answered.

Carew prepared a written order which included a finding that Little Gloria's life before June 1932 was "in every way unsuitable, unfit, improper, calculated to destroy her health, and neglectful of her moral, spiritual and mental education." Burkan begged him to explicitly reject the very public charges of immorality leveled against Gloria. He was not usually a Bible spouter, but for Carew he made an exception:

> She may have been a neglectful mother. That is for Your Honor to find. That is a serious thing. The charge of immorality and these other offenses is very serious. It is branding her down to the third generation. The day will come, it must come, when this issue must be tried out between this child and her mother, no matter what disposition Your Honor makes as to these charges. . . . There cannot be a reconciliation of these two people, certainly not if the mother is as she has been branded. Neither Your Honor nor any living man can reconcile these two people.

Carew's answer was peremptory and final. "I do not intend to make a finding on those charges and I do it out of consideration for the mother and the child." The less said about Gloria's moral character, as far as Carew was concerned, the better.

Twilight of the Music Trust

The Vanderbilt case took an immense toll on Burkan. The emotional seven-week trial was followed by months of legal motions and the preparation of an appeal based on the 3,500-page record. Little Gloria's first weekend visit with her mother, which included a pre-Christmas trip to the F.A.O. Schwartz toy store to break the ice, had to be carefully managed in accordance with the terms of Justice Carew's decree. Gloria's allowance for 1935 had to be set by Surrogate Foley, after a struggle with the now overtly hostile Thomas Gilchrist. And in the midst of all that, Burkan's younger brother Benjamin, a pharmacist with whom he had always been close, died suddenly at the age of fifty-two.

In home movies made at the Great Neck mansion during the summer of 1935, Burkan appears as a frail man with stooped posture, an unsteady gait, and labored breathing. He looks at least twenty years older than his actual age of fifty-six. Looking at those pictures eight decades later, Nathan Jr. was struck by how prematurely his father had aged. He remembered vividly that bending over was so difficult for Nathan Sr. that he needed his butler's help to tie his own shoes. His father's severe hypertension went essentially untreated, consistent with state of the medical arts.

Burkan appeared before the Appellate Division of the New York Supreme Court for two days in early June 1935 to argue Gloria Morgan Vanderbilt's appeal. As he concluded his argument on June 6 with a plea for the court to clear his client's name, Burkan was, one reporter wrote,

Nathan Burkans, Sr. and Jr., at the Great Neck mansion, summer 1935. (Courtesy, Nathan Burkan Jr.)

"almost incoherent in his emotion." Yet on the following Monday morning, June 10, he was back in a sweltering, makeshift federal district courtroom in the Woolworth Building, where an antitrust lawsuit that the United States Department of Justice had filed against Ascap less than a year earlier was scheduled to go on trial. Burkan moved to have the case postponed until autumn, and made an uncharacteristically personal argument:

> I have lived with this proposition for twenty years, this is not something which springs up overnight. . . . I do not think it is fair, Your Honor, to yourself or to us, to try to sweat through the summer with this case, and I am certainly in no

position to try this case through the summer. I have been in court since last September almost continuously. I am at present worn and exhausted.

He went on to point out that the government had been granted an early trial date for an extremely complex case on the ground that industry-wide Ascap contracts with radio broadcasters were set to expire on September 1. The parties, however, had now agreed to extend those contracts to the end of 1935, removing any urgency. The court denied Burkan's motion.

He then asked for, and was refused, a one-week continuance to complete his preparations for trial. Burkan was clearly stunned by the court's intransigence. "Do I understand we are going on now, Your Honor?"

"Yes."

"Now, Your Honor?"

With Ascap's continued existence once again in jeopardy, Burkan drew deep from an unfathomable reservoir of energy and soldiered on.

Notwithstanding the national depression, the early 1930s had been boom years for Ascap. By 1935, according to *Variety*, performance rights had become "the principal source of income for both writer and publisher." Radio and movies were thriving as relatively cheap forms of diversion and the society's treasury was overflowing. Annual revenue had reached $4 million, writer membership passed the one thousand mark, and publisher members numbered more than a hundred. "The second quarter royalty melon to be divided this week will be a record high," *Variety* reported in July 1935. "Its total of $860,105 exceeds by $100,000 the melon split up by Ascap for the first quarter." The society moved to spacious new offices on the forty-fifth floor of the just-opened RCA Building at 30 Rockefeller Center.

This prosperity, and the new set of troubles that came with it, can in significant measure be traced to the death of general manager J.C. Rosenthal, at age forty-six, in December 1931. The lawyerly, cautious Rosenthal, Burkan's protégé in every respect, was replaced by the pugnacious, street-smart Claude Mills. Mills believed the society was not getting its fair share of the public's entertainment dollar, and he was determined to right the situation. He promptly upended Ascap's five-year truce with radio broadcasters, forcing through a three-year license that imposed a levy of 5 percent on advertising revenues in addition to larger base fees. The result was that, for most stations, total annual fees at least tripled and Ascap's yearly take from broadcasters alone approached $3 million.

The National Association of Broadcasters, which for several years had been rather quiescent on copyright matters while concentrating on its own antitrust problems and passage of the Federal Communications Act, was reawakened. At its November 1932 convention, the NAB resolved to protect radio, "by legislation, litigation, or otherwise," against "any organization which may undertake to levy an arbitrary and extortionate tribute upon the users of music under the pretense of a copyright monopoly." The NAB began to raise a war chest from its members, exhorting them to contribute 10 percent of their then-current Ascap fees with the slogan "Ten Percent Now or 300% in 1935!"

Success was creating another problem for Ascap. With broadcasters and most other commercial music users locked into blanket licenses that provided unlimited access to the entire Ascap repertoire for a flat fee, there was a strong disincentive to incurring the cost and administrative fuss of using any other copyrighted music. It was not necessary for Ascap to wag the imaginary "long warning finger" that the NAB's lawyer had once evoked before a congressional committee; the disincentive was built into the system. As a result, membership in Ascap had become more than a nice way to supplement a composer's income; rather, it was a practical necessity for those hoping to have their music performed publicly and, if performed, to collect a royalty for it. "For publishers and composers, to be outside of Ascap was to be a nonentity in the music business," writes John Ryan, a sociologist who studied the industry. Few of the new applicants, however, could add marginal value to Ascap's blanket license; most would simply dilute the pot available for distribution to existing members.

Ascap's articles of association stipulated that "every composer of music and every author of musical works who regularly practices the profession of writing music or the text of lyrics of musical works shall be eligible" for membership. An unwritten rule required that an application be endorsed by two members. The membership committee, chaired by Raymond Hubbell in those years, had discretion to reject applicants who met these objective requirements if it subjectively believed the published works were not "in vogue," that is, "sufficiently popular to bring income to the Society." Therein lay the catch. With Ascap membership virtually a prerequisite to getting music publicly performed, how could an applicant's music come into vogue in the first place? Those who were blackballed included not only kitchen-table amateurs, but also prodigious talents who toiled in disfavored genres such as "race" or "hillbilly" music, Jelly Roll Morton and Gene Autry being two egregious examples.

Complaints from the NAB and from composers and publishers who were rejected for membership put Ascap back in the crosshairs of the U.S. Department of Justice. The society had fared well under the laissez-faire administrations of Harding, Coolidge, and Hoover. Now a new generation of regulators had arrived on the scene, New Dealers with a more skeptical view of business combinations and a more expansive view of the federal government's power to curtail them.

On August 30, 1934, Franklin Roosevelt's Department of Justice filed an action against Ascap under the Sherman Antitrust Act. Federal action was proper, the complaint alleged, because the society restrained interstate traffic in "energy, entertainment, and ideas" by dictating "the manner in which radio broadcasting stations may be operated" and by "depriving those owners of copyrighted compositions who are not members of defendant Society the opportunity of transmitting their musical compositions to the ear of the purchasing public." The case marked the first time that Ascap was forced to respond in court to a fully wrought theory of antitrust liability, although it was essentially the same legal theory that Charles Tuttle had outlined in his testimony before Congress a decade earlier.

The government conceded that a centralized enforcement mechanism for performing rights was legal and probably necessary, and it disclaimed any intent to seek the dissolution of Ascap. But it attacked Ascap's central business practice, blanket licensing of pooled copyrights. The government argued that it was a form of price-fixing; that it restrained competition, both among Ascap's members and from nonmembers; and that it was therefore illegal "per se."

If the government prevailed on such a theory, it would not matter whether Ascap's intentions were laudable, whether the prices it demanded were objectively reasonable for the value provided, or whether its blanket license was demonstrably more efficient than a system in which prices were individually negotiated—all things that Burkan could have easily proved. Burkan, moreover, had no idea how he could restructure Ascap to conform to the remedy that the government was seeking: a perpetual injunction against licensing performance rights on any basis "other than free and open competition between copyright owners," with the royalty on each individual composition determined by the copyright owner "acting independently in his or its own discretion." That seemed to be the very antithesis of the principle of collective rights enforcement on which Ascap was founded.

Claude Mills was reenergizing not only broadcasters, but all of the society's old nemeses. In 1931, Ascap had made its second trip to the U.S. Supreme Court. The issue this time was whether the LaSalle Hotel in Kansas City, which retransmitted radio broadcasts from a master receiver to various public and private rooms—a common hotel amenity at the time—was giving public performances for profit by doing so. In a unanimous decision, authored by Justice Louis Brandeis, the court held that it was, reasoning that "the reception of a radio broadcast and its translation into audible sound is not a mere audition of the original program. It is essentially a reproduction." (Burkan, sidelined for four months in early 1931 by an unspecified illness, likely a major heart attack, had not been able to argue the case.)

Despite that victory, J. C. Rosenthal had been reluctant to collect fees for hotel retransmissions; Mills did so with relish. Long grandfathered into a rate structure that topped out at $180 per year since Ascap's earliest days, hotels suddenly found themselves paying as much as ten times that. After nearly two decades of good relations, the hotel interests concluded that, under Mills, Ascap "had become so arrogant and dictatorial that bargaining was impossible."

Mills turned his attention to movie exhibitors. Burkan had made a good trade-off with Mills back in 1926, when he ceded collection of synchronization royalties to the Music Publishers Protective Association in exchange for a requirement that theaters showing sound pictures be licensed by Ascap. As a result, some 80 percent of movie theaters held Ascap licenses in the early 1930s. Mills upset the long-standing equilibrium by doubling the annual per seat rate for movie theaters, which had been ten cents for the previous fifteen years.

Complaints about Ascap began pouring into the offices of state legislators and attorneys general. Several states passed statutes creating a phalanx of taxes and regulations, nominally directed at "any" performing rights organization, which were "so onerous and so complicated and so impossible of compliance," one Ascap executive wrote, that they would "actually operate as an absolute prohibitive against two or more copyright owners combining" to collect performance royalties. Burkan called these state anti-Ascap measures the "Snide Acts."

Wisconsin, especially, became what radio star Rudy Vallee termed a "hotbed of sedition" against Ascap. Ascap's regional agent there had a reputation for being particularly aggressive with small-venue operators. One Wisconsinite wrote to his Congressman in 1933: "For a number of years, I and all other owners of dance halls have been forced to pay tribute to these Jew racketeers. . . . The Federal Govt. took Capone. Can't it take the Ascap?" Wisconsin's state legislature voted to impose a 5 percent tax on the revenues of performing rights organizations, regardless of where the revenue was collected. The Wisconsin tax would have substantially exceeded Ascap's total revenues from the state of Wisconsin.

Wisconsin's junior U.S. senator at the time, Democrat F. Ryan Duffy, was chairman of a Senate Foreign Relations subcommittee tasked with writing legislation that would enable the United States to enter the international Berne Convention for the Protection of Literary and Artistic Works. Having heard his share of constituent complaints about Ascap, Duffy was receptive to lobbying from music user associations that were seeking to attach to his bill various unrelated measures to "reform" American copyright law. The "Duffy Bill," introduced in the Senate on April 1, 1935, included many provisions that had been on commercial music users' wish-list, but one item became the focus of Ascap's ire: the elimination of a provision for minimum statutory damages of $250 in copyright infringement cases. Minimum statutory damages had long been a vital weapon in Ascap's enforcement arsenal. The actual monetary harm from an infringing performance of a musical composition, if it could be measured at all, was negligible. Litigation against infringers would have been economically impracticable without this guaranteed minimum recovery. Burkan rallied Ascap's membership for another arduous legislative battle.

"Ascap seems to be very much on the defensive these days," one of the radio trade journals observed on the eve of the federal antitrust trial in June 1935. "What a change from its arrogant, domineering, and take-it-or-leave-it attitude of the past. . . . Ascap appears to be on its last legs as a hard-hearted music trust."

As exhausted and unprepared as Burkan was when the antitrust action came on for trial, he easily took control of the courtroom. One witness for the government after another, mostly radio industry lackeys, wilted under long hours of his cross-examination. "What has impressed observers of the trial most," *Variety* reported, "has been the success Nathan Burkan has had in getting a wealth of the Society's side of the case into the record through the Government's own witnesses."

The program director from one NBC-affiliated station, for example, testified that he could not use public domain music as a substitute for

Ascap-controlled music. Nearly all available arrangements and orchestrations of public domain pieces, he explained, were under copyright and published by Ascap members. (Even if, say, Stephen Foster's "Old Folks at Home" is in the public domain, a particular arrangement of the song could be protected under its own copyright.) Over two days of cross-examination, Burkan confronted the witness with a seemingly endless parade of counterexamples, and then suggested that the radio industry could easily create its own arrangements:

> *Burkan.* You could engage a staff of arrangers to score for you and in the form in which you required it, any work in the public domain provided you are willing to pay the price?
>
> *Witness.* If you can stand the expense and still operate.
>
> *Q.* So what it gets down to is purely a question of expense, that is true, isn't it?
>
> *A.* Primarily, yes, sir. . . .
>
> *Q.* The average arranger, how much a week does he get?
>
> *A.* From $75 to $100.

Burkan had previously established that broadcasters' annual revenues exceeded $100 million. It would have been fatuous to deny that the radio industry could absorb the cost of a few $5,000-a-year arrangers as an alternative to the $3 million it was then paying Ascap. It was an economically plausible option that at least cast doubt on the government's contention that Ascap had the market power to fix prices above a market rate.

Burkan was also able to use the government's witnesses to dramatize the effect that requiring composers to negotiate royalties individually would entail in the real world. NBC stations required individual, non-Ascap composers who wanted any of their music played over the air to assign to the network the performing rights to their entire catalogs, gratis:

> *Burkan.* Did you ever pay any songwriter anything?
>
> *Witness.* For individual numbers?
>
> *Q.* Yes.
>
> *A.* No.

When songwriters are forced to negotiate individually, Burkan argued, they are reduced to virtual "peonage."

The government lawyers had relied excessively on the NAB in preparing their case, and Burkan, who one observer noted "has been doing little else for the past 20 years and knows all the answers," rode rough-shod over them. "The case at the present moment seems weaker than at any other time," was *Billboard*'s take. "Broadcasters in attendance are inclined now to be pessimistic." The government lawyers, Burkan later gloated, were just "carrying the bag" for the broadcasters, when they suddenly realized that the bag "was loaded with dynamite."

Progress was slow; frequent recesses were taken to open the windows and air out the courtroom. After seven days of trial, the government asked for an adjournment. The court granted four months. It was spec-ulated in the trade press that the trial would never resume, government lawyers not being "in the habit of picking up a case that has already been botched up or proved a cropper."

Burkan was looking forward to getting some rest and relaxation in Great Neck, but bad news just kept coming. On July 3, 1935, the appel-late court affirmed Justice Carew's custody order in the Vanderbilt case. "It is difficult to see how the court below could have made any different disposition than it did," the court wrote. "It could hardly have directed that, against her vehement protest, this child should be taken from the wholesome life which she is now leading, among people to whom she has become attached, and consigned to the life of neglect and loneliness which had alienated her affection."

The only consolation for Burkan was the court's comment with respect to the Milford-Haven encounter, but even that contained a needling reminder of his famous blunder: "We think that the charge which rests upon the testimony of the maid Caillot, elicited on cross-examination, is so detrimental to the petitioner and the evidence to support it so unsubstantial that she was entitled to unqualified and complete exonera-tion." It is otherwise an unrelievedly damning opinion. "Not until the allowance, which was provided for the child's support, appeared to be endangered by the fact that the child no longer lived with her, does the petitioner appear to have manifested any strong desire for her daugh-ter's companionship." It ended with the admonishment that "if the peti-tioner shall avail herself fully of her rights under the order, she will spend more time with her child than for many years past." News accounts of the decision were accompanied by photos of the two Glorias frolicking in Long Island Sound on their first court-sanctioned July holiday.

The news that Burkan was getting on the Ascap front was no better. The Senate approved the Duffy Bill and sent it to the House of

Representatives. In the state of Washington, the attorney general filed an antitrust action, a copycat case using the federal complaint as a template. A court there enjoined Ascap from doing business within the state and placed it in receivership. The NAB was now encouraging other state attorneys general to do the same.

And then the Music Publishers Holding Corporation, the Warner Brothers subsidiary that had, in the earliest days of sound pictures, purchased three of Ascap's most important publishers—Witmark, Harms, and Remick—announced that it would be withdrawing from the society upon the expiration of its existing five-year commitment on January 1, 1936. This fulfilled the prophecy that *Variety* had made when Warner first went into the publishing business in 1929.

Warner Brothers made no secret of why it was taking this step. As Gene Buck explained, "They wanted more money, plain greed, g-r-e-e-d." Warner believed that its catalog—including much of the music of Victor Herbert, Sigmund Romberg, George Gershwin, Jerome Kern, Harry Warren, and Cole Porter—was responsible for 40 percent of Ascap's revenue, but it was receiving only about 20 percent of the distributions. As of January 1, music users would have to license that music directly from Warner, for a license fee equal to 40 percent of Ascap's going rate.

Burkan knew that if the Warner Brothers group succeeded as an independent performing rights licensing organization, other publishers would follow suit and Ascap would enter a death spiral. It was a dire threat that merited a bet-the-company response. Burkan went for broke. He had Ascap announce that it would not recognize Warner Brothers' legal right to withdraw any music from its repertory as long as the writers of that music (or, as in the case of Victor Herbert, their estates) remained members of the society. Ascap would grant no reduction of its licensing rates, but it would defend and indemnify any licensees who were sued by Warner publishers for copyright infringement.

It was a bold gambit. Twenty years earlier, by insisting that Ascap's membership include both publishers and writers, Burkan had elided the uncertain legal question whether a publisher who receives an assignment of copyright under the standard writer-publisher agreement holds it as a mere trustee for the benefit of the songwriter. Now he would have to test that proposition head on. Under the headline "Repercussions Brewing in WB Copyright Suits; Which Side Is Burkan On?" *Variety* reported that some publishers were outraged to learn that Burkan "had fathered a legal theory which questioned the right of a publisher to claim 100% ownership of its copyrights." (Burkan had actually first advanced this theory as far back as 1907, when he used it to argue to Congress that the contracts publishers had made with the Aeolian Company with respect to mechanical reproductions were null and void.)

There was no guarantee that Burkan's theory would prevail, but failure would have bankrupted the society. Solidarity among Ascap's remaining publisher members was essential to pulling this off. Burkan had wanted to hold Warner Brothers' Ascap distributions in escrow, consistent with his theory that its withdrawal was a legal nullity, but to quell the publisher revolt he allowed them to divvy up among themselves the $170,000 that Warner would have received in the first quarter of 1936. Writers who received distributions from the Warner licensing agency agreed to turn them over to Ascap for reallocation in accordance with its established classifications.

Burkan's uncompromising stance, with Ascap's membership unified behind him, dissuaded most broadcasters from taking licenses from Warner. Some were cautious about using Warner music—bandleader Paul Whiteman dropped his theme song, the most famous on radio, "Rhapsody in Blue"—while others continued to do so freely in reliance on Ascap's indemnity. Warner responded with a wave of copyright infringement litigation. During the first months of 1936 it filed more than one hundred lawsuits against broadcasters, seeking the *maximum* statutory damages of $5,000 for each alleged copyright infringement. The CBS radio network was sued for a total of $1.5 million and NBC for $1 million. All those cases were tendered to Burkan's office for defense, with Ascap on the hook for any damages awarded.

The House Committee on Patents convened for hearings on the Duffy Bill in February 1936. It had been thirty years since Burkan—a mere "stripling," as he recalled—made his first appearance before a committee of Congress. Back then, he had been outflanked and outprepared by his opponents as he struggled to get a word in edgewise before members who could not seem to remember who he was. Now he was past master at the art of the congressional hearing.

With the help of his well-connected Washington lobbyists, Burkan had arranged for Ascap to dominate the first days of the hearings. George M. Cohan, Guy Lombardo, Sigmund Romberg, and Rudy Vallee testified in between the by-now obligatory, but still-effective, appearances of Gene Buck and Claude Mills. George Gershwin and Irving Berlin took bows from the gallery. One of the radio trade journals was gracious in giving the devil its due:

Burkan spars with members of the House Committee on Patents during hearings on the Duffy Bill, February 25, 1936. (Queens Borough Public Library Archives, New York Herald–Tribune Photo Morgue Collection)

The truth is the broadcasters were caught napping. The committee and its chairman were stacked by Ascap before the hearings got under way. Ascap, as opponent of the Duffy Bill, was permitted to bring forward its witnesses first, contrary to customary procedure. They monopolized the first two weeks of the hearings, adroitly parading their "big-name" members who could add nothing to the evidence on the legislation, but who could put on a good vaudeville show.

Burkan was not scheduled to speak, but one committee member, Thomas O'Malley of Wisconsin, baited him into quite a donnybrook by referring to Ascap as a "legal racket." "Mr. O'Malley, you can do anything you please and vote for this bill any way you like," Burkan said, "but in the name of common decency and fair play do not put through this iniquitous bill by calling us 'racketeers.'" Burkan charged that Wisconsin officials were attempting to nullify federal copyright law:

Burkan. Your state is the most flagrant in this Union. . . . I am shocked and
surprised that men holding public office in these United States tell these
tavern people and these restaurant people to throw us out on our ear.

O'Malley. You came here to give testimony, and I do not want you lecturing
me.

Burkan. I am not lecturing you, but I want the facts on the record. . . . We
have been having a lot of trouble in your state.

O'Malley. I know, and you are going to have some more.

Burkan. Because you kick our people out on their ear.

O'Malley. That is right.

A host of weighty legal issues separated U.S. copyright law from
copyright law elsewhere in the world under the Berne Convention. But
Ascap managed to make the rather parochial matter of minimum statutory damages the dominant issue over the course of what turned out to
be twenty-five hearing days spread over two months. Was this provision, as Ascap argued, a necessary deterrent to copyright infringements,
the vast majority of which would go undetected and for which actual
damages would be nominal? Or was it a "club" by which Ascap could
extract exorbitant license fees from music users who feared being sued
for accidental infringements? The hearing transcript contains hundreds
of pages devoted to this one interminable debate.

As the hearings were winding down, the chairman announced that
"the committee has, at the instance of several of the members, invited
Mr. Burkan, counsel for Ascap, to our meeting in order that he might
give a presentation of the legal aspects." Indeed, the entire final day had
been set aside for Burkan to give a "rebuttal." Calling this "the most
asinine situation in the history of hearings before Congress," one member objected: "The opponents of all this legislation, including Ascap,
had the first two weeks of the hearing. I do not think it is fair. . . . I know
half a dozen of the most brilliant and scholarly attorneys, representing
various phases of this whole proposition, who would like to come in
here for 10 minutes, or 20 minutes, or 30 minutes." Representative
O'Malley objected that if the committee "is to be enlightened on the
legal aspects of the bills, it ought to be enlightened by attorneys who are
not receiving, let us say, any fees from any particular source that is
interested in the legislation."

The objections were overruled. A battle-worn and weary Burkan
enlightened the committee at great length. His presentation was barely
interrupted with questions from the members. It had the unmistakable

air of a valediction. He had come to Washington a mere stripling in 1906; he would take his leave as a consummate insider in 1936.

At the close of the hearings on the Duffy Bill, a subcommittee was named to try to hash out compromises. Burkan returned to New York to find that there were now 180 Warner Brothers suits on his desk, seeking damages totaling $4 million. Coming up on his calendar were the Democratic National Convention in Philadelphia in June, where he would be a member of the New York delegation, and the opening ceremony for the Triborough Bridge in July. Another busy summer lay ahead.

Animus toward Ascap was continuing to mount at the state level. In the state of Washington, even though the society was already in the hands of a receiver and unable to conduct business, an enterprising district attorney in Everett, Snohomish County, filed a criminal indictment against Buck, Mills, Burkan, and other officers. It charged them with using intimidation to interfere with the pursuit of lawful occupations by others—racketeering, as it were. "The prosecutor asked extradition of the New York men," it was reported, "and the judge set bail at $1,250 for each."

A few days later, on March 30, 1936, the U.S. Supreme Court denied Gloria Morgan Vanderbilt's petition for review. Burkan's argument, born of desparation, was that Gloria had been denied due process of law under the U.S. Constitution because she had not been afforded the administrative procedures, including warnings and interventions, required before taking custody of a child from a parent under the public welfare law of New York State. The brainchild of Louis Frohlich and Herman Finkelstein, it was not a frivolous theory, but they had not raised it in a timely fashion in the lower courts.

The Vanderbilt case had become Burkan's last deeply personal crusade. He never collected a fee from Gloria for his legal services; she paid only out-of-pockets costs from the money she inherited from Alice Vanderbilt. "He was sure he could vindicate Gloria Vanderbilt," Herman Finkelstein told Barbara Goldsmith. "After he had exhausted every resource, it killed him."

When Burkan left his office in Manhattan on June 4, 1936, headed for his summer home in Great Neck, Ascap—his brainchild and cherished legacy—was still under siege on multiple fronts. The Department of Justice's antitrust action was hanging over the society like the sword of Damocles. The outcome of his Warner Brothers gambit was still highly uncertain. Reports leaking from the House subcommittee indicated that Ascap's priority item, minimum statutory damages, might be sacrificed in the name of compromise. The society was unable to conduct business under the Snide Acts of a growing number of states. And in Snohomish County, Washington, Burkan was a wanted fugitive from justice.

Exeunt

Burkan died at his Great Neck mansion just past 8 A.M. on Saturday, June 6, 1936, after suffering a massive heart attack and losing consciousness the day before—a "sudden attack of acute indigestion" in the quaint diagnostic vocabulary of the time. He was surrounded by his wife, Marienne, age thirty-eight, and son, age five. All that Nathan Jr. would recall of the death vigil were the cylinders of liquid oxygen that stood near his father's bed like oversized votive candles.

Within days, obituaries filled with lavish encomiums gave way in the trade papers to speculation on the business and legal ramifications of Burkan's untimely passing. He had carried so much weight on his shoulders, his reputation was so towering, the sudden void was palpable. Lawyers at the Department of Justice, who had been trying to work out stipulations of fact with Burkan before resuming the antitrust trial, which had been on hold a full year, told reporters that his death "threw the case into confusion." They "exhibited little optimism as to the chances of obtaining further action in the case in the near future."

Variety detected "uneasiness among broadcasters, particularly in NBC and CBS quarters," in the wake of Burkan's death:

> The networks and associated station defendants had, in turning over their cases to Burkan, felt secure about the outcome, since there was no one who knew better than Burkan the circumstances that led to Warner Bros. breakaway and . . . the argument to be used in upholding the Ascap writers' rights to the catalogs withdrawn. Another factor that made them confident was Burkan's No. 1 rating as a trial lawyer on issues of musical copyright.

A week later, *Variety* reported that the "breakoff of cordial relations between Ascap and the networks which was anticipated with the death of Nathan Burkan has already happened." Claude Mills, no longer restrained by Burkan, was pushing a new plan for reconciliation with Warner that would impose onerous new obligations on broadcasters in order to raise additional revenue. For all practical purposes, it would have been an abandonment of Burkan's strategy and a surrender to the demands that the Warner publishers had been making before they withdrew from the society.

At the same time, however, it was becoming apparent that Burkan's plan was working. Reports had emerged that Warner Brothers was hurting financially. Not only was it collecting less in performance rights money than it had been with Ascap, but the vaunted Warner movie musical franchise was feeling the repercussions as songs from its releases were getting less play on the airwaves and top songwriters were declining to work for the studio. Its stock price suffered. Warner was learning the hard way, as Ascap had learned over many trying years, that licensing performing rights is not easy money.

Many tributes to Burkan invoked Ralph Waldo Emerson's aphorism "An institution is the lengthened shadow of one man." Strategies that Burkan had set in motion in the winter and spring of 1936 averted catastrophes for Ascap on multiple fronts in the summer, as though he were continuing to cast his long shadow from the grave.

Even before Burkan's burial, an appellate court in the state of Washington reversed the injunction that had been entered against Ascap and dissolved the receivership, finding that Ascap was a necessary and lawful organization. The indictments against Ascap's officers were dismissed in due course. "The Washington state suits were the target of the last fight made by Nathan Burkan on behalf of the Society before he died recently," one trade journal reported. "Mr. Burkan also had planned to move against 'snipe' [sic] legislation in various localities."

A few weeks later, Congress adjourned without taking any action on the Duffy Bill. It was reintroduced in the next Congress, but with the deteriorating situation in Europe, it went nowhere. Senator Duffy, defeated in his bid for reelection in 1938, was appointed to the federal bench in Milwaukee. The United States did not join the Berne Convention until 1989. And statutory damages remain an important remedy under U.S. copyright law. Indeed, in 1999 the minimum was raised to $750 and the maximum to $30,000 (and up to $150,000 for willful infringement).

The Warner Brothers music publishers surrendered and rejoined Ascap in August 1936 on essentially the same terms that were in place when they withdrew. The two hundred or so copyright infringement lawsuits Warner had filed were dismissed, and Paul Whiteman resumed using "Rhapsody in Blue" as his theme. There had been no court ruling on Burkan's theory that the publishers did not possess the right to withdraw the works of Ascap's writer-members. Nine years would pass before a court would adopt Burkan's view. In a case arising out of the defection of old-time Tin Pan Alley publisher Edward B. Marks from Ascap, a court held that a publisher's obligation to act as the writer's trustee was "expressed and implied in the very structural arrangement of Ascap itself." For a publisher to withdraw without the consent of the songwriter "would amount to a ruthless violation of the underlying pact made between publishers and creators when they became members of Ascap, to divide such compensation equally between them; and it would shock the sense and spirit of equity."

The hiatus in the federal antitrust suit eventually stretched to five years, but the case remained on the court's docket and the more antagonistic attitude that the Department of Justice had assumed toward Ascap was irreversible. The fight against state Snide Acts, which were proliferating, was just beginning. Florida, for example, adopted a law that required Ascap to file with the state a schedule of fees for the performing rights to each individual composition, "with affidavit that such price was fixed by the copyright owner alone and not in combination with other owners." "Ascap is being assailed on all sides," one executive wrote in 1937; "the fight at the present time is a bitter one, and a hard one and a costly one, and it looks as though it might also be a long one."

Ascap, as an institution, seemed to lose its way without Burkan's steadying hand. By 1940, Ascap's overreaching had prompted the broadcasting industry to form a competing performing rights organization, Broadcast Music, Inc. (BMI), and in 1941 radio mounted a successful boycott of Ascap music. At the same time, the Department of Justice brought a criminal antitrust indictment that resulted in guilty pleas by Ascap board members, fines, and a consent decree that continues to regulate Ascap to this day, subjecting its prices to judicial review and requiring it to offer membership to all qualified applicants.

The Justice Department pointedly chose to file the criminal case in Wisconsin, that "hotbed of sedition." Gene Buck, Claude Mills, and other officers and directors had to suffer the humiliation of appearing before the Honorable F. Ryan Duffy to enter their "no contest" pleas. Among other gratuitous indignities he heaped upon them, Judge Duffy questioned the prosecutor in open court about the appropriateness of jail time, before imposing fines totaling more than $35,000.

It was a stunning fall from grace. But it was also a turning point in the history of popular music. In time, as one empirical study concluded, it was "the birth of BMI and the breaking of Ascap's hold on the industry that gave country music, rhythm and blues, and, ultimately, rock 'n' roll a wider media exposure, a financial base from which to develop, and a new found respectability."

There has never been a bear market in performing rights; today it is a billion-dollar industry. Most fees are set in judicial proceedings, where competing economists present sophisticated valuation models. Performing rights, impossible to monetize when Burkan took on the problem at the beginning of the twentieth century, were nearly as portable, transferable, and money-good as Federal Reserve notes by the beginning of the twenty-first.

On February 5, 1936, Burkan attended his final Charlie Chaplin premiere. It was Chaplin's first new film in five years. Burkan had to navigate through a large and unruly mob that had gathered to gape at the film industry notables who strode the red carpet and addressed a national radio audience from microphones stationed in front of the Rivoli Theater.

For his farewell to the art of silent pantomime, *Modern Times,* Chaplin's theme was survival of the human spirit in an ever more mechanized and depersonalized world. With Burkan's passing, Chaplin himself seemed adrift in that world, unable to dust himself off and sally forth to the horizon after a pratfall like the Tramp of old. A spurious 1943 paternity suit did Chaplin's public image far more harm than his all-too-real relations with teenage girls had in earlier years. By 1952—without Burkan to stiffen his backbone—Charlie lacked the fortitude to fend off the FBI's political harassment, choosing instead to sell his beloved Chaplin Studio and live in exile in Europe, making only three more films in the remaining twenty-five years of his life.

Like many a child caught in the middle of a custody dispute, Little Gloria Vanderbilt had a troubled adolescence. Gloria Morgan Vanderbilt was at her daughter's mercy: a single false move and she could lose contact altogether. Contrary to a prediction made by Herbert Smythe, however, it was never necessary to straitjacket Little Gloria to get her to see her mother, and some degree of rapprochement was reached. Tired of the petty bickering between Gloria and guardian Gilchrist, Surrogate Foley had granted Gloria a $21,000 a year allowance. But when Little Gloria turned twenty-one in 1945—by then already in her second marriage, to sixty-three-year-old conductor Leopold Stokowski—she cut off her disapproving mother. "The money my mother wants is now going to blind children," she told the press, "and to help feed children who are homeless and starving in many countries." She continued, however, to provide monthly stipends to Naney and Dodo for the remainder of their lives.

Hollywood made biopics of Victor Herbert, Flo Ziegfeld, Charlie Chaplin, and Al Jolson without even a cameo for the distinguished legal counsel they shared. But when Barbara Goldsmith's classic account of the Vanderbilt custody case, *Little Gloria ... Happy at Last,* was adapted for television in 1982, Nathan Burkan was a principal player. Martin Balsam's screen interpretation of Burkan was an avuncular, bow-tied, preternaturally calm presence, around whom an all-star cast that included divas Bette Davis, Angela Lansbury, and Maureen Stapleton devoured the scenery. Except for the bow tie, it was a pretty good take.

Burkan must have played the role that Fiorello LaGuardia had in mind for him on the Triborough Bridge Authority satisfactorily. At the time of his death, just one month before the bridge's ceremonial opening on July 11, 1936, it was reported that LaGuardia was planning to reappoint Burkan for a second three-year term as chairman. Upon his death, the title of chairman devolved to Robert Moses, and the Triborough Bridge Authority (later the Triborough Bridge and Tunnel Authority) remained the seat of Moses's power for another thirty years. Ironically, as Robert Caro writes in *The Power Broker,* the young, anti–Tammany Hall reformer Moses merely became a new kind of political boss. Collecting tolls from seven bridges and two tunnels within the five boroughs, the Authority gave Moses the financial wherewithal to bend several generations of New York's movers and shakers to his iron will. "He kept these men in line by doling out to them, as Tammany ward bosses had once handed out turkeys to the poor at Thanksgiving, the goodies in which such men were interested."

Charles Schwartz and Louis Frohlich formed a new law partnership, together with Arthur Schwartz and Herman Finkelstein, which carried

Formal portrait, circa 1932. (Courtesy, Nathan Burkan Jr.)

on Burkan's practice until the early 1970s, continuing to represent Ascap, Chaplin, Jolson, the Victor Herbert estate, and, for a time, Gloria Morgan Vanderbilt. Finkelstein left in 1943 to become Ascap's first fulltime general counsel, a position he held until 1973. For many years, Schwartz & Frohlich maintained a telephone listing under "Burkan Nathan lwyr" in the Manhattan directory, a fitting act of homage and a smart piece of professional marketing.

Burkan left an estate valued at $1.5 million (the equivalent of more than $25 million in 2020) to his wife and son. He specially bequeathed to Nathan Jr. the oil portrait of Charlie Chaplin that the Marchioness of Queensbury had painted during Chaplin's prolonged 1927 cohabitation with Burkan. Burkan prized it not because of its "intrinsic value," but as a memento of his "sincere and true friendship" with Chaplin. The painting still hangs in Nathan Jr.'s Park Avenue living room.

Marienne Burkan remarried in 1937. Her second husband could not have been more different from the first. A "society" dentist, Harry Weiss was young, handsome, and totally carefree. Nathan Jr. considered him a great stepfather, but it was not a happy marriage for his anxiety-prone mother, who had worshipped his father and never got over losing the life they led together. Marienne died in 1983.

As a young man, Nathan Jr. was an indifferent student. He believes that had his father lived a few years longer, their relationship would have become strained. But he eventually followed his father into the law and, after a brief stint with Schwartz & Frohlich and forays into Democratic politics, had a long career in the office of New York City's Corporation Counsel.

From its very beginnings, Ascap took justifiable pride in its meaningful and tasteful commemorations of fallen members and friends. When it came time to create a permanent memorial to its founding father, Ascap surpassed even itself. It established the Nathan Burkan Memorial Competition to perpetuate his name and "to encourage the study of Copyright Law, analyses of the need and justification for, the social benefits derived from, and the wise public policy of enacting such law, and to induce original and impartial thinking upon the whole subject." The program offered students at law schools throughout the country cash prizes and an opportunity to publish their research papers. Judging was objective and rigorous. Winners over the ensuing seventy-five years included such giants of copyright scholarship as Melville Nimmer and Paul Goldstein.

The popular culture complex that Nathan Burkan had been so instrumental in creating—a web of laws, institutions, and attitudes—has been remarkably durable. Only recently, at the dawn of the digital millennium, with the rise of a new generation of disruptive media, have the commercial and legal structures he engineered begun to fray. Still, the legal debates of today eerily echo the arguments of a century ago, and the solutions often have the bouquet of new wine in old skins.

The most lasting and important of all Burkan's legacies, collective rights enforcement, seems certain to survive in some form. New technologies have made exploitation of all sorts of entertainment content even more ubiquitous, fleeting, ephemeral, and fugitive than Burkan could have imagined. New collective enforcement organizations have proliferated. SoundExchange was founded in 2003 to collect and distribute digital performance royalties for sound recordings. The Music

Modernization Act of 2018 provides for the creation of a Mechanical Licensing Collective (MLC) for collectively administering mechanical reproduction royalties paid by digital streaming services. The Copyright Office is in the process of establishing the MLC as this is being written. No one has ever replicated Nathan Burkan's unparalled knack for mediating between conflicting stakeholders. Every effort to amend the copyright law and every administrative proceeding under it is more arduous than the last.

Burkan's lifetime body of work stands as a testament that the technological dislocation, creative ferment, and shattering of social taboos roiling popular culture today is not a singularity, but rather just one phase in a historical continuum that slowly lurches toward greater creative freedom, artistic achievement, and cultural diversity.

Acknowledgments

One of the pleasures of undertaking a project like this after a career spent in the snake pit of litigation is finding that there are no opponents, only friends and even strangers more than willing to lend a helping hand, no questions asked. I am especially grateful for the material contributions of Nathan Burkan Jr., Kate Guyonvarch, Lauren Iossa, Zvi Rosen, Robert Brauneis, and Judge Albert Rosenblatt, and for the candid and conscientious critiques and advice of Peter Decherney, Philip Furia, Peter Jaszi, Kevin Parks, Robert Spoo, John Wright, Chris Calhoun, William Frucht, and Ben Yagoda. All errors, omissions, and bad ideas that remain are my responsibility alone.

Numerous archivists and librarians have gone above and beyond the call of duty to help me. Thank you Jenny Romero (Academy of Motion Picture Arts and Sciences); Andrea Dresseno and Celeste Cenciarelli (Chaplin Archive); Scott Pagel, Ken Rodriguez, and Karen Wahl (George Washington University); Greg Plunges, Trina Yeckley, Kelly McAnnaney, and Cary Stumm (National Archives, New York); Grace Schultz (National Archives, Philadelphia); Dan Jordan (New York County Lawyers Association); Joseph van Nostrand, Kimberly Sulik, and the Records Room staff at the New York County Municipal Archives; Meredith Mann (New York Public Library); Nancy Horan (New York State Archive); Sylvia Wang (Shubert Archive); Brett Service (Warner Brothers Archive); and Erik Huber (Queens Borough Public Library).

My editor at University of California Press, Raina Polivka, saw potential in a raw proposal and has been there every step of the way in bringing it to fruition. Her editorial assistants, Zuha Kahn, Elena Bellaart, and Madison Wetzel, have been unfailingly helpful, responsive, and efficient, as were Kate Hoffman (production), Alexandra Dahne (publicity), and Aimée Goggins (marketing). Anne Canright's copyedit was meticulous, insightful, and immensely beneficial.

My wife, Lisa, and daughter, Emily, have sustained me, over the past fifteen years, through two books, with saintly if bemused patience, only occasionally having to intervene to prevent me from losing all sense of perspective. The memory of our son and brother, Greg, is a blessing. His laughter and humanity are missed every day.

Chronology

1916 Feb. 25: NB witnesses Chaplin's signature on Mutual Film contract

Apr. 4: NB elected Tammany Hall leader for 26th Assembly District

1917 Jan. 10: NB argues *Herbert v. The Shanley Co.* before U.S. Supreme Court

June 19: Chaplin signs First National contract negotiated by NB

1918 Apr. 4: Injunction denied in Motion Picture Exhibitors League antitrust suit against Ascap ("*174th Street v. Maxwell*")

Dec. 16: Injunction granted in *Carmen v. Fox Film Corp.* (Federal)

1919 Feb. 5: United Artists Corporation organized

June 17: Bench trial in *Carmen v. Fox Film Corp.* (Federal)

1920 Nov. 12: Mildred Harris granted divorce from Chaplin

Dec. 3: NB reaches agreement with First National for *The Kid*

1921 Jan. 1: New Ascap articles of association take effect

1922 Apr. 30: NB renders opinion on broadcasts as public performances for profit

1923 Apr. 12: NB takes deposition of Sir Arthur Conan Doyle

1924 Apr. 16: Ascap gives concert for congressmen at National Press Club

Nov. 22: United Artists Corporation reorganization agreement signed

Nov. 25: NB attends wedding of Charlie Chaplin and Lita Grey, Empalme, Mexico

1925 Apr. 27–30: Jury trial in *Carmen v. Fox Film Corp.* (N.Y. State)

July 4–Aug. 31: NB travels to Europe; takes cure in Karlsbad

1926 Aug. 5: Warner Brothers gives first Vitaphone demonstration

Aug. 6: Department of Justice closes first antitrust investigation of Ascap

Sep. 14–21: Jury trial in *D. W. Griffith, Inc. v. Jolson*

Oct. 6–15: Jury trial in *Kelly v. Jolson*

1927 Jan. 3–20: Jury trial in *United States v. Costello*

Jan. 10: Lita Grey files for divorce from Charlie Chaplin

Jan. 14: Chaplin suffers "nervous breakdown" in NB penthouse

May 4–11: Jury trial in *Loeb v. Chaplin*

May 11: NB elected special member of Academy of Motion Picture Arts and Sciences

May 26: NB signs *Jazz Singer* contract on Al Jolson's behalf

Aug. 22: Lita Grey granted divorce from Charlie Chaplin

Oct. 6: Premiere of *The Jazz Singer*

Oct. 8: NB marries Marienne Alexander in New York penthouse

Oct. 9–15: The Burkans honeymoon at the Greenbriar

1928   Apr. 26–May 1: Jury trial in *Nayfack v. Nayfack*

Oct. 1: Police raid opening of Mae West's *The Pleasure Man*

Nov. 17: NB appointed counsel to temporary administrators of Arnold Rothstein estate

1929   Jan. 2: Jell-O heir Orator Woodward "kidnaps" children in Paris

Sep. 26: LaGuardia attacks NB over Rothstein "little black books"

1930   Mar. 17–Apr. 3: Jury trial in *People v. Mae West*

1931   Jan.–Apr.: NB incapacitated by illness, likely heart attack

May 3: Nathan Burkan Jr. born

1932   May 25–26: NB accompanies Mayor Walker before Seabury Commission

1933   Jan. 4: NB casts presidential electoral vote for Franklin D. Roosevelt

Apr. 22–23: Bench trial in *Sheldon v. MGM*

June 27: NB delegate to New York convention to ratify 21st Amendment

Nov. 23: President Franklin Roosevelt approves NRA Code of Fair Competition for Motion Picture Industry

Nov. 28: NB appointed chairman of Triborough Bridge Authority

1934   Sep. 20: NB hosts "Night of Stars" benefit for German Jewry

Sep. 28–Nov.14: Hearing on writ of habeas corpus in Vanderbilt case

1935   Apr. 3–5: Jury trial in *Collette François v. Arthur Loew*

June 5–6: Appellate argument in Vanderbilt case

June 10–19: Abortive bench trial in *United States v. Ascap* antitrust case

Nov. 13: Appellate argument in *Sheldon v. MGM*

1936   Jan. 1: Warner Brothers music publishers withdraw from Ascap

Mar. 20: NB and other Ascap officers indicted, Snohomish Cty, WA

Mar. 30: Supreme Court denies review in Vanderbilt case

Apr. 15: NB makes final appearance before congressional committee, on Duffy Bill

June 6: NB dies at Great Neck, New York home

June 9: Funeral at Temple Emanu-El; interment Union Field Cemetery

Notes

ABBREVIATIONS: ARCHIVAL COLLECTIONS

B/F/I   Box/Folder/Item

ASCAP   Ascap Collection, Jacob Burns Law Library, George Washington University, Washington, DC

BGC   Barbara Goldsmith Collection, New York Public Library Rare Books and Manuscripts Division

CCA   Charlie Chaplin Archive, Cineteca di Bologna, IT (www. charliechaplinarchive.org)

DOJ   U.S. Department of Justice File 60–22–5, National Archives and Records Administration, College Park, MD

JTP   Jim Tully Papers, University of California, Los Angeles Library

LACA   Los Angeles County Archives

LCR   Lambs Club Records, New York Public Library Performing Arts Branch, Lincoln Center

LGA   LaGuardia and Wagner Archives, LaGuardia Community College, New York, NY (www.laguardiawagnerarchive.lagcc .cuny.edu)

LHP   Learned Hand Papers, Harvard Law School Library

MPP   Mary Pickford Papers, Academy of Motion Picture Arts and Sciences Library, Los Angeles, CA

NARA-NY   National Archives and Records Administration, New York, NY

NARA-PH   National Archives and Records Administration, Philadelphia,

PA

NYCLA	New York County Lawyers Association Library
NYCMA	New York City Municipal Archives
NYSA	New York State Archives, Albany, NY
SA	Shubert Archive, New York, NY
SCT	U.S. Supreme Court Records and Briefs, 1832–1978 (www.gale.com/c/making-of-modern-law-us-supreme-court-records-and-briefs-1832–1978)
VHC	Victor Herbert Collection, Library of Congress, Washington, DC
VHP	Victor Herbert Papers, New York Public Library Performing Arts Branch, Lincoln Center
WB	Warner Brothers Archive, School of Cinematic Arts, University of Southern California, Los Angeles, CA
WSC	William Selig Collection, Academy of Motion Picture Arts and Sciences Library, Los Angeles, CA

ABBREVIATIONS: PERIODICALS

AMAJ	American Musician and Art Journal
BB	Billboard
BE	Brooklyn Eagle
BEN	Buffalo Evening News
BES	Baltimore Evening Sun
CE	Cincinnati Enquirer
CT	Chicago Tribune
DFP	Detroit Free Press
EH	Exhibitors Herald
ETR	Exhibitors Trade Review
FD	Film Daily
LAH	Los Angeles Herald
LAR	Los Angeles Record
LAT	Los Angeles Times
LAX	Los Angeles Examiner
MC	Musical Courier
MPD	Motion Picture Daily
MPH	Motion Picture Herald

MPM	*Motion Picture Magazine*
MPN	*Motion Picture News*
MPW	*Moving Picture World*
MT	*The Music Trades*
MTR	*Music Trade Review*
NYA	*New York American*
NYC	*New York Clipper*
NYDN	*New York Daily News*
NYH	*New York Herald*
NYHT	*New York Herald Tribune*
NYMT	*New York Morning Telegraph*
NYP	*New York Post*
NYS	*New York Sun*
NYT	*New York Times*
NYTr	*New York Tribune*
NYW	*New York World*
PDP	*Pittsburgh Daily Post*
PP	*Pittsburgh Press*
PPG	*Pittsburgh Post-Gazette*
SLPD	*St. Louis Post-Dispatch*
VAR	*Variety (Weekly)*
WP	*Washington Post*

PROLOGUE

1 *More than two thousand mourners:* "Notables of City at Burkan Service," *NYT,* June 10, 1936, 23.

"Today he will be buried": Phil M. Daly, "Along the Rialto," *FD,* June 9, 1936, 4.

2 *"'The travail, the pangs, the agony of politics!'":* Tierney, "Nathan Burkan Tempers," 4.

Roosevelt was reported to be considering Burkan: "Mahon, Burkan Show Strength in Bench Bids," *BE,* November 29, 1935, 3; "Tammany Leader Slated as New U.S. Judge," *NYP,* November 29, 1935, 6.

"many of Hollywood's most famous stars": Parsons, "Famous Lawyer Mourned," 8.

3 *"I love him, but I'm afraid of him":* C. Chaplin, *My Trip Abroad,* 13.

"One or two newspaper writers": Dixon, "Sidewalks of New York," 22.

4 *"loved Nat because he found in him a young crusader":* Buck, "Eulogy for Nathan Burkan," 1–3.

"I never knew a man of greater heart": ibid., 4.

"Stories of the man's capacity for friendship": Red Kann, "Insiders' Outlook," MPD, June 10, 1936, 2.

"He was fearless, yet friendly": "Nathan Burkan Rites Will Be Held Today," MPD, June 9, 1936, 1, 8.

5 *"remarkable in his freedom from embitterment and bias":* "Mr. Nathan Burkan," MPH, June 13, 1936, 6.

"an endless capacity for friendship": Dixon, "Sidewalks of New York," 22.

"serene in manner, dynamic in thought": Nizer, "A Couple of More," 22.

"He is said to know just when": Tierney, "Nathan Burkan Tempers," 4.

6 *"Before it reaches the stage of actual warfare":* Jack Alicoate, "The 'Wideies' Present a Problem," FD, January 7, 1930, 1.

"Nathan Burkan trying to negotiate a merger": James P. Cunningham, "Putts," FD, May 23, 1929, 10.

CHAPTER ONE. IMMIGRANT PASSAGES

10 *"not so much a political party":* Parkhurst, *Our Fight with Tammany,* 64.

"Tammany Hall's leaders delivered social services": Golway, "The Forgotten Virtues," A23.

prostitution and gambling rackets: "Passing of Martin Engel, A Unique Figure in Politics," *Chicago Inter-Ocean,* December 8, 1901, 33.

11 *"made himself visible in the clubrooms":* Howe, *World of Our Fathers,* 369.

"gorgeously gowned women": "Martin Engel Gives a Ball," NYMT, March 10, 1900, 12.

"his robust charm, his ready Irish ribaldry": Gould, *Victor Herbert,* 78.

13 awash with military-style brass bands: G. Martin, *Opera at the Bandstand,* 27–35, 57–58.

Herbert embraced the lowbrow conventions: Kaye, *Victor Herbert,* 59–66.

"It was as Gilmore's successor": Gould, *Victor Herbert,* 25.

By 1894, Herbert was reported to be making: E. J. Edwards, "In the Musical World," *Helena Daily Independent,* February 4, 1894.

He entered into a contract: Herbert-Bostonians Agreement, June 21, 1894 (VHP, B4/F5).

"an inept and inane libretto": Bordman, *American Operetta,* 57.

"When he knows the operetta field better": "'Prince Ananias' Produced," NYT, November 21, 1894, 2.

"not to write over the heads of his audience": Ellis, "London Letter," 230.

14 *"turning cheap sheets of music paper":* Gould, *Victor Herbert,* 161.

"lay claim to any extraordinary purposes": Dreiser, "The Lambs," 14.

"the Lambs' Theater became the center": Annals of the Lambs, 1899, 39 (LCR, B166/F3).

Once each year, as a fundraiser: Lambs v. Dressler, Case on Appeal, 33–37; Star Gambol of the Lambs, May 1898 (VHC, B189/F9).

15 *His practice was typical of the mix:* Wald, "The Rise and Fall," 1833–36.

CHAPTER TWO. THE PITTSBURGH TROUBLES

17 *"My operas and other work":* "Victor Herbert Here," PDP, February 22, 1898, 1.

"his brass band work and his light opera antics": "The Orchestra Changes," PP, February 13, 1898, 4.

18 *"lamenting Herbert's 'vulgarity'":* PP, February 21, 1898, 1.

"The Musical Courier *affords a great variety:* Matthews, "Music Journalism," 240.

"the violence of its antipathies": "Musical Journalism," BE, October 26, 1902, 16.

suspicion that the paper's editorial judgments were for sale: Schwab, James Gibbons Huneker, 42.

"genteel tradition": Seldes, Seven Lively Arts, 349.

"not radically" but "gradually": Herbert v. Musical Courier, Case on Appeal, 60.

19 *"I never came in contact with a more agile intellect":* Huneker, Steeplejack, 23.

"scholarly, musicianly manner": "Cincinnati," MC, November 3, 1897, 19.

"generally trashy and extremely noisy": "Herbert's Band Concert," MC, November 24, 1897, 36.

"Pittsburgh will find out about Victor Herbert": "Herbert for Pittsburgh," MC, February 16, 1898, 20–21.

"That is, symphony in Pittsburgh": "Pittsburgh on Herbert," MC, March 2, 1898, 27.

"The people of Pittsburgh will get a first-class idea": "Frisky Lambs," MC, March 23, 1898, 22.

20 *"The same man who is at the head of a theatrical frolic":* "Pittsburgh," MC, June 15, 1898, 11.

"The Pittsburgh Troubles": MC, July 17, 1901, 19.

21 *"almost beneath criticism":* "Monday Night's Novelties," MC, October 27, 1897, x.

22 *"confine himself to criticism":* Triggs v. Sun Printing & Publishing Ass'n, 179 N.Y. 144, 154, 71 N.E. 739 (1904).

"The critic can call a painting": quoted in *Knickerbocker Life Ins. Co. v. Ecclesine,* 6 Abb.Pr.N.S. 9 (N.Y. Super. Ct. 1869).

"as broad as the charge": Skinner v. Powers, 1 Wend. 451, 456 (1828).

to take the oath of citizenship: Certificate of Naturalization, October 14, 1902 (VHP, B2/F4).

23 *"what is technically called in the trade":* Recker v. Windsor, Affidavit of Edwin S. Brill, February 2, 1902, 1.

"shoved the papers in his safe": "Court No Judge of Rag-Time," *NYT,* February 8, 1902, 16.

"had better use of his time": "Judge Lacombe and Rag-Time," *NYT,* February 9, 1902, 6.

"Coon songs, like coons": "The Genesis of Ragtime," *St. Paul Globe,* June 22, 1903, 4.

The court eventually denied a restraining order: Robert Recker Co. v. Windsor Music Co., 114 F. 1024 (S.D.N.Y. 1902).

died unexpectedly of complications from surgery: "Julius Lehmann, Well Known Lawyer, Dead," *NYH,* May 23, 1902, 14.

CHAPTER THREE. TO VICTOR BELONG THE SPOILS

24 *"packed to the doors with musical and theatrical folk":* "Herbert Wins Libel Suit," *NYT,* October 29, 1902, 16.

25 *"the mouthpieces, if not, as was often asserted, the brains":* Rovere, *Howe & Hummel,* 27, 39, 54.

"I'm an American!": "Jury's Musical Puzzle," *NYT,* October 23, 1902, 7.

Hummel had been promising: "Victor Herbert's Libel Suit," *NYT,* October 10, 1902, 16; "Plagiarism in Music," *NYW,* October 10, 1902, 12.

"What a peety eet ees": "Discord in Herbert's Suit," *NYT,* October 25, 1902, 5.

"Then what struck your notice": Herbert v. Musical Courier, Case on Appeal, 104.

26 *"Mr. Hummel, who says he has taken lessons in music":* "Jury's Musical Puzzle," *NYT,* October 23, 1902, 7.

"Walter Damrosch was the most enlightening witness": "Musical Journalism," *BE,* October 26, 1902, 16.

"The sonorous tones of the symphony leader": "Three Experts Pass on Herbert," *NYH,* October 25, 1902, 5.

"cannot legitimately aspire": Herbert v. Musical Courier, Case on Appeal, 47 (emphasis added).

"Such a man cannot be in an aesthetic condition": ibid., 51.

"The two pursuits are contradictory": ibid., 58.

27 *"no necessity for verifying":* ibid., 56.

"money kills inspiration": ibid., 61.

true musical genius: ibid., 53.

"Is it true in all cases": ibid., 72–73.

"not a good composer as a composer": ibid, 74.

"that any physical or mental peculiarities": ibid., 156.

28 *his copying was likely "unconscious":* ibid., 52.

"weary of the atmosphere of petty intrigue": Schwab, *James Gibbons Huneker,* 135.

29 *"Did you say to Mr. Weil":* Herbert v. *Musical Courier,* Case on Appeal, 60.

"snake in the grass, ready to pounce": "Victor Herbert Is Awarded $15,000 Damages in His Libel Suit against the 'Musical Courier,'" *The Concert-Goer,* November 1, 1902, 1–3.

"mild way in which the judge rebuked": Herbert v. *Musical Courier,* Brief of Appellant, 48.

30 *"To the Victor Belong the Spoils":* "A Fifteen Thousand Dollar Verdict against the 'Musical Courier,'" *MT,* November 1, 1902, 17.

"will continue to be published": [Untitled], *MC,* November 5, 1902, 20.

"any musician who feels as if he or she": "Music Papers," *MC,* November 5, 1902, 21–22.

"stone dead agglomerations": "A Healthful Libel Verdict," *BE,* October 29, 1902, 4.

"scurrilous and 'slang-whanging' style": "Plagiarism in Music," *NYT,* October 30, 1902, 8.

31 *affirmed the judgment on the condition:* Victor Herbert v. Musical Courier Co., 86 A.D. 627, 83 N.Y.S. 1107 (1903), aff'd, 180 N.Y. 520 (1904).

"five crisp $1,000 bills": "Victor Herbert Gets His $5,900," *MTR,* February 4, 1905, 29.

"Although the stated intention of the arbiters": Levine, *Highbrow/Lowbrow,* 235.

pulling down twice that amount in a week: Lewis M. Isaacs, "The Musician as a Money-Maker," *The Bookman,* January 1909, 429, 433.

32 *"those who enthuse over simpler music":* quoted in Gould, *Victor Herbert,* 160.

"I don't know that he is any relation to Nathan Hale": "The House of Witmark on the Herbert Suit vs. The 'Musical Courier,'" *MT,* November 8, 1902, 45.

CHAPTER FOUR. TIN PAN ALLEY

37 *"Our business is run scientifically":* "The Interviewer Talks with Edward B. Marks," *AMAJ,* August 28, 1908, 14.

38 *"The publishers of popular music":* Recker v. Windsor, Affidavit of Herman F. Vorbeck, February 5, 1902, 1.

"If a songwriter is ethical": Marks, *They All Sang,* 172.

"The immediate effect of our copyright law": Twentieth Century Music Corp. v. Aiken, 422 U.S. 151, 156 (1975).

the Copyright Act of 1790: U.S. Copyright Office, *Copyright Enactments,* 22–24.

In 1831, the initial term: ibid., 27–31.

39 *In an 1856 amendment:* ibid., 33.

In the waning days of the Civil War: ibid., 34–42.

The Supreme Court, however, upheld the copyright: Burrow-Giles Lithographic Company v. Sarony, 111 U.S. 53, 58 (1884).

An 1897 amendment: U.S. Copyright Office, *Copyright Enactments,* 56–57.

40 *Through the vagaries of the legislative drafting process:* Z. Rosen, "Twilight of the Opera Pirates," 1200–1216.

"If they command the interest of any public": Bleistein v. Donaldson Lithographing Co., 188 U.S. 239, 252 (1903).

41 *"interesting reports of the various officers":* "Music Publishers' Meeting," *MTR,* June 24, 1891, 12.

"it would seem at times": "Convention Music Publishers Association of the United States," *MTR,* June 16, 1901, 27.

He left as the first general counsel: "Music Publishers' Annual Convention," *MTR,* June 17, 1905, 40–42.

the New York State Penal Code made it a crime: N.Y. Penal Code § 364 (10th Rev. Ed. 1891).

42 *Burkan maximized the impact:* "Big Music Fight On," *MTR,* August 19, 1905, 18; "Couchois Held for the Grand Jury," *MTR,* September 9, 1905, 43.

Couchois's only defense: "Music Is Merchandise," *NYT,* September 16, 1905, 9, 43.

44 *"lawyer's moral autonomy":* Altman, "Considering the ABA's 1908 Canons," 2472.

CHAPTER FIVE. CANNED MUSIC

45 *"Our copyright laws urgently need revision":* Theodore Roosevelt, Fifth Annual Message to Congress, December 5, 1905. The American Presidency Project, www.presidency.ucsb.edu/documents/fifth-annual-message-4.

45 *Putnam's invitations only went to:* June 1906 Hearings, 151.

46 *"the present law will be sufficient":* Brylawski and Goldman, *Legislative History,* vol. 1, part C, 12.

"acquitted itself splendidly": "Music Publishers' Annual Convention," *MTR,* June 17, 1905, 40.

47   *New York State "right-of-privacy" statute:* N.Y. Civil Rights Law, §§ 50–51.

"worth a volume of logic": New York Trust Co. v. Eisner, 256 U.S. 345, 349 (1921).

48   *A single lower federal court precedent:* 33 F. 584 (D. Mass. 1888).

The deal was contingent on two things: White-Smith v. Apollo, Transcript of Record, 345–47.

49   *"The idea of recorded sound":* Brooks, "Columbia Records," 9.

"the player piano was widely seen": Suisman, *Selling Sounds,* 92.

50   *"question here presented for decision": Stern v. Rosey,* 17 App.D.C. 562 (1901).

51   *"poured out money like water": June 1906 Hearings,* 167.

52   *Aeolian's learned experts: White-Smith v. Apollo,* Transcript of Record, 40–43, 50–56.

the federal district court ruled: White-Smith Music Publishing Co. v. Apollo Co., 139 F. 427 (S.D.N.Y. 1905), *aff'd,* 147 F. 226 (2d Cir. 1906), *aff'd,* 209 U.S. 1 (1908).

53   *"If I had been attorney": March 1908 Hearings,* 367.

"interests which are likely to be benefitted": Brylawski and Goldman, *Legislative History,* vol. 3, part E, 278–79.

CHAPTER SIX. MR. BURKAN GOES TO WASHINGTON

54   *"many hundreds of poor fellows": June 1906 Hearings,* 25–26.

55   *"Is not the real reason":* ibid., 31.

"This committee will try to represent": May 1906 Hearings, 12.

"a complete monopolistic octopus": June 1906 Hearings, 98.

"so ingenious that it does not violate any law": ibid., 169.

56   *a few minutes to offer rebuttal:* ibid., 202–6.

"doomed": "The Man on the Street," *MTR,* December 15, 1906, 48.

57   *Much of their oratory:* "Music Publisher's Dinner to Hon. T.P. O'Connor," *MTR,* October 27, 1906, 47.

59   *"writing can be protected": December 1906 Hearings,* 203.

"It is the intellectual production that is entitled to protection": ibid., 208.

60   *Like students in a graduate seminar:* ibid.

"The whole bugaboo": ibid., 266.

"If anybody's ears would tingle": ibid., 353.

61   *"the right to have the horse of the Chairman":* ibid., 267.

"Did you ever hear of any of them": ibid., 364.

62 *"if the music publishers received":* Witmark and Goldberg, *Story of the House,* 299–300.

"nine-tenths of the composers of the country": Burkan, "The Charge That the Passage," 8.

"had no right to dispose": ibid., 7.

63 *Through Representative Barchfeld, Herbert gained access:* Witmark and Goldberg, *Story of the House,* 304–5.

"Manufacturers who have invested many millions": 1907 *Senate Rep.,* Views of Minority, 4.

"further legislation regarding this matter": 1907 *House Rep.,* 9.

"The divergence of views on the subject": "Copyright Fight is Tied up Tight," *Washington Times,* February 6, 1907, 6.

so Burkan ghost-wrote one: Witmark and Goldberg, *Story of the House,* 298.

Burkan's House minority report: 1907 *House Rep.,* Views of Minority, 1–7.

CHAPTER SEVEN. THE TWO-CENT SOLUTION

65 *In anonymous comments:* "Annual Meeting of Association," *MTR,* May 25, 1907, 48.

"Despite the anticipation of a war": "Annual Meeting of Music Publishers' Association," *MTR,* June 15, 1907, 44.

66 *"It was no trouble to get that dollar":* Witmark and Goldberg, *Story of the House,* 301–2.

"composers are more direct parties": White-Smith v. Apollo, Petition of Victor Herbert to Be Admitted as a Co-Appellant, 10.

"My friend and legal advisor": "Isadore Witmark's Itinerary," *MTR,* September 14, 1907, 44.

67 *The court of appeals had acknowledged:* White-Smith Music Publishing Co. v. Apollo Co., 147 F. 226, 227 (2d Cir. 1906), aff'd, 209 U.S. 1 (1908).

"Notation serves as one means": White-Smith v. Apollo, Brief for Victor Herbert, 21, 24.

Justice William Day's opinion: White-Smith Music Publishing Co. v. Apollo Co., 209 U.S. 1 (1908).

68 *Justice Holmes wrote a separate concurrence:* ibid., 18–20.

69 *"We would like your position well defined":* March 1908 Hearings, 192.

"Are you prepared to let the bill go to wreck and ruin": ibid., 245.

"We are men who just write the ordinary popular songs": ibid., 247.

"You should get what you can": ibid., 238.

"I, for one, would advise my people": ibid., 367.

70 *"If you reached an agreement":* ibid., 368.

a "Compromise Agreement" that was widely disseminated: "Important Developments in the Copyright Situation," *MTR,* April 4, 1908, 25.

decried two cents as "confiscatory": "Latest Phase of Copyright Situation," *MTR,* April 11, 1908, 23.

71 *"no lukewarm attitude of neutrality":* "Harris on Copyright," *AMAJ,* December 13, 1907, 10.

"Burkan has been my most inveterate enemy": Burkan v. Musical Courier, Case on Appeal, 187–88.

"egged on by Mr. Blumenberg": ibid., 205.

"Some Plain Truths about Copyright": AMAJ, June 26, 1908, 7–8.

72 *"to smoke people out":* Burkan v. Musical Courier, Case on Appeal, 163–64.

In a fake letter to the editor: "Takes Exception to Copyright Article," *AMAJ,* August 14, 1908, 10–11.

"Answer to 'a Popular Music Publisher'": AMAJ, August 14, 1908, 11–12.

"a knave" of the "meanest and most pronounced type": "Anent Our Position on Copyright," *AMAJ,* August 28, 1908, 8.

"any lawyer, much less a lawyer of national reputation": [Untitled], *AMAJ,* October 9, 1908, 12.

"It is very apparent that under the pretext": "Nathan Burkan Replies," *AMAJ,* September 11, 1908, 9–10.

"Is it not high time for him to indulge": "Reply to Nathan Burkan," *AMAJ,* September 11, 1908, 10–11.

"arguments would have brought discredit": "The Mistakes of Casad," *AMAJ,* October 9, 1908, 11.

"attorney of obscure and misty origin": Burkan v. Musical Courier, Case on Appeal, 48, 176–77, 198–99; "The Destructive Work of a Decoy Duck and a Judas," *AMAJ,* August 27, 1909, 24–25.

73 *"There was once a little lawyer":* [Untitled], *AMAJ,* December 11, 1908, 10.

74 *The committee explained that it was seeking: 1909 House Report,* 9.

75 *"It took quite a while":* Burkan v. Musical Courier, Case on Appeal, 195–96, 206.

tried on the Illinois libel charge: "Admits Trying to Hold Up Steger," *CT,* January 25, 1913, 3; "'Czar of Steger,' Denies His Power," *CT,* January 26, 1913, 7; "Trial of Trade Paper Man Charged with Conspiracy," *MTR,* February 1, 1913, 25.

But he died in Paris, still on the lam: "Fugitive Editor Dies in Hiding," *CT,* March 29, 1913, 15.

CHAPTER EIGHT. ENTR'ACTE

80 *"the physical articulation of Tammany's ad-hoc ideology":* Golway, *Machine Made,* 154.

81 *"It is abhorrent to believe":* Record of the Constitutional Convention, 3152–53.

Barnes amendment: Proposed Amendments of the Constitutional Convention, May 26, 1915, No. 319.

"of that reserve, that Puritanism": Record of the Constitutional Convention, 1912.

"I represent a district": ibid., 1915.

82 *"If there has been a demand":* ibid., 1919.

"The aspirations of our city": ibid., 594.

"persistent discrimination": ibid., 4305–6.

"a real man and a real Democrat": Malone, "Tribute to Nathan Burkan," 1.

CHAPTER NINE. THE LONE STAR

84 *"When Chaplin bumped into a tree":* Robinson, *Chaplin,* 113.

85 *The barebones one-year contract:* Chaplin-Essanay Contract, December 1914 (CCA, ECCI00313942).

86 *"all the patents known by experts":* "Facts Concerning the New Arrangement of the Principal Factors of the Motion Picture Manufacturing Interests in America," *MPW,* December 26, 1908, 519.

"The Trust sought to standardize the industry": Decherney, *Hollywood: A Very Short Introduction,* 15–16.

87 *The 1912 amendment:* U.S. Copyright Office, *Copyright Enactments,* 87–90.

"the machinery is different and more complex": 222 U.S. 55, 62 (1911).

88 *In a typical exchange:* O'Neill v. General Film, Case on Appeal, 101–2.

"industry and skill worthy of a better cause": O'Neill v. General Film Co., 152 N.Y.S. 599, 602 (Sup. Ct. N.Y.Cty. 1915).

Burkan persuaded an appellate court: O'Neill v. General Film Co., 171 App. Div. 854, 157 N.Y.S. 1028 (1916).

89 *they struck a deal to make a film version:* Lasky, *Blow My Own Horn,* 89–99.

"whether the cutouts are made or not": Lasky v. Celebrated, Affidavit of Samuel Goldfish, May 13, 1914, 6.

"too anxious to get matters": Jesse L. Lasky Feature Play Co. v. Celebrated Players Film Co., 214 F. 861, 866 (S.D.N.Y. 1914).

90 *which ordered Sam to continue:* Goldfish v. Goldfish, 193 A.D. 686, 184 N.Y.S. 512 (1920), aff'd, 230 N.Y. 606, 130 N.E. 912 (1921).

Sam Goldfish "dragooned": Berg, *Goldwyn,* 125–26.

As King later told the story: Thompson (ed.), *Henry King Director,*

"Nathan Burkan has so many clients": Phil M. Daly, "And That's That," *FD,* December 6, 1929, 4.

91 *Charlie Chaplin gag coins:* "Slot Machine Men Fight Chaplin Coins," *NYT,* January 19, 1916, 8.

"the shoulders of the dancers are held stiffly": "Chaplin Dance Is Latest," *Wichita Daily Eagle,* January 16, 1916, 4.

"Any form of expressing Chaplin": Charles J. McGuirk, "Chaplinitis," *MPM,* July 1915, 121.

"Chaplin's Enormous Offers": *VAR,* January 21, 1916, 1, 19.

"Tell Charlie not come east": S. Chaplin to Harrington, January 21, 1916 (CCA, ECCI00314044).

a "big combine" on the hook: S. Chaplin to C. Chaplin, January 31, 1916 (CCA, ECCI00314077).

92 *"Syd Chaplin has power to sign":* S. Chaplin to C. Chaplin, January 31, 1916 (CCA, ECCI00314076).

Burke's first two movie contracts: Hayter-Menzies, *Mrs. Ziegfeld,* 79–86.

Charlie left Los Angeles for New York: "Charley Chaplin Quits Essanay— Has Own Firm," *LAT,* February 1, 1916, 26.

"Famous Comedian Dozes": "Chaplin in City," *Wichita Daily Eagle,* February 4, 1916, 5.

"practically every film manufacturer in the business": "Chaplin Here Listening," *VAR,* February 11, 1916, 28.

93 *sightings of Syd and Charlie in the company of Loew:* "Film Ball Aftermaths," *VAR,* February 25, 1916, 25; "Chaplin to Go with Loew?" *NYC,* February 19, 1916, 1.

Freuler's "imposing height": Ramsaye, *A Million and One Nights,* 734.

"one of the most ponderous and intricate documents": quoted in Robinson, *Chaplin,* 158.

94 *"sole charge of the artistic direction":* Chaplin–Lone Star Contract, February 25, 1916, 2–3 (CCA, ECCI00314248).

"Nathan Burkan demonstrated his genius": Ramsaye, "Romantic History," 120.

"a murmur of disappointment went around": "Very Well, Agnes," *Reel Life,* March 18, 1916, 12.

"means that I am left free": "Chaplin Signs with Mutual," *MPW,* March 11, 1916, 1622.

"We have been startled rightly": "It's All about Charlie's Pay," *Motography,* April 1, 1916, 745.

95 *"press agent coinage":* "Chaplin Gets $670,000 Year," *Beckley [W.Va.] Messenger,* April 4, 1916, 6.

"inhale spaghetti": "The Sky's the Salary Limit," *Motography,* April 8, 1916, 789.

96 *"could work within the capitalist machine":* Decherney, *Hollywood's Copyright Wars,* 68.

CHAPTER TEN. CHARLIE IN THE HAREM

97 *not a "world-beater":* Chaplin v. Essanay, Papers on Appeal from Order, 103.

98 *"The literal kicks":* "A Monotony of Chaplin," *BE,* April 9, 1916, 9.

"The disappointment of unsuccessful bidders": ibid., 101.

"had the effect of retarding the action": Chaplin v. Essanay, Papers on Appeal from Order, 44.

"the first suit ever filed": ibid., 101.

99 *"gives up the results":* Frohlich and Schwartz, *Law of Motion Pictures,* 27.

had the effect of limiting it: Chaplin v. Essanay, Papers on Appeal from Order, 176–77.

"an unfavorable and disappointing impression": ibid., 8–13.

Courts have from time to time been receptive: Decherney, *Hollywood's Copyright Wars,* 108–54.

"his eccentricities and peculiarities": Chaplin v. Essanay, Papers on Appeal from Order, 91.

100 *"Chaplin comedies are not made":* quoted in Robinson, *Chaplin,* 169.

"His insatiable appetite": Chaplin v. Essanay, Papers on Appeal from Order, 212–14.

"Charlie loves power": Goldwyn, *Behind the Screen,* 159.

"Whether plaintiff will suffer any damage": Chaplin v. Essanay, Papers on Appeal from Order, 220.

"of all the imitations": advertisement, *VAR,* July 2, 1915, 26.

101 *"We have secured Chaplin's latest":* "Charlie Chaplin to be at the Paramount Saturday," *Winston-Salem Journal,* August 10, 1916, 9.

approached Burkan about taking legal action: S. Chaplin to Burkan, October 9, 1916 (CCA, ECCI00314243).

Burkan prudently declined: Burkan to S. Chaplin, October 18, 1916 (CCA, ECCI00314245).

103 *It was Grauman:* Burkan to S. Chaplin, September 15, 1917 (CCA, ECCI00314277).

"No more likely situation": "Savoy Theater Offers Good Bill for Entire Week," *Atlanta Constitution,* August 19, 1917, 3.

"The effect created": Burkan to S. Chaplin, September 19, 1917 (CCA, ECCI00314278).

"It is a pity": Burkan to S. Chaplin, October 22, 1917 (CCA, ECCI00314556).

"universally known and recognized": Chaplin v. New Apollo, Bill of Complaint, September 22, 1917, 4.

"It will mean a great deal more work:" Burkan to S. Chaplin, October 22, 1917 (CCA, ECCI00314556).

104 *"We will not miss Chaplin":* "What the Picture Did for Me," *Motography,* October 20, 1917, 799.

"ran off for my benefit": Burkan to Wright, February 26, 1918, 4–5 (CCA, ECCI00314413).

"If my many years of experience": ibid., 1.

"The plan is simple": "Restrain Alleged Imitators of Chaplin," *MPN,* October 27, 1917, 2884.

105 *"The happiest period of my career":* C. Chaplin, *My Autobiography,* 188.

A few months later, she was Adolph Zukor's partner: Wilkening v. Moore, Transcript of Record, 360–74.

"By working for myself": C. Chaplin to "Gentlemen," circa December 1916 (CCA, ECCI00314058).

106 *"Paramount is the program":* "Attacks the Open Booking System," *MPW,* August 12, 1916, 1088.

"offer its arm of protection": "First National," *MPN,* July 28, 1917, 541.

"If you still waver and debate": Freuler to C. Chaplin, May 17, 1917 (CCA, ECCI00028356).

CHAPTER ELEVEN. THE PRICE OF A GOOD TIME

107 *"Everything splendid":* S. Chaplin to C. Chaplin, June 21, 1917 (CCA, ECCI00314165).

even when "Burkan agreed with them": quoted in Robinson, *Chaplin,* 224.

"the largest salary ever paid": "Charley Chaplin May Get $1,000,000 a Year," *NYT,* July 1, 1917, 5.

exclusive, worldwide distribution license: Chaplin–First National Agreement, June 19, 1917 (WB, 2724B-F008793_002).

108 *"decide and know exactly":* quoted in Robinson, *Chaplin,* 225.

"I had to do something to prove I had it": C. Chaplin, *My Autobiography,* 189.

"I love him, but am afraid of him": C. Chaplin, *My Trip Abroad,* 13.

109 *"one of his most perfect films":* Robinson, *Chaplin,* 229.

"every debtor would be touring": "Chaplin Can be Sued while Boosting Loan," *NYTr,* April 13, 1918, 8; "Loan Work Doesn't Shield Mr. Chaplin from Court Action," *NYH,* April 13, 1918, 11; "Action against Chaplin Called a 'Burning Shame,'" *NYS,* April 13, 1918, 14.

110 *"as Fairbanks' leading lady":* "Fairbanks to Return East," *MPW,* December 30, 1916, 1985.

"I had been caught": C. Chaplin, *My Autobiography,* 230.

111 *"At the rate Charlie is traveling":* S. Chaplin to Burkan, January 7, 1919 (CCA, ECCI00314569).

"serve to stabilize conditions": "First National Is Still in Session," *MPW,* February 1, 1919, 615.

"The addition of hundreds of theaters": Balio, *United Artists,* 11.

"We think that this step": "Star Combination Was Unexpected," *MPW,* February 1, 1919, 619.

papers organizing the United Artists Corporation: Chaplin-Fairbanks-Griffith-Pickford Agreement, February 5, 1919 (CCA, ECCI00012165).

He was obligated to contribute: Chaplin–United Artists Agreement, February 5, 1919 (CCA ECCI00313821).

Syd asked Burkan to confirm this: S. Chaplin to Burkan, February 5, 1919 (CCA, ECCI00314597).

112 *Charlie would be incurring:* Burkan to S. Chaplin, February 17, 1919 (CCA, ECCI00314620).

"quantity and speed to quality": "Chaplin Policy Is Explained," *FD,* September 23, 1918, 1.

"become the scene of bustling activity": "Chaplins Abandon Trip Abroad," *MPW,* February 22, 1919, 1020.

"Mr. Chaplin was with the baby": "Finds.Chaplin Is Not Funny as a Husband," *BEN,* March 19, 1920, 25.

"That kid's immense!": Emma-Lindsay Squier, "Charlie Chaplin's Partner," *Picture-Play,* January 1921, 32.

"Chaplin never shone more brightly": Goldwyn, *Behind the Screen,* 171.

113 *"I shall wait a year to prove to him":* "Won't Sue Film Star, Says Wife," *LAT,* March 24, 1920, II-1.

"The whole trouble arose": "Wife Denies Blame for Chaplin Fight," *LAH,* April 8, 1920, 1, 14.

114 *"When told that her husband had been in a fight":* "Mrs. Chaplin Dances with Prince of Wales," *BEN,* April 9, 1920, 21.

filed suit for divorce: "Chaplin's Wife Asks Divorce," *LAT,* August 3, 1920, II-1.

an intrepid Los Angeles Times *reporter:* "Corners Chaplin in Salt Lake Hotel," *LAT,* August 10, 1920, II-11.

"In one of the bedrooms": C. Chaplin, *My Autobiography,* 241.

115 *"I do not propose to lose":* quoted in "Chaplin in 'The Kid,'" *FD,* August 18, 1920, 1, 3.

First National reponded with a full-page open letter: "Regarding Charles Chaplin and 'The Kid,'" *MPN,* September 4, 1920, 1840.

They found that the coffee tins: Lyons (ed.), "Totheroh Interviewed," 268.

"on the ground that he is a British subject": "Chaplins Here to Fight Out Marital War," *NYTr,* September 13, 1920, 1, 3; "Threatens to Put Charlie Chaplin in Hands of Receiver," *NYW,* September 13, 1920, 1, 11.

116 *"The Bolsheviki believe in dividing":* "Chaplin Spurns Wife's Peace Parley Offer," *NYTr,* September 14, 1920, 1, 8.

"We were planning to let the couple": ibid.; "Chaplin Does a Fadeout, Taking to the Mountains," *NYH,* September 16, 1920 , 11.

"I hope there will be no further unpleasantries": "Girl Takes a Big Chance in Marrying an Artist," *New York Evening Telegram,* September 19, 1920, 6.

Burkan quickly negotiated a settlement: "Mildred Harris Chaplin Gets Divorce and Cash," *LAT,* November 13, 1920, II-1.

"Since he arrived in New York": Frank P. Donovan, "Things You Won't Read Anywhere Else," *Camera!* October 30, 1920, 9.

"being seen almost nightly": "Charlie Chaplin Divorced," *NYC,* November 24, 1920, 29.

"metaphorically with their hats in their hands": C. Chaplin, *My Autobiography,* 245–46.

"buying lawsuits": "After 'The Kid,'" *FD,* September 17, 1920, 1; "Not Buying Law Suits," *FD,* September 18, 1920, 1.

117 *"His action in refusing to deliver":* Martin J. Quigley, "The Case of Mr. Charles Chaplin," *EH,* November 9, 1920, 33.

Burkan struck a deal with First National: Chaplin–First National Agreement, December 3, 1920 (WB, 2724B_F008793_001).

Chaplin returned to Los Angeles: "Chaplin again Working," *EH* , February 5, 1921, 48; "Chaplin Delivers Print of 'The Kid,'" *Camera!,* January 8, 1921, 5.

"The picture, besides being his most interesting": "Charlie Chaplin Funnier Than Ever," *NYH,* February 7, 1921, 9.

"moments of unbelievable tension": Seldes, *Seven Lively Arts,* 50.

"face the strain of having his mother near him": Robinson, *Chaplin,* 270.

118 *"The old lady will soon be on her way over":* Hughes to Burkan, March 5, 1921 (CCA, ECCI00314702).

"I am eager to bring poetry to the screen": Parsons, "In and Out of Focus," 5.

CHAPTER TWELVE. THE GOSPEL OF PERFORMING RIGHTS

121 *the exclusive right to publicly perform:* U.S. Copyright Office, *Copyright Enactments,* 56–57.

"ephemeral, fleeting, and fugitive": April 1926 Hearings, 355.

122 *"repeal the statute":* May 1906 Hearings, 22.

As early as 1904, Sacem had urged: "French Composers Retaliate," *MTR,* April 2, 1904, 47.

"for the purpose of protecting copyrights": "Organized for 'Protection,'" *MTR,* December 3, 1910, 45.

123 *"Managers of concerts in New York":* "Demand Royalty for French Music," *NYT,* January 11, 1911, 13.

"this demand for a sum all out of proportion": "Francis Roger's Recital," *NYT*, November 17, 1911, 8.

"The attitude of the Society of French Authors": "Royalty on French Songs," *MTR*, December 2, 1911, 47.

"It is the performing rights that last": "Comments by 'the Man on the Street,'" *MTR*, December 23, 1911, 48.

"Can you imagine": ibid.

124 *"a hungry and thirsty lot":* "Epidemic of Music Halls to Strike New York City," *VAR*, May 6, 1911, 6.

By the middle of 1912, large cabaret-restaurants: Erenberg, *Steppin' Out*, 114–24.

"rendezvous for those to whom the witching hour": "The Century Roof Opens Its Doors," *NYT*, January 20, 1917, 9.

"Thomas Shanley has the best cabaret show in town": "Shanley's Cabaret," *VAR*, November 28, 1913, 21.

"caterers rather than impresarios": Chapman, "By Special Permission," 12.

Their curiosity was piqued: "Mme. Nordica Refuses," *MTR*, December 30, 1911, 63.

125 *When Victor Herbert nominated Burkan: The Lambs Candidates Book, 1907–1911*, 318 (LCR, B35).

As a first step, Burkan deputized Hubbell: Hubbell, "From Nothing," 1.

126 *"The big laugh in Tin Pan Alley":* ibid.," 9.

127 *"A cabaret show gets":* "Leaning toward Cabaret," *VAR*, February 3, 1912, 10.

It was reported that Tom Shanley: "'Cabarets' Mean Big Money; Some Costing $1,000 Weekly," *VAR*, February 3, 1912, 5.

Music Publishers Board of Trade: "Music Publishers Board of Trade Now a Reality," *NYC*, July 4, 1914, 7; "Popular Publishers Organize," *MTR*, July 4, 1914, 52.

articles of association: April 1926 Hearings, 56–67.

128 *"The society has not been formed":* "The Society of Authors, Composers and Publishers," *MTR*, February 21, 1914, 54.

"we shall not burden the musician": "The Realm of Music," *Oregon Daily Journal*, March 22, 1914, 48.

"Anyone," Burkan naively predicted: "Dinner of the Publishers a Great Success," *MTR*, June 13, 1914, 146.

"A feature of the meeting at which the organization was perfected": "The Society of Authors, Composers and Publishers," *MTR*, February 21, 1914, 54.

129 *"It would seem to be true that Mr. Burkan":* Brann, "Summary Report," 9.

"never received or wanted": Hubbell, "From Nothing," 38.

CHAPTER THIRTEEN. SHANLEY'S CABARET EXTRAORDINAIRE

131 *the hotel would not have incurred the expense:* Church v. Hilliard, Judge's Handwritten Notes, August 13, 1914 & Order, August 31, 1914.

spending more than $1,000 each week: "Big Cabarets' Big Business Warrants Big Vaudeville," *VAR*, October 25, 1912, 7.

"would not submit to the ultimatum": "Defy Song Composers," *NYTr*, October 1, 1914, 7.

"When October 1 came in with midnight": "Big Cabarets Now Pay for Their Tunes," *NYS*, October 2, 1914, 9.

132 *"The assessment has been quickly called":* "Higher Music Standards," *PDP*, October 4, 1914, 2.

"bites the innards of the average American": Hubbell, "From Nothing," 26.

"instead of giving the public": "Publishers Start Copyright Suit," *BB*, October 17, 1914, 5.

"It was decided to confine the musical entertainment": " 'Blue Danube' Deemed Only 'Safe' Music at Composers' Dinner," *LAH*, November 30, 1914, 2.

133 *"turns upon the meaning":* John Church Co. v. Hilliard Hotel Co., 221 F. 229 (2d Cir. 1915), rev'd, 242 U.S. 591 (1917).

134 *"purely incidental to the restaurant business":* Herbert v. Shanley Co., Transcript of Record, 17–20.

135 *"We now have it":* Herbert v. The Shanley Co., 222 F. 344 (S.D.N.Y. 1915), aff'd, 229 F. 340 (2d Cir. 1916), rev'd, 242 U.S. 591 (1917).

"I was a little unhappy": Hand to Burkan, February 1, 1917 (LHP, B15/F6).

"a copyright case was a joke": "Interesting Addresses at the Banquet," *MTR*, June 17, 1916, 61.

136 *"The main thing that impressed me":* Boosey v. Empire Music Co., 224 F. 646 (S.D.N.Y. 1915).

"economic interests of the incipient American music industry": Cronin, "Hear America Suing," 1209.

"it would be absurd": Haas v. Leo Feist, Inc., 234 F. 105 (S.D.N.Y. 1916).

"Did you ever hear Pinafore?*":* "Mysteries of 'Popular' Music Productions," *NYTr*, June 18, 1916, IV-5.

137 *"an established place among composers":* Fred Fisher, Inc. v. Dillingham, 298 F. 145 (S.D.N.Y. 1924).

"The more popular a musical composition is": Herbert v. Shanley Co., Petition for a Writ of Certiorari, 9.

138 *"But the showman in Burkan":* Hubbell, "From Nothing," 38.

the court had "flitted lightly": "Supreme Court to Decide Question, 'What is Cabaret?' " *PP*, January 10, 1917, 9.

139 *"may have driven more patrons"*: Herbert v. The Shanley Co., 242 U.S. 591, 592–93 (1917).

"If the rights under the copyright": ibid., 594–95.

"There was jubilation plenty among the writer gang": Hubbell, "From Nothing," 42.

CHAPTER FOURTEEN. THE MUSIC TAX

140 *"play-and-pay campaign"*: Frederick James Smith, "Chances of Escaping Tax for Use of Music are Slim," *New York Dramatic Mirror*, September 29, 1917, 9.

141 *The courts had no trouble: Hubbell v. Royal Pastime Amusement Co.*, 242 F. 1002 (S.D.N.Y. 1917); *Harms v. Cohen*, 279 F. 276 (E.D. Pa. 1922).

"The only way to treat an exhibitor": "Cohen Highly Enthused over Reception in Central West," *EH*, December 31, 1921, 39, 42.

"overcome the noise of shuffling feet": *174th Street v. Maxwell*, Affidavit of Samuel M. Berg, November 1, 1917, 3.

142 *"didn't take Mr. Woods's word"*: Ochs v. Woods, Case on Appeal, 34.

Burkan prevailed on appeal: Ochs v. Woods, 160 A.D. 740, 146 N.Y.S. 4 (1914), rev'd, 221 N.Y. 335, 117 N.E. 305 (1917).

"At the end of Burkan's speech": "Film Men Will Not Pay Fee for Music," *NYC*, July 25, 1917, 5.

"to fix prices and to coerce": 174th Street v. Maxwell, Memorandum in Support of Motion, 10 (emphasis in original).

143 *"the action contemplated by the society"*: "Music in Theaters," *Motography*, August 4, 1917, 228.

preparing to file over one hundred lawsuits: "Composers Sue First of 100 Film Houses," *NYC*, August 1, 1917, 5.

144 *"for it is easy enough to evade them"*: "Must Exhibitors Pay for Music Rights?" *MPW*, June 9, 1917, 1616.

"The easiest and most effective means": "Mutual's Music Expert Is Also against the Tax," *MPN*, November 24, 1917, 3618.

"If I thought it was going to do me any real good": "Harry von Tilzer Resigns from American Society as Direct Result of Fight on Music Tax by Trade Review and League," *ETR*, November 10, 1917.

145 *"It should be kept in mind"*: 174th Street v. Maxwell, Defendants' Brief, 24.

would effectively gut those rights: 174th Street & St. Nicholas Ave. Amusement Co., 169 N.Y.S. 895 (N.Y. Sup. Ct. 1918).

"Little Napoleon of the Steam-Roller": "Those Babies Will Get Theirs—Ochs to New Association," *MPN*, August 4, 1917, 813.

"The experience of both music publisher": "Music Tax," *FD*, June 2, 1919, 1.

146 *Variety went overboard:* "M.P. Theatre Owners to Seek Relief from Publishers' Tax," *VAR*, December 10, 1920, 5.

Nearly all of the Protective Association's popular music publishers: Certificate, February 18, 1922 (WB, 16083A_F008795_002); Announcement to "All Concerned," January 31, 1924 (DOJ, B219).

"to carry out the plans": "Composers, Authors and Publishers Hold Meeting," *MTR,* November 27, 1920, 55.

"had no stomach for it": Hubbell, "From Nothing," 53.

147 *devising systems of classification:* Memorandum of Resolution of Writer Members, April 14, 1921 (ASCAP, B5/I117); Memorandum of Resolution of Publisher Members, April 8, 1921 (ASCAP, Box Finkelstein-E/I200).

148 *"we intend to go to Congress":* "Decide to Fight Music Tax," *EH,* June 26, 1920, 38.

ran full-page warning messages: "Exhibitors! A Friendly Notice!" *MPN,* February 26, 1921, 1670; "The Law," *MPN,* March 5, 1921, 1821; "Music Free," *MPN,* March 12, 1921, 1961; "For Three Weeks," *MPN,* March 19, 1921, 2075; "The Last Word!!," *MPN,* March 26, 1921, 2219.

"I urged patience, and another sincere try": E. C. Mills, "The Other Side of the Movie Tax," *MPW,* May 27, 1922, 384.

"Sydney Cohen's checks in payment": ibid.

"despite the fact that he has urged exhibitors": "No Formal Complaints Filed by Cohen against So-Called Music Trust," *ETR,* December 23, 1922, 169.

"inasmuch as our boys had been martyrs": "Evans Attacks Cohen on Music Tax," *ETR,* February 3, 1923, 487.

149 *"take every dollar away from the public":* F. J. Rembusch to Senator H. S. New, February 18, 1922 (DOJ, B219).

"turn around and sue us": R. A. Grombacher to S. Cohen, January 26, 1923 (DOJ, B219).

"They notified us that on a western serial picture": P. K. Peters to S. Cohen, October 27, 1922 (DOJ, B219).

The FTC declined to intercede: April 1924 Hearings, 195–96.

knew of only two songwriters: ibid., 180.

CHAPTER FIFTEEN. THE ETHER TOY

151 *2.25 million radio receiving sets:* "How Many Sets?" *Radio Age,* December 1923, 4.

152 *"Do we hear Jolson, Belle Baker":* April 1924 Hearings, 163.

"He will interpret the law": "Opinion on Radio by Nathan Burkan," *VAR,* March 3, 1922, 1.

"On this radio matter": April 1924 Hearings, 128–29.

153 *a disingenuously saccharine circular:* Rosenthal to Radio Broadcasting Stations, May 24, 1922 (DOJ, B219).

Even to Sarnoff's "lay mind": Sarnoff to W. Brown, September 11, 1922 (DOJ, B219).

"We render our broadcasting services": I. J. Adams to Sarnoff, March 3, 1922 (DOJ, B219).

"Who is to pay the bills?": April 1924 Hearings, 131.

154   *"The radio plug may be the biggest plug":* May 1924 Hearings, 242.

"the majority of the large publishers are resorting": April 1924 Hearings, 195.

"simply because I have got that fever": ibid., 9.

"pay no heed to the protests of Ascap": "National Broadcasters to Use Copyright Music," *Atlanta Constitution*, April 27, 1923, 8.

"If the development or enlargement": M. Witmark & Sons v. L. Bamberger & Co., 291 F. 776 (D.N.J. 1923).

155   *"more telegrams have come in":* April 1924 Hearings, 4–5.

their preferred copyright amendment: May 1924 Hearings, 5.

"Just the moment they put obvious advertising": April 1924 Hearings, 11–12.

156   *"King Tut":* May 1924 Hearings, 88.

"not in sympathy": H. Waterson to P. Klugh, February 5, 1924 (DOJ B219).

"They have the ability to fix the price": April 1924 Hearings, 27.

"We are in the same position as the mouse": April 1924 Hearings, 248.

"perverted into a legal blackjack": April 1924 Hearings, 53.

157   *"smothered" such slanders:* Hubbell, "From Nothing," 90–91 ; "Publishers Appear Against the Dill Bill in Senate," *MTR*, April 26, 1924, 57.

"there are not going to be many song writers": April 1924 Hearings, 63.

"We think that radio is the greatest contribution": ibid., 74.

158   *"One of our men wrote a song called 'Over There'":* ibid., 81.

"share fairly and equitably": ibid., 73.

"It is a pathetic history": ibid., 180.

159   *"And why do they call us a monopoly?":* ibid., 190.

"police court" tactics: ibid., 253.

"an American-born and -bred boy": ibid., 259.

"the moron music of the Yiddish popular song trust": "Jewish Jazz Becomes Our National Music," *Dearborn Independent*, August 6, 1921, 8.

"Shylock tactics": "Copyright Parley Hears Movie Plea," *NYT,* July 9, 1925, 40.

160   *"If we are an illegal combination":* May 1924 Hearings, 211.

"Judas Iscariot of the music business": April 1924 Hearings, 61.

"In order to constitute a public performance": Jerome H. Remick & Co. v. American Automobile Accessories, 298 F. 628, 631 (S.D. Oh. 1924), rev'd, 5 F.2d 411 (6th Cir. 1925).

"the whole country was whistling": "Victor Herbert Dies on way to Physician," *NYT*, May 27, 1924, 1, 3.

161 *"Herbert would have been a great man"*: quoted in Gould, *Victor Herbert*, 548.

"The radio broadcaster renders entertainments": *April 1926 Hearings*, 145.

"is no less public": *Jerome H. Remick & Co. v. American Automobile Accessories*, 5 F.2d 411, 412 (6th Cir.), *cert. denied*, 269 U.S. 556 (1925).

162 *"a wise man changes his mind"*: *April 1926 Hearings*, 2.

"We are here in the position": ibid., 33.

"the Bank of Bunk": ibid., 253–54.

"I am ashamed of it": *February 1925 Hearings*, 155.

"Our bitter experience": *April 1926 Hearings*, 376.

"You are going to be staggered": ibid., 384.

163 *"Assume for a minute"*: ibid., 375.

"While today they are supporting": ibid., 382.

publicly expressed his hope: "Senator Dill, Radio's Friend, Urges Treaty with Music Men," *VAR*, September 22, 1926, 44.

even the tide of resistance from movie exhibitors: "'Music Tax' Being Paid, Nathan Burkan Says," *FD*, October 3, 1926, 1.

"actuated solely by a desire": Brann, "Summary Report," 64.

164 *The investigation was closed:* Donovan to Buck, July 26, 1926 (DOJ, B219); Thompson to Donovan, April 22, 1926 (DOJ, B21).

"a kind of authors' agents": Marks, *They All Sang*, 216.

165 *"along about this time"*: Hubbell, "From Nothing," 102.

CHAPTER SIXTEEN. THE SILENT SCREEN

169 *Although August Lüchow:* "Luchow Estate $1,258,025," *NYT*, October 17, 1925, 17.

"would as soon (and did formerly)": "Theatrical Attorneys," *VAR*, December 31, 1920, 15, 18.

170 *"If there is any lawyer"*: "Chief Justice of Celluloidia," *Photoplay*, December 1919, 121.

"ate a plate of ice cream so toothsomely": "Jewel Carmen," *MPM*, March 1918, 34.

"a lily as it were in a bed of flaming poppies": Parsons, "Snow White," 34.

171 *"I was underpaid"*: *Carmen v. Fox Film I*, Affidavit of Jewel Carmen, October 10, 1918, 6.

Frank Keeney announced: Advertisement, *MPN*, August 31, 1918, 1335.

"a fighter by nature": Gabler, *Empire of Their Own*, 67.

172   *"if the defendants believe themselves":* "Player Wins First Round in Fox Suit," *MPW,* December 14, 1918, 1188.

    decided all issues in Jewel's favor: Carmen v. Fox Film Corp., 258 F. 703 (S.D.N.Y. 1919), *rev'd,* 269 F. 928 (2d Cir. 1920).

    "to place herself on the auction block": Carmen v. Fox Film II, Respondents' Brief in Opposition to Application for a Writ of Certiorari, 12–13.

    "Her action in repudiating her pledged word": Carmen v. Fox Film Corp., 269 F. 928, 931 (2d Cir. 1920), *cert. denied,* 255 U.S. 569 (1921).

173   *essentially treating the title as a trademark: Outcault v. Lamar,* 135 A.D. 110, 119 N.Y.S. 930 (1909).

    such unremarkable titles: Dickey v. Metro Pictures Corp., 164 N.Y.S. 788 (Sup. Ct. 1917); *Selig Polyscope Co. v. Unicorn Film Service,* 163 N.Y.S. 62 (Sup. Ct. 1917).

174   *ought simply to lay them out: Gillette v. Stoll,* Papers on Appeal, 182–83.

    he submitted affidavits from a who's who: ibid., 125–31, 140–43.

    The court was not persuaded: Gillette v. Stoll Film Co., 120 Misc. 850 (N.Y. Sup. Ct. 1922), *aff'd,* 206 A.D. 617, 198 N.Y.S. 916 (1923).

175   *"It was chatty": Gillette v. Stoll,* Deposition of Sir Arthur Conan Doyle, 5.

    "You can marry him": ibid., 7.

    "committed suicide": ibid., 4.

    "No, the question of exclusion did not come at all": ibid., 21.

176   *"Before delivery of either":* "Idea," circa November 1922 (CCA, ECCI00314723).

    "Cannot entertain proposition": C. Chaplin to Burkan, November 14, 1922 (CCA, ECCI00007844).

    "Proposition ridiculous": C. Chaplin to Burkan, November 21, 1922 (CCA, ECCI00007854).

    "failed to offer suitable conditions": C. Chaplin to Burkan, December 7, 1922 (CCA, ECCI00007861).

    "fully and faithfully performed": First National to C. Chaplin, January 8, 1923 (CCA, ECCI00314727).

177   *"Funny, I have to read the papers":* "Deals," *FD,* March 13, 1924, 2.

    When Chaplin balked at participating: Supplemental Agreement, February 21, 1923 (MPP, 258.f-2396); Balio, *United Artists,* 42–43.

178   *"Charlie Chaplin has not entered into the spirit":* "United Artists Plan for Elaborate Expansion," *ETR,* November 15, 1924, 9.

    "should be a closed corporation": "In Conference," *VAR,* November 12, 1924, 19.

    "did not pass with the smoothness": ibid.

179   *Schenck was named chairman of the board:* Schenck–United Artists Agreement, November 22, 1924 (CCA, ECCI00313957).

Chaplin complained loudly: "Chaplin Blocking M-G-U-A Deal," *VAR,* November 25, 1925, 27; "M-G-U-A Deal Called Off by Protests of Exhibitors and Chaplin," *VAR,* December 2, 1925, 27.

It was later rumored: Maurice Kann, "The Infant Approaches Manhood," *FD,* May 24, 1928. 21, 37–39.

significant pretrial legal rulings: Carmen v. Fox Film Corp., 204 A.D. 776, 198 N.Y.S. 766 (1923).

180 *"near the post office in Blaine": Carmen v. Fox Film I,* Affidavit of Jewel Carmen, October 10, 1918, 1.

The auto dealer's trial: "Disagreement; La Casse Jury," *LAT,* July 26, 1913, I-10.

181 *"Well the only way I know": Carmen v. Fox Film III,* Case on Appeal, 61.

"Now gentlemen, the parents of this plaintiff": ibid., 403–4.

"This amuses you?": ibid., Case on Appeal, 262–63.

182 *"Bring to your minds this whole situation":* ibid., 406–7.

"Who says lawyers are heartless?": Phil M. Daly, "And That's That," *FD,* March 1, 1927, 3.

"take the cure": "Burkan Sails Saturday," *FD,* July 3, 1925, 1.

CHAPTER SEVENTEEN. THE JAZZ SINGER

183 *"Mr. Fairbanks and Miss Pickford were almost carried off their feet":* "Fairbanks Returns; Greeters Jam Pier," *NYT,* August 26, 1926, 21.

Jeddu Krishnamurti, an Indian mystic: "'New Messiah' Comes with Love Doctrine," *NYDN,* August 26, 1926, 9.

184 *"agitation against American pictures":* "Burkan Warns," *FD,* August 26, 1926, 3.

"Amazing Invention": NYT, August 15, 1926, sec. 7, 2.

"no single word . . . is quite adequate": "Audible Pictures," *NYT,* August 8, 1926, 57.

"smallest hamlets": Crafton, *The Talkies,* 10, 72.

"do not intrigue us personally": Elizabeth Greer, "Have You Heard About the Vitaphone?" *MPM,* December 1926, 70, 105.

185 *Rosenthal had told the press:* "Demand Royalties on Vitaphone Songs," *NYT,* August 24, 1926, 19.

"You are to enact before the camera": Jolson-Vitaphone Agreement, August 25, 1926 (WB, 1099A-F008792).

he accumulated enough of them that by 1928: ASCAP Payments to Members, 1921–1934 (DOJ).

"Jolson is driven by a power beyond himself": Seldes, *Seven Lively Arts,* 196.

186 *"You must not lose sight of the fact":* J.J. Shubert to Jolson, November 30, 1913, 4 (SA, F3109).

"Under no consideration have your picture taken": J.J. Shubert to Jolson, March 29, 1914 (SA, F3109).

187 *"long nursed the idea that this generation":* "Griffith's Next Production Will Have Al Jolson as Star," *VAR,* May 30, 1923, 1.

"I was delighted with his work": "Griffith and Al Jolson May Settle $100,000 'Walk-Out,'" *VAR,* June 26, 1923, 18.

"everything seemed to go according to schedule": "Jolson Has 'Screen Fright,'" *NYC,* June 27, 1923, 7.

"But most broken-hearted of all": "Griffith and Al Jolson May Settle $100,000 'Walk-Out,'" *VAR,* June 26, 1923, 18.

188 *Mills objected:* Mills-Vitaphone Correspondence, 1926 (WB, 1099_F015890).

"could handle the industry's interests in the same manner": Hubbell, "From Nothing," 103–5.

189 *deal for motion picture synchronization rights:* "Vitaphone Will Pay $104,000 for Music," *FD,* October 14, 1926, 1.

190 *"Everybody at Trial Gets a Laugh":* "Griffith Reels Off Comedy as Witness in Jolson Suit," *NYDN,* September 15, 1926, 3.

"I thought you had more brains": ibid.

"That's rotten": "Jolson Screen Tests 'Rotten,' Lawyer Says," *NYT,* September 15, 1926, 26.

"Just let it go at rotten": "Jolson's a Comedian, Even on the Stand," *NYDN,* September 21, 1926, 33.

"Have you ever appeared": *Griffith v. Jolson,* Affidavit of Benjamin Pepper, November 8, 1926, 4.

"his face suffused with a broad smile": ""All Jolson Must Pay in Film Suit," *NYS,* September 21, 1926, 19.

"Al Jolson promised": "Jolson Forgot Pearls Pledge New Suit Says," *NYDN,* October 7, 1926, 31.

191 *"The golden voice of Jolson":* Martin Dickstein, "The Cinema Circuit," *BE,* October 8, 1926, 36.

"Mr. Jolson is no less than sensational": Robert E. Sherwood, "Feature Pictures," *Minneapolis Star Tribune,* October 17, 1926, 55.

"hypnotized me into believing": "Hypnotized, He Forgot Flop, Says Jolson," *NYDN,* October 12, 1926, 24.

"I knew Jolson was not a motion picture actor": *Griffith v. Jolson,* Affidavit of Samuel L. Warner, November 17, 1926, 3.

192 *Warner Brothers purchased the screen rights:* Raphaelson-Warner Brothers Agreement, June 2, 1926 (WB, F12721); "'Jazz Singer' for Jessel," *FD,* August 1, 1926, 11.

193

194

195

196

the story was given a new epilogue: Knapp, "Sacred Songs Popular Prices," 316.

"Jessel's singing in a synagogue": "Jessel to be Vitaphoned," *EH,* April 2, 1927, 52.

"reproducing vocal numbers and their accompaniments": [Unitled], *EH,* April 23, 1927, 29.

Jolson did not say anything: Goldman, *Jolson,* 149.

The agreement called for Jolson to perform five songs: Jolson–Warner Brothers Agreement, May 26, 1927 (WB, 12624A-F027136_006).

"When this chance to portray a role which so vitally concerns me": "Al Jolson Signs with Warners," *LAT,* May 26, 1927, II–A.

"An explanation of the mystery": "Jolson—'Jazz Singer' Mystery Is Explained," *BB,* July 23, 1927, 5.

"My Dear Nat": Jolson to Burkan, May 23, 1928 (WB, 12624A-F027136_005).

"The picture biz is a life-saver": "See Passing of Music Tax Collecting Agent as Film Trade Builds Own Library," *VAR,* March 27, 1929, 4, 19.

superseded in 1927 by a similar, five-year agreement: Mills-ERPI Agreement, September 5, 1927 (WB, 16076B_F008797_001).

A boycott by other studios: Crafton, *The Talkies,* 129.

The limitations of the arrangement soon became apparent: Internal correspondence, July–October,1928 (WB, 1107A_F02775).

"This certainly is a darn shame": Starr to Quigley, December 13, 1928, (WB, 1107A_F02775–002).

"Music Publishers Holding Corporation": Acquisition Digest, August 15, 1929 (WB, F002440_001).

Warner Brothers created the Looney Tunes*:* Goldmark, *Tunes for 'Toons,* 17–18.

"Tin Pan Alley is rapidly changing its colorful tune": "A Day in New York," *Arizona Daily Star,* May 4, 1929, 6.

"Tin Pan Alley Goes West en Masse": NYDN, June 23, 1929, 48.

"There is not much left of Tin Pan Alley": "New York, Day by Day," *Modesto News-Herald,* June 2, 1929, 22.

"Which has absorbed which?" Hoffman, "Westward the Course," 38.

"will inevitably create their pictures free of any copyrights": "See Passing of Music Tax Collecting Agent as Film Trade Builds Own Library," *VAR,* March 27, 1929, 4.

CHAPTER EIGHTEEN. RUMRUNNERS

199 *"with all the careful attention to detail":* "Rum 'Trust' Code Told by Witness," *NYP,* January 4, 1927, 3.

200 *"Working for thirty-six dollars a month":* Okrent, *Last Call,* 279.

201   *enthusiastic assistance:* "Says U.S. Cutters Aided Rum Gangs," *NYW,* January 6, 1927, 5; "Coast Guards' Rum Row Aid Bared at Trial," *NYHT,* January 7, 1927, 7.

captured, looted, and sank: "Hijacking by Coast Guard Revealed in Rum Ring Trial," *NYA,* January 11, 1927, 8.

"Everybody down at Freeport": "Rum Boat Agent a Bielaski Spy," *NYS,* January 5, 1927, 11.

202   *"an angel of vengeance":* Goldsmith, *Little Gloria,* 324.

"Does everybody *at Freeport run booze?":* "Rum Boat Agent a Bielaski Spy," *NYS,* January 5, 1927, 11.

"seemed greatly interested": "Once Rum-Runner, Now with Bielaski," *NYT,* January 6, 1927, 10.

"His skill at cross-examination was a revelation": "Nathan Burkan's Victory," *VAR,* June 23, 1926, 38.

203   *"I got drunk":* "Rum Ring Witness in Chains on Ship," *NYP,* January 7, 1927, 2.

"The hatches were battened down": "Tells of Coast Guard Cruelty," *NYS,* January 7, 1927, 3.

"Cold Storage Treatment": *CT,* January 8, 1927, 8.

"poison in every pretzel": Talk of the Town, *New Yorker,* February 26, 1927, 18.

204   *"The Combine":* Miller, *Supreme City,* 72–90.

"vast system of espionage": "LaGuardia Charges Dry Unit Blackmail," *NYT,* January 6, 1927, 3.

"served hundreds of customers a day": "Urges Indictment of 3 Dry Officials," *NYT,* January 16, 1927, 29.

"Mr. Bielaski is not on trial": "Jury Is Locked Up in Rum Bribe Trial," *NYW,* January 11, 1927, 6.

205   *"going to state's prison or to the federal prison":* "Bielaski's Agent Jailed in Rum Trial," *NYT,* January 12, 1927, 12.

CHAPTER NINETEEN. THE BINDLESTIFF

206   *that the groom had abandoned his bride:* Harrison Carroll, "Charlie Amazes Mexicans," *LAT,* November 27, 1924, I-2.

told a tale as old as time: Chaplin v. Chaplin, Complaint for Divorce, January 10, 1927, § V.

207   *"Eluding Charlie's Wives":* Lyons (ed.), "Totheroh Interviewed," 273.

"Bestial Acts Charged": *Twin City Reporter,* March 11, 1927, 1.

208   *"a lot of nonsense":* "'Nonsense,' Says Chaplin Lawyer," *LAR,* January 12, 1927.

"That's Charlie's story": Joseph Cowen, "Chaplin to Fight Back," *NYDN,* January 12, 1927, 3.

"dejected and disconsolate figure": "Suit 'Terrible,' Says Chaplin," *NYHT*, January 13, 1927, 7.

"I'm going there to write": "Chaplin Calls it 'Too Terrible,'" *NYS*, January 13, 1927, 15.

"when he finds a human brain that has something to give": St. Johns, "Can a Genius," 117.

209 *"He is frightfully depressed"*: Bern to C. Chaplin, January 16, 1924 (CCA, ECCI00022303).

"wholly in discussing political movements": D. Ryan, "Chaplin—the Genius," 89.

Tully and Chaplin had their inevitable falling out: Bauer and Dawidziak, *Jim Tully*, 162–163.

"what his forebears did with a shovel": "Charlie Chaplin Flays Tully as 'Ex-Bindle Stiff,'" *NYDN*, September 24, 1933, 53-C.

210 *attorneys for James Joyce:* Spoo, *Without Copyrights*, 193–232.

Burkan had been the losing attorney: Ellis v. Hurst, 128 N.Y.S. 144 (Sup. Ct. 1910), aff'd without op., 130 N.Y.S. 1110 (App. Div. 1911).

"eccentricities of genius": Chaplin v. Pictorial Review, Affidavit of Arthur C. Vance, January 12, 1927, 3.

211 *To pass time he entertained the press corps:* Austin O'Malley, "Charges Plot to Ruin His Reputation," *NYA*, January 14, 1927, 1, 4; James Doherty, "Chaplin Fights for Name," *CT*, January 14, 1927, 1, 4.

"The desire to tell someone:" James Doherty, "Chaplin Lets Out Secrets of Nightmare Marriage," *LAT*, January 15, 1927, I-1.

"A ray of sunlight": Austin O'Malley, "Chaplin Traces Woes to Mother-in-Law, Sees Plot for Riches," *NYA*, January 15, 1927, 1, 6.

"You've got to marry me": James Doherty, "'My Whole Story': Chaplin," *CT*, January 15, 1927, 1.

212 *"Like many fool men"*: James Doherty, "Chaplin Lets Out Secrets of Nightmare Marriage," *LAT*, January 15, 1927, I-1.

"seemed like one seeking solace": ibid.

"big, well-developed girl": ibid.

"think mostly of sex": James Doherty, "His Marriage Nightmare, Two Listeners Told," *NYDN*, January 15, 1927, 3, 4.

"Melpomene, the muse of tragedy": "'It Ain't So!' Charlie Tells His 'Kid' Fans," *NYA*, January 15, 1927, 6.

"half-antagonistic, half-ribald": "'All Vixen's Pack of Lies,' Chaplin Calls Wife's Suit; To Seek Divorce Himself," *NYW*, January 15, 1927, 1.

"vanished into some burrow": "Chaplin Arrives, To Take Children from Wife, His Aid," *NYP*, January 14, 1927, 1, 6.

213 *to argue for a preliminary injunction:* "Chaplin Asks Injunction," *NYT*, January 15, 1927, 11; "Celeb Natural Target for Publicity, Chaplin," *VAR*, January 19, 1927, 4.

214 *"feminine among the scribes":* "Charlie Holds First Council of War," *NYDN,* January 15, 1927, 4.

CHAPTER TWENTY. NEW YORK'S SPOTLIGHT LAWYER

215 *"Cruelty kills love":* "Chaplin Here, Plans Fight for Children," *NYT,* January 15, 1927, 1, 11.

"I like fifty women": "'All Vixen's Pack of Lies,' Chaplin Calls Wife's Suit; To Seek Divorce Himself," *NYW,* January 15, 1927, 1, 4.

"primitive, instinctively healthy outlook": "Chaplin Charges Wife's Family with Plot to Get His Millions," *NYHT,* January 15, 1927, 1, 3; "Chaplin Ill in Bed, Worn by Troubles, Lawyer Declares, *NYP,* January 15, 1927, 1, 11.

"I am completely crushed": "'All Vixen's Pack of Lies,' Chaplin Calls Wife's Suit; To Seek Divorce Himself," *NYW,* January 15, 1927, 1, 4.

"the lies that have been broadcast": Jack Rielly, "Strain Fells Chaplin," *NYDN,* January 16, 1927, 3.

216 *"Chaplin Takes Gravely Ill":* NYA, January 16, 1927, 5.

"Chaplin Hides in Lawyer's Home": NYS, January 15, 1927, 1.

"a mysterious and invisible power": "Rum Conspiracy Jury Locked Up," *NYW,* January 20, 1927, 3.

Why wasn't Bielaski called: "'Liquor Plot' Jury Charged by Court," *NYP,* January 19, 1927, 3.

"The depraved character of the witnesses": Compare "Liquor Ring Case in Hands of Jury," *NYT,* January 20, 1927, 25, *with* "Bielaski Is Assailed at Rum-Ring Hearing," *WP,* January 20, 1927, 3.

"modishly dressed, but with less elegance": "Chaplin's Wife Granted $4,000 a Month Alimony," *NYA,* January 18, 1927, 1, 5.

217 **"screening of the second** *Gold Rush"*: "Suit Digs into Chaplin's Gold," *LAT,* January 18, 1927, A1, A8.

"there would be due me": "Large Bond Set in Chaplin Case," *LAT,* January 20, 1927, A1, A2.

the IRS liens had priority: "Taxes Held First Lien," *NYS,* January 21, 1927, 29.

"haggard and worn": "'Undercover' Methods Beat Rum Ring Trial," *NYW,* January 21, 1927, 1.

218 *"A complete loss for the government":* "Jurors Take Dig at Secret Dry Snoopers," *CT,* January 21, 1927, 1.

"Rum Jurors Repudiate Bielaski": NYDN, January 21, 1927, 3.

"we'd have held out until doomsday": ibid.

"reliably informed that the jury": [Untitled], *NYT,* January 22, 1927, 15.

the indictment was dismissed: U.S. v. Costello, Nolle Prosequi, March 2, 1942, 2.

withdraw the company's entire balance: "Chaplin Saves $500,000 From Lien," *NYA,* January 22, 1927, 1.

Burkan moved quickly to dissuade: "Chaplin to Give Bond for Tax of $1,135,000," *NYW,* January 22, 1927, 1, 6; "Chaplin Out Again, Much Bewildered," *NYW,* January 22, 1927, 1, 6.

219   *kept up for months the ruse:* "Chaplin Will Finish 'Circus' around N.Y.," *VAR,* April 13, 1927, 9.

He was permitted to post a bond: "Chaplin Cash Here May Be Freed Today," *NYT,* January 25, 1927, 25.

Lita's pleas for help: "U.S. Turns Lita Down," *CT,* January 22, 1927, 5.

220   *soft-spoken and terse:* "Wife 'Misguided,' Chaplin Asserts," *NYA,* January 22, 1927, 1; "Chaplin Done with Women? Certainly Not!" *BE,* January 3, 1927, 2A.

"New York's Spotlight Lawyer": Dixon, "Sidewalks of New York," 22.

221   *"Work in the courthouse was virtually suspended":* "Chaplin Draws Many to Court," *DFP,* May 10, 1927, 7.

"Are you at perfect ease?": Loeb v. Chaplin, Stenographer's Minutes, 400.

"I had been to many cantonments": ibid., 404.

"I don't think anybody who is sensitive": ibid., 412.

"general conception of a framework": ibid., 407.

"on my cuff": ibid., 436–38.

222   *"Chaplin scrutinized the paper":* "Chaplin Stages Comedy in Court," *Salt Lake Telegram,* May 11, 1927, 1, 4.

"Do you see three pages": Loeb v. Chaplin, Stenographer's Minutes, 439.

the jury's vote was 10–2: "Chaplin Just Missed 'Shoulder Arms' Rout," *Wilmington [Del.] News-Journal,* May 13, 1927, 22.

In his answering papers: Chaplin v. Chaplin, Answer of Defendant, May 27, 1927; Cross-Complaint, May 27, 1927.

223   *"We'd lose our bankroll":* "Mrs. Chaplin Gets Alimony," *LAT,* April 30, 1927, II-1.

224   *"two of the most expensive legal minds":* "Cost Chaplin $2,000,000 In All for Divorce," *VAR,* August 31, 1927, 4.

"Charlie summoned Nathan Burkan to Los Angeles": L. Chaplin and Cooper, *My Life with Chaplin,* 269.

"a few sensation-hunters": "Mrs. Chaplin Wins Divorce and $825,000," *NYT,* August 23, 1927, 1, 8.

CHAPTER TWENTY-ONE. LOVE'S UNDERTAKER

227   *"Despite his reputation":* Arthur Mefford, "Lawyer Burkan, 49, Succumbs in Re Nate v. Love," *NYDN,* October 9, 1927, 43.

"a reception": "Nathan Burkan Wed at 'Reception,'" *NYT,* October 9, 1927, 26.

"following an extended honeymoon": "Lawyer Burkan, 49, Succumbs in re Nate v. Love," *NYDN,* October 9, 1927, 43.

"for years, Burkan was cynical": Parsons, "Famous Lawyer Mourned," 8.

228 *hearing on temporary alimony:* "Query on Alcohol Stirs Leary's Ire," *NYS,* October 20, 1927, 26; "Lawyers in Row at Leary Hearing," *NYT,* October 20, 1927, 14.

229 *"a Mecca for wealthy and distressed gentlemen":* "Woodward Case for This County," *NYS,* January 31, 1929, 2.

"looked more or less pleased with himself": "Woodward Denies He and Wife Separated; Silent on Divorce," *Rochester [NY] Democrat and Chronicle,* January 25, 1929, 1.

230 *"an obvious attempt to put up a bluff":* "'We'll Finish It,' Says Malone," *Rochester [NY] Democrat and Chronicle,* January 24, 1929, 2.

"some sort of potentate": Alexander Orban, "Jelly King Evades Writ Hunt by Wife," *NYDN,* January 30, 1929, 2, 4.

"she has thick black hair": ibid.

"But there is one thing the sleuths won't gainsay": ibid.

"conventional ballroom steps": Douglas Cameron, "$30,000,000 Jelly Magnate Fights Wife for Children," *NYDN,* February 3, 1929, 3; Alexander Orban, "Jelly King Embroiled Anew by Mother-in-Law's Visit," *NYDN,* February 4, 1929, 14.

231 *"To all reporters, greetings":* "Woodward Faces Writ for Children," *NYT,* January 30, 1929, 14.

"tell of Paris parties and love rodeos": "5 Arrive on Liner to Aid Jello King," *NYDN,* February 9, 1929, 4.

At a hearing on the writ of habeas corpus: Alexander Orban, "Jelly Magnate Tells How to Discard Wife Quietly," *NYDN,* February 1, 1929, 3.

"But the detectives convoying the foreigners": Alexander Orban, "Jelly King Pays Wife $1,650,000 Ending Kidnap-Divorce Fight," *NYDN,* March 16, 1929, 3, 4.

"sweeping victory" for Persis: "$3,800,000 Frees Jelly King," *NYDN,* July 24, 1929, 3.

232 *Burkan and Malone split a $100,000 fee:* "Judgment Names Malone," *NYT,* November 24, 1932, 30.

"I realize how much you are in love": Nayfack v. Nayfack, Papers on Appeal, 101–5.

"Dear Friend Jules": ibid., 49–50.

"Don't be discouraged": "$65-A-Day Dancer Hit Mate for More," *NYDN,* May 1, 1928, 36.

233 *"I had deluded myself":* Nayfack v. Nayfack, Papers on Appeal, 62–63.

He adhered to a strict policy: P. Martin, *Private Life of a Private Detective,* 79.

Kerin saw Sebastian buttoning the curtain: Nayfack v. Nayfack, Papers on Appeal, 192–95.

"While there was some discrepancy": "Peeper Pulls a Pip on Pullman," *NYDN,* April 26, 1928, 2.

234   *"In their modesty and propriety": Nayfack v. Nayfack,* Papers on Appeal, 160.

"For Dr. Nayfack to cast such aspersions": ibid., 154.

"I was dancing with Mrs. Nayfack": Alexander Orban, "Camera's Evil Eye Traps Dancer," *NYDN,* April 27, 1928, 18.

"Like a picador baiting a bull": Alexander Orban, "Mrs. Nayfack Weeps for Love of Sonny," *NYDN,* April 28, 1928, 25.

The jury came back: Alice Medill, "Trip in Pullman Berth Divorces Mrs. Nayfack," *NYDN,* May 2, 1928, 2; "Dr. Jules Nayfack Wins Divorce Suit," *NYS,* May 1, 1928, 6; "Mrs. Nayfack Held Guilty; 'Gigolo' May Be Deported," *BE,* May 1, 1928, 2.

235   *"heart balm racket":* Robin Harris, "Hardy Balm Racket Dies with Boots On," *NYDN,* June 30, 1935, 46–47.

"subjected to grave abuses": quoted in Kane, *Heart Balm and Public Policy,* 63.

"petite Parisian ma'mselle": "Ma'mselle Tres Polite, She Says in Loew Suit," *BE,* April 5, 1935, 2.

236   *"Didn't she use the word 'rendezvous'?": François v. Loew,* Stenographer's Minutes, 29–30.

"As she told of these events": Grace Robinson, "Roses Loew's Solitary Gift, Says Colette," *NYDN,* April 5, 1935, 3, 10.

"Please tell the jury": François v. Loew, Stenographer's Minutes, 107, 111, 113, 144.

237   *"Phoo-ey, give that to the fund for abandoned babies":* Grace Robinson, "Colette Suit Thrown Out by Judge; 'Sorry,'" *NYDN,* April 6, 1935, 3.

"houris of the hist": O. O. McIntyre, "Drab Days for Shakedown Art," *New Castle [Pa.] News,* February 22, 1938, 7.

238   *"must watch their step":* "$$? Proof! Loew's Accuser Sails with Moral Victory," *NYP,* April 6, 1935, 5.

"Colette reached up and kissed her lawyer": ibid.

CHAPTER TWENTY-TWO. NIGHTSTICK CENSORSHIP

239   *"Diamond Lil is a scarlet woman":* "'Diamond Lil' Is Lurid and Often Stirring," *NYT,* April 10, 1928, 32.

240   *"I didn't think he would die":* Schlissel (ed.), *Three Plays,* 200.

"the true picture of a man": Irene Kuhn, "Mae West and Co. to Play in Court Today, Show's Free," *NYDN,* March 17, 1930, 3.

"Smeared from beginning to end": Robert Littell, "They Don't Come Any Dirtier," *NYP,* October 2, 1928, 18.

"This is a community of liberal people": "Mayor Takes a Hand, Show Again Raided," *NYT,* October 4, 1928, 1, 15.

241   *"the advertisement and prolonged runs":* "Police in New Drive to Clean Up Stage," *NYT,* February 14, 1925, 1, 6.

stage regulation law dating from 1909: New York Penal Code § 1140a, L. 1909, ch. 279.

242   *"a prostitute who is more or less true to the British navy":* Burns Mantle, "Authoress of 'Sex' Stumps the Police," *NYDN,* May 1, 1926, 22.

"will not be more than a week's delay": "Banton Abandons Play Jury for Law," *NYT,* February 5, 1927, 1, 12.

Wales Padlock Law: New York Penal Code, § 1140a, L. 1927, ch. 690; "New Wales Law State's Whip in Mae West Case," *NYDN,* October 3, 1928, 3.

"invites all sorts of narrow-minded bigots": Robert Littell, "Two on the Aisle," *NYP,* October 5, 1928, B6.

243   *"has made more motions":* "Clash Marks Move to Free Mae West," *NYT,* March 20, 1930, 24.

"Roman holiday": "'Pleasure Man' Plea Lost," *NYT,* December 14, 1928, 8.

"Why can't a jury of laborers": "Mae West Trial Feb. 17," *NYT,* February 6, 1930, 17.

"piping falsetto": Lindesay Parrott, "J.S. Sumner at Trial of Mae West," *NYP,* March 18, 1930, 1, 20.

244   *"foulest-minded pervert":* "Mae West's Jury is Completed," *NYS,* March 19, 1930, 3.

"It is no crime": Irene Kuhn, "Cop Critic a Hit as 'Pleasure Man,'" *NYDN,* March 21, 1930, 6.

245   *"if they insist on bringing in filth":* "State's Charges Shock Mae West," *New York Evening Graphic,* March 20, 1930, 4, 11.

"The court room will be treated to unusual maneuvers": "Mae West's Jury is Completed," *NYS,* March 19, 1930, 3.

"Selig's head to a point approximately where": People v. West, District Attorney's Bill of Particulars, September 1929, 4.

"Once Coy got going": Irene Kuhn, "Cop Critic a Hit as 'Pleasure Man,'" *NYDN,* March 21, 1930, 6.

"He put his left hand on his hip": Wilbur E. Rogers, "Mae West's Censor Once Actor Himself," *BE,* March 21, 1930, 2.

246   *"chronic love affair":* People v. West, Defendants' Requests for Charge, nos. 66, 67.

"You 'whoop' pretty well": Tom Pettey, "Dean of Police Drama Critics Fails as Singer," *CT,* March 22, 1930, 9.

"Isn't it true that your recollections": "Mae West Counsel Assails Capt. Coy," *NYT,* March 22, 1930, 12.

"You have had a lot of experience": "So Modest!" *CE,* March 28, 1930, 5.

"If the questionable phrases": Mildred Gilman, "Sleuth Ready to Spice Up Mae's Trial," *Syracuse Journal,* March 28, 1930, 17.

247   *the jury would be instructed: People v. West,* Defendants' Requests for Charge, no. 22.

"a double, dire, sinister and objectionable meaning": "New Play Weapon in Mae West Ruling," *NYT,* March 29, 1930, 7.

"Nathan Burkan saw no reason why": Irene Kuhn, "Want Sexpert Opinion on West Trial," *NYDN,* March 28, 1930, 10.

"Miss West, at counsel table": "New Play Weapon in Mae West Ruling," *NYT,* March 29, 1930, 7.

"The jury retired while the two acrobats": Irene Kuhn, "Pleasure Man Does Flips; Fails to Thrill," *NYDN,* April 1, 1930, 8.

248   *"Why didn't you take the trousers":* "Burkan Sums Up in Mae West Case," *NYP,* April 2, 1930, 3.

His two-and-a-half-hour closing: "Charges Police 'Framing' Mae West," *Indiana [Pa.] Gazette,* April 3, 1930, 2; Irene Kuhn, "Cops Framed Mae West, Her Last Plea to Jurors," *NYDN,* April 3, 1930, 3, 4; "Burkan Says Police 'Framed' Mae West," *NYT,* April 3, 1930, 15.; Dixie Tighe, "Pleasure Man Case Goes to Jury Some Time Today," *PPG,* April 3, 1930, 2.

"The test is whether": "Jury Fails to Agree at Mae West Trial," *NYT,* April 4, 1930, 1, 14.

"no longer can the new spring moon be used": "Moon in Bad," *CE,* March 29, 1930, 17.

"In view of the expense": "Jury Fails to Agree at Mae West Trial," *NYT,* April 4, 1930, 1.

"broad-gauged and intelligent men": "Bertini Sees Need for Stage Censor," *NYT,* April 5, 1930, 13.

249   *"The Police Department has no place":* Lindesay Parrott, "And Now Who'll Censor?" *NYP,* April 12, 1930, 1, 5.

"I was the one who held out for a not guilty verdict": "One Juror Saved 'Pleasure Man,'" *NYDN,* April 16, 1930, 11.

"any show she writes in the future": "Bertini Sees Need for Stage Censor," *NYT,* April 5, 1930, 13.

Burkan did have to sue: Burkan v. West, Affidavit of Sol A. Rosenblatt, January 30, 1932, 1–3.

"Mae West, the box-office champ": Denby, "Sex and Sexier," 71.

CHAPTER TWENTY-THREE. THE BIG BANKROLL AND
THE LITTLE FLOWER

250   *"no sense at all": In re Rothstein,* Examination of Elizabeth F. Love, December 7, 1928, 15.

251 *"Arnold, this is your will":* ibid., 7–9, 39.

"in order to get him out": ibid., 21.

252 *"symbolized his period as perhaps no other man could":* MacKaye, *Tin Box Parade,* 3–4.

"200 gayly decorated automobiles": "Film Men Hosts to Walker," *NYT,* September 10, 1925, 3.

"That means trouble": Pietrusza, *Rothstein,* 14.

"When Rothstein's safe deposit boxes are opened": "Hot Rothstein Tips Turn Icy," *BE,* November 23, 1928, 2.

"The Rothstein case, they have concluded": Frank Dolan, "Mayor Joins Rothstein Sleep Club," *NYDN,* November 24, 1928, 2, 3.

253 *"For years to come students":* Rice, "Amazing Record in Rothstein Case," 1.

"the richest prize": Frank Dolan, "Rothstein Slayer Identified by Chicago Cloak Model," *NYDN,* November 22, 1928, 3, 4.

"The task," Banton said, "is too dreary": Frank Dolan, "Rothstein Files Ignored," *NYDN,* November 23, 1928, 2, 6.

254 *"Among the files and papers":* "LaGuardia Quizzes Banton on Missing 'Black Books,'" *NYP,* September 27, 1929, 1, 25.

"the strategy of a desperate man": ibid.

"no notes or any documents": "Proof in Gambler's Files," *NYT,* September 28, 1929, 1, 2.

"Judge Vitale is at this very moment": ibid.

255 *Burkan never saw a penny: Rothstein Estate,* Petition of Marienne Burkan and Charles Schwartz, March 3, 1939.

"keep any incriminating documents from seeing the light of day": Pietrusza, *Rothstein,* 307.

"had probably been visited": Rice, "Amazing Record in Rothstein Case," 1.

256 *"brought down the avalanche":* MacKaye, *Tin Box Parade,* 37.

"I hope he proves": F. Raymond Daniell, "Walker, Concluding, Derides Charges," *NYT,* May 27, 1932, 1.

"someone is seeking my political life": Doris Gleeson, "Mayor Disowns $964,063," *NYDN,* May 27, 1932, 3, 4.

257 *"I feel that Mr. Roosevelt's liberal views":* "Welcome Extended by Film Leaders to F. D. Roosevelt," *FD,* March 4, 1933, 8.

gave an interview to the New York Post: Tierney, "Nathan Burkan Tempers," 4.

258 *"at the sacrifice of a lucrative law practice":* "Burkan Won't Resign from Tri-Boro Body," *Long Island Press,* February 4, 1934, 8.

"Democrats who have not been identified": Preliminary Report on the Triborough Bridge Authority, circa December 1933, 1 (LAG, B3 137/F2).

"I am always glad to get suggestions": "Mayor Outlines Charter Moves," *BE,* January 18, 1934, 1, 2.

"We are going to build a bridge": "LaGuardia to Try a Bridge Official as Tool of Bosses," *NYT,* January 14, 1934, 1, 13.

"unwarranted, despicable and low": "Triborough Writ Argued in Court," *NYT,* January 18, 1934, 6.

259   *"Mr. Burkan has the authority":* "Can't Halt German Steel Order," *NYS,* November 12, 1935, 21.

"That's fine": "German Steel Threatens Halt of Triboro Span," *BE,* November 13, 1935, 2.

"My dear Nathan": "Mayor Orders Ban on German Steel," *NYT,* November 15, 1935, 4.

CHAPTER TWENTY-FOUR. NEW DEAL DAYS

264   *"they used the making of the code":* Cohen, "Struggle to Fashion," 1039.

"we just want to be 100% represented": "100% Screen Actors' Guild," *VAR,* October 10, 1933, 7.

265   *"as a matter of principle":* U.S. National Recovery Administration, *Report Regarding Investigation,* 5.

$301 in the bank: "Acad Almost Down, but Not Out; Fights for Chance to Stay Alive," *VAR,* January 23, 1934, 2.

"one of the most iniquitous of all codes": "Nye Resumes Attack on Code 'Monopoly'" *MPH,* June 23, 1934, 86.

"injustice, oppression, and favoritism": April 1935 Hearings, 2.

"Prior to the time that Burkan became active": ibid., 2026.

266   *"The innuendos made":* ibid., 1973.

struck down the Recovery Act: A.L.A. Schechter Poultry Corp. v. United States, 295 U.S. 495 (1935).

Finkelstein was, in fact, the first law clerk: Interview of H. Finkelstein by Gerald Gunther, July 28, 1970, 4–5 (LHP, B233/F3).

267   *"If Burkan liked a person":* "Industry Loses One of its Noted Attorneys in Nathan Burkan," *MPH,* June 13, 1936, 66.

"that was light years removed": Goldsmith, *Little Gloria,* 261–63.

"he was not at all like them": Notes of Adelaide Bodow Interview, ca. 1978 (BGC, B48/F7).

"sprawled in untidy profusion": Goldsmith, *Little Gloria,* 262.

268   *"fond of long walks":* Nizer, "A Couple of More," 22.

"with any other actress": Sheldon v. MGM, Transcript of Record, 75.

269   *"seek to recover on a theory":* Sheldon v. MGM, Brief of Defendants-Appellees, circa November 1935, 43.

"will pass a good deal of his vacation": "To Pass on 'Ulysses,'" *NYT,* August 30, 1933, 16.

270 *"the basic plot, after passing through"*: Sheldon v. Metro-Goldwyn *Pictures*, 7 F.Supp. 837, 841 (S.D.N.Y. 1934), *rev'd*, 81 F.2d 49 (2d Cir.), *cert. denied*, 298 U.S. 669 (1936).

"At once he falls to wooing her": Sheldon v. Metro-Goldwyn *Pictures*, 81 F.2d 49, 50–51 (2d Cir.), *cert. denied*, 298 U.S. 669 (1936).

271 *"The dramatic significance of the scenes"*: ibid., 55.

"of the utmost importance to authors": Sheldon v. MGM, Petition for a Writ of Certiorari, April 4, 1936, 20.

"a later adaptor must forsake": Sheldon v. MGM, Memorandum of Amici Curiae on Petition for Certiorari, April 13, 1936, 4.

"If his name does not spring at you": Johnston, "Blumey—I," 19.

272 *"His wife asked him what was the matter"*: Sinclair, *Presents William Fox*, 193.

"God will strike you dead": Johnston, "Blumey—II," 22.

"the premier of Jimmy Walker's nocturnal cabinet": Johnston, "Blumey—I," 19.

"when A. C. Blumenthal sails": Ed Sullivan, "Broadway," *NYDN*, June 12, 1933, 28.

"Peggy Fears, sobbing wildly": Ed Sullivan, "Broadway," *NYDN*, June 14, 1933, 40.

273 *Blumey was "squiring" Gloria:* [Untitled], *NYDN*, December 7, 1933, 30.

CHAPTER TWENTY-FIVE. GLORIA

274 *"a bride whose pulchritude"*: "Social Happenings of the Week," *DFP*, December 21, 1924, 4.

275 *"one of the cleverest matchmaking mammas"*: Jack Alexander, "Battling the Vanderbilts for Her Own Child," *SLPD*, Sunday Magazine, September 9, 1934, 2.

"The marriages of the Morgan girls": "How Do the Morgan Girls Win Such Matrimonial Prizes?" *PP*, American Weekly Section, June 24, 1923, 12.

"If horses, yachts, automobiles": ibid.

"Reginald C. Vanderbilt Dies": *CE*, September 5, 1925, 1.

276 *"Only a dimpled, playful baby"*: "Millions for Baby Vanderbilt," *NYDN*, October 18, 1925, 4.

"World's Most Expensive Baby": *Galveston Daily News*, May 13, 1928, 14.

"keep up appearances": Vanderbilt Guardianship, Affidavit of Gloria M. Vanderbilt, January 2, 1935, 8.

277 *"living at a pretty extravagant rate"*: Vanderbilt Habeas, Record on Appeal, 3449.

"beautiful stranger glimpsed only fleetingly": Cooper and Vanderbilt, *The Rainbow Comes,* 30.

"Naney and Dodo's feelings toward her": ibid., 41.

"She objected to my marrying": Vanderbilt Habeas, Record on Appeal, 2215–16.

"the allowance was extremely generous": ibid., 3384–85.

278 *"to bring the child to this country":* ibid., 3441–42.

279 *"Your prolonged absence":* ibid., 3444.

"remote control": Author's interview with Nathan Burkan Jr., October 13, 2013.

280 *"Possession is nine-tenths of the law":* Goldsmith, *Little Gloria,* 264.

"Just a few more months": Vanderbilt Habeas, Record on Appeal, 2481.

"this being the advice": ibid., 3396.

281 *"the right of a surviving parent":* People ex rel. Beaudoin v. Beaudoin, 126 A.D. 505, 507, 110 N.Y.S. 592, 593 (1908).

"immoral or amoral or a prostitute": Notes of James A. Murray Interview, ca. 1978 (BGC, B50/F29).

"Mrs. Vanderbilt's continued friendship": Nancy Randolph, "Vanderbilts Move to Halt Child Fight," *NYDN,* July 26, 1934, 20.

"somebody is desirous of keeping Little Gloria away": Robert McNamara, "Vanderbilts Fight for Golden Gloria," *NYDN,* July 25, 1934, 3, 14.

"No less than three women": ibid, 3.

282 *"It did not escape the attention of society":* Nancy Randolph, "Vanderbilts Move to Halt Child Fight," *NYDN,* July 26, 1934, 20.

"I told him where he came off": Vanderbilt Habeas, Record on Appeal, 1452, 1462.

"For some unknown reason": In re Vanderbilt, 153 Misc. 884, 885–86 (N.Y. Cty. Surr. 1934).

"absolutely and unequivocally": Vanderbilt Guardianship, Affidavit of Gloria M. Vanderbilt, January 2, 1935, 3.

283 *"The Jew in Germany today":* Burkan, "United Jewish Appeal," 1.

"As midnight approached": "35,000 Hear Stars to Aid Reich Jews," *NYT,* September 21, 1934, 28.

"To permit the child": Vanderbilt Guardianship, Affidavit of Gloria M. Vanderbilt, January 2, 1935, 6.

284 *"looking as happy and serenely confident":* Nancy Randolph, "That Guardianship Fight Doesn't Affect Mrs. Reggie," *NYDN,* September 25, 1934, 43.

"The little girl, having black bobbed hair": "Mother Opposes Mrs. Vanderbilt," *NYT,* September 29, 1934, 34.

"the glittering world of glamorous Mrs. Gloria Morgan Vanderbilt": Julia McCarthy, "Mother Brands Daughter as Unfit to Raise Gloria," *NYDN,* September 29, 1934, 2.

285 *"the tide of irreligion"*: "Carew Urges a Check on Tide of Irreligion," *NYT*, November 3, 1930, 11.

"my daughter paid absolutely no attention": *Vanderbilt Habeas,* Record on Appeal, 22–25.

CHAPTER TWENTY-SIX. BLUE BLOODS MEET
THE HOI POLLOI

286 *"Tall, ruddy, immaculately dressed"*: "Opposites Battle in Vanderbilt Case," *BES,* October 5, 1934, 12.

287 *"It discredits a witness"*: *Vanderbilt Habeas,* Record on Appeal, 53.

"painted her former employer": Julia McCarthy, "Prince's Affair Bared, Gloria To Strike Back," *NYDN,* October 2, 1934, 3.

"Was that the word she used": *Vanderbilt Habeas,* Record on Appeal, 79–80.

"Wealth brings greed": ibid., 168–69.

288 *"Certainly, if they are good ones"*: ibid., 215–21.

"she was an influence": ibid., 208–9.

"is a dynamo of energy on cross-examination": "Opposites Battle in Vanderbilt Case," *BES,* October 5, 1934, 12.

"He is a forcible gentleman": *Vanderbilt Habeas,* Record on Appeal, 520–21.

"this Calvary on earth!": ibid., 801.

"the Paris that Mrs. Gloria Morgan Vanderbilt knew": Julia McCarthy, "Ex-Maid Bares Gloria's Hectic Life in France," *NYDN,* October 3, 1934, 3.

289 *"You saw nothing improper"*: *Vanderbilt Habeas,* Record on Appeal, 366.

"his face in death looked no more stricken": Vanderbilt and Wayne, *Without Prejudice,* 290.

"So you told Mr. Smythe": *Vanderbilt Habeas,* Record on Appeal, 368.

290 *"warfare in haughty pantomime"*: Julia McCarthy, "Mrs. Whitney, Gloria's Pals Trade Chills," *NYDN,* October 17, 1934, 14.

"Mr. Burkan gave her a long cross-examination": "Mother Discredits Mrs. Vanderbilt," *NYT,* October 10, 1934, 4; Julia McCarthy, "Nurse Recants Part of Story Against Gloria," *NYDN,* October 10, 1934, 3.

"It is not my daughter's fault": *Vanderbilt Habeas,* Record on Appeal, 609.

"Didn't you hate this man": ibid., 782–83.

291 *"all of its motives and cross-purposes"*: Vanderbilt and Wayne, *Without Prejudice,* 295.

"nothing new": "Mother Pensioned by Mrs. Vanderbilt," *NYT,* October 11, 1934, 9.

Justice Carew told reporters: "Servant Defends Mrs. Vanderbilt," *NYT,* October 12, 1934, 29.

292 *"Were those pictures of naked women?":* Vanderbilt Habeas, Record on Appeal, 891–92.

"Instead of Ivory Soap": Goldsmith, *Little Gloria,* 389.

"One of the reporters began: "New Secrecy Rule in Vanderbilt Case," *NYT,* October 16, 1934, 16.

Whitney's "nude conscious" mind: "Gloria to Put Spotlight on Mrs. Whitney," *NYDN,* October 14, 1934, 3.

293 *Burkan had little choice but to accept:* Goldsmith, *Little Gloria,* 416–18.

"I think we can pass all that": Vanderbilt Habeas, Record on Appeal, 1252.

294 *"God awful nurse":* ibid., 1110–11.

"French generals": ibid., 1714.

"the cool distant look of an affronted aristocrat": "Aunt Whitney Tells Her Side in Gloria Suit," *NYDN,* October 23, 1934, 3.

"The question accompanying this action": "Gloria in Court Picks Aunt, Rejects Mother," *NYDN,* October 25, 1934, 3, 4.

"Looking at a picture of a naked woman": Vanderbilt Habeas, Record on Appeal, 1770.

295 *"if I was to remain with Auntie Ger":* Cooper and Vanderbilt, *The Rainbow Comes,* 67.

"He was getting quite old": Vanderbilt Habeas, Record on Appeal, 1822.

"And look!": ibid., 1857.

"on the lap of the Gods": ibid., 1771.

296 *"The child made it plain she did not dislike her mother:* "Vanderbilt Girl 'Visits' with Judge; Wishes to Stay with Mrs. Whitney," *NYT,* October 25, 1934, 1, 2.

"the Duke of Boloney": ibid., 2088.

"the child's spiritual and religious education": ibid., 1930.

297 *"We are not all liars":* ibid., 218.

"Don't shrink from me": ibid., 220–21.

"make her eat it with catsup": "Mrs. Vanderbilt Denies She Ever Neglected Gloria," *BES,* November 10, 1934, 3.

"sportive nudes playing leapfrog": "Gloria Cries Defiance at Blumey Quiz," *NYDN,* November 8, 1934, 3, 11; "Art Photos Shown in Vanderbilt Case," *NYT,* November 8, 1934, 19.

"She could always dance all night": "Blumey's Parties Gay but Proper, Gloria Testifies," *NYDN,* November 2, 1934, 3, 4.

298 *"If she has to be carried in on a litter":* "Mrs. Vanderbilt's Witnesses Testify, but She Leaves," *NYDN,* October 26, 1934, 3.

"With a catch in her voice": Julia McCarthy, "Mrs. Vanderbilt Sobs Defending Self as Mother," *NYDN,* October 31, 1934, 3.

"How did it happen": *Vanderbilt Habeas,* Record on Appeal, 2775–76.

299 *"HAVE HANNAH REMOVE":* ibid., 2983–84, 3443.

"Did you spend one percent": ibid., 2755.

"I will not send the child back": ibid., 3091.

"You will insist you are licked": ibid., 3103–4.

300 *"It was designed to keep you from finding out":* "Vanderbilt Child to Get a New Life," *NYT,* November 15, 1934, 1; Julia McCarthy, "Gloria's Old Life Barred by Court," *NYDN,* November 15, 1934, 3, 4.

"The nurse goes?": *Vanderbilt Habeas,* Record on Appeal, 3116.

Carew prepared a written order: ibid., 5–9.

"She may have been a neglectful mother": ibid., 3114–15.

CHAPTER TWENTY-SEVEN. TWILIGHT OF THE MUSIC TRUST

301 *Nathan Jr. was struck by:* Author's interview with Nathan Burkan Jr., October 13, 2013.

302 *"almost incoherent in his emotion":* "Gloria's Future Now Rests with Appellate Court," *BE,* June 7, 1935, 3.

303 *"I have been living with this":* U.S. v. Ascap, Trial Transcript, 5.

Do I understand: ibid., 10.

"the principal source of income": "Ascap Collected $19,363,000 in 14 Years; Distributed $12,410,800," *VAR,* July 24, 1935, 48.

"The second quarter royalty melon": "Ascap Cutting 860G Melon, But Fighting 'Snide' State Taxes," *VAR,* July 10, 1935, 53.

304 *"by legislation, litigation, or otherwise":* Resolution Adopted by the National Association of Broadcasters at the Annual Convention Held in St. Louis, Missouri, November 14–16, 1932 (DOJ, B223).

"Ten Percent Now or 300% in 1935!": February 1936 Hearings, 123.

"For publishers and composers, to be outside of Ascap": J. Ryan, *Production of Culture,* 80.

"who regularly practices the profession": April 1926 Hearings, 57.

"sufficiently popular to bring income": J. Ryan, *Production of Culture,* 53.

305 *"energy, entertainment, and ideas":* U.S. v. Ascap, Petition, August 30, 1934, 20–22.

"other than free and open competition": ibid., 33.

306 *In a unanimous decision:* Buck v. Jewell-LaSalle Realty Co., 283 U.S. 191, 199–200 (1931).

"had become so arrogant": February 1936 Hearings, 597.

"so onerous and so complicated": J.C. Paine to R. Jeanne, August 27, 1937 (DOJ).

"Snide Acts": "ASCAP Cutting 860G Melon, but Fighting State 'Snide' Taxes," *VAR,* July 10, 1935, 53.

"hotbed of sedition": *February 1936 Hearings,* 145.

307 *"For a number of years, I and all other owners":* J. Ellis to Rep. J. Hughes, July 8, 1933 (DOJ).

"Ascap seems to be very much on the defensive": "Old Ascap—Last Curtain," *Broadcasting,* June 1, 1935, 28.

"What has impressed observers of the trial most": "Burkan Scores with Gov't Witness," *VAR,* June 19, 1935, 63.

308 *"You could engage a staff":* U.S. v. Ascap, Trial Transcript, 636, 719.

"Did you ever pay any songwriter": ibid., 677.

309 *"has been doing little else":* "Ascap Trial Sidelights," *BB,* June 22, 1935, 7.

"The case at the present moment": "U.S. vs. Ascap Looks Weak as Trial Gets Under Way," *BB,* June 22, 1935, 7.

the bag *"was loaded with dynamite":* *February 1936 Hearings,* 57.

"in the habit of picking up a case": "Ascap Suit Off Till Nov. by Gov't Request; Looks Like U. S. Has Given Up, But Radio Still Wants C't Ruling," *VAR,* June 26, 1935, 49.

affirmed Justice Carew's custody order: In re Vanderbilt, 245 A.D. 211, 281 N.Y.S. 171 (1935), *cert. denied,* 297 U.S. 724 (1936).

310 *This fulfilled the prophecy:* "See Passing of Music Tax Collecting Agent as Film Trade Builds Own Library," *VAR,* March 27, 1929, 4.

"they wanted more money": *February 1936 Hearings,* 80.

"Repercussions Brewing in WB Copyright Suits": *VAR,* March 4, 1936, 47.

311 *to quell the publisher revolt:* "Record $935,000 Royalty Split by Ascap for First Quarter, Publishers Divvy Up Warners' $170,000 Share," *VAR,* April 15, 1936, 47; "Ascap to Hold WB Coin Aside, Pubs Ponder, for Split," *VAR,* April 8, 1936, 47.

a mere "stripling": *February 1936 Hearings,* 1089.

312 *"The truth is the broadcasters were caught napping":* "Right and Copyright," *Broadcasting,* March 15, 1936, 32.

baited him into quite a donnybrook: February 1936 Hearings, 45–59.

313 *As the hearings were winding down:* ibid., 1020–26.

314 *"The prosecutor asked extradition":* "Intimidation by Composers Society Charged in Criminal Indictments," *MPH,* March 28, 1936, 24.

"He was sure he could vindicate Gloria Vanderbilt": Goldsmith, *Little Gloria,* 567.

CHAPTER TWENTY-EIGHT. EXEUNT

316 *"threw the case into confusion":* "Federal Ascap Suit Is Delayed," *MPH,* June 27, 1936, 78.

"uneasiness among broadcasters": "Burkan a Loss to Ascap," *VAR,* June 10, 1936, 49.

317 *"breakoff of cordial relations":* "Death of Nathan Burkan, Diplomat of Ascap, Brings Doubts to Networks," *VAR,* June 17, 1936, 38.

Warner Brothers was hurting financially: "Agreement on Warner Return to Ascap Believed to Be Near," *Broadcasting,* July 15, 1936, 60; "WB's $500,000 Loss," *VAR,* August 5, 1936, 39.

"The Washington state suits were the target": "Superior Court Says Ascap Is Legal Group," *MPH,* June 20, 1936, 72.

318 *on essentially the same terms:* Ascap–M. Witmark & Sons Agreement, August 4, 1936 (WB, 16083A-F008795).

"expressed and implied in the very structural arrangement": Broadcast Music, Inc. v. Taylor, 10 Misc.2d 9, 19–22, 55 N.Y.S.2d 94 102–104 (N.Y. Sup. Ct. 1945).

"with affidavit that such price": Bucks v. Gibbs, 34 F.Supp. 510, 513 n.3 (N.D. Fl. 1940), *aff'd in part, rev'd in part,* 313 U.S. 387 (1941).

"Ascap is being assailed on all sides": J.C. Paine to R. Jeanne, August 27, 1937 (DOJ).

to form a competing performing rights organization: G. Rosen, *Unfair to Genius,* 193–214.

319 *among other gratuitous indignities:* "Wisconsin Fines against ASCAP Total $35,250," *VAR,* March 19, 1941, 39.

"the birth of BMI and the breaking of Ascap's hold": J. Ryan, *Production of Culture,* 115.

320 *"The money my mother wants":* "Gloria Vanderbilt Says Mother Can Go to Work, or Starve," *Miami News,* March 13, 1946, 10-A.

"He kept these men in line by doling out": Caro, *Power Broker,* 17–18.

321 *He specially bequeathed: Estate of Burkan,* Last Will and Testament of Nathan Burkan, February 23, 1934, para. II.

322 *"to encourage the study of Copyright Law":* 2 *Ascap Copyright Law Symposium,* Foreword (1940).

Selected Bibliography

BOOKS, ARTICLES, AND MANUSCRIPTS

Altman, James M. "Considering the ABA's 1908 Canons of Ethics." *Fordham Law Review* 71, no. 6 (2003): 2395–2508.

Balio, Tino. *United Artists: The Company Built by the Stars.* Madison: University of Wisconsin Press, 1976.

Bauer, Paul J., and Mark Dawidziak. *Jim Tully: American Writer, Irish Rover, Hollywood Brawler.* Kent, OH: Kent State University Press, 2014.

Beauchamp, Cari, ed. *Adventures of a Hollywood Secretary: Her Private Letters from Inside the Studios of the 1920s.* Berkeley: University of California Press, 2006.

Berg, A. Scott. *Goldwyn: A Biography.* New York: Alfred A. Knopf, 1989.

Bordman, Gerald. *American Operetta: From H.M.S. Pinafore to Sweeney Todd.* New York: Oxford University Press, 1981.

Brann, John A. "Summary Report: Ascap Alleged Violation of Sherman Anti-Trust Act." June 2, 1925. Manuscript in DOJ.

Brooks, Tim. "Columbia Records in the 1890's: Founding the Record Industry." *ARSC Journal* 10, no. 1 (1978): 5–36.

Brylawski, A. Fulton, and Abe Goldman, eds. *Legislative History of the 1909 Copyright Act.* South Hackensack, NJ: Rothman, 1976.

Buck, Gene. "Eulogy for Nathan Burkan." June 9, 1936. Manuscript in possession of author.

Burkan, Nathan. "Memorandum in Support of Articles Offered by the Academy of Motion Picture Arts and Sciences in Substitution for the Articles Contained in the Proposed Basic Code of Fair Competition for the Motion Picture Industry." September 1933. Legal brief available at digitalcollections.oscars.org/cdm/compoundobject/collection/p15759coll4/id/3014/rec/19.

Burkan, Nathan. "The Charge That the Passage of the Copyright Bill, Senate Bill 6330, Will Create a Monopoly in the Manufacture of Automatic Musical Devices Is False." January 8, 1907. Legal brief available at archive .org/details/TheChargeThatThePassageOfTheCopyrightBillSenateBill6330 WillCreateAMonopolyInTheM.

Burkan, Nathan. "United Jewish Appeal Night of Stars." September 1934. Manuscript in possession of author.

Canney, Donald L., *Rum War: The U.S. Coast Guard and Prohibition*. Washington, DC: U.S. Coast Guard, 1989.

Caro, Robert A. *The Power Broker: Robert Moses and the Fall of New York*. New York: Alfred A. Knopf, 1974.

Chaplin, Charles. *My Autobiography*. New York: Simon & Schuster, 1964.

Chaplin, Charles. *My Trip Abroad*. New York: Harper & Brothers, 1923.

Chaplin, Lita Grey, and Jeffrey Vance. *Wife of the Life of the Party*. Lanham, MD: Scarecrow Press, 1998.

Chaplin, Lita Grey, and Morton Cooper. *My Life with Chaplin: An Intimate Memoir*. New York: Grove Press, 1966.

Chapman, John. "By Special Permission." *Elks Magazine*, April 1932, 12–46.

Cohen, Harvey G. "The Struggle to Fashion the NRA Code: The Triumph of Studio Power in 1933 Hollywood." *Journal of American Studies* 50, no. 4, (2016): 1039–66.

Cooper, Anderson, and Gloria Vanderbilt. *The Rainbow Comes and Goes: A Mother and Son on Life, Love, and Loss*. New York: HarperCollins, 2016.

Crafton, Donald. *The Talkies: American Cinema's Transition to Sound, 1926–1931*. New York: Charles Scribner's Sons, 1997.

Cronin, Charles. "I Hear America Suing: Music Copyright Infringement in the Era of Electronic Sound." *Hastings Law Journal* 66, no. 5 (2015): 1187–1256.

Decherney, Peter. *Hollywood: A Very Short Introduction*. New York: Oxford University Press, 2016.

Decherney, Peter. *Hollywood's Copyright Wars*. New York: Columbia University Press, 2012.

Denby, David. "Sex and Sexier." *New Yorker*, May 2, 2016, 66–72.

DeStefano, Anthony M. *Top Hoodlum: Frank Costello, Prime Minister of the Mafia*. New York: Citadel Press, 2018.

Dixon, Grant. "Sidewalks of New York." *Albany Evening News*, February 14, 1927.

Dreiser, Theodore. "The Lambs." *New York Times Magazine*, October 10, 1897, 14–15.

Ellis, Horace. "London Letter." *Music* 13, no. 2 (1897): 229–30.

Erenberg, Lewis A. *Steppin' Out: New York Nightlife and the Transformation of American Culture, 1890–1930*. Chicago: University of Chicago Press, 1984.

Frohlich, Louis D., and Charles Schwartz. *The Law of Motion Pictures*. New York: Baker, Voorhis, 1918.

Gabler, Neal. *An Empire of Their Own: How the Jews Invented Hollywood*. New York: Anchor Books, 1989.

Goldman, Herbert G. *Jolson: The Legend Comes to Life.* New York: Oxford University Press, 1988.

Goldmark, Daniel. *Tunes for 'Toons: Music and the Hollywood Cartoon.* Berkeley: University of California Press, 2007.

Goldsmith, Barbara. *Little Gloria . . . Happy at Last.* New York: Alfred A. Knopf, 1980.

Goldwyn, Samuel. *Behind the Screen.* New York: George H. Doran, 1923.

Golway, Terry. "The Forgotten Virtues of Tammany Hall." *New York Times,* January 17, 2014.

Golway, Terry. *Machine Made: Tammany Hall and the Creation of American Politics.* New York: Liveright, 2014.

Gould, Neil. *Victor Herbert: A Theatrical Life.* New York: Fordham University Press, 2008.

Hardee, Lewis J., Jr. *The Lambs Theatre Club.* Jefferson, NC: McFarland, 2006.

Hayter-Menzies, Grant. *Mrs. Ziegfeld: The Public and Private Lives of Billie Burke.* Jefferson, NC: McFarland, 2009.

Hilmes, Michele. *Radio Voices: American Broadcasting, 1922–1952.* St. Paul: University of Minnesota Press, 1997.

Hoffman, Jerry. "Westward the Course of Tin Pan Alley," *Photoplay,* September 1929, 38.

Houchin, John H. *Censorship of the America Theatre in the Twentieth Century.* Cambridge: Cambridge University Press, 2003.

Howe, Irving. *World of Our Fathers: The Journey of the East European Jews to America and the Life They Found and Made.* New York: Simon & Schuster, 1976.

Hubbell, Raymond. "From Nothing to Five Million a Year! The Story of ASCAP, by One of Its Founders." Circa 1937. Manuscript at New York Public Library Performing Arts Branch, Lincoln Center.

Huneker, James Gibbons. *Steeplejack.* New York: Charles Scribner's Sons, 1922.

Johnston, Alva. "Blumey—I." *New Yorker,* February 4, 1933, 19–23.

Johnston, Alva. "Blumey—II." *New Yorker,* February 11, 1933, 21–25.

Kammen, Michael. *The Lively Arts: Gilbert Seldes and the Transformation of Cultural Criticism in the United States.* New York: Oxford University Press, 1996.

Kane, Frederick L. "Heart Balm and Public Policy." *Fordham Law Review* 5, no. 1 (1936): 63–72.

Kaye, Joseph. *Victor Herbert.* New York: G. Howard Watt, 1931.

Knapp, Jeffrey. "Sacred Songs Popular Prices." *Critical Inquiry* 34, no. 2 (2008): 313–35.

Lasky, Jesse L., with Don Weldon. *I Blow My Own Horn.* New York: Doubleday, 1957.

Levine, Lawrence W. *Highbrow/Lowbrow: The Emergence of Cultural Hierarchy in America.* Cambridge, MA: Harvard University Press, 1988.

Lyons, Timothy, ed. "Roland H. Totheroh Interviewed." *Film Culture,* nos. 53–55 (Spring 1972): 229–85.

MacKaye, Milton. *The Tin Box Parade: A Handbook for Larceny.* New York: Laugh Club, 1934.

Malone, Dudley Field. "Tribute to Nathan Burkan." May 17, 1916. Manuscript in possession of author.

Marks, Edward B. *They All Sang: From Tony Pastor to Rudy Vallee.* New York: Viking, 1935.

Martin, George W. *Opera at the Bandstand: Then and Now.* Lanham, MD: Scarecrow Press, 2014.

Martin, Pete. "The Private Life of a Private Detective." *Saturday Evening Post,* August 24, 1946, 22–80.

Massock, Richard. "Nathan Burkan, Actor's Friend." *Gettysburg Times,* May 7, 1930.

Matthews, W.S.B. "Musical Journalism and Journalists." *Music* 2, no.3 (1892): 231.

Miller, Donald L. *Supreme City: How Jazz Age Manhattan Gave Birth to Modern America.* New York: Simon & Schuster, 2014.

Nizer, Louis. "A Couple of More Pen Sketches." *New York State Exhibitor,* March 10, 1932, 22.

Okrent, Daniel. *Last Call: The Rise and Fall of Prohibition.* New York: Scribner, 2010.

Parkhurst, Charles H. *Our Fight with Tammany,* New York: Charles Scribner's Sons, 1895.

Parks, Kevin. *Music and Copyright in America: Toward the Celestial Jukebox.* Chicago: American Bar Association, 2012.

Parsons, Louella O. "Famous Lawyer Mourned Here." *Los Angeles Examiner,* June 7, 1936.

Parsons, Louella O. "In and Out of Focus." *New York Morning Telegraph,* September 4, 1921, sec. 5.

Parsons, Louella O. "Snow White and the Movie 'Vampire Trust.'" *Buffalo Morning Express,* March 3, 1918.

Pietrusza, David. *Rothstein: The Life, Times, and Murder of the Criminal Genius Who Fixed the 1919 World Series.* New York: Basic Books, 2011.

Ramsaye, Terry. *A Million and One Nights: A History of the Motion Picture through 1925.* New York: Touchstone, 1986.

Ramsaye, Terry. "The Romantic History of the Motion Picture." *Photoplay,* November 1924, 66–122.

Rice, Thomas S. "Amazing History Record in Rothstein Case by Police and District Attorney Has No Equal in History of City." *Brooklyn Eagle,* March 31, 1929.

Robinson, David. *Chaplin: His Life and Art.* New York: McGraw-Hill, 1985.

Rosen, Gary A. *Unfair to Genius: The Strange and Litigious Career of Ira B. Arnstein.* New York: Oxford University Press, 2012.

Rosen, Zvi S. "The Twilight of the Opera Pirates: A Prehistory of the Exclusive Right of Public Performance of Musical Compositions." *Cardozo Arts and Entertainment Journal* 24, no. 3 (2007): 1157–1218.

Rovere, Richard H. *Howe & Hummel: Their True and Scandalous History.* New York: Farrar, Straus, 1947.

Ryan, Don. "Chaplin—the Genius." *Picture-Play,* March 1926, 88–90.

Ryan, John. *The Production of Culture in the Music Industry: The Ascap-BMI Controversy.* Lanham, MD: University Press of America, 1985.

Sanjek, Russell. *Pennies from Heaven: The American Popular Music Business in the Twentieth Century.* New York: Da Capo, 1996.

Schlissel, Lillian, ed. *Three Plays by Mae West.* New York: Routledge, 1997.

Schwab, Arnold T. *James Gibbons Huneker: Critic of the Seven Arts.* Stanford, CA: Stanford University Press, 1963.

Seldes, Gilbert. *The Seven Lively Arts.* Mineola, NY: Dover, 2001.

Sinclair, Upton. *Upton Sinclair Presents William Fox.* Los Angeles: published by author, 1933.

Spoo, Robert. *Without Copyrights: Piracy, Publishing, and the Public Domain.* New York: Oxford University Press, 2013.

St. Johns, Adela Rogers. "Can a Genius Be a Husband?" *Motion Picture Magazine,* January 1927, 31–117.

Suisman, David. *Selling Sounds: The Commercial Revolution in American Music,* Cambridge, MA: Harvard University Press, 2009.

Thompson, Frank, ed. *Henry King Director: From Silents to 'Scope.* Los Angeles: Directors Guild of America, 1995.

Tierney, Paul A.. "Nathan Burkan Tempers the Wind to Shorn Lambs in Tiger's Fold." *New York Post,* March 10, 1933.

Vanderbilt, Gloria Morgan; and Palma Wayne. *Without Prejudice.* New York: E. P. Dutton, 1936.

Wald, Eli. "The Rise and Fall of the WASP and Jewish Law Firms." *Stanford Law Review* 60, no.6 (2008): 1803–66.

Waters, Edward N. *Victor Herbert: A Life in Music.* New York: Macmillan, 1955.

Watts, Jill. *Mae West: An Icon in Black and White.* New York: Oxford University Press, 2003.

Willoughby, Malcolm F. *Rum War at Sea.* Washington, DC: Government Printing Office, 1964.

Witmark, Isadore, and Isaac Goldberg. *The Story of the House of Witmark: From Ragtime to Swingtime.* New York: Lee Furman, 1939.

COURT RECORDS

Burkan, *In re Estate of Nathan,* N.Y. Cty. Surrogate Ct., 1607/1936 (NYCMA) (*"Burkan Estate"*).

Burkan, *Nathan v. Mae West,* N.Y. Sup. Ct., 1147/1932 (NYCMA) (*"Burkan v. West"*).

Burkan, *Nathan v. Musical Courier Co.,* N.Y. Sup. Ct., 92–1910 (NYCMA) (*"Burkan v. Musical Courier"*).

Carmen, *Jewel v. Fox Film Corp., et al.,* S.D.N.Y., E-15-254 (1918) (NARA-NY) (*"Carmen v. Fox Film I"*).

Carmen, *Jewel v. Fox Film Corp., et al.,* U.S. Sup. Ct., 685, Oct. Term, 1920 (SCT) (*"Carmen v. Fox Film II"*).

Carmen, *Jewel v. Fox Film Corp., et al.,* N.Y. Sup. Ct. App. Div., 148–911 (1921) (NYCLA) (*"Carmen v. Fox Film III"*).

Chaplin, Charles v. Julius Potash, et al., S.D.N.Y., E-15-296 (1918) (NARA-NY).

Chaplin, Charles v. New Apollo Feature Film Co., et al., S.D.N.Y., E-14-299 & -341 (1917) (NARA-NY) (*"Chaplin v. New Apollo"*).

Chaplin, Charles v. Otis Lithograph Co., et al., S.D.N.Y., E-14-344 (1917) (NARA-NY).

Chaplin, Charles v. Pictorial Review Co., S.D.N.Y., E-40-13 (1927) (NARA-NY) (*"Chaplin v. Pictorial Review"*).

Chaplin, Charles v. Vitagraph-Lubin-Selig-Essanay, Inc., et al., N.Y. Sup.Ct., 10883/1916 (NYCMA) (*"Chaplin v. Essanay"*).

Chaplin, Charles v. Western Feature Productions, Inc., et al., L.A. Sup. Ct., 103571 (1922) (LACA).

Chaplin, Lillita Louise v. Charles Spencer Chaplin, et al., L.A. Sup. Ct., D-52298 (1927) (LACA) (*"Chaplin v. Chaplin"*).

D. W. Griffith, Inc. v. Al Jolson, S.D.N.Y., L-33-261 (1923) (NARA-NY) (*"Griffith v. Jolson"*).

Essanay Film Mfg. Co. v. Charles Chaplin, et al., S.D.N.Y., E-13-244 (1918) (NARA-NY).

François, Colette v. Arthur Loew, N.Y. Sup. Ct., 23403/1930 (NYCMA) (*"François v. Loew"*).

Gillette, William, et al. v. Stoll Film Co., et al., N.Y. Sup. Ct., 30293/1922 (NYCMA) (*"Gillette v. Stoll"*).

Goldfish, Samuel v. Blanche Goldfish, N.Y. Ct. Appeals, 230/606 (1920) (NYSA) (*"Goldfish v. Goldfish"*).

Grossman, Moses H., et al. v. Sacem, N.Y. Sup. Ct., 31326/1919 (NYCMA).

Herbert, Victor v. Musical Courier Co., N.Y. Sup. Ct., M-530 (1902) (NYCMA) and N.Y. Ct. Appeals, 2240 (1904) (NYSA) (*"Herbert v. Musical Courier"*).

Herbert, Victor v. The Shanley Co., S.D.N.Y., E-12-237, 2d Cir., 5470 (1915) (NARA-NY) & U.S. Sup. Ct., 427, October Term 1916 (SCT) (*"Herbert v. Shanley Co."*).

Irving Berlin, Inc. v. John S. Evans, E.D.Pa., 2259, March Term 1921 (NARA-PHL).

Jerome H. Remick & Co. v. General Electric, S.D.N.Y., E-29-102 (1924) (NARA-NY).

Jesse L. Lasky Feature Play Co. v. Celebrated Players Film Co., S.D.N.Y. E-11-179 (1914) (NARA-NY) (*"Lasky v. Celebrated"*).

John Church Co. v. Hilliard Hotel Co., et al., S.D.N.Y., E-11-247, 2d Cir. 5625 (1914) (NARA-NY) & U.S. Sup. Ct., 433, October Term 1916 (SCT) (*"Church v. Hilliard"*).

Kelly, Anthony Paul v. Al Jolson, N.Y. Sup. Ct., 39546/1923 (NYCMA).

Lambs, Inc. v. Marie Dressler, N.Y. Ct. Appeals, 1914 (ASCAP, Box Finkelstein-A/I177) (*"Lambs v. Dressler"*).

Loeb, Leo v. Charles Chaplin, S.D.N.Y. (1921) (CCA, ECCI00011003) (*"Loeb v. Chaplin"*).

Loveman, Herbert v. Al Jolson, S.D.N.Y., E-24-287 (1922) (NARA-NY).

M. Witmark & Sons v. Miller, E.D.Pa., 2229, March Term 1921 (NARA-PHL).

Nayfack, Jules S. v. Emily Nord Nayfack, N.Y. Sup. Ct., 37301/1927 (ASCAP, Box Finkelstein B/I179) (*"Nayfack v. Nayfack"*).

174th Street & St. Nicholas Ave. Amusement Co. v. George Maxwell, et al., N.Y. Sup. Ct., 33938/1917 (NYCMA) (*"174th Street v. Maxwell"*).

Ochs, Lee A. v. A.H. Woods, N.Y. Ct. Appeals, 221/335 (1912) (NYSA) (*"Ochs v. Woods"*).

O'Neill, James v. General Film Co., N.Y. Sup. Ct. (1915) (WSC, 8.f-121–124) & N.Y. App. Div., 854–869 (archive.org/details/ONeillVGeneralFilm) (*"O'Neill v. General Film"*).

People of the State of New York v. Mae West, et al., N.Y. Cty. Gen. Sess., 174820/1928 (ASCAP, B7/30) (*"People v. West"*).

Robert Recker Co. v. Windsor Music Co., S.D.N.Y., Eq.-P-7994 (1902) (NARA-NY) (*"Recker v. Windsor"*).

Robillard, Ovide v. Sacem, N.Y. Sup. Ct., 31325/1919 (NYCMA).

Rothstein, In re Estate of Arnold, N.Y. Cty. Surrogate Ct., 2802/1928 (NYCMA) (*"Rothstein Estate"*).

Sheldon, et al. v. Metro-Goldwyn Pictures Corp.,, et al., S.D.N.Y., 2d Cir. and U.S. Sup. Ct.(1932) (ASCAP, Box Finkelstein C/ I184) (*"Sheldon v. MGM"*).

Society of Authors, Composers & Publishers of New York v. Sacem, N.Y. Sup. Ct., 31324/1919 (NYCMA).

T. B. Harms and Francis, Day & Hunter v. John S. Evans, E.D.Pa., 2261, March Term 1921 (NARA-PHL).

T.B. Harms and Francis, Day & Hunter v. William Cohen, E.D.Pa., 2271, March Term 1921 (NARA-PHL).

United States v. Ascap, et al., S.D.N.Y., E-78–388 (1934) (NARA-NY) (*"U.S. v. Ascap"*).

United States v. Frank Costello, et al., S.D.N.Y., C-45–985 (1926) (NARA-NY) (*"U.S. v. Costello"*).

Vanderbilt, In re Guardianship of Gloria Laura Morgan, Surrogate—N.Y. Cty., G-1314/1925 (NYCMA) (*"Vanderbilt Guardianship"*).

Vanderbilt, In re Application of Gloria Morgan for Writ of Habeas Corpus, N.Y. Sup. Ct., 37959/1934, N.Y. App. Div. and N.Y. Ct. Appeals (ASCAP, Box Finkelstein B/I178, Box Finkelstein F/I204) (*"Vanderbilt Habeas"*).

Waterson, Berlin & Snyder v. Gene Buck, S.D.N.Y., E-29–77 (1924) (NARA-NY).

Waterson, Berlin & Snyder v. Shanley Co., S.D.N.Y., E-12–11 (1914) (NARA-NY).

White-Smith Music Publishing Co. v. Apollo Co., U.S. Sup. Ct., 110 & 111, Oct. Term 1907 (SCT) (*"White-Smith v. Apollo"*).

Wilkening, Cora C. v. Gladys Mary Moore (a/k/a Mary Pickford), S.D.N.Y., L-21–93 (1919) (NARA-NY) (*"Wilkening v. Moore"*).

LEGISLATIVE AND ADMINISTRATIVE MATERIALS: FEDERAL (CONGRESSIONAL MATERIALS ARRANGED CHRONOLOGICALLY)

U.S. Congress. House of Representatives Committee on Patents. *Arguments on H.R. 11943 to Amend Title 60, Chapter 3 of the Revised Statutes of the*

United States Relating to Copyright. 59th Cong., 1st sess., May 2, 1906 (*"May 1906 Hearings"*).

U.S. Congress. Senate and House of Representatives Committees on Patents. *Arguments on the Bills S. 6330 and H.R. 19853 to Amend and Consolidate the Acts Respecting Copyright.* 59th Cong., 1st sess., June 6–9, 1906 (*"June 1906 Hearings"*).

U.S. Congress. Senate and House of Representatives Committees on Patents. *Arguments on the Bills S. 6330 and H.R. 19853 to Amend and Consolidate the Acts Respecting Copyright.* 59th Cong., 2d sess., December 7–11, 1906 (*"December 1906 Hearings"*).

U.S. Congress. Senate. Committee on Patents. *To Consolidate and Revise the Acts Respecting Copyright (to Accompany S. 8190).* 59th Cong., 2d sess., 1907. S. Rep. 6187 (*"1907 Senate Rep."*).

U.S. Congress. House of Representatives. Committee on Patents. *To Amend and Consolidate the Acts Respecting Copyright (to Accompany H.R. 25133).* 59th Cong., 2d sess., 1907. H.R. Rep. 7083 (*"1907 House Rep."*).

U.S. Congress. Senate and House of Representatives Committees on Patents. *Hearings on Pending Bills to Amend and Consolidate the Acts Respecting Copyright.* 60th Cong., 2d sess., March 26–28, 1908 (*"March 1908 Hearings"*).

U.S. Congress. House of Representatives. Committee on Patents. *To Amend and Consolidate the Acts Respecting Copyright (to Accompany H.R. 28192).* 60th Cong., 2d sess., H.R. Rep. No. 2222 (*"1909 House Report"*).

U.S. Congress. Senate. Committee on Patents. *Hearings on S. 2600 a Bill to Amend Section 1 of the Copyright Act.* 68th Cong., 1st sess., April 9, 17, 18, 1924 (*"April 1924 Hearings"*).

U.S. Congress. House of Representatives. Committee on Patents. *Hearings on H.R. 6250 and 9137 Bills to Amend Section 1 of the Copyright Act.* 68th Cong., 1st sess., April 25, May 6–8, 1924 (*"May 1924 Hearings"*).

U.S. Congress. House of Representatives. Committee on Patents. *Hearings on H.R. 11258 to Amend and Consolidate the Acts Respecting Copyright, Part 2.* 68th Cong., 2nd sess., February 3, 1925 (*"February 1925 Hearings"*).

U.S. Congress. Senate and House of Representatives. Committees on Patents. *Joint Hearings on S. 2328 and H.R. 10353 Bills to Amend Section 1 of Copyright Act.* 69th Cong., 1st sess., April 5–9, 1926 (*"April 1926 Hearings"*).

U.S. Congress. Senate Committee on Finance. *Hearings Pursuant to S. Res. 79 for an Investigation of Certain Charges Concerning the Administration of the Industrial Codes by the National Recovery Administration.* 74th Cong., 1st Sess., vol. I: March 7–April 4, 1935, vol. II: April 5–16, 1935 (*"April 1935 Hearings"*).

U.S. Congress. House of Representatives. Committee on Patents. *Hearings on Revision of Copyright Laws.* 74th Cong., 2nd sess., February 25–April 15, 1936 (*"February 1936 Hearings"*).

U.S. Copyright Office. *Copyright Enactments: Laws Passed in the United States Since 1783 Relating to Copyright.* Washington, DC: GPO, 1973 (*"Copyright Enactments"*).

U.S. National Recovery Administration, *Code of Fair Competition for the Motion Picture Industry,* November 23, 1933.

U.S. National Recovery Administration. *Report Regarding Investigation Directed to be Made by the President in his Executive Order of November 23, 1933, Approving the Code of Fair Competition for the Motion Picture Industry*, July 7, 1934.

LEGISLATIVE AND ADMINISTRATIVE MATERIALS: STATE

The Convention Manual of Procedure, Forms and Rules for the Regulation of Business in the Seventh New York State Constitutional Convention 1915 (Albany, NY: J.B. Lyon Co., 1915).

Proposed Amendments of the Constitutional Convention of the State of New York, April 6 to September 10, 1915 (Albany, NY: J.B. Lyon Co., 1915) ("*Proposed Amendments of the Constitutional Convention*").

Revised Record of the Constitutional Convention of the State of New York April 6 to September 10, 1915 (Albany, NY: J.B. Lyon Co., 1916) ("*Record of the Constitutional Convention*").

Index